Magdaragat

Magdaragat

An Anthology of Filipino-Canadian Writing

Edited by

Teodoro Alcuitas,
C.E. Gatchalian &
Patria Rivera

Cormorant Books

We acknowledge financial support for our publishing activities: the Government of Canada, through the Canada Book Fund and The Canada Council for the Arts; the Government of Ontario, through the Ontario Arts Council, Ontario Creates, and the Ontario Book Publishing Tax Credit. We acknowledge additional funding provided by the Government of Ontario and the Ontario Arts Council to address the adverse effects of the novel coronavirus pandemic.

LIBRARY AND ARCHIVES CANADA CATALOGUING IN PUBLICATION

Title: Magdaragat : an anthology of Filipino-Canadian writing / edited by Teodoro Alcuitas, C.E. Gatchalian, & Patria Rivera.
Names: Alcuitas, Teodoro, editor.
Description: Essays and short stories.
Identifiers: Canadiana (print) 20230443133 | Canadiana (ebook) 20230443184 | ISBN 9781770867178 (softcover) | ISBN 9781770867185 (HTML)
Subjects: LCSH: Canadian literature—21st century. | CSH: Canadian literature (English)—21st Century | CSH: Canadian literature (English)—Asian Canadian authors
Classification: LCC PS8235.F55 M34 2023 | DDC C810.8/089921—dc23

United States Library of Congress Control Number: 2023934887

Cover and interior design: Marijke Friesen
Manufactured by Friesens in Altona, Manitoba in September, 2023.

MIX
Paper from responsible sources
FSC® C016245

Printed using paper from a responsible and sustainable resource, including a mix of virgin fibres and recycled materials.

Printed and bound in Canada.

CORMORANT BOOKS INC.
260 ISHPADINAA (SPADINA) AVENUE, SUITE 502,
TKARONTO (TORONTO), ON M5T 2E4

www.cormorantbooks.com

To the memory of Jim Wong-Chu (1949–2017);
And to all our Kapwa, living and dead, on Turtle Island,
the Archipelago, and Everywhere

Table of Contents

Introduction   /xi

The Homeland

Hari Alluri | Body Is Not a Thing to Escape   3

Isabel Carlin | Wedding vows for a revolution   5

Karla Comanda | Buruja   7

Deann Louise C. Nardo | Where do you come from?   8

Rafael Palma |

Balikbayan box   9

NAIA Terminal 3   11

Marc Perez |

Papuri   12

Body of Water   13

Steffi Tad-y | Cruel Strokes   14

Jellyn Ayudan | Manila, 1993   15

Renato Gandia | Tubigan, tumbang preso, taguan, and other preludes
to a trauma   17

Christopher Nasaire | Eskinita   26

The Big Picture

Isabel Carlin |

Welcome! Long life! Good health! Big smile!   35

Foreign aid   38

Lazarus in the age of war   39

Steffi Tad-y |

Third Person Singular   42

Real Talk   43

Kaia M. Arrow | Dreams of Pinoy Joy: Decolonial Rage and Disabled
Resistance in the Diaspora   44

Teodoro Alcuitas | Accidental Journalist   47

C.E. Gatchalian | Fuck You: Selfishness, Big Girls, and the (Mis) Education of Hidilyn Diaz   54

Hannah Balba | "As Opposed to Other Races": Filipino-Canadians in Care Work and the Politics of Legibility   63

Alexa Batitis | Living a Life of Hybrid Languages   69

Mila Bongco-Philipzig | White Lies My Elders Told Me   73

Davey Samuel Calderon | Magic Sing, Or, What I Want to Say to You, But I'll Sing Instead   82

Maribeth Manalaysay Tabanera | Pagpasok Sa Sarili Ko / Coming Into Myself   92

Patria Rivera | LANDING AND ARRIVAL: A map of no return   106

Proximity

Adrian De Leon | Ship Time   119

Hari Alluri | Oracle Card: Toward Wonder   121

Shirley Camia | To the dep*rted   128

Steffi Tad-y | Islands Along Mount Pleasant   131

Jellyn Ayudan | Roots   133

Erica Dionora | Cutscene   136

Angelo Santos | boxes   140

Leon Aureus | Just My Imagination   146

Kay Costales | If I Talked to Death   156

Made in Canada

Hari Alluri | The Problem Is I Actually Love Mountains   171

Rachel Evangeline Chiong | Desidido   174

Karla Comanda | arrival   176

Ariel de la Cruz | in little manila   177

Deann Louise C. Nardo | Mimosa pudica   179

Carolyn Fe | I clearly remember   184

Marc Perez | Bones are Seeds   187

Rafael Palma |

Lunch box   189

OPM   192

Rani Rivera |

All Violet   194

Night and Day   195

A Dereliction of Line   197

Aileen Santiago | Phantom Pains   199

Hari Alluri, Sol Diana & Carlo Sayo | Offering for Eric   201

Primrose Madayag Knazan | Where. Are. You. From.   206

Jim Agapito | Punk As F*ck   213

Jennilee Austria-Bonifacio | Seven Steps to Reuniting with Your Teenage Daughter   230

Christine Añonuevo | roots & routes   245

Isabela Palanca Aureus | Finding Home   249

Gemma Derpo Dalayoan | First Few Years in Winnipeg, Manitoba, as Immigrants Climbing the Educational Ladders in Canada   263

Yves Lamson | Reliquary   272

Remilyn "Felix" Policarpio | Over the Grave and Back Again   283

Alma Salazar Retuta, MD | My journey as a doctor in Canada   298

Lorina Mapa | First Winter   302

Monica Batac | Sisters in Practice: A Readers Theatre Script   305

Kawika Guillermo | Untouchable, Or, The Most Filipino Story You'll Ever Read   310

José Romelo Lagman | A Day in the Life of a Meatpacker   320

Grace Sanchez MacCall | Wild West   337

Leah Ranada | Foragers   341

Nathalie De Los Santos | Over the Rainbow   349

Vincent Ternida | Acacia   367

Contributor Biographies   377

Acknowledgements   391

Introduction

"[Filipinos are] mystic wanderers in the land of perpetual departures."
— Karl Gaspar, author, professor, Redemptorist brother, Filipinologist

MAGDARAGAT IS FILIPINO for "seafarer" or "mariner." Its dictionary meaning is straightforward enough, and even those with only cursory knowledge of the lands colonially known as "the Philippines" will understand why one would choose that word as the title for an anthology of Filipino diasporic writing. After all, the Philippines is an archipelago of approximately 7,000 islands in the South Pacific; the sea, as both literal and metaphorical entity, has dominated Filipino life — economically, politically, and culturally — since time immemorial.

The realities currently facing all folks of Filipino ancestry — both in the homeland and in the diaspora — deepen and complicate the idea of *magdaragat*. According to a 2022 study released by the Philippine government, approximately 1.83 million of the Philippines' 110 million citizens were overseas Filipino workers (OFWs).[1] In terms of "overseas Filipinos" — a broader term referring to people of Filipino ancestry, regardless of citizenship, who live outside the Philippines — the number jumps to approximately 12 million.[2] The phenomena of Filipinos forced out of their homelands because of political corruption and poverty, and of Filipino women leaving their own children behind to care for others' children abroad, are well documented. What isn't as well documented is the extreme disconnection felt by many

---

1 "Overseas Filipino Workers are estimated at 1.83 million," *Philippine Statistics Authority*, December 2, 2022, https://psa.gov.ph/statistics/survey/labor-and-employment/survey-overseas-filipinos.
2 "Event: We Find Ways for Overseas Filipinos ft. BDO," *Remitbee*, January 29, 2021, https://www.remitbee.com/blog/event-we-find-ways-for-overseas-filipinos-ft-bdo.

second-generation diasporic Filipinos — the children of Filipino immigrants — from the culture of their ancestral homeland, a disconnection intensified by colonialism and white supremacy. For second-generation Filipinos on Turtle Island (North America), the ocean is simultaneously that which divides us from, and binds us to, the homeland, whose shores many have never seen and whose culture and ethos have historically been denigrated.

Ocean, sea, water — apt metaphors, then, for the contemporary diasporic Filipino experience. Water as both separator and melder, as symbol of cultural fluidity, of the protean adaptability that is both our blessing and curse.

Filipinos on Turtle Island have a particularly complicated relationship with Filipino-ness. Of the 12 million diasporic Filipinos scattered on every continent of the globe (including Antarctica), more than a third live in North America. On Turtle Island is lodged the Philippines' most recent colonizer — the United States (not counting the Japanese occupation of the islands during World War II), whose economic, political, and cultural influence on the Philippines continues to be overwhelming. Filipino-Americans wrestle regularly with the implications of holding citizenship in the colonizer's country, one that has whitewashed Filipino cultural life with the blue-eyed goddesses and gods of Hollywood. This wrestling has spawned an impressive and almost century-long tradition of Filipino-American literature, boasting a number of award-winning, critically acclaimed books and plays.

But what of Filipinos living north of the forty-ninth parallel? The Philippines' relationship to the nation-state of Canada is far more oblique than the one it has to the United States. There is, of course, the commonality of language. Due to colonialism, both Canada and the Philippines are predominantly English-speaking countries. (With approximately 175 dialects scattered across its over 7,000 islands, English has become the Philippines' default common language.) The two countries also — technically — share a common colonizer, Great Britain. (The British occupied Manila for twenty months in the mid-eighteenth century as part of the Seven Years' War.) Far more importantly, they share a common *cultural* colonizer, the United States. But the conflict-laden, love-hate, Stockholm Syndrome aspects of the Philippines' relationship with the United States are not found in its relationship with

Canada. It's the *American* Dream, after all, that Filipinos chase; Canada is the consolation prize if America, for whatever reason, doesn't pan out.

While, according to historical records, the first Filipinos arrived in what would eventually become the United States in 1587, Filipinos didn't arrive on Canadian shores (Bowen Island, BC, to be exact) until close to three centuries later, in 1861.[3] In addition, Canada's population is a tenth of the United States'. Filipino-Canadian history is, thus, of a smaller scope than Filipino-American history. But within that scope are issues unique to Filipinos in Canada that makes Fil-Can history a distinct subject in its own right, not merely an ancillary of Fil-Am history.

There is, to begin with, the different circumstances in which Filipinos arrived in Canada. While many Filipinos saw the United States as the logical destination for providing a better life for themselves and their families, they often "wandered into" Canada by accident, so the rationale for settling in Canada was more oblique and, therefore, less easily co-opted into predictable triumph narratives. To wit, stories of Filipino settlement in Canada are less burdened by ubiquitous abstractions like "the American Dream" and more grounded in the practical particulars of day-to-day survival.

Part of day-to-day survival are the physical conditions in which people live. For most Filipino immigrants, the most jarring thing about moving to Canada is adjusting to the climate. Much of Canada is buried in snow for six months (or more) of the year. In a stunning stroke of irony, the oldest — and still, by percentage of the population, largest — Filipino community is in Winnipeg, jokingly nicknamed "Winterpeg" because of its extraordinarily harsh and long winters. That a tropical people would be found in significant numbers in such a locale may be fodder for comical narratives but is, more significantly, a testament to this sombre fact: that desperation for a better life has led Filipinos to self-uproot even to climates that are the complete opposite of what they are familiar with.

Another, more insidious, survival issue Filipinos in Canada have to navigate: the passive-aggressive racism of white Canadians. The brazenness of

---

3 Joseph Lopez, "First Filipino Canadians: The Filipino in Me — Insights into Living Heritage," Philippine Arts Council (website), May 31, 2022, https://www. philippineartscouncil.com/post/first-filipino-canadians.

white American racism is well documented (and spotlighted and hyperscrutinized because of the United States' status as an imperial power); in contrast, white Canadian racism often slips under the radar because it is more typically characterized by microaggressions. The favourite Canadian refrain vis-à-vis racism — "We're not as bad as Americans" — constitutes what might be called "maple-washing": the relentless washing over of all instances of Canadian racism with the claim that it's still not as horrible as what has transpired in the United States. Accordingly, the racism Filipinos in Canada experience — and which makes its way into some of the pieces in this anthology — is more insidious than its American counterpart and is characterized by shocking ruptures in a strenuously maintained politesse.

As mentioned, Filipino-Canadian history — and activism — is much younger than Filipino-American history; therefore, the evolution from playing supporting roles in white people's stories to leading roles in Filipino-centric ones is, inevitably, at least two decades behind the American trajectory.

SUPPORTING PLAYERS IN *white people's stories*. Certainly, north of the forty-ninth parallel, the image most white people have of Filipinos is that of caregivers of various kinds (nurses, housekeepers, nannies). White Canadians have, in general, a benign view of Filipinos as cheerful, friendly, family-oriented, and unthreatening. ("Good Christians" is a descriptor most Filipino-Canadians have heard at one point or another.) Other comments commonly heard about Filipinos, all lifted from the lived experiences of this book's editors, include:

"Filipino women are loyal and faithful."

"I love how Filipino people are always smiling."

"I so admire how Filipinos always send money back to their families in the Philippines."

"Why is everyone trashing the nanny program? I was raised by a Filipino nanny and she was happy to work for us. I'm glad that we could provide her with a better life."

White people — alongside privileged, "white-adjacent" non-whites — even "thingify" Filipinos. A friend of a member of the editorial team mentioned how, at the hospital in which they worked as a nurse, a colleague once asked the head of a white family whose matriarch was being released if they required an in-house nurse. "No, we're fine," replied the head. "We have a Filipino at home."

The inner lives of Filipinos — especially those who have just immigrated to Canada and are working service jobs to make ends meet — remain a mystery to most white Canadians. For example, the majority have little to no idea of the high levels of education Filipinos typically achieved prior to arriving in this country; many were practising doctors, lawyers, or architects in the Philippines. It's lives of personal agency and fulfillment — not ones dedicated to caring for others in wealthy foreign countries — that most Filipinos hope and train for. But extreme poverty in the homeland — exacerbated by corrupt politicians embezzling money from the public coffers and a World Bank unforgiving of debts that its own colonial projects caused, layered over by an ongoing pas de deux with post-colonial melancholia — have driven Filipinos overseas, taking all varieties of work to survive. Thus, the widespread conception of Filipinos as "supporting players," happy to take on the jobs no one else wants because of our humble and self-effacing natures.

What's ultimately effaced is the truth behind the smiles we're known for: the stories of our parents, grandparents, and great-grandparents, informed by the colonial trauma every Filipino carries in their DNA — so many stories buried under the rubble of colonialism, under the smiles we wear out of regard for others.

THE FILIPINO WORD *hiya* is a core concept in Filipino psychology. As Filipino psychologist Dr. Elizabeth de Castro explains, "*Hiya*, literally translated, again by Western scholars, is 'shame.' If you are ashamed, you must have sinned. If you sin, then you are guilty. If you are guilty, then … you have to apologize. If you apologize then there is repentance or penance. Down the line of the sin, guilt, and repentance framework. And that is why we are all feeling guilty. But *hiya* is not that. It is a kind of sensitivity, a sense of propriety in order to not offend the other. Actually, *hiya* is not easy to translate — there is no one word translation."[4]

---

4 Elizabeth de Castro, "Filipino Psychology and Crisis Leadership," Bridging Leadership Institute, April 17, 2020, YouTube video, 24:48, https://youtu.be/8sog9LhzxDE.

A language is not only a means of communication; it is a manifestation of a world view. White colonizers who learned Filipino but understood little to nothing of the indigenous Filipino world view interpreted *hiya* in a manner inflected by Western Christianity. So, with the passage of time and the consolidation of white supremacy in the islands — resulting in colonizers teaching us *their* version of Filipino culture — *hiya* came to denote something very different from its original meaning. As mentioned, the word is now commonly understood to mean "shame," and to be *walang hiya*, or "without shame," is a major moral transgression. One of the most enduring consequences of colonialism has been our collective inferiority complex, so shame has come to be not only about things we do, but who we *are*.

The poems, stories, essays, think pieces, speeches, and plays that comprise this anthology are textured testimonies to *all that we are*, the full humanity of an uprooted and traumatized people creating a syncretic culture from the rubble of melancholia and displacement.

THE COVID-19 PANDEMIC brought the world to a virtual standstill. In that standstill, issues customarily lost in the static of capitalist colonialism got overdue airtime: the durability of white supremacy, manifesting, on Turtle Island, in anti-Indigenous, anti-Black, and anti-Asian racisms.

As Asians, Filipino-Canadians were not exempt from the harm caused by the broad stroke perception of COVID as an "Asian" disease; furthermore, as a disproportionately large percentage of front line labourers in general and health care workers in particular, Filipinos played a significant role in keeping Canadian society going during the pandemic. To be simultaneously demonized and heroized, after decades of invisibility, had yet another displacing effect on an already chronically displaced community. A positive consequence of this has been a new — or renewed — motivation to assert one's Filipino-ness — most especially of the "pure" ilk, that which pre-existed Spanish and American colonization. No doubt this indigenizing shift has been greatly inspired by #LandBack and other Indigenous rights movements, which were foregrounded dramatically in the midpoint of the pandemic with the discovery of the unmarked graves of residential school children.

Needless to say, this emphasis on "purity," with its eugenic connotations, is deeply problematic, but it generates a more quotidian question: is there even such a thing as a "pure Filipino"? The question is mostly rhetorical (science has proven that the notion of absolute racial and ethnic purity is a supremacist pipe dream) but, for Filipinos, can serve as a framework in which to think about identity.

To begin with, the term "Filipino" is itself colonial, derived from the name imposed on the islands by Spanish conquerors, so the phrase "pure Filipino" is conceptually nonsensical. But, more importantly for our purposes, the majority of Filipinos are ancestrally multi-ethnic, a mix of the peoples indigenous to the islands with the traders and, later, the colonizers who settled there. The resultant culture is similarly mixed, a syncretism of the world views and life practices of these peoples. (Just a few examples: indigenous animism melding with Roman Catholicism, American Protestantism, Hinduism, and Islam; Chinese, Japanese, and Indian influences peppering native culinary traditions; languages native to the islands absorbing Spanish and English genderedness, expressions, and words.) Most Filipinos still have Spanish surnames, thanks to the Spanish colonial requirement that all natives take Spanish names for tax registration purposes. To further complicate matters, in the Philippines the term "indigenous" is used differently from what we are accustomed to in North America, applying specifically to members and descendants of tribes that resisted Spanish colonization and who have remained in their ancestral domains. Since most Filipinos do not trace their ancestries to these tribes, the majority of Filipinos are, in this context, "non-indigenous" to their own land. Readers can extrapolate for themselves the social, cultural, and psychological implications of this formulation.

FILIPINO. FILIPINA. FILIPINX. *Philippine. Maharlikan.* The complexity of Filipino identity is evident even in the variety of terms we use to identify ourselves. *Filipino* and *Filipina* remain the most used in common parlance. However, many younger and academically inclined diasporic Filipinos are opting out of those terms, pointing to their genderedness as remnants of Spanish colonization (virtually all languages indigenous to the islands are non-gendered), as well as expressing solidarity with queer-identifying Filipinos alienated by the Western gender binary. This awareness has given rise to the term *Filipinx*, inspired by the term *Latinx*, increasingly used by people of Latin American ancestry for similar reasons. The push back against Filipinx is that it, too, is a Western imposition, as the letter *x* doesn't exist in the Filipino alphabet and the Filipino language already demonstrates gender neutrality. *Philippine* — a derivative of the name of the sixteenth-century Spanish monarch in power when Spain colonized the islands (Philip II) — is, of course, laden with colonialism and no longer commonly used as an identifier. *Maharlikan* comes from the term *Maharlika*, which refers to the feudal warrior class in ancient, pre-colonial Filipino society. While its pre-colonial origins may seem compatible with the drive to indigenize, its close association with right-wing Filipino nationalism, in particular former President Ferdinand Marcos (who advocated changing the country's name to Maharlika, as did, decades later, populist President Rodrigo Duterte), causes extreme wariness among liberal and progressive Filipinos. Others eschew broad national modifiers altogether and root themselves to specific tribal ones, such as *Tagalog*, *Ilocano*, and *Visayan*.

IN SUM, IT's complicated. Filipino-ness is complicated. This anthology makes no attempt to disguise this complicatedness. Our aim, as this book's editors, is to unroll a polytextural tapestry that reflects as many modes of Filipino-Canadian life as possible.

The operative phrase here is, *as possible*. And what is possible is inevitably constrained by circumstances beyond any editorial team's control, such as budget, maximum page count, and the systemic barriers that prevent writers from marginalized communities from responding to calls for submissions. Hence, this anthology is by no means a comprehensive one. There are voices and experiences that have unfortunately been excluded. We especially regret the lack of Muslim representation in this anthology.

That said, we are proud that the book's contributors hail from every region of Canada, including the remote north. We are proud of the roster's diversity in terms of gender and sexual identity. We are proud of the sheer breadth of stories and experiences in this volume, and of the singular qualities of the voices telling them. When faced with the choice between longer contributions from fewer authors or shorter contributions from more authors, we opted for the latter: the value of inclusion was paramount.

We've divided the book into four parts; the contributions are grouped together by theme. Part One, "The Homeland," contains pieces set in the Philippines; the pieces in Part Two, "The Big Picture," wrestle with the systemic struggles of Filipino-Canadians, furnishing a clear socio-political context for the book as a whole; Part Three, "Proximity," explores the liminality of having one's body in one's new (adopted) country while mind, heart, and most of one's family remain in the homeland; and Part Four, "Made in Canada," illuminates the polychromatic realities of being Filipino in Canada.

A content warning is in order: pieces about mental illness, sexual abuse, addiction, and racist violence take their place alongside ones of success, family (both biological and chosen), recovery, and joy. If a project such as ours is to have integrity, it must capture the broadest possible spectrum of *all that we are*, not just the parts that are benign, reassuring, or comforting.

THIS ANTHOLOGY WOULD not have been possible without the steadfast urging of Asian-Canadian poet, community organizer, arts advocate, and literary pioneer Jim Wong-Chu (1949–2017). A few years before he died, Jim encouraged one of our co-editors, Teodoro Alcuitas, to set in motion an anthology of Filipino-Canadian literary writing, which they both felt was long overdue. Teodoro was hesitant, uncertain about doing it on his own; but, shortly after Jim's passing, Teodoro revived the idea after coming into contact with C.E. Gatchalian and Patria Rivera, and soon after, work on the book began in earnest.

Pakikisama — "togetherness" — is a core value for Filipinos. Indeed, this collectivist tilt is perhaps the element of the Filipino mindset that is most at odds with the decidedly individualist tenor of North American culture. In line with Filipino-Canadians' hyphenated identities, the book's overall spirit is a hybridized one: it celebrates individual voice, style, and artistry while upholding not just common themes, but a spirit of mutual seeing, truth sharing, and affirmation. *Kapwa* is another core Filipino value, meaning "neighbour" or "kindred." Pre-colonial Filipino culture placed all living beings — human or otherwise — under the same loving umbrella. Hence, while this anthology is about, and primarily for, Filipino-Canadians, it by no means eschews "the universal." This book, therefore, is meant for everyone.

The Homeland

HARI ALLURI

Body Is Not a Thing to Escape

My sister in navigation, from another migration, lights up a childhood
    story,
passes me a drag. That's when Lolo's ghost appears — to take one also.
    Ripples

in this working river at the pier below us, and I tell the one about the nail
    clipper
interviewing Nanay for a job. Picture the clippings. The man in the suit
allowing them to fall, discarded moons instead of questions.

That was already over here, and I already existed, but before I started to
    haunt
whatever Lolo pictured to keep his feet moving. In April's warming rain

as he Death-Marched from Bataan. Years before my future nanay
    shimmered
into view. The log ripples subside. Too many rivers, their memory also just
    for them,
have watched somebody's lolo scour a rock — or turning rooster vane —

for signs of coming blood. My sis knows all too well
when *body* isn't sign of love, when it doesn't mean *worth grieving*.

This is for the ground that pushed up at his feet and hers, that pushed our
    nanays

into another haunting; elsewhere from those islands; those islands
whose roots are centipedes of flame.

This, for cardboard boxes on weigh-scales at airports troubling the sepia
    rhyme
with nostalgia. Lies we forge begin us again from paleness at the mouth of
    sleep
(nothing gets passed down through generations like silence)

If I didn't raise my cup in this story, help me raise it now. Cheers
any moment that brings back the heckle of Lolo's cough. The bacon oil
hop-burn, at my forearm from before my sister's telling. Thanks be

to this joy that haunts like a raft undone, to tunnels we leave
each other in our stories. Between us, the smoke

improvises its own lineage. Lolo, do you see? I also have a sister you never
    got to meet.
When she sings, I hear the lullaby's rev
the Death March failed to take from you. I see your body walking

on any day but that and getting up to walk on that day, too.
My sister, you would recognize anting-anting in her: the engine of her
    work: a hunger
that turns a spoon into a hand: your hand

at my mouth: feeding me something your words can't,
keeping me from biting my tongue.

For & After Cynthia Dewi Oka

ISABEL CARLIN

Wedding vows for a revolution

We met at the fire escape, in use,
At the dawnbreak of lethal.

It was love at first sight, I think;
Your mouth moved and I heard song.

And every day since then a crispness
In our fingertips, hearts buzzing.

Your land will be my land, your people
My people, your struggle my struggle.

Would you take my feet if I offered them,
My restless throat and uncorked chest?

If I vowed to you — and I do —
The power of my wrists,

Would you take it? My wrists, my knuckles,
The skin of my palm, my nose,

My knees, my ankles, my clicking lungs,
Survivalist chin and unflinching elbows.

I give you my first-breath sunrise,
My deathbed magpie visit.

I lay my homeland at your feet,
I dream of our children.

For you, I will crack open
Golden clouds of Pacific sundown

I will grow rice. I will brush a thousand
Mount Tais from under your feet.

At high noon, I will bake pandesal,
Boil tinola for your stuffed-up nose.

I will write a thousand letters to you.
Each one will say I love you.

I will cut ten yards of ocean for our
Pillowcases, weave rain for curtains.

When you change with greying years,
Take me with you, my love.

Let me be there in the tiger charge
Symphony of armed revolt.

I'll hold your gun. I'll break your chains.
I'll sharpen your knife. I'll build your tent.

Your home is my home; your home is me.
From now, 'til death do us part.

KARLA COMANDA

Buruja

si grita dao lejos, ese cerca
si grita dao suena, ese lejos

if you are wondering
what this means
in english don't ask me
as i will forget (maybe
by choice) would it
help you remember
this riddle and its answer
if i imprint images not
semantics mamang hated
nanay believed she hexed
tatay mamang hated
us too i wonder if i looked
more suspicious than
my younger sisters my hair
broke all brushes and combs
i attacked the apartment's
walls with crayola destroyed
dolls with costume changes
don't ask me to speak
in chavacano i can't
i never believe
textbooks when they say
bien facil lang gayot

DEANN LOUISE C. NARDO

Where do you come from?

I COME FROM dirt and sand, the scribbled writing of an ancestor in a trance, the sound of droplets on skylights, unopened buds on trees, and the sleep dust in my mama's eyes. I come from cacao beans and the callouses on fishermen's hands, the arthritic crackle of my grandmother's hands as she tends to the garden and mends nets. I come from the silver iridescence of stretch marks, the swirl pattern inside tree barks, the razor-thin whiskers of cats, and eerie creaking of maple wood floors. I come from lengthwise half-cut bamboo wall sheathing, river mud and buried shards of broken glass, of broken tsinelas and confused roosters singing *tik-ti-la-ok* at three in the morning. I come from the welcoming scent of frying garlic, stinging hot oil, ocean beat glass, shiny black sand in company with gold. I come from every flap of birds' wings, yellow legal pages, and cassette tape the length of my small intestine carrying her voice. I come from women's shelter unrestrained phone calls and hidden baby photos, of home lonely near possibilities and nonsense. I come from all the stories and memories and the lattice of truths in between because all I'm made up of are impressions left behind by kin not afraid of the unknown, brave enough to choose to go deep in darkness to find me. I am co-created, imaginary, an in/out process. I come from all the voices released into the ether and the ones stifled. From ideaspheres and afterlives. From wounds and wombs. I come from it all and none of it all.

RAFAEL PALMA

Balikbayan box

Written in Daquioag, Marcos, Ilocos Norte

It stands in the middle of the living room,
its sides are taped carefully, mummified in clear
packing tape, almost four feet tall,
set to ship the Pacific for you.

A set of china,
plates laced with cloth
and brown paper in between.
Each one, covered in rim-woven patterns
and branches of blue columbines,
drooping to the concave centre.
Underneath it is a gilded mirror.
Wrought, antiqued, and thrifted
twenty by ten.
Just enough class
for an elevated aesthetic.
A collection of letters and poems,
slid on the side to compact it tightly.
In an envelope,
ten thousand dollars,
scraped up from long hours.
Shoes of assorted sizes,
twelve pairs to be exact.

Tubs of face cream, lipsticks,
eyeshadows, soap, toothpaste,
pumps of shampoo and conditioner,
thrift-store designer clothes,
old tablets and phones,
multivitamins,
toys for the little ones,
sweaters and hoodies
even in the now-searing summer.

I stood over the box,
almost bursting,
contemplating what else
I could put inside
to send to you.
I couldn't talk or scream loud enough,
to cram my lauds, love, and concerns.
And I couldn't close the box
fast enough to keep it echoing inside.

I've put inexpensive wafers inside,
chocolates, caramels,
precautious of melting points.
Two bottles of spirits, and three bottles of wine,
for the social drinkers, scattered
through the age spectrum.
I stand over it again, before the final pass
of tape, wishing I could fit inside too.

NAIA Terminal 3

There is a never-ending hum,
revived by the fast talkers,
small talk is never a challenge,
the "passed-on" conversations
start a revolution. The city is
a witness to this. The dust
from cars and volcanoes is
biding its time to settle.
It puts a grey-faded filter upon
the city. Covering commercial
complexes and old stone strongholds.
The low prevalent noise,
the singing of our hearts,
or our impertinent sorrow.

The familiarity fazes me.
The headache of letting go,
or the constant gridlock,
held hands, locked in struggle.

It could also just be
the slow crawl
of the North Bound Highway.

You see almond-curved eyes
over brown-skinned people,
peddling on centuries-old
stone and wood, burned
and salvaged through wars.

I was let go of this land.
Before I came of age.
Before the land could claim me.
And yet, I still miss home.

MARC PEREZ

Papuri

Praise the bread.
— Martin Espada, "Alabanza: In Praise of Local 100"

Praise the hospital worker clad
in white armour, mask, and face shield,
breathing life despite knee-bending
exhaustion, poor wages. Praise
the housekeeper, steering her cart
through sinuous rooms and hallways
with the skill of a jeepney driver
singing Top 10s in deadened air. Praise
to the proof that greatness
is faceless. Praise the jeepney
drivers. Praise the peasants
who till land during dead season,
and the labourers for roads
under our feet. The high-noon
for lunch of steamed rice
and dried fish. A drizzle, torrential
downpour, cyclone — rain
will pass. Praise the silver lining,
spotted from the minuscule window
of a seafarer, eight months aboard
an oil tanker, at home in open sea,
no one to talk to except for low-lying

clouds & elusive seabirds. Praise
the migrant worker, a modern-day exile
blanketed with snowflakes or desert dust,
toiling past midnight with a worn-out

pair of rubber shoes. Praise also
the shoes, gifted by a son to his mother,
purchased with his first paycheque
as a grape picker in wine valley. The sap
of loneliness and sacrifice. At night,
praise the stars and moon, sing
praise with the rhythm of a childhood tune.

Body of Water

Home is a place where rivers meet
the sea. Fill my lungs with brackish delta
water. *Estero de Tripa de Gallina*, childhood
memory's tributary, stagnant in black silt
& methane — only the dead remember
your lilies. But this is no longer
about drowning. I've outgrown my fear of
letting go. This is surrender, a body
defying buoyancy — sunken & supine on
the seabed like the sedimented hull
of a
capsized ship. Reel in my feet
from a
cerulean reef, swathed in seaweed.
There's room for you here — a crevice
among corals. Come, I'll breathe you in.

STEFFI TAD-Y

Cruel Strokes

For Ben Ramos

When I found out that my tongue

could be a scythe
on a shearing spree

I decided I would only eat
what would make my mouth

bloom. Later on I learned

that to speak only in flowers
in a field that kills

is the sharpest blade of all.

JELLYN AYUDAN

Manila, 1993

"1 … 2 … 3 … 4 … 5 … 6 … 7 … 8. Look alive, ladies, and smile," Mark instructs the line of girls, all slim and eager. Not eager, hungry.

Girls from every corner of the country arrived in this agency in droves, all awaiting a chance to be chosen to go to Japan. She knows coming to the big city to be trained as an entertainer will have her branded as a *Japayuki-san*,[1] and while she may be desperate, she knows she'll never stray that far. Last year, Sol's day-to-day locations consisted of her college, her brother's monastery, and her home. Now, she's subjected to daily lessons on when to pour drinks or laugh at dumb jokes. Plus, there's the complicated choreography to Gary Valenciano's "Natutulog Ba ang Diyos?" that Mark continually adds on to. Sol stumbles and hopes that God is sleeping.

Her older sister, Luz, is waiting for her in Japan, and she swears that the fastest way to get there is to be an entertainer. Her other sister, Nora, is also applying in another agency. Nora's aiming for Dubai as a domestic helper. Cousin Rosa is aiming for Australia, dreaming about the day her pen pal will ask her to get married. Sol's been in this agency for almost six months and daydreams about what her life had looked like before Luz didn't send enough money for her tuition.

She recalls taking the jeepney[2] to the market with her sister Nora, who accidentally suffocated the Mother Hen in her market bag. She was too ashamed, but Sol had long let go of trying to keep up pretenses when other

---

1 A derogatory term for Filipino women who travel to Japan as entertainers, often mistakenly believed to be prostitutes.
2 A popular mode of transportation in the Philippines, similar to the bus systems in North America.

schoolgirls mocked her banana-leaf-wrapped lunch. Welcome to the Philippines, where even Tupperware is considered a status symbol! Sol knew that there was no shame in selling the Mother Hen to cover some of their tuition for the year. She asked her sister to let the Mother Hen breathe. After all, that's what they're all trying to do: survive. As she peeked in the bag, she knew the Mother Hen would be a little too dead to be a farmer's livestock.

So, Sol has adjusted her sails, knowing she can't move against the wind. She practices the choreography every day and laughs at all the dumb jokes — she does both to the beat of eight counts. However, this Choosing Day she doesn't make the cut again. The agency official's verdict: "It's good that you're slim, but we're looking for someone a bit more exotic. I'm afraid you might look too local for their tastes." Like the Mother Hen, Sol is a little too pale to be on the market.

RENATO GANDIA

Tubigan, tumbang preso, taguan, and other preludes to a trauma

LET'S JUST SAY *I didn't move to Canada when I was twenty-seven years old, confused about how my life was going to turn out after I pissed off an entire community of would-be priests, their loving parents, family, and relatives — an entire community of priests who didn't think I had a bone of a snitch in me, my friends who didn't see it coming, and the rest of the community at St. Augustine School of Theology, who knew something was wrong with me, but they just couldn't put their fingers on it.*

Let's also just say that I didn't believe in second chances, that as long as I was willing to do the work and master being selfless instead of being selfish, things could change, and the course of my life would eventually turn toward my childhood dream of becoming a priest. Although my mother was convinced by a numerologist that I would never become a priest no matter how many times I tried to go in and out of the seminary, she agreed it was for the best that I moved to Kamloops, British Columbia. I had no idea what life would be like away from my family, from my former friends, from my enemies, from people who hated me for valid reasons, from people who hated me for no reason at all. All I wanted was a fresh start.

Let's just say that when I attended a seminary in Edmonton, I chose to keep my secrets to myself as a typical Pinoy would. Let's just say I'd stuck to "I'd rather die than lose face for airing out my dirty linens" to someone who had no idea about the arduous struggle I already went through, keeping a lid on this mistake I made fifteen years ago. Let's just say I didn't emerge from being a victim and didn't claim my chance at redemption. Let's just say

I didn't tell my shrink about that night when I was a foolish, impressionable fifteen-year-old high school student in my hometown. Then I wouldn't have to remember every detail of that Friday night in October 1986.

THERE WAS SOMETHING about the blowing wind that Friday night when my friends and I rode our bikes along the bay in my hometown of Calauag, Quezon. Old people often said it meant rain was afoot. We, the kids, didn't believe it. We thought it was simply a ploy to keep us home, to keep us from our bicycles at night. Growing up, we played physical games, such as *taguan*, a local version of hide-and-seek, *tumbang preso*, which involved hitting an empty can of milk with a sandal or a flat stone, or *tubigan*, a group game involving a skillful passing through ground-drawn lines without being tagged by the guards. *Tumbang preso* and *tubigan* were played mostly by younger children. Youngsters my age — I was fifteen at that time — had usually graduated to riding bikes. On a night leading to the weekend, we usually rode our bikes until everyone was bone tired and nobody could kick the pedal anymore.

We rode across the urban area that night, stopping at spots where there were other kids to see and chat with. Since there was no school the next day, the streets in town were alive. There were all kinds of people wandering about. Some kids engaged in a boisterous *tumbang preso*; another group played hide-and-seek near a school ground. Some adults sat in front of their houses exchanging the latest about the neighbourhood. Everyone in my house had gone to bed. I was the only one still out and about.

Along our bike route, we came upon a makeshift eatery selling *bibingka*, a type of rice cake baked in a clay pot, topped with burning coconut husk. Even today, the smell of burning coconut husk still conjures up memories of my childhood. We could only afford to buy one cake, so we shared and each got a bite. After chowing down the *bibingka*, we pedalled away from the eatery and headed back to our hangout near the school, where we chatted a little more.

Earlier that day, I was in the school library when an official from the provincial education department dropped by for an impromptu visit. I was researching an article I was writing for the school paper. I had seen this man before. A six-footer, which was unusually tall for a Filipino. He was wearing a short-sleeved *barong*, signalling he was a person in an important position. His smiley face showed friendliness and an air of being approachable. He sported a receding hairline. I threw a glance at the visitor. He smiled at me. I respectfully bowed my head and said, "Good afternoon, Mr. Guillermo."

"Is this an *obra*?" he asked, glancing at the research notes I'd scribbled on index cards. I laughed perfunctorily. I thought that was supposed to be a joke. "It's nothing, sir, just a piece for the school paper." Saying that it was nothing was a way of showing politeness, self-deprecation perhaps, and somehow saying that I was a person of no consequence compared to the man speaking with me. The principal, who briefly left the guest by himself so she could speak to the librarian, saw that I was speaking with the man. She approached us.

"This is Renato," the principal introduced me. "He's one of the students we chose to compete in the upcoming school paper writing competition. He's also one of our top honour students among our juniors."

"A bright student. I like bright students," Mr. Guillermo said without missing a beat. I also noticed a smile on his face that was somehow puzzling. I blushed, a tad embarrassed, but I also felt proud I'd been called a bright student and that somebody liked me.

I forgot about that friendly encounter until that night when Mr. Guillermo and a teacher from another school passed by where my friends and I were hanging out. They stopped briefly near us and then kept walking.

"Wasn't that the visitor at school today?" asked my friend Ramon. "My brother knew about him."

"How did your brother know about him?" I asked.

"Nestor was in boy scouts. He went on a lot of camping trips and that shit that they do, what was that again?" he said, scratching his head, trying to remember what it was. "Scout forums. Right, scout forums. He got sent to a couple of those, and Mr. Guillermo was one of the guest speakers. The scouts slept in the school, and apparently, Mr. Guillermo asked the boys to bring him a 'crying banana' at night."

Guffaws ripped through the deserted streets. People had gone home. Kids stopped playing *taguan*, *tumbang preso*, or *tubigan*.

"He promised unsuspecting kids stuff to get what he wanted. But he never lives up to them," Ramon added.

"If he proposed to me something like that, he'd get a kick in the shin and another in the groin," chimed another kid, which elicited even louder reactions.

We were still in a banter when Mr. Guillermo's sidekick teacher came back and approached us. Mr. Guillermo was half a block from us, heading toward a guest house where he was staying for the night. The teacher pointed out to us that it was time to go home and that our parents would soon be looking for us because it was late. We all got up, picked up our bikes, and headed our separate ways. My house was about three blocks east of the guest house. I was just about to mount my bike when I felt a tight grip on my left wrist. The heavy-set teacher, who was slightly taller than me, had wrapped his hand around my wrist.

"We have a visitor who wants to talk to you," he said. I felt disturbed. Nervous. He held my wrist tightly as if I was going to escape.

"Did I do anything wrong, sir?" I asked.

"Do you want to graduate at the top of your class?" he asked me.

That confused me. What did the visitor have to do with me graduating at the top of my class?

"He can make it happen, you know," said the teacher.

IT'S STILL SOMETIMES *difficult to talk about that night. Every time I do, it means reliving that experience. It means feeling the same guilt over and over. It means going through the thousand ifs and buts in one vicious cycle.*

"Leave it up to the Lord. Lift your worries to the high heavens." That's how my grandaunt, a Catholic nun, would have advised how to deal with things like this. "Go to confession. Leave all your burdens to the Lord," I could hear her insistent but calm voice. I've lost track of how many priests I've told about this in the past. I've lost count of how many times I've left this burden for the Lord to bear. I feel better temporarily, but the pain comes back. The burden reappears. The fidgeting of my hands recurs. And there I am again. Back in that room. With that man.

MY HANDS WERE fidgety and my knees were shaky when Mr. Guillermo came out of the washroom. The teacher who fetched me was gone. The door behind me was shut. With that, I convinced myself that I was simply going to talk. There was nothing wrong with talking. It would be over soon, I thought. Mr. Guillermo was powerful and he could change the course of my future. If I could graduate at the top of my class, I'd get scholarships.

It started to rain. The old people were right about the blowing wind by the bay. I could hear raindrops pelting the glass jalousies as the shadow of swaying coconut leaves was projected on the windows. The diaphanous fabric of Mr. Guillermo's *barong* rose above his head, eventually landing on the floor. He was a big man, definitely taller than me. His head was balding. He asked me to grab a chair while he opened a bottle of beer and asked if I wanted one. I declined. There was no legal age limit to consume alcohol in the Philippines. At least there wasn't at that time. Anyone could buy beers or liquor from a corner store. Some of my classmates had begun drinking at age fifteen. I had not. Given my experience with my alcoholic father and grandfather, I didn't want to partake in any of that.

Mr. Guillermo asked me to tell him something about myself. I didn't exactly know what to tell him, so I bored him with school stuff. I mentioned I was number two in my class, that I was active in extracurricular activities, that I was a student leader, that I loved to write, and I was this and that.

"You're ranked number two? I can change that," he said with a particular sparkle in his eyes.

"What do I have to do to make that happen?" I asked.

"You don't have to do anything. I will do all the work," he said, again with that smile.

I fidgeted more. It felt as if my knees were shaking more vigorously, although they were not. My eyes avoided his stare. There was something off, but my fifteen-year-old self could not forget the prize of being at the top, the prospect of being a winner for a change.

The rain reinforced with gusty winds grew stronger. The coconut leaves slapped the windows more violently. I could hear water gushing from a downspout, crashing onto a rain barrel.

"Do you think you taste salty?" Mr. Guillermo asked me before taking a swig from the bottle of beer in his hand. "I heard the water supply in town was cut." It had been two days since the supply of running water was cut. There was a problem with the source, and the whole town had to resort to using water from the wells.

"I showered today," I said as a matter of fact.

"I was just kidding. You didn't look salty," he said laughing, seemingly amused by my naïveté.

I felt his toes touch mine. I swallowed my spit. Perturbed. No one had ever played with my toes that way. My discomfort intensified, but I seemed to have been bolted to the chair. I couldn't move. I felt stuck and helpless, but I knew I could get up and walk out of the room. I could bolt and run home, forget about Mr. Guillermo's offer to change things for me. But my feet felt heavy. They seemed to have grown roots and become planted on the floor. They seemed to become irreversibly attached to the wood and onto the ground.

Someone knocked at the door. Mr. Guillermo looked at me. I looked at the door. I hoped it was the teacher who brought me here. I hoped he came back to take me out of this pickle. Mr. Guillermo told me to open the door. It was the maintenance staff.

"Is there anything else that you need, Mr. Guillermo?" he asked. He didn't acknowledge my presence.

"That would be all," said Mr. Guillermo. "I noticed that you replenished the water container in the washroom. Thank you very much."

The maintenance guy smirked and disappeared before I could say anything. My mind raced between grabbing the doorknob and running, and staying and finding out what Mr. Guillermo was really offering me. But I was glued to the floor. The wind outside was picking up speed.

"I'm not forcing you to do anything," said Mr. Guillermo, as he emptied the beer to his mouth. He was right. I had the chance to leave, but I stayed. As his face became blurry to me, so was my resolve to take off. I could see his lips spouting words. "I don't want you to do anything against your will. You came here voluntarily. Nobody forced you." He came around me. Put his hands on my shoulder. I could smell the beer from his breath when his lips planted an unwanted kiss on my nape. His hand slid between my underwear and my skin.

He turned off the light switch by the door. The room darkened. My mind dimmed. The rain raged even harder. I wondered when it was going to end. I wondered how I was going home.

FINE.

I'm going to deal with this the right way. Not with the prescribed confessions to priests and spiritual direction that often suggested the Lord would heal me, would heal my wounds. And so, let's just say I did talk to a shrink about that night. Let's just say that my exposure to a plurality of thoughts in Canada led me to the comfortable chair in a therapist's office somewhere in Edmonton, because if I didn't, I would have relied upon the deep religious beliefs of my parents that someday the grace of God would heal me and make we well and whole again. And because if I didn't, every time I saw a red bike tied outside a house anywhere in the world, I would be back to that house over and over.

MY BIKE WAS still outside, standing by the fence, when I got out of the guest house. There was no other choice but to ride it home through the pouring rain. I loved the rain, but that night the drops of water were daggers hitting my skin. I had nothing to diffuse them with. They hit my head, intent on splitting it open. At least that was how it felt. My vision was blurry. The torrential rain made it impossible to see the street. I passed by a group of teenagers taking shelter from the downpour in front of the Muelsa, the town's movie house. We lived just behind it. Although it was just a few kicks in the pedal, my legs felt they were ready to give up. Stormwater covered the street. It was difficult to plow along with my bike. I passed another group of bystanders in a makeshift shelter beside the wall of the movie house. Despite the sheets of rain, I caught a whiff of marijuana.

I was ready to collapse when I reached our house. It was dark. Everyone was in bed. The only light inside was an electric votive candle in the altar atop a dresser in my parents' bedroom. My parents had left the wooden jalousies of their bedroom open. The rain wasn't spilling into the bedroom.

An extended roof protected the windows from rain spills. My father usually shut the door at night, knowing I was still out and about. The door didn't have a doorknob. I didn't need a key to get in. I just had to pick a contraption he made and the door would open. I did the trick as quietly as possible. I didn't want to alert anyone I was returning home quite late and soaking wet. When I got in, I tiptoed my way to the washroom and scrambled to find a dry towel. I found one hanging on a covered clothesline in my father's furniture shop at the back of the house. The washroom, more like an outhouse, was adjacent to the shop. There was no light in it. Although I was afraid of the dark, that night I didn't mind that I could barely see anything. I didn't want to see anything. I wanted to stay in the dark. I was ashamed of what I had just allowed to happen to me.

For a moment I sat on the washroom floor, hugging my legs close to my chest, with all my clothes on. I sobbed like I had been mugged, like someone had stolen something from me. I wasn't sure if I was sobbing for losing my innocence or for realizing that I had been had. The cold radiating from the cement floor seeped into my wet skin. I peeled off my shirt, shorts, and underwear and showered. I scrubbed every inch of my body with a bar of Irish Spring as if I could wash away that encounter.

I stopped sobbing. There was no use crying over something I had allowed to happen to me. It was partly my fault. If I hadn't gone out on a bike ride, I wouldn't have been spotted. If I had just ridden away on the bike. If I had just turned the doorknob when I had the chance, I wouldn't have been nursing a broken innocence. I don't remember how long I showered that night. It felt like forever, and even after scrubbing myself raw, I didn't feel clean at all. While I was drying myself off, I heard someone get up from bed and go into the shop. It was my father. He was going to take a leak, but I was in the washroom. I heard a stream of water hitting a pile of firewood just outside. He called my name, probably checking if it was me in the washroom and not some unwanted intruder.

"I got wet in the rain on my way home," I said. I felt the need to explain why I was showering that late. He said I should go to bed soon. I wanted to tell my father to stay and wait for me to get out of the washroom. I wanted to tell him what had happened, but I realized I didn't have a change of clothes.

It would be awkward to come out of the washroom with just a towel draped around my waist. I had always felt awkward being half-naked around anyone. I wanted to tell him I was hurt. I wanted him to hurt the man who hurt me, but I didn't want to give him the impression I wasn't man enough to defend myself. I didn't want to face the consequences of telling my father, so I just wrapped myself in silence, in the dark washroom, where the evidence of any crime against my innocence had been washed with soap and water.

The rain abated. I got out of the washroom. My father left the kitchen light turned on. I didn't have to grope in the darkness trying to find my dresser to get a fresh shirt, a pair of underwear, and shorts. When I had put on clean clothes, I climbed to the top of the double-decked bunk bed in the room I shared with my siblings. Somebody had set up the mosquito net for me. My mother probably told one of my sisters to do it. I wrapped myself in a blanket. I closed my eyes, though I didn't want to fall asleep yet. My hair was still wet. I didn't want to wake up the next day a crazy, mad young man. My grandmother had always advised us not to sleep with wet hair. "You will go crazy, the water will seep into your brain," she cautioned.

I didn't want to fall asleep, though I didn't want to remember what had happened. I closed my eyes. I didn't want any sensory memory from that encounter. But no matter how hard I tried, the smell of beer from his breath became indelibly inked in my consciousness.

LET'S JUST SAY *I didn't move to Canada when I was twenty-seven years old. Chances are, I would have become a bitter fifty-one-year-old priest caught up in an eternal* tubigan, tumbang preso, *and* taguan *back in my hometown. But I already told you I moved to Kamloops because Honolulu would have been boring.*

CHRISTOPHER NASAIRE

Eskinita

THIS IS THE eskinita, this long labyrinthine corridor formed by all the city's scraps, sprawling like lilies. It is an intricate patchwork blistering with shacks on stilts, towering over muddy waters, no taller than the taro shrubs, no more structured than parched earth. Though, of course, here the earth is never parched. It buries the feet with soil softened by the short afternoon rains and the constant flow of water from the mountains scrambling for the sea. Here is where the tides once swelled in, though now it is a huge busy port, paving the way for a dozen manufacturing plants. Corn milling. Pineapple canning. Cola bottling. The coast has gone farther. That's why in this eskinita, the water is all flooded, turning the land into mud.

What keeps my feet from the mud is a long stretch of footbridge made out of wood planks placed on top of cement blocks. Above, a canopy of rusty iron roofs protects from the heat or rain. Yet there's an air of heaviness. It must be the dampness, the eternal misting of all the water that's giving the air weight so tangible to the skin, as if absorbing everything around. There's the funky smell building up in the nose that I know I'm long too familiar with, the stench of something that's been decaying for a long time: a dead rat, a haluan — snakehead fish — I'm sure I've once seen jump out of these waters, onto someone's floor. And there are heaps of trash. All sorts of them: plastic, glass containers, empty shampoo sachets, ice tubig cellophanes. Everything is thrown down the mud through a hole somewhere — a door, a window, a chink on a floor. It's the closest one can be with nature. Nothing comes in between. Everything that thrives here feeds off the mud and all that's in it; everything that falls into it sustains it, becomes it.

Here, in this eskinita, is where we once were, Victor. Do you remember?

I'm back here because your mother called me. She said you've not been seen since the raid — when armed men forcibly closed a Lumad school in southern Bukidnon accused of indoctrinating children into communism. They rounded up everyone — village leaders, teachers, parents, volunteers, and even some of the children — and detained them for several days. Since then no one has gotten any news from you. Your mother is deeply worried. Your wife and child too.

I'm back here in search of you. I don't know how. I don't know where. But, I'm here.

THE MORNING FINALLY reaches the eskinita, though in small scatterings of light, ones that a few fissures between the shacks allow. Still there is no movement. No sign of life. Only satisfying peals of kitchen wares striking against each other. And the firewood smoke escaping from a few latticed windows, carrying the all too familiar aroma of boiling rice and salted fish.

As I make my way through the footbridge in search of your shack, a white dog emerges. It's scratching one side of its ear, the one dappled with a big brown spot extending to its eye, giving it a little shadow. It looks impervious to me watching, though I stand only a few feet away. Glowering, it bares its little teeth and buries them into its scabby skin, trailing the length of its hind leg. Its purpled teats dangle like a row of laburnum flowers kissing the ground.

Askal, they call it in Tagalog. I don't think there's any direct word for that in Bisaya. It's a portmanteau of asong kalye, literally "street dog," an indistinct breed, mongrels you could say. They're everywhere in the eskinita; whether they have a family or are abandoned, all of them are free to roam the streets, like the children playing in the day or the women and men under the pink lights at night.

"Toy, toy," I call the dog's attention. Now on my knees, I throw a hand out in front. The dog stops scratching, looks at my hand, and for a brief moment, slightly wags its tail before nearing close. The dog is trying to sniff whatever I have in my hand. There's nothing. I reach for my pocket, thinking whether I still have a piece of Sky Flakes from the flight earlier, though what's left is the foil wrapper that I haven't thrown out. I look around to see whether there are any sari-sari stores where I could buy a piece of bread, but none of them are open. I move closer to pet the dog. But as I beckon to touch the top of its head, it lets out a loud angry bark. Panicked, I immediately pull back. And I stay still. Though its teeth are still bared, the dog, in turn, starts to back off and eventually runs away.

IN THE ESKINITA the mud looks back. I peer over my reflection upon the surface of the water, and my faint silhouette appears against the backdrop of a whiteout sky. All around, a kaleidoscope of election posters show President Rodrigo Duterte raising the right hand of his close personal aide, who is now running for senator. They give the place colour, a vertigo-inducing blue and red. You can still see Duterte's own election posters from three years ago, now becoming some sort of a house fixture, a wallpaper to protect doors and walls from heat and humidity and rain, as if they are written histories themselves, curated only by time and the people paid to paste them on other people's shacks.

During the 2016 presidential election, I was excited for the possibility of President Duterte. He would be the first from Mindanao, a huge change from establishment politics, whose power almost always points north: Tagalogs, Ilocanos, Kapampangans — never a Mindanaoan. It would be the first time in recent years that the highest official of the country speaks my native tongue, however questionable his choice of words. For twenty years Duterte was the mayor of Davao, where he took a crime-ridden, murderous city and made it one of the cleanest and safest in the country. He ran on a platform of law and order.

There's one photograph that lent a painful face to Duterte's drug war. It's called the Pietà: the woman cradles in her arms the body of her dead husband. Her face furrows, half shown, as her cheek lies close to his, and her legs almost clutch the entirety of his body, feet bare, soles blackened by the dirt from the asphalt street. Behind them, as though witnessing her pain, torsos beyond the yellow police line and a "No Loading and Off-Loading Passengers" sign provide a backdrop. In front, a crumpled piece of brown cardboard reads, "Pusher Ako. Wag Tularan" (I'm a drug pusher. Don't follow my example). It's the first image I saw of Duterte's drug war, the first that hits me with fear.

Life imitating art.

WHAT I DO remember of your shack is the tree beside it, the one you said your mother planted the year she was pregnant with you. It was the tuba-tuba, whose leaves she used as antiseptic for open wounds. Remember that, Victor? She used it on me when I fell through a big gap on the footbridge fronting your door, where I scraped my thigh against its sharp edges. You were with me then, and you laughed when I fell and got myself covered in mud, and you laughed the second time when I was crying for pain as your mother washed and cleaned my wounds. It doesn't take me too long to find the tuba-tuba, and your home, now barely anything you can make of, besides the four pieces of plywood walls standing, and a roof on top almost ready to collapse. I push your door lightly to open and bring myself in. I know nobody's here, but I come in like I used to, without saying a word.

Your room hasn't changed much: the same dim cavern, no more than a hard bed and an old study table, except for a duyan, a white flour cloth wrapped into a baby hammock, hovering over your bed. The only colours, your rainbow mosquito net and your red coffee mug — your favourite, now nothing but a ring of coffee residue and a small heap of cigarette butts. Below, a small drawer, once a Pandora's box of anything barely legal you wanted to show me. What's left of it now, a call centre employment contract, a thick photocopy of Lenin's *Imperialism*, pediatric prescriptions, monthly copies of your electric and water bills.

As I leaf through your things, I see a folded piece of paper. It opens to a familiar loose and loopy penmanship. It is a letter from you to me.

I CAN'T BELIEVE *I'm writing you this letter with your new Canadian address. How's your new home treating you? I know how much you've waited and prayed for it, where you are now, finally with your entire family together. I know — I've been there with you every Sunday at the Nazareno Church. We heard the mass, and as if it wasn't enough, we offered flowers, lit candles, went to that quiet, red-carpeted, air-conditioned Eucharist room because you wanted so much to be there. Canadian, I teased you. And I liked it when you gave me that annoyed don't-call-me-that look you make, as if you didn't want it, but I knew deep inside you did.*

How time flies! Sorry, it took a lot of time for me to muster the courage to write to you. But I hope you're doing well. As for me, I am. I'm with Elisa. We met her during our immersion trip to Talaingod a few years back in college. Do you remember her? In those couple of weeks, the two of you spent so much time together; like lovers, I thought you were. You just had a way with people and with women; they'd like you almost as immediately as you opened your mouth. I envied you for that. You know, that trip wasn't the last time I saw her. I travelled back and forth. No, it wasn't just you. I spent more time with her and her family. They are very good people.

After we get married, Tatay — I call her father — has promised to give us a small tract of land where we could build our own home not too far from theirs. And he wants me to help with their farm. You won't believe the crops they grow here: asparagus, cabbages as large as a punch bowl, and carrots like your forearms. Right now, I'm helping Tatay plant strawberries. It'd be a first on this farm, and I'm doing the research.

I also spend much of my time teaching the children here. Tatay, as the community leader, helped build a school here with his bare hands alongside other members of the community. It's for their own children and even adults who want to learn how to read and write. They're all amazing. When I teach, I always think of you. How I wish you were here. You're way more of a natural teacher than I am. I'm sure you'd love teaching these kids too.

I love it here. Here is far more different from the life I knew. What they have here is a deep connection to the land and the people around them. I don't think we'll ever run out of food here, not just because we grow our own food, but because there is a strong sense of community; neighbours know each other, look out for each other, protect each other. Frankly, I don't think that there's any more I could teach these kids, or all of the people here. They are the ones teaching me, in ways I never could've imagined, to roam freely with your own feet and set your sight far and wide. Here, I've never felt closer to home. This is home.

"BU-ANG NA IRO! BU-ANG NA IRO!" I hear someone bellow from not so far. Loud and limpid, it's a familiar din that on some distant mornings had let my heart slip out of my chest. Outside the shack, I can see the sun is already high, now coming into view like a giant fire bird perched on the blue contours of the nearby Malasag hills. I follow the ruckus. The doors creak. Windows open. Rubber slippers brush against floors. The wood planks under my feet tremble slightly. I now share this eskinita with someone.

I tuck the letter safely inside my back pocket. I climb up the tuba-tuba, and from there I see, behind a rusty tin wall, a stream of men gushing down like water. Top naked, their skin dark in the high sun. Some gaunt. Some bulbous, their bellies sticking out and their bodies writhing like sea waves collapsing into each other, drifting with the steam of midmorning air, bawling, heaving. Armed with whatever objects they found: pieces of wood, broomsticks, large stones, a baseball bat, a digging bar. I watch them, with all their feet buried in mud, scour beneath the shacks, these muddy recesses filled with debris dipped in mud. Their knees and hands press against the soft earth as it starts to creep into their body.

"Naa ra, Naa ra," a young boy shouts, beckoning everyone to the part where he's found the dog. The crowd opens, and the man with the digging bar approaches the boy, walking with his tool, almost as tall as him, leaving a perforation trail on the mud. He then bends down and inspects the gap beneath a shack.

An old man with shiny grey hair holds a long bamboo stick with an iron wire looped on one end. He goes to the same spot and does a similar inspection. "I'll pull it out," he tells the man with the digging bar, who in turn gives him a subtle nod. Then the old man sticks his bamboo pole underneath the shack, reaching for the dog, careful and calculated in manner. As he aims for a catch, everyone's eyes shuffle in intense anticipation, not a word let out from their lips. The silence burns like wildfire forming at the ear tip, throbbing erratically as if all the body's energy collected in one place. The old man jerks and his bamboo pole whisks like the surface of a deep water. Gathering strength, he gives his pole a much firmer grip, with both of his hands pulling it harder and harder after every breath.

Then a big thud. The old man pulls the dog out of hiding and flings it into the crowd like a piece of meat, the iron wire still squeezing its neck. Mud replaces its coat, though the big spot on its ear still shows. The dog lets out a loud howl as the men press in.

The man with the digging bar throws his first blow. The dog cowers, shrieking and shaking violently as it tries to pull its head out, only to tighten even more the wire wrapped around its neck. With rump lowered and tail tucked between its thighs, it hobbles inch by inch in a futile attempt to escape. The other men come in with all their found tools, targeting the dog's body. Soon the dog drops, head down. Now narrowed by the swelling and the blood leaking out of its temple, the dog's eyes flounder as if searching for the light of day that's now dimmed by the mad crowd. Every bat, every whip, every kick razes until it can barely stand, stumbling with every mean force placed upon its body, the very weight of which it could no more carry.

Seeing the dog no longer moving, all the men fall silent. The man with the digging bar draws himself close to the dog's body to check for the slightest movement.

"Buhi ba, buhi?" one person in the crowd asks.

Then with one hand, the man holds his digging bar to the ground like a staff, and with another, he wipes a thick blob of mud and blood off his face, then his arms and torso, his chest revealing a fading blue-and-red tattoo of the Sacred Heart of Jesus. He turns his head to the other men around him, and they look at him earnestly in return. Quickly, he takes a big step back, raises the digging bar over his head, and with a soft grunt, hurls it finally into the dog's head.

Above, what was once a bright sky dims out. Suddenly, the early afternoon rain starts to pour heavily, washing the mud off the men's bodies. Then the crowd begins to scatter, one by one, leaving the dead dog in the mud. I come down from the tuba-tuba and run for shelter as quickly as I can toward your shack. There I stand still. The eskinita is now quiet. The only sound left is the drumming of rain against the roofs. And as it goes on, this place heaves anew in the rising flood waters. Soon the dead dog's body will disappear — buried, interred in the thickness of mud.

FROM MY POCKET I grab your letter, which is now a crumpled piece of paper. It unveils your last words: *Here, I've never felt closer to home. This is home.*

The Big Picture

ISABEL CARLIN

Welcome! Long life! Good health! Big smile!

Note: Every time I read this poem, I am compelled to add new names to the footnote at the end. I hope one day to write poems in a world where grief is a relic, where we can build monuments to the dead without leaving space for future martyrs.

Mabuhay, ghost!

on sabbath day noon i went into a staggering courtyard felt
the bells of trinite earrings past/pass me by,
the birds of Balangiga.

the neon nuke our parents built made a big Pacific crater
i sat with Death in it (we were wearing bikinis) She said it's too hot
for a hot tub, like we were in a rooftop jacuzzi swimming
and bubbling with air.

did you hear in that water the gurgling throatchimes of your
self which is not a self, your bodynotbody
windshot and gunswept, run afoul of
shore and run aground of evil men —
did you hear them?

Mabuhay, ghost!

at two minutes before midnight on the doomsday
clock let's meet at the park bench under
the willow weeping for Billie Holiday.

on my way to you a curled-up housebroken cornstalk
will strangle me around the throat — an act of
war — you'll cry in the streets with an upright banner
shouting, I survive! the whole thing passing through your spectral hands.

what is it that i meant to tell you? what smokestack
lightning would we have pressed palm-to-palm
like lovers under that willow? were we once bodies? did we
not have hands to write letters to our own mothers
who most likely did not receive them?

Mabuhay, ghost!

on feast day noon i held the silent vigil which is
of course loud in its own way (speaking vigilantly
to the unghosting instinct of a browbeaten press)
      your name aloud afoul aground:
      Kerima!

      Zara!

      Lorena!

      River!*

at the plowing prow of that riverbend liner
i saw the aching marrow of southern bodies
overturned deep in shallow water
as the cruise line undrowned a disappeared thousand.

as the machinic canyonmaker scrapes fruit from labour
wholly and efficiently in lethal-fertile valleys
i shoulderpress plunge into the canefield dirt-earth.
a shovel hits once for twelve bodies and more
salvaged and saved from the spectre who haunts to this day.

Mabuhay, ghost!

i saw you in that world-ending archipelago-alley where two gunmen
shot you at dawn or bombed out your school or bulldozed your house
or rezoned your neighbourhood for nuke-making —

*a short footnote on names: it was indeed true and in fact irrefutable that Kerima
Lorena Tariman and Zara Alvarez and Maria Lorena Barros and River Nasino
once had hands and once were bodies although River certainly did not write
letters to her mother — a political prisoner — as she was three months old when
she died after being separated from her mother — who attended her funeral in
shackles — salvage bears a unique sense in the Philippines as a euphemism for
forced disappearances — other people who had hands and were once bodies and
presumably wrote letters to their own mothers include — Fidel Agcaoili — Randy
Echanis — Macliing Dulag — Reken Remasog — Jennifer Laude — Liliosa Hilao
— Edgar Jopson — Tandang Sora — Juan Escandor — Archimedes Trajano — Bae
Merlin Ansabo Celis — Emmanuel Lacaba — Randy Malayao — Amado Khaya
Canham Rodriguez — Ricardo Mayumi — Ben Ramos — Rex Fernandez — Ka
Oris — Ka Pika — Kian delos Santos — Carl Arnaiz — Reynaldo de Guzman —
Chad Booc — Jurain Ngujo — Elgyn Balonga — Robert Aragon — Tirso Añar.

Foreign aid

Tonight's prairie sunset over the Trans-Canada
blockades the freight trucks plying the empty road.

The black snake-eye warps the shifting mud-land
beneath it; smells fear and lurches for parts
snakelike and tar-slurried: lung cancer dancefloor, atom
Lumily anupon of Ferdinand Marcos, deteriorating liver.

Our snake is full. It has eaten all that can be
eaten in the world. It takes aim at the immaterial rest:

The 120th meridian east arcing disconsolately over
the bloated globe from end to end, always itself, wondering
is there not a thing to be seen one degree to the west?
No! Not for our snake, our attic ghost, our albatross.

Black snake wires empire to colony via the Pacific Rim,
near-bioluminescent with its crackling underwater sparks.

Eating. Always hungry, our snake, our Llorona, our amour damné.
Watching. Always watching, our Galil Ace 5.56 mm, our fatherland.
Watch the black snake spread oilspill-like along four cascading
highway tiers from downtown Manila to uptown West Point.

Palm down fingers stretched curling into the ocean; tsunamis
spilling past the webs of our fingers dissolving eating gnashing

Swallowing the world we built and killed and ate

in nine lonely stanzas.

Lazarus in the age of war

i. DEATH OF X — AT DUSK

Yukawa signalled at the watchtower yesterday —
Strike! one brassborn song for your
Late unladen corpse.

Our moon eclipsed twice that night winking
Back and forth like the delicate ankle in our
Argentine tango.

Our stars fell to earth, prostrate, kissed the soil
And our earthworms and ants with mouths
As so many waterfalls.

Our sun broiled the earth open and cracked it
Deeply, subversively, so that your body was
Buried by the sky itself.

ii. FLOODING OF THE TOWN OF X —

Big trout knew it first:
the vengeance of our rivers.

Fish quarrelled in seven tongues
With blacksmiths and soothsayers
Inside the mouths of nuns and priests
Between couch cushions, electric outlets:
salmon at war.

Whales, then, crushed great vehicles
Hauling forests by the log
Slipped into clubs dressed as college kids

Married ten thousand of our men
Here! the wretched augurs cried:
the vengeance of our rivers.

Sea snakes rained down from the sky
In torrents, died inelegant deaths publicly,
Smashed to pieces by eavestroughs
Cornwallis and soon after gunned down
By firing squad, who hoped to keep them
In the sky where they belonged:
executioner-style.

Even the hot cooked-earth marsh which was
Your divan now, your bed, your pillow,
Was filled with it:
the vengeance of our rivers.

iii. AROUSAL OF THE CORPSE OF X —

Uneasy to snap open   Pearl-sky
dew   Kokytos howl in your   throat
Knife-perch   your thigh slice through
Father Geiger's aureole glow
make   you   alive

iv. RETURN OF X — AT SUNRISE

Palm breaches the surface of our
Hymn-organ wrist, lifeline first.

Each fingertip haloed for its own
Virtue. Verging on the obscene.

Our cold wristvein spills into our lap
Via this opening, *sangserpent.*

Rizal's palm at the stone warmed
By our stars, our moon, our sun.

Kitchenuhmaykoos watches the
Firing squad kill *serpents de mer.*

Your palm sunskinned by utopian vision
Wincing against hot stone, cold metal.

Some archer you are, turret-perched,
Hailing a military response to the flood.

Your uran-crown rings each brass fingertip
Already-grieving, beatitude-wearied,
Signalling at the watchtower:

FLOODING WORSE BY RAIN
OUR SUN HAS LEFT THE AUGURS
DROWNED BY SKY ITSELF

STEFFI TAD-Y

Third Person Singular

What if hysterical
had historical roots

What if arrival does not mean
a departure from roots

What if we talked
about the departed

What if roots
were an unrestrained
show of colour

What if we moved
slow & furious
like a windmill dunk

What if we kept writing
about violets

If we can't (yet)
about the violence
(What if we wrapped ourselves
in *other than*, in *other than*)

What if we removed
the knife

What if we stopped
the blow

Real Talk

Dear Jesus, I am ticked off by that passage where you suffer for my transgressions. First of all, they are mine. Even soggy mulch in the gutter once shimmered gold. I can get behind the cross and crown of thorns but what moved me the most was when you took the fallen ear on the ground and put it back on to the soldier about to arrest you. The book of John says there is no greater love than for a man to lay down his life for his friend. So did you ever have feelings for John? Why must love be premised on self-annihilation? I was flustered when you replied, "It's okay, Girl. I'll live."

KAIA M. ARROW

Dreams of Pinoy Joy, Decolonial Rage and Disabled Resistance in the Diaspora

I need you to know

I am privileged
That my survival
Depends on asking questions
Instead of swallowing them down.

This is our intergenerational wealth.
Passed down by parents who survived on a steady diet of silence.

I tried to succeed under white judgment; now I survive white surveillance/ignorance/fragility. Sick & disabled Pinay, too familiar with how folks feel our rights are optional, are favours, are unfair — at the cost of our inconvenient humanity.

My body is an act of defiance
That I'm an un/willing accomplice to

> *Sometimes I revel in how uncomfortable it makes other people.*
> *Sometimes I have to, to keep going.*

They "play along" with our personhood until it's too much work, too tiring, too challenging. They "tolerate" and "allow," these so-called allies of anti-racism and anti-colonialism. They tell me (token Brown woman, token crip, token queer) about their token learnings, as if they're gifts I should be grateful to receive. As if unlearning white normativity, capitalism, and colonization isn't work to free us all.

For many of us, we live here on stolen land because colonialism and racial capitalism have had direct destructive effects on our homelands. Land still being ravaged by colonial capitalism.

Sometimes I never want to step foot in the Philippines again
What it's supposed to mean to me
Who I'm supposed to be
Will this Land embrace me
Or spit me back, unknown daughter

I'm afraid to find out.

The destruction continues every time whiteness is positioned as normal, as unquestionable, as standard; when whiteness receives the benefit of the doubt, while the rest of us are subject to scrutiny. And it continues every time our people and our cultures are positioned as abnormal, as subject to judgment, as extraneous.

I grieve what has been taken from us. I don't know what holidays my ancestors celebrated before Spanish galleons broke the horizon in 1521. I don't know what songs they sang, the rituals they had, or the lives they lived. These stories were systematically destroyed by Spanish colonists, American imperialists, and Japanese occupiers. I don't imagine some pre-colonial utopia. There is precious little left to imagine at all.

At night
My guides and ancestors rock me to sleep
In a bangka they weave around my bed.

Daughter of infinities, descendant of multitudes
They speak in my Lola's voice.
Anak, they say.

Close your eyes
Rest now.

Now I am grown
When I reach out for yakap
Only the ancestors respond.

I learned my culture in negatives. Don't speak Tagalog at work, don't make trouble, don't flinch when white men eye my (crip) body like a toy they can take home. We were taught just enough to survive with feet in two worlds. I can still dance the tinikling, and placate a self-righteous white woman with a deferent tone and words to soothe the ego.

The gift I receive from my lineage is to do more than lay low in white supremacy, but to revel in Pilipinx joy and defiance.

The word Brown feels like an anthem
> *These days*
Our rage/pride/love/joy feels like singing

You need to know that this is urgent and painful and necessary for all of us. That my dreams are full of loud Pinoys rebuilding what has been taken, of abundance where we can all hold room for softness and for rage, of our children free and fierce and proud in a world that demands we shrink.

I dream of celebrating in tandem with our ancestors once again, to sing their songs and write new ones.

This is what I need you to know: It starts with naming that things are not as they should be. It ends with us.

TEODORO ALCUITAS

Accidental Journalist

I WAS DRIFTING in my career as an architect after arriving in Canada with my family in 1968 and, like most immigrants, was lost in the new country.

After moving to Winnipeg from Saskatoon, I switched to life insurance sales.

The Filipino community numbered seven thousand at the time, and like them, I was hungry for news from the Motherland. The only means of news were by mail from relatives or the television, as the Internet had not been invented yet. There were no Filipino newspapers in Canada at the time.

The idea of starting one came when I saw high school students assembling their paper by the traditional "cut and paste" method. On a whim, my brother-in-law and I decided we could do a paper for the Winnipeg community. Neither of us had journalism experience, although Flor Cadigal was an English teacher back home.

We agreed to name the paper *Silangan*, as it embodied our vision. "*Silangan*" in Filipino is where the sun rises — the east. We wanted the newspaper to be a beacon to our community to inspire them to greater heights. From the beginning, our goal was clear: the paper was to be a voice and a beacon and not just a mere chronicler of events,

I was editor, with Florentino "Flor" Cadigal Jr. and Ric Sumaling as the editorial staff.

Cadigal did his column — "Bato-Bato sa Langit ang Tamaan Huwag Magalit" — and Sumaling did the artwork, while I did content writing and production as well as distribution.

The first issue of the twenty-four-page tabloid came out in February 1976 and it became a sensation. The excitement of the first issue was like expecting a first baby!

It was a "labour of love" for me, as I had to do most of the work running the paper, and I neglected my selling job.

My basement served as the editorial and distribution centre. I would stay up all night to put the issue to bed and then drive to Steinbach, sixty kilometres away, to the printers. I would deliver copies to the different outlets in the city and then prepare the mailing to subscribers. The intensive labour needed to produce and distribute *Silangan* was eclipsed by the euphoria of its popularity among its readers.

I did not have the foggiest idea about the basics of journalism except the bare five Ws — Who, What, When, Where, and Why — so I had to learn it on my own.

Published once a month, *Silangan* became a staple of the community. People eagerly awaited copies at grocery stores and other outlets. It was distributed free, and whatever little income it generated from ads was just enough to cover printing costs.

From initially focusing on the Winnipeg community, it gradually expanded to other centres as I recruited more contributors and writers. Soon, I had people sending their contributions from Saskatoon, Calgary, Edmonton, and Vancouver.

The paper covered topics from social issues to politics. I did not shirk from commenting on so-called controversial community issues like the Philippine Association of Manitoba (PAM). PAM was the self-proclaimed association representing Filipinos in Winnipeg. My criticism was that it was a "song and dance" organization that was not really involved in societal issues that affected the community.

When the community faced a racial backlash, for example, PAM did not speak up, preferring instead to not "rock the boat." They also catered to the typical Filipino propensity for "gala" affairs, hosting events where attendees come out in their lavish fashion outfits. Added to this was the organization's lack of diversity in their officers, who were mainly medical professionals. Workers in the garment industry and other sectors were not represented in the organization's leadership.

I was preoccupied with issues of discrimination and racism. It was common during those days to label Filipinos and other minorities or racialized people as the "bad apples" in society, much like how the mainstream media portrayed Indigenous people. I wrote and fought against openly racist treatment and once told a CBC reporter, "I am one Filipino that will not allow myself to be a doormat." He tried to describe the way the media was treating us by replying, "They [the media] did it to the Italians and Irish before. Now it is Filipinos."

Being a community journalist posed some very difficult dilemmas for me, including having to decide whether to cover stories about people in the community that I knew personally. One example I can remember was when a prominent member of the community was accused of a crime. The news came out in the mainstream media and callers inquired whether I was going to write about it in my paper. I agonized over the decision but realized I had no choice but to cover it as news.

My obsession to improve the community took its toll on me by the time the paper was five years old. While the paper had a growing readership and influence, the physical and emotional stress began to surface, not to mention the financial burden it was putting on me. As I devoted all my time to running the paper, I neglected my own insurance selling and relied solely on my wife's income to sustain the family.

The advertising revenues were not sufficient to pay me or the other staff a salary, and it could barely pay for printing and other costs. By this time, I was also beginning to feel that my advocacies were not influencing the community.

The straw that broke the camel's back was the reaction to my criticism of PAM's sponsorship of a nationwide conference in Winnipeg. The aim was supposedly to talk about the problems faced by the community. The day before the conference, I asked several people to join me in demonstrating at the hotel where the conference was taking place. I believed the conference was a waste of money and that the organizers should not have paid travel costs for delegates from out-of-province to find out what the problems were in the Winnipeg Filipino community.

To my dismay, on the morning of the conference, no one showed up to demonstrate. I ended up alone with my family — my wife and three daughters shivering in the Winnipeg cold with our placards. People shouted at us as they passed by: "You are an embarrassment for demonstrating ... *nakakahiya kayo.*" When we went home, the family talked about the experience; we were all bitterly disappointed.

I did a lot of soul-searching, asking myself if the struggle was worth it. That night I decided to give up the paper and called a few people to break the news. It was a shock to the community, and I knew it would be hard to face them at that moment, so I decided to withdraw to an undisclosed location to get away from the incessant phone calls.

After a few days, I received feelers that a group of Filipinos were interested in negotiating with me to buy the paper. I accepted an offer made by a group that consisted of Rod Cantiveros, Fred de Villa, and Epoy Tawagin. We agreed on a "goodwill value" for the paper as there were no physical assets nor receivables to talk about. Among the conditions of the sale was that I would stay on for several issues to help the transition. I also agreed to a two-year "no competition" clause.

The last issue of *Silangan* came out in July 1982, and a brief announcement came out in the *Winnipeg Free Press*. Cantiveros became the paper's editor, and after a year its name was changed to *Filipino Journal*, presumably because *Silangan* had a controversial reputation. *Filipino Journal* continues to this day, making it one of the oldest Filipino newspapers in Canada. The other is *Atin Ito* of Toronto.

After the closure of *Silangan*, I was offered a column in the *Winnipeg Sun*, which I declined as I had no confidence in my writing ability.

And while my pen lay idle after the sale, things were happening fast in the homeland. Senator Benigno "Ninoy" Aquino, the dictator Ferdinand Marcos' main rival, was assassinated on August 21, 1983, and the country was in turmoil. I was itching to cover this event, but I had no platform.

A day after the Aquino assassination, I rang up *Winnipeg Sun* editor Paul Sullivan and asked if he was interested in an opinion piece.

"If you can do it in two hours or so, we can use it," he said. I stayed up late that night, frantically ransacking my files about Aquino and Marcos, and my piece came out the next day.

I was becoming increasingly restless over not being able to write about the Philippine situation, so I thought of venturing into another publication. In February 1983, *Kalayaan* was born. "*Kalayaan*" means freedom in Filipino, and it was appropriate for the times as the Motherland was under Martial Law and fighting to regain its freedom.

A modest eight-page tabloid, *Kalayaan* featured articles about the Filipino people's struggle and the fight against the Marcos dictatorship and Martial Law.

Defying traditional journalistic standards, I reluctantly took up the leadership of the anti-Marcos movement that formed in Winnipeg soon after the Aquino assassination on August 21, 1983. The August Twenty-One Movement (ATOM) was the vanguard of the anti-Marcos opposition in Canada.

Kalayaan had a busy time covering the series of events in the city that included the visits of Agapito "Butz" Aquino, brother of the slain senator, and other Philippine personalities.

When *Kalayaan* carried advertising from the Bank of Nova Scotia, I was asked by the local anti-apartheid group if I was willing to withdraw the bank's ad as it was doing business in South Africa. It was a lucrative contract for a small paper like mine, but I did not hesitate to cancel it in support of the anti-apartheid movement.

The paper exposed the extravagance of the Philippine government in maintaining a large consulate in Winnipeg. A poor country like the Philippines did not need to rent a whole floor of a downtown office building and employ ten people. I compared it to the Japanese Consulate, which occupied only a quarter of the space in the same building. The story was picked up by the *Winnipeg Free Press* and the controversy erupted. Soon after the consulate was closed, I bore the brunt of the blame for its closure from some people in the community. My exposé perhaps contributed to the consulate's demise, although it was a decision made by the Philippine government.

But it was in issues related to racism that I found myself most embroiled. The Indigenous community and people of colour were fair game for the mainstream media, and headlines screamed of crimes allegedly committed by them. I could not understand why only Indigenous people and people of colour were identified in crime reporting. Our race was always identified, while the race of people of European ancestry was not.

I helped organize a meeting with mainstream media and community leaders to discuss the issue of racialized reporting of crime news in the city. Media representatives argued that there was no racism in their reporting, as the identification of race was "germane" to the story.

One incident involving some Filipinos during Folklorama was reported by the *Winnipeg Sun*, whose headlines screamed "Filipinos in fracas," and whose articles warned of potential trouble during Folklorama, a practice of sensationalizing news involving people of colour.

This happened after our meeting with media representatives, and I thought if the media would not respond to our concerns, maybe we should hurt them in their pocketbooks. I called for a boycott of the paper and invited some people to call and cancel their subscriptions. Some Filipino mothers called the *Winnipeg Sun* to tell them that their boys would no longer be distributing the paper if the discriminatory practice continued. Corner stores that sold the paper also called to say that they would stop selling the *Sun*.

The editor at the time, Kelly Armstrong, called and asked me to hold off on my call for a boycott. I said it was too late, as *Kalayaan* was on its way to the printers with my editorial for a boycott on it. The move prompted an editorial response from the *Sun* explaining their side. It was the first time a major media outlet in the city had acknowledged their actions, which was a major victory for the Filipino community.

I thought of expanding *Kalayaan* to other ethnic communities in Winnipeg in the hope of increasing circulation. The paper became a magazine, and I named it *Mosaik* to reflect the diversity of the city. Personalities that were featured included Elijah Harper, the first Indigenous member of the Manitoba legislature, and Evelyn Lau, the acclaimed Chinese-Canadian poet and author. Despite my efforts, however, the publication did not become a viable financial operation and folded after a year.

In 1992, my family moved to the west coast and settled in Vancouver. Since I had contacts in the city while publishing *Silangan*, I was invited to write for the *Philippine Chronicle*, then published by Boding and Erly Juatco. When the paper changed ownership, I became its new editor until it folded.

In early 2009, I tried to revive *Silangan* with a first tabloid issue in April. It lasted for ten issues until January 2010. I then moved to *Philippine Asian News Today* (PNT), published by Rey Fortaleza in 2009 as the Senior Editor, until December 2014 when I started my own online paper: philippinecana-diannews.com. The vision is to link the Filipino diaspora in Canada.

Today, at eighty-three years old, I am still doing what I love to do: telling and sharing the stories of our community.

We haven't reached one million views yet, but I will keep writing with that goal in mind, one click at a time.

Working for forty-six years now as an "accidental journalist" in Canada has not always been easy, but I have thoroughly enjoyed it, and I am truly grateful that I have chosen this path.

C.E. GATCHALIAN

Fuck You. Gutlfishness, Big Girls, and the (Mis) Education of Hidilyn Diaz

This think piece was originally commissioned by fu-GEN Asian Canadian Theatre Company and presented by the author as part of fu-GEN's series *Digital Connections* in 2021.

HELLO EVERYONE. I'M C.E. Ga*tcha*lian — my apologies, C.E. Gatcha*lian*, I'm pronouncing it the original Tagalog way now — but you can call me Chris.

First off, I'd like to acknowledge that I'm livestreaming today from the unceded — meaning unsurrendered — and occupied territories of the Musqueam, Squamish, and Tsleil-Waututh peoples, colonially known as Vancouver.

I just started this webinar with a land acknowledgment. A friend of mine, a settler, is of the belief that unless we truly intend to completely dismantle the colonial nation-state as we know it and return all the land to its traditional caretakers, such acknowledgements are meaningless and, worse, hypocritical. I know that some Indigenous folks share this view.

And this leads me to reflect on some of the issues the last eighteen months have brought up for me — issues related to how we moved in the world prior to the pandemic.

Okay, let me rephrase that: issues related to how *I* moved in the world prior to the pandemic.

(Prior to the pandemic, for example, I would have been less reluctant to use the royal, colonial "we." See how quickly I corrected myself just there? I'm learning.)

So. Looking back at my modus operandi shortly before the pandemic, I was moving on the surface of things, going through the motions, putting only as much effort as was necessary to get by.

Simply put, the first two months of 2020, I was exhausted. I felt it in my body. One could attribute it to SAD — seasonal affective disorder — a condition that Vancouverites are particularly prone to, given our unremittingly grey winters.

But it was more than that, I think. I was running on empty. My raison d'être — or my life mission, the Nietzschean "heroic goal" that gets me up in the morning — had lost its lustre, had become a dreary wake-up call rather than a lofty riff from angels' trumpets. I was forcing every gesture. Everything felt heavy. But I'm a mullard. And a pleaser. So as empty as I felt — as empty as I was — I kept rowing and rowing. Forcing. Producing.

Then on March 16, 2020, the world stopped. Do you remember what you were doing that day? As in, *exactly* what you were doing that day? Like how you remember what you were doing when John Lennon died, or Princess Di, or Kobe Bryant?

Well, I don't, and if you don't either, maybe it's because it wasn't a crash out of nowhere, but something that felt inevitable and boringly, numbingly *right*.

On March 16, 2020, I think I shrugged. I just shrugged.

I don't think I gave it much or any real thought the first two weeks of the lockdown, except as an opportunity to reboot before returning to the proverbial treadmill.

And then, as the lockdown dragged out and on, and as each one of us — sorry, old habit, and a bad one, I was totalizing — as *I*, like a scorpion, tuned out and turned *in*, there was nothing but thoughts. Thoughts were all I had.

Some of these I remember with crystalline clarity. Despite the whirl of them in my head, multiplied and magnified by the external deadness of lockdown, some managed to stand out from all the rest, like pinkish pearls in a flurry of snow.

Such was the tragic beauty of a mind in lockdown.

Some of these thoughts were, oddly enough, about Ayn Rand.

Like many, I first discovered Ayn Rand when I was in my teens. She is most famous for two enormous doorstops of books: *The Fountainhead* and *Atlas Shrugged*, both of which I devoured in hungry, predatory succession.

I wasn't particularly bothered about their cartoonish plots and turgid prose; these two novels were like intellectual cocaine, filling a need that for me at age fifteen was insatiable: affirmation and validation in the face of a hostile and hateful world.

Coz I was bullied as a kid. K to 12, bullied. Some years were worse than others. But yeah, it was my baseline. Macro and micro. Bruised eyes, bruised ego. A brown queer bookworm. An obvious, easy target.

This isn't something I've talked about much — I think I downplayed it even in my memoir — because I've been conditioned by neo liberalism to never "play victim" and conditioned by cis-hetero-misogyny to be ashamed of weakness.

In *Atlas Shrugged*, the world stops. The world's corporate, artistic, scientific, and intellectual elite go on "strike" to teach the useless, brainless, and, God forbid, altruistic masses a lesson: that, without the selfish elite, the world would go to shit. Rand's dystopian vision kinda came true eighteen months ago, but for a different reason, I think, than what *Atlas Shrugged* posits. Reality went on strike against the very creatures who've turned a blind eye to it, grinding industry to a temporary halt so that Nature could come up for a bit of air.

Atlas Shrugged celebrates a world in ceaseless, perpetual motion where nothing matters but achievement, where we're only as good as what we produce. Therein, according to Rand, lies the path to transcendence. And, like just about everyone, I was hungry for transcendence.

My reasons for adoring Ayn Rand — and why I still, despite my long, messy, hard-earned political evolution from classical liberal to neo-Marxist, have a soft spot for her — can be summed up in two simple words: "fuck you." Coz despite the occasional well-taken insights her philosophy offers on such lofty topics as metaphysics, epistemology, and aesthetics, "fuck you" is, essentially, what her world view boils down to.

And for a brown queer bookworm who was convinced the entire world despised him, the words "fuck you" were pure and utter magic.

Rand wrote another book called *The Virtue of Selfishness*. My ex half-jokingly calls that book my Bible. And you know what? He's right. It *was* my Bible for a few years. And when the pandemic forced us to retreat inside our houses, behind our walls, a lot of us — sorry, *I* — went deeper still: into our*selves*. Into, to paraphrase Tennessee Williams, the solitary confinement of our own skins. The world stopped precisely where the inside of my skin began.

Hence, the virtue of selfishness. And reflections on Ayn Rand.

As an only child, being alone was always my default. Since the outer world rolled out no welcome mat, I fetishized the inner. So down the path of unchecked, spiralling narcissism I went. Everything I encountered in the outer world simply confirmed what I already thought of it. This, though, was true: the world *was* racist and homophobic. My choice: I could jump off a cliff and die, or claw out some way to survive.

Unbreached will-to-power. Unfettered personal liberty. Trust your mind, trust yourself. Screw the masses, screw conformity.

Egoistic, ego*tist*ic, anti-social, narcissistic.

Filipinos have a massive inferiority complex.

Sorry. Filipin*x* have a massive inferiority complex.

Sorry. *I* have a massive inferiority complex.

As a brainy queer kid from a single-income, working-class brown household, the philosophy of Ayn Rand pointed a way out. Her books were what neo-liberalism made most readily available for poor kids like me with a decent brain and healthy ambition. If there were alternatives, they weren't on offer. *But Ayn Rand got me through.*

So, during the pandemic, I've been thinking about how I'd been living with an Ayn Rand mindset long after I thought I had discarded her, and, more generally, about the paradox of things being simultaneously horrible and empowering: about how something that is ultimately poison can be necessary medicine in the short term.

Narcissism as medicine. *It got me through.* And honestly, this occurred to me: is narcissism such a bad thing if one believes, beyond a shadow of a doubt, that no one else can possibly love them? Narcissism is the consequence, not the cause, of social ills. Even if the world doesn't actually hate you, even if it *is* just in your head, there are *reasons* they're in your head — neurological predispositions being only half the story. Society is fucked up, and it's fucked up our minds. So ... why *not* narcissism? Why not *anything*, short of murder, that might provide some comfort? That society pays so much lip service to condemning narcissism is pretty rich given how, for the last 250 years, it's been shredding itself into billions of unrelated individual selves.

Narcissism. The first Asian I lusted after was Tony Leung Chiu-Wai, the handsome, hunky star of such Wong Kar-Wai films as *In the Mood for Love* and the queer classic, *Happy Together.* In my twenties, I justified not sleeping with Asian men on the grounds that it would be "narcissistic" to pursue fellow Asians. I became very creative around rationalizing my internalized white supremacy.

In late June, when things started opening up in Vancouver, I got wind of a Wong Kar-Wai retrospective at my favourite movie theatre. Most of the films starred Tony Leung Chiu-Wai. Single and sex-starved, I promptly bought my ticket to the 1994 gem, *Chungking Express.*

I left the movie theatre with "California Dreamin'" stuck in my head, playing as it did through much of the second half of *Chungking Express.* Life, via this film, was beckoning again, cracking my shell and gently taking my hand.

But that song, that song though. Who did that song?

(This is a quiz. Audience participation. Who did that song? Those of you old enough to know.)

The Mamas & the Papas. The band that defined the 60s counterculture. Its breakout star was the last of its members to be asked to join, coz they thought her unbankable. Read: too heavy. The fiercely intelligent, sharp-witted, silken-voiced Mama Cass.

Mama Cass, who died when I was eight weeks old, who everyone still thinks died from choking on a ham sandwich. Actually, she died of heart failure, caused most likely by years of yo-yo dieting.

And I think about the heavy girls I gravitated toward when I was a kid, coz they seemed to gravitate toward *me* — or at least, not think any less of me coz I was a bookworm and burgeoning queer.

And I think about this phenomenon of gay men and their "fag hags," how the women we chose for this role were often, though by no means always, heavy.

My hag certainly was. A rich straight white girl. Unlucky in love. One of the first people I came out to.

And she'd hang out with me and my buddies, go to the clubs and get drunk with us. She'd gently counsel us on the travails of our love lives, and we'd drunkenly voice our undying gratitude to her.

And I think about the fat jokes we'd tell behind her back — some of which she was the subject of — and how much we pitied her.

And I think about how we told those jokes, with a relish that was also a release — of the pain that had been inflicted on us, that we were helpless to not pass on to others.

And just as I'm about to self-flagellate over how badly I treated my friend, it dawns on me that she very well could have been making jokes behind *my* back, that for all her declarations of allyship, it was all joyous slumming.

And I think about all the reasons why people come together, fragile alliances against common enemies. And I wonder if bonding always has to be negative, if we can ever come together out of love instead of fear.

Then I think, is coming together out of fear such a bad thing? Maybe, as marginalized folx, we have no choice in the matter. And maybe, as marginalized folx, it's not our problem to solve.

I think about the misogyny and transmisogyny of many gay men, how our public trans-inclusive feminism is belied by our private banter.

I think about fatphobia, my own and gay men's in general, and our narcissistic desire to look as buffed as our high school torturers.

And how this is yet more evidence of the vicious cycles we need to liberate from, and, for a second, I wonder if it's truly possible to escape them.

Just for a second, though. I'm an optimist at heart.

I told one of my writer friends that I was researching Ayn Rand for a novel. He said, "Don't be ashamed. If nobody studied cancer, we wouldn't have oncology!"

"The white race is the cancer of human history," Susan Sontag — a white woman — once wrote. She later apologized for that statement, saying it was insensitive to cancer patients.

In my memoir, I call Sontag's statement extreme. Some of my readers have responded that it's the hard, ugly truth.

Not all white folks are bad, I remind myself — ever conscious of white fragility, even when there are no white people around. And then there are folks like the well-to-do white family my friend — a doctor — told me about a while ago. She asked them if they required additional "house help" to care for their recently hospitalized matriarch. "We're good," they replied blithely. "We have a Filipino at home."

And the white guy on the bus whom I overheard talking about his Filipinx girlfriend. "Filipinas are the best," he said. "They're so loyal and faithful."

And the white people over the years who've told me how much they "love" Filipinx folks — like this wealthy West Side white woman whom I worked for briefly. Lighting up when I told her of my ancestral background, she said, "I love Filipinos! You're all so family oriented and Christian." A comment "young me" would have taken as the highest compliment.

Two months ago, Hidilyn Francisco Diaz, a weightlifter from Zamboanga City, Philippines, made history by being the first Filipino athlete *ever* to win an Olympic gold medal.

Lest you further interrogate my leftist creds now that I've admitted a lingering soft spot for Ayn Rand, let me be very clear: I couldn't care less about the Olympics. However, this particular "Olympic moment" struck a chord with me for reasons that are undeniably atavistic and tribal.

Coz someone forgot to tell Hidilyn Diaz: you're not supposed to do this.

Coz someone forgot to tell Hidilyn Diaz: Filipinos can't be anything other than upholders of other people's privilege.

Coz someone forgot to tell Hidilyn Diaz: Filipino women shouldn't expect any selfish rewards for literally carrying the world on their shoulders.

On July 26, 2021, Hidilyn Francisco Diaz, a four-foot, eleven-inch member of the Philippine Air Force, lifted a combined weight of 224 kilograms over her head — a feat she performed in Tokyo, capital of Japan, one of the many countries that colonized the Philippines over the years.

A woman is her macho country's first ever Olympic champion.

A revenge fantasy on multiple fronts. Which is why I kinda get Duterte.

He's a thug and I condemn him. But I won't lie and say I don't get him.

He's not much of a Christian, and — surprise — neither am I. And I'm certainly not enough of one to always turn the other cheek.

When I'm wronged, it's "Duterte-energy" that emerges in my stomach, unresolved trauma masquerading as big-boy rage. "Big boys" rarely acknowledge the true source of their rage. And when you don't acknowledge the truth, you ultimately feed on yourself.

Ayn Rand would call trauma — any trauma — "accidental," not "essential." And your feelings, she would say, are neither here nor there. Neither, for that matter, are your race, gender, class background, etc. All that matters, ultimately, is what you *achieve*.

In an interview she gave after receiving her gold medal, Hidilyn Diaz got all effusive about God and Jesus. I sighed and rolled my eyes. *Oh, God, she's one of those*.

And then the very next day she did another interview, voicing her support for trans athletes competing at the Olympics.

Duterte is pro-queer. There are open queers in his administration.

Machismo is rampant in the Phils, a country that's had two female presidents.

"It's complex." A take so common it's almost a truism — or is it? Have we so completely forgotten complexity that it bears constant repeating?

I think it could go both ways. We could just *shrug* and say everything's complex and sit perpetually on the sidelines. Or we could go in, parse, dig, and get dirty.

When Hidilyn Diaz made that lift that won her the gold medal, what was she lifting besides cast iron and stainless steel?

The spirit of a traumatized and impoverished people? Sure.

AND. *It was just a lift*. In a sports pageant that's the walking, talking embodiment of neo-liberalism, organized by an outfit whose greed and corruption know no bounds.

THAT SAID. It *was* a long-awaited "fuck you" to the world on behalf of Filipinos both in the homeland and dispersed in all seven continents of the globe — including Antarctica.

As in: *fuck you*, we're more than upholders of other people's privilege.

So, all my fellow Filipinos and Filipinx who are watching this, altogether now, just to get it out of our collective system: "fuck you."

Pause.

May I offer?

The next time you say "fuck you" to someone, make it mean something new. Make that "you" not the personal, singular, individual you of Ayn Rand, but a collective "you," which includes *all* of who you're talking to, the systems they were reared in, and all the different histories — their own and others — they carry in their bodies.

And as for the word "fuck," remember that people fuck — for love. It's messy and there's pain, but, after and always, one way or another, there's clarity.

So, fuck you all. Thank you for watching.

HANNAH BALBA

"As Opposed to Other Races": Filipino-Canadians in Care Work and the Politics of Legibility

THERE ARE TWO topics that often dominate discussions within the Filipino diaspora: visibility and representation. In my time observing and engaging with such conversations, I am met with silence around discussions about Filipino *legibility*. Being *seen* is different from being *read*. The former entails the ability for our existence to be readily *noticeable*; the latter predicates on the act of deciphering in order for others to *make sense* of our existence.

Virtually, Filipinos are everywhere — we are the fourth largest visible minority in Canada. It is easy to talk about Filipino-Canadian visibility, which I believe cannot happen without discussing the overrepresentation of Filipino-Canadians in care work. The Philippines is the largest exporter of nurses worldwide.[1] In the article cited, the quote reads: "Among immigrants [to Canada] from Southeast Asia, immigrants from the Philippines stood out with a high proportion (13%) and a large number (44,380) of people employed in nursing or health care support occupations. In 2016, they accounted for nearly one-third (30%) of adult immigrants in these occupations", with Filipino women comprising an overwhelming majority of these jobs.[2] The overrepresentation of Filipinos in caregiving cannot be seen in isolation from the historical legacies of American education systems imposed on the Philippines, which consisted of training Filipino nurses to

1 Fely Marilyn E. Lorenzo et al., "Nurse Migration from a Source Country Perspective: Philippine Country Case Study," Health Services Research 42, no. 3 (2007): 1406-1418, https://doi.org/10.1111/j.1475-6773.2007.00716.x.
2 Louis Cornelissen, "Profile of immigrants in nursing and health care support occupations," Statistics Canada, released May 28, 2021, https://www150.statcan.gc.ca/n1/pub/75-006-x/2021001/article/00004-eng.htm.

satisfy nursing shortages in postwar America — a project of U.S. colonialism that remains highly consequential to the socio-economic state of the Philippines. These historical conditions have directly shaped how Foreign Domestic Worker movements developed in Canada. From the eighteenth to nineteenth century, Canada limited Indigenous women and enslaved Black women to domestic servitude.[3] From the beginning of the twentieth century to the mid-twentieth century, Canada recruited European women mostly from Britain and Ireland, to work as nannies, but they are automatically granted Permanent Residence status, distinguishing them from most racialized caregivers who are barred from landed immigrant status upon arriving in Canada.[4] Throughout the latter half of the twentieth century, Canada shifted its recruitment prospects toward women from British colonies in the Caribbean, where this led to the legislation of the Foreign Domestic Movement (FDM) to increase recruitment from foreign countries, as most Canadians do not want to work these jobs.[5] In the early 1970s, the Labour Export Policy (LEP) was implemented by the Marcos dictatorship in the Philippines in response to widespread unemployment and growing social unrest. This was a policy development regulating the export of Filipino workers abroad, while reaping the foreign remittances of Overseas Filipino Workers (OFWs) — with care workers occupying a large portion of OFWs. Following the country's established reputation of producing American-trained nurses, together with the increasing rate of Filipino emigration during the Marcos era, Canada shifted its recruitment for care workers toward Filipinos, notably women. By the early 1990s, Canada started the Live-in Caregiver Program (LCP), with Filipino women constituting the majority of recruited caregivers. The LCP was replaced by the Caregiver Program in 2014; Filipinos still comprise the majority of those recruited. These historical developments work in synthesis to explain the hypervisibility of Filipino-Canadians in care work today.

Filipinos are easily *seen* in Canada, but how are we read?

---

3 Althea Balmes and Jo Simalaya Alcampo, "Preview #10: Kwentong Bayan: Labour of Love," Graphic History Collective, January 20, 2015.

4 Ibid.

5 Ibid.

I argue that the visibility of Filipinos in caregiving shapes Filipino *legibility* — that is, how Canadian public consciousness *makes sense* of Filipino existence in Canada. This is exemplified in the ways Filipinos are often discussed in public discourse. For instance, in 2013, *Pacific Rim Magazine* published an article titled: "Filipino Nannies: The Cost of Caring."[6] The article aims to contextualize the prevalence of Filipino caregivers in Canada through the personal story of Marilou Tuazon, a Filipino caregiver living in Canada, who is pictured smiling with a white child — who I presume is the child she is employed to look after — in the article backdrop. One section in the article called "Why Filipino Nannies Are Popular" describes how "Canada's love for Filipino caregivers is tied to Filipino culture." To support this cultural assumption, the article includes a quote from Adelina Deloeg, a Filipino caregiver. "We learn from our families at a very early age to respect everyone," she says. "That is what was put in our minds and hearts and that's what we have to do from generation to generation. When you are growing up, everyone is caring for you — parents, uncles and aunts, all the extended family — and if we don't have anything, everyone shares." In October 2020, *Inscol* released "Reasons Why Hiring Filipino Nurses Is Popular in Canada,"[7] a piece that explains why Canada prefers recruiting Filipino nurses "as opposed to other races." They write: "Canada nurse hiring was reliant on Filipino nurses because they have always been considered as the best nursing professionals among internationally educated nurses. Filipinos are looked upon all over the world because of them coming from a caring culture. They are empathetic, kind, emotionally, and socially pleasing people which are some of the qualities important for being a successful nurse." The article continues: "The Canadian government has seen and respected this ability of the Filipino nurses to connect with patients at such a deep level. When it comes to helping nurses gain the Canadian experience in the nursing field, the ability of Filipino nurses to adjust and adapt anywhere they go sets them apart from all others. They have a remarkable capability to adapt to

---

6 Janis Letchuman, "Filipino Nannies: The Cost of Caring," Pacific Rim Magazine, 2013.
7 "Reasons Why Hiring Filipino Nurses is Popular in Canada," Inscol, October 12, 2020, https://www.inscol.com/canada/blog/reasons-why-hiring-of-filipino-nurses-is-popular-in-canada.

the new environment in Canada." In January 2022, the Saskatoon Ministry of Health announced that the Saskatchewan Health Authority hopes to recruit at least 150 and as many as 300 international health care workers, with a focus on workers from the Philippines, in order to upheave Canadian health care services exhausted by COVID-19.[8] Tracy Zambory, Saskatchewan Union of Nurses President, states, "We could not be without our Filipino nurses. They are a gigantic asset and we could not run without them."[9] The aftereffects of such value judgments are not immaterial, as they translate into Canadian policy. In April 2021, Canada administered the Health-care Workers Permanent Residence Pathway, an immigration program meant to provide an expedited pathway towards permanent residence for health care workers employed during the COVID-19 pandemic. In tandem with this are the conditions of the Caregiver Program, a stream that offers a pathway to permanent residency, provided that caregivers complete a full two years or equivalent of caregiving experience in Canada. There is a clear "love" for Filipinos in Canada — demonstrated through these affections toward Filipino care workers located in public communication and state programming.

How are Filipino-Canadians made legible through this discourse? That is, how does our existence as Filipinos in Canada occupy political and public registers? And what does this legibility imply? It seems as though we are made legible to the extent that our movements affirm these subjugated identities of "care," "empathy," and willingness to "please others" — qualities that are seemingly "tied to Filipino culture." While there is nothing inherently wrong or problematic about identifying as "empathetic," "kind," or "caring," what is worth problematizing is how these qualities have become essentialized within the Filipino body. Essentialism is convenient, as it removes the responsibility of critically evaluating the conditions that lead to peoples' social patterns. We are discouraged from engaging with the historical and global conditions that assimilate Filipinos under caregiving and lead thousands

8 Jonathan Charlton, "Here's why Sask. may be in a tough spot to recruit Filipino nurses," CTV News, January 7, 2022, https://saskatoon.ctvnews.ca/here-s-why-sask-may-be-in-a-tough-spot-to-recruit-filipino-nurses-1.5743359.
9 "Saskatchewan, Canada hiring nurses from PH but unions say it's not enough," USA Inquirer, January 14, 2022, https://usa.inquirer.net/91330/saskatchewan-canada-hiring-nurses-from-ph-but-unions-say-its-not-enough.

to leave their lives and families in the Philippines to seek better economic opportunities elsewhere. Unseen as desperation or a means of survival — the results of lasting economic and political destabilization inherited from centuries of imperial and colonial violence — and instead seen as the product of the Filipino nature: sacrificial, caring, eager to serve, and willingness to go above and beyond for others.

Willingness.

Who then benefits from this legibility? Filipinos are, at worst, ignored and invisibilized, and at best, our racial difference is only ever acknowledged when the West can capitalize off of these representational differences. We are conditioned to perform within the representational figurations that construct, enforce, and maintain our subjugation as racialized "Others" that exist for Western consumption. As Kimiko Inouye writes in *Conditional love*: "Workers are perceived as acceptable and loveable, but only to the extent that they are grateful and obedient. Otherwise, when they raise critiques about their conditions, love towards them is absent."[10] Inouye continues, "This love is more about the creation of an ideal national multicultural subject, rather than a genuine and respectful bond with the stranger, the other, the migrant. At the same time, the subject becomes invested in the creation of a loveable object."[11] Our legibility — or the ability for others to easily understand our existence in Canada — rests on how well we assume these cultural assimilations of care and servitude.

Why does legibility in these terms matter for Filipino-Canadians? Because the existence of our "Othered" form as racialized people itself resists white dominance; our racial form is in need of being recognizable under terms that work within racial logics that champion white supremacy in the age of the multiculturalist state. We are afforded recognition for our ability to ascribe to these imposed-upon representations of "care" and eagerness to

---

10 Kimiko Inouye, "Conditional love; representations of migrant work in Canadian newsprint media," *Social Identities: Journal for the Study of Race, Nation, and Culture,* 42, no.5 (2012): 573-592.

11 Sara Ahmed, *The cultural politics of emotion* (Edinburgh, Edinburgh University Press, 2004), quoted in Kimiko Inouye, "Conditional love; representations of migrant work in Canadian newsprint media," *Social Identities: Journal for the Study of Race, Nation, and Culture,* 42, no.5 (2012): 580.

"socially please" — an act of compliance that our livability is determined by. Because we are easily *read* in these terms, we are then worthy of being included in the Canadian socio-political fabric, as demonstrated by these discursive appraisals, and in the material, legal consequences of acceding to such logics — namely permanent status and citizenship.

It is as if to ask: why *else* would Filipinos exist if not in service to others?

I end with fewer answers and more questions. Our legibility as Filipino-Canadians will continue to shift, subject to ever-changing cultural moments and state needs. Would there be so many Filipinos in Canada if the Philippines had not developed a history of producing nurses, domestic workers, and caregivers? Canada cannot "make do without" us — but what happens to us when we do not appear in ways that are "caring" and "socially pleasing"? What follows when the Other fails to be perceived as loveable?

What will happen when we refuse to be legible?

ALEXA BATITIS

Living a Life of Hybrid Languages

MY FAMILY HAS a funny quirk when it comes to speaking with each other. Well, I'm not sure what you'd call it — others might call it a quirk, which I would agree with. Nonetheless, I can say that somewhere, somebody along the line made a decision, and to this day I can't point any fingers or determine who exactly decided that we would do this. Six-year-old me certainly did not have an explanation for when this came up during a class activity about birthdays.

It was September, so school had started fairly recently, and I was probably trying to make a good impression on the other first graders in my class. Talking about birthdays sparked a memory of my mom rhyming off our weekend schedule, and I raised my hand to offer my input.

"My Tita Bernadette and Uncle Nestorio both have birthdays this weekend," I shared in excitement. I remember that my teacher gave me a bit of a perplexed look. She replied, "Thanks for sharing, Alexa, that's great — but exactly *what* is a tita?"

Okay, maybe it wasn't that dramatic, and I can't remember if those were her exact words. And honestly, that teacher was fantastic, and I have fond memories of that class. However, that moment felt like an end-of-the-world embarrassment for shy little me. At the time, I obviously didn't have the words for the feelings I had; looking back now, I realize that being othered (intentionally or not) made me feel a plethora of feelings that I couldn't express as a six-year-old.

All because someone taught the cousins to call the aunts Tita, but decided to stop short of teaching us to call our uncles Tito. (Don't listen to any of my titas and uncles, by the way — they didn't try hard enough to make Tito a thing.)

I knew that, like all families, my family had quirks; my family was a bunch of larger-than-life Filipinos living in Ottawa, Canada's frosty capital, so I felt that our quirks seemed to stick out more than others'. I, my sister, and many of my cousins were "born here," as I say to the busybodies — both of my parents were under eighteen when they immigrated to Canada from the Philippines with their families in the mid and late 1970s. Neither of my parents really encountered other Filipinos growing up, and many Filipinos that they did meet had lost their native language, speaking English to integrate with their friend groups in Canada. At a certain point, my mother forgot the language completely. It was more important to blend in, to assimilate.

While growing up in the late 1990s and 2000s offered a higher level of multicultural acceptance, I still found myself in awkward situations where I couldn't explain the way I spoke and the words I used, especially with my family. See, another quirk about my family is that none of the cousins can speak Tagalog fluently, but we use just enough key words to confuse the average English speaker. Our family's conversations growing up were peppered with Tagalog and Ilocano words, with what felt like no rhyme or reason. I used to not understand the difference between Tagalog and Ilocano and, up to a point, did not realize that my dad spoke the former with his family and my mom spoke the latter with her family. Didn't even notice! In my household, we were throwing a bunch of words together as we pleased, since it got the point across anyway. Besides that, I like to joke that knowing the curse words in Tagalog is good enough in itself.

My family, like many other Filipino families living in Canada, lives this unintended, but quite common, "hybrid" life of languages. I believe that this stems from wanting to fit in and belong in Canadian society, as well as from an unconscious shame of being Filipino. A visible other, an ethnicity guessing game associated with nannies and nurses, the idea of being Filipino in Canada has changed as my parents and I have grown up. I am a firm believer in the idea that the language you use shapes the world around you — having grown up with Filipino words tossed with English all around me, I am all too familiar with this hybrid life of languages. I was surprised to discover that this was more common among Filipino-Canadians than I had previously thought, showing me that we should be collectively embracing this as a part of our identity and community.

Some of the first Tagalog words I learned were words that referred to body parts. This made some early childhood encounters a bit strange, but I think most people were willing to gloss over the particular words I used, given the context. I don't think any supervising adults or friends wanted to risk having me explain my special word (but yeah, I probably did mean to say "vagina"). These words reinforced the fact that my body was Filipino. Dark unruly hair and tanned skin made me feel so different from my classmates and peers. The same shame of being Filipino that my parents felt growing up once they got to Canada, that was what I started to feel from a young age. The idea of the body, and by consequence my own body, was a reminder that no matter how Canadian I acted, people would always see me as a Filipino first.

One might think that coming across other Filipinos would remedy feeling down about fitting in. But as a kid, I felt almost *more* ashamed when meeting other Filipino kids. I threw up a defensive wall if language was ever mentioned; I didn't know how to deal with not knowing Tagalog, I didn't know how to respond to *kamusta na,* and I was nervous about finding another space where I didn't belong. Nobody really addressed this formally either — at best, meeting other Filipino kids happened in one of my lola's random friends' basement at a party. On our way home, I would casually tell my parents about the other kids and their language levels, but it was never made to be a big deal. My parents shrugged it off and I was encouraged to do so too. I got the impression that it was better if I knew as little as possible.

In fact, as I got older, my parents started to focus on prioritizing my learning of French. Living in Ottawa, which straddles the Ontario/Québec border, my parents believed that learning French would benefit my career possibilities (something they considered greatly as I turned twelve). I was on board, as some of my titas and uncles knew French — my dad's family actually landed in Québec first, and one tita used to say *tabarnak* so often I thought it was a Tagalog word. I have reaped the benefits of being educated in French and have had jobs using French; I even worked in Québec for a short period of time. My French, though nothing special, is still what I would consider much better than my Tagalog. Sometimes I wonder what it would be like to know as much Tagalog as French, and I wonder why my parents might have thought that learning French would impede my capacity to learn Tagalog. Again, there was this underlying shame of being Filipino resurfacing — as if to deem our language inelegant and not worth knowing.

With this unconscious shame, I drove headfirst into a direction that panicked my parents: English literature and the arts. Language had become so important to me, and I was bent on diving deeper. We had *so* many arguments — *all* of the arguments — about it. I got my wish, but truthfully, it felt like I was digging for something missing; I was feeling incomplete and didn't have the words to describe how I was feeling, even to myself. A component of literature is knowing history for context. At times, in certain texts, I could see a glimpse of my ancestry, but it was never at the forefront. I read and studied so much about the histories and cultures of what my ancestors would consider the world's biggest bullies. And still, it took much more time and coming to terms with myself before I realized that the most healing would come from connecting to my roots — exploring my family history and, very slowly, considering the idea of learning Tagalog.

I don't actually place blame on anyone for not making the Filipino language a priority in our family. My family's experience of being immigrants and first-generation Canadian had a quiet impact on their Filipino identity. Joking that the kids didn't want to learn the language or saying that we were too lazy to commit to learning, I think subconsciously, was our family's way of trying to save the next generation from being othered in the same way they were when they were growing up in Canada. Knowing how they struggled and couldn't put their feelings into the right words, I want my generation and the next generation of Filipino-Canadians to be able to share our experiences, no matter what language they speak, no matter which words they choose (but, extra points if you toss in *putang ina mo*). There are so many of us living these hybrid lives of languages, starting to feel comfortable with exploring our Filipino roots, desiring to feel more connected to the homeland.

I believe we can heal by realizing that we can exist without shame in this in-between, hybrid life. We can embrace this as part of our collective identity as a community. I'll be over here with my titas and uncles, waiting to welcome more people into this strange club.

MILA BONGCO-PHILIPZIG

White Lies My Elders Told Me

"AY NAKU, DON'T ever go to that area. *Puno ng mga pana*. They're mostly homeless and drunk, nothing but trouble there."

"Oh no, don't rent in Millwoods. That's the curry community. If you rent a room there, you will come out smelling like them, *sige ka*."

"Why would you even think of doing that? *Kababae mong tao!* You should be thankful *nasa* Canada *ka na*. Don't draw any attention to yourself."

These were some of the advice given to me — more than once — from people in my heritage community during my first few years in Canada.

In 1984, I arrived in Edmonton with a scholarship to study at the University of Alberta. I was on my own, young, and still impressionable. Like most newcomers to a distant land, I gravitated toward people from my home country as I sought to find my footing in a new city, as I tried to settle and establish myself. People from one's native land provide familiarity and a cultural safe haven for immigrants in a new place, especially for those arriving without families. Not having a single relative in Edmonton nor in all of Canada, I relied heavily on the proximity and wisdom of my heritage community, which became my extended family — my kin network — in this new environment. I soaked up the pronouncements of the titos and titas who were here before me without any hesitation because like many Filipinos, especially at that time, I was raised to listen to people older than me, to obey them without question, and to not challenge them or talk back at all.

When you move to a new land as an adult, you tend to bring your home country with you, and it serves as your frame of reference. How can you not? This is all you have known, especially if this is the first time you've moved away. Exploring, discovering, and taking on new experiences can be exhilarating but also confusing and disconcerting. Turning to people from your own heritage community provides security, predictability, and a sense of belonging, including a framework for what you can inherently trust and rely on. I was happy to be in a group where I could loosen up and not constantly be decoding actions and intentions, then planning and assessing my reactions. I was thankful to be where I could speak Filipino because speaking in another language and constantly being mindful of the proper words, pronunciations, and accent can be exhausting.

However, doubts started forming in my mind about the soundness of the information and advice I was getting from my kin network after I started settling into university, taking courses on comparative literature and cultural studies, and having discussions with professors and other graduate students. I could not shake the niggling feeling that there was something wrong with the perspectives my community elders were handing down to me and sharing with each other. After being immersed in studying the sociological, cultural, and environmental developments in Canada and other Commonwealth countries, I started doubting and questioning the mindset of these people I respected, the very same people who warmly welcomed me into their homes, who fed me, who invited me to their family parties, who encouraged and uplifted me when I felt homesick and alone. I had a sinking feeling, but my conviction was strong that my community elders were harbouring and circulating damaging stereotypes and prejudices, most probably without really understanding what they were doing. It was an alarming and disheartening discovery — that the people I relied on from my heritage community were so poorly informed about other cultures and persisted on believing harmful ideas that were racist and misogynistic. It was only after I was deep into my graduate studies that I recognized and understood this. And I realized that my awareness took some time because I, myself, was all these as well: poorly informed, misogynistic, racist.

Philippine Education and Whiteness

In the 1960s, while growing up in the Philippines, I went to a school run by nuns, reading books in English about people, places, and activities that were completely strange to me, in words unfamiliar to my tongue. And we had no choice; these were the books we had to read for school. These were also the only books available to us then. In addition, we were not allowed to speak in any language other than English in school. Otherwise, we'd get fined. That fine was a major setback for students like me who did not even get an allowance, who sometimes even had to go to school without lunch.

Being schooled in English was commonplace in the Philippines then, not only in the urban areas. Since the early 1900s, the school system in the Philippines was founded and designed by our American colonizers. The curriculum and school materials were patterned after the U.S. school system and disadvantaged the school children in the Philippines, because not only were they trying to learn new concepts in a foreign language, but they were also being forced to do so from the point of view of a different culture. Although the Philippines started in 1974 to aim for bilingual education (English and Filipino), it was not until the school term 1978–79 that it was nationally mandated to teach areas like social studies, character education, and health and physical education in our native language, in addition to a Pilipino subject. The progress for the new program, however, was slow, as materials were sorely lacking in quantity and quality, and the teachers needed training to teach in the Filipino language. As for me, most subjects like math, natural and social sciences, religion, history, and language arts were all taught in English. Especially for literature, all the way up to university, we went from English classic to English classic written by non-Filipinos. The only exception was studying excerpts of *Noli Me Tángere,* written by a Filipino, Jose Rizal. But even this, we read the English translation, and we were not made to read the whole book.

The world view, mindset, and aspirations instilled in us for many, many years by those books in English, as well as the influence and instructions from both our religious and secular teachers, were all structured to uphold a foreign ideology that centred on whiteness, on the belief that white culture, values, and norms were the standard centre of the world. This was taken for granted in the Philippines then — the root, causality, or context never clearly clarified why white culture was deemed superior to ours. However, the ideas endorsed in these imported books — the way of living, concepts of beauty, criteria for success — were not only foreign but elusive and inaccessible to us. The activities and aspirations depicted did not resemble what we saw or experienced in our immediate environment, did not come near to the realities of our families, neighbours, community. Nevertheless, we were made to absorb concepts and values toward accepting that white culture was better and preferred. Moreover, a social system organized around patriarchy came bundled with the white, colonial culture that we ingested. Men were favoured from birth, and there were marked differences in what was permissible or encouraged between men and women in terms of aptitudes, career choices, social status, overall life experiences, and access to power, wealth, and privilege.

The predilection toward venerating white and male cultures and ideals was echoed outside school as well, for this was what our elders learned and passed on down the generations. In hindsight, this was also why I was not critical of those divisive and derogatory remarks from the titos and titas in Edmonton in the 1980s, instructing me not to associate with Indigenous people, who were generalized as homeless and worthless, as well as to avoid other heritage communities while making fun of them. I accepted these precepts without questioning them because they were simply extensions of what I had heard my whole life before coming to Canada, which I had already internalized as status quo.

"If you don't behave, *kukunin ka ng bumbay.*"

"No, girls can't do it. That's only for boys."

"*Ay, ang puti!* And what a nice nose. She will go far."

"Let your *kuya* have more, because he's a boy."

"Why did you stay out under the sun? You're so dark, *mukha ka ngayong busabos*" (you look poor and dirty).

I grew up surrounded by uncritical belief and blind adherence to white colonial and patriarchal standards that made me feel inferior, insecure, and fearful about my future. Without truly understanding the underlying reasons, I felt that I was never good enough, that I could never measure up to the ideals and aspirations required of me. There was an incessant mantra in my head, "I will never be beautiful nor rich nor successful enough," and it was echoed by many around me as well — my siblings, classmates, friends, and relatives, even those who were older. As a response, we all kept striving to be better, we all kept trying harder and harder, not fully understanding that the playing field and rules were not conceived for us to win. I did not realize then that this was intentional and bolstered by systems and structures that profited by intentionally making people like me feel deficient and anxious. We were indoctrinated into believing that our identity and worth were premised upon some standards set and controlled by others, not ourselves. Our precarious self-esteem drove us to constant self-surveillance and self-management mode, and it made us vulnerable to outside approval and submission to authorities.

I believe that generations and generations of Filipinos constantly made to feel inadequate and powerless by colonial principles gave rise to attitudes and values that became embedded in our psyche, which, in turn, were deemed as cultural traits, when, actually, these were responses to trauma caused by inequality and distress: complaisance, deference to authority, conflict avoidance, self-restraint, persistence, determination to work hard, and the urge to excel. For me, this inadequacy complex is a major reason why being a Filipino can feel like we lead a life of constant striving, a life where we always need to be productive, where we need to keep improving ourselves. And we keep orienting the definition of improvement and success on colonial standards, which are mostly unattainable. In the 1980s, to "go abroad" was one of the most prominent signs of success for Filipinos. Specifically, it was to go to America. Many difficult years under a dictatorship contributed to Filipinos wanting to immigrate and "finally make it" in America. America was so revered, I remember some people's response when I told them I was leaving with a scholarship to study at a university in Canada: "Okay *na rin yan*, at least you can go abroad. *Malapit na yan sa* America, maybe you can transfer later." Not knowing any better then, I secretly wished the same: to someday "make it" to America.

Choosing to Belong in Edmonton
I did not know much about Canada when I arrived in 1984. This was pre-Internet, pre-cellphone days, and a time when travel was very expensive and not as commonplace. Canada seemed harmless. I had not heard of Canada colonizing or being at war with any country. In my limited experience, the people seemed kind and friendly enough. However, as I mentioned earlier, I quickly learned that in a colonial country like Canada, whiteness and white

superiority are deeply embedded in its policies, structures, values, and systems, so that racialized groups are negatively impacted in many aspects of our lives: employment, housing, education, justice, social participation, and access to goods and services. Even some of the kind, friendly Canadians I met were not aware or uncritically accepting of the gaps and hierarchies between the dominant white population and those who were non-white. After I learned this, I tried sharing my apprehensions with my heritage community about the power dynamics being sustained in Canada that favoured the colonists' culture and led to racism. I encouraged the community to fight the systems and values that kept us marginalized and exploitable, instead of comparing and pitting ourselves against other heritage groups. But I was not successful in raising awareness or understanding. Compared to their lives in the Philippines, the Filipinos in Edmonton had jobs, houses, access to health care, schools, and churches. So, they did not perceive the inequality of access to wealth and social participation that I was pointing out. Instead, they told me, "That's the way it's always been and will be for us," and advised me to be grateful to Canada. There was nothing that needed to change, other than Canada should allow more of our relatives to easily immigrate here. People also pointed out that Canada encouraged immigration and multiculturalism and was the first country to pass a national multiculturalism law in 1988. Hence, Canada must love people like us. My contention that multiculturalism did not equate to inclusion and equity fell on deaf ears.

When one is used to being passive and constantly told to sacrifice for the family and community, assertiveness may be perceived as aggression and disrespect. When one is not used to being self-confident, confidence can be misconstrued as arrogance. My dissent and talking back to those who were older than me and who had been in Edmonton longer than me was construed exactly as such — arrogance. I think my confidence was taken for arrogance because it triggered some fear that I was challenging the status quo, just when more and more Filipinos were getting established in Edmonton, enjoying the fruits of their labour and wages. The dream to pursue when we go abroad is to find a job, buy a house and car, raise a family comfortably, and send money back home. At that time, there was really no one in the Filipino community who understood why I was deviating from this immigrant's dream and asking them to divert their time and energy toward addressing inequality, misogyny, and racism. I think it also did not help that I was a cash-strapped academic living in a rented studio apartment, did not have a car, and was unmarried and childless, which all belied the idea of success within our community.

Still wanting to belong to and be accepted by my kin network, I succumbed to normative social adjustment and toned myself down. To be safe, I tried to only chat about movies, food, people, clothes, children, and houses. I tried to not be critical of conversations and actions even as I perceived them as biased and prejudiced. I tried to make excuses or explain away some behaviours, especially from the older people, in view of their generation's upbringing and hardships. But it was really difficult to keep ignoring the double standards between genders, the preference for white patriarchal culture and values, the push to conform to white standards of beauty, the constant striving to assimilate into a culture of intensified consumption.

I believe that there is no neutral space between being a racist and diligently fighting racism, no neutral space between sexism and relentlessly fighting misogyny. White centring, together with its patriarchal and consumption-focused ideals, is so pervasive and harmful that we need to be intentionally and actively fighting it daily. It is not enough to stop laughing at some jokes, to keep quiet when someone says a racist or sexist statement, or to ignore news harmful to a group due to race or gender. There is no neutral space. One is either supporting whiteness as a dominant culture or actively opposing it. When I mentioned earlier that my heritage community was racist and misogynistic, and so was I, it was because, by refusing to accept how colonial and patriarchal mentality had impacted racialized groups and we needed to change, my heritage community was being complicit in sustaining the dominant culture. As for me, by being selective in my opposition, by choosing to sometimes stay quiet and not do anything, I was also furthering the damage caused by racism and misogyny.

Edmonton and Change

In 1989, I left Edmonton to move to Germany for a scholarship toward my PhD. I ended up working in Europe, as well as Asia, for quite some time and came back to Edmonton only in 2007 with my husband and son to stay in Canada permanently. Working at the University of Alberta and raising a young child while establishing roots in a new city kept me busy for the first few years after coming back. It was not until 2014 that I slowly started being more involved again with the Filipino community in Edmonton. After twenty-five years, the community had changed tremendously. There were only about six thousand Filipinos in the early 1980s, and this grew to sixty-five thousand by 2016. It was also a much more diverse group in terms of age, profession, educational achievement, and artistic abilities, as well as gender orientation. I was happy to note a marked increase of more progressive, open-minded, and forward-thinking Filipinos, mostly younger than me. I surmised they were not as strongly bounded by the strict colonial education we had pre-1980s.

I had also changed. In 2014, I was not a fledgling academic anymore, trying to lecture my elders out of a world view and mindset that took decades of indoctrination. I had a better grasp of how big and complex socio-racial hierarchies and processes are, the myriad ways both locals and immigrants position themselves within them, and how it will take a very long time to unpack centuries of inequality created by the preference for whiteness. I also learned that it was better to choose a different starting place — to situate all these through a lens of understanding, compassion, and healing, rather than anxiety and anger. With this, I was able to join together once more with my heritage community, gain allies, and better move forward on raising awareness about systemic inequalities.

Now, in 2022, I remain an avid advocate for equity, inclusion, and diversity, and not only for people of Philippine heritage. I believe it is imperative that we go past heritage, past ethnicity, past single socio-cultural categorizations and show how closely intertwined the factors, causes, and impacts of widespread inequalities are: Black Lives Matter, #MeToo movement, rise in Asian hate, LGBTQ+ struggles, the heartbreak of residential schools, climate change and climate migrants, and so on. We get a more comprehensive picture of what needs to be addressed for society to change if we see the interconnectivity among all these. This way, we also better understand the need to bring communities together, sharpen our solidarity work, and transition from organizational silos to wider community-based solidarity. It is encouraging to see many cross-community events and discussions promoted not only in Edmonton, but Canada-wide, many available and shared online. It is encouraging to see there are more and more relevant materials available from diverse sources, from treatises to personal stories showing how real people, real families have been impacted. It is encouraging to see more young people aware of the systemic causes of these inequalities and wishing to be involved in effecting change. It is crucial that we move from our silos and focus on working together to learn, share, and take appropriate action. Only when we amplify each other's voices and expand spaces for each other, can we offer up and understand truths from many angles, from different perspectives, from a truly diverse population. Then, we are more discerning and do not have to accept one truth from a single white centre.

DAVEY SAMUEL CALDERON

Magic Sing, Or, What I Want to Say to You, But I'll Sing Instead

Five instrumental beats until performance
In the Style of Pinoy Angst
Year: 1990
Duration: Lifetime
Key: D minor

I HEAR A click, and I'm rewarded with seeing the flat black screen give way to an image of a generic beach. I see two blues compete for dominance in the frame and a small sliver of pristine sand differentiates the blues, showing what is the ocean and what is a glorious clear sky. The focal point of the background picture is an impressive coconut tree, curving out in a pleasing shape into the sky. Could this actually be a photo taken in the Philippines? Probably not, but what is most important comes next.

"Okay, okay here use this!" Tita Darling thrusts a microphone at me. A Frankenstein microphone with remote control buttons on it. I start mashing buttons until I can search for songs by letters instead of by number codes. I signal to everyone in the room that we're all set up.

"What are you going to sing? Hmm?" my father asks me. He strokes his chin and brushes his salt-and-pepper moustache. He appears complacent as he slouches on the couch, but I see a twinkle in his eyes. He can't hide his anticipation from me.

"Papa, you sing the first song. Perry Como? Buddy Holly? What about Sinatra?" He smiles and raises his eyebrows in approval to some Sinatra. I input Frank Sinatra into the search bar and all of his song titles appear, in no particular order. The cursor hovers over "My Way."

"Bold, bold …" mutters Tito Charlie, who has just entered with a plate of cake and takes a bite.

My father slowly shakes his head and tells me to put on "All My Tomorrows."

The track starts, and we can hear the MIDI notes attempting to imitate the dramatic orchestral intro. The odd bleeps fail to capture the grandness of the song, but that doesn't faze my father. He sings the first line of lyrics, which are highlighted from white to blue.

The room hushes slightly to appreciate my father's voice, but he doesn't notice this. For him, the world has slowed down, and the people at the party momentarily fade into the background. And with a shaking yet soft timbre, my father continues to sing about tomorrow. Reminiscing as he sings, I can't help but be enthralled by this man's performance. The man who has somehow transcended time and space as he sings and exists simultaneously in both the past and the present moment.

Verse 1

If someone placed me in front of a microphone on a stage and a crowd of people and asked me, "What does Filipino Canadian mean to you?" I'm certain I would whip up a satisfactory answer to the question. A convincing speech of: "I'm a Canadian of Filipino descent. I grew up with an understanding of my culture. What Fil-Can identity means to me is how Filipinx immigrants, like my parents, forged ahead against adversity in this new land. Thus, I am a product of that work ethic, that pain, that perseverance, blah, blah."

I would push that story because it sounds heroic and empowering, but it's a story I can't take full ownership of. I may be a product of their work and sacrifice, but, born and raised here and unable to speak the language, I lack a real connection to the Philippines. If I were to answer the question "What does Filipino-Canadian mean to you?" my answer would be a lie.

I wonder if all second-generation Filipinx have the same thoughts. Thoughts of living in an unsettling duality become ambivalent clouds floating above our heads. They dictate the forecast of our emotions around our identity, which become turbulent at pinoy family events, where the Filipinx party becomes the epicentre of all mental and social pressures, spiralling into a personal identity storm. Let's imagine it. The quintessential Filipinx celebration.

Verse 2

Filipinx open our homes up and come together for all occasions, be it an anniversary, a graduation, a christening, or a birthday for every family member and friend; there is always a reason to celebrate. Even when there is a death or death anniversary, we still come together to celebrate the lives of our loved ones.

It is at these parties where that force of duality presses down on us second-gen kids. Although not true for everyone, some may be in situations similar to how it's like for me showing up at my parents' place:

There's always some hesitation when I walk through their door. When the door opens, there's always a cacophony of Tagalog or Ilocano or another language spoken by the folks at the party. And when I make my way inside, at first, I feel pretty good hearing all the boisterous laughter and friendly voices and seeing Filipinx folks everywhere.

There are the titos in the corner playing poker while they peel boiled peanuts in one hand and flick them in the mouth, followed by a swig of Coors lager (although they wish it was Red Horse beer). There are the titas on the other side of the room, where one is giving a presentation about Korean herbal diet tea. Her expertly manicured red nails and her extra-white bleached teeth expertly click and clack together during her presentation, creating a tempting siren song drawing folks in. Then there are the kids going up to Lola to ask for "blessing po," and after they gently touch their forehead to Lola's outreached hand, they run off to join the myriad of cousins playing throughout the house. Then as I make my way to the kitchen, I see the dining room table and kitchen counters covered with every food imaginable: KFC fried chicken, sweet-and-sour pork, macaroni salad, Costco Nanaimo bars, garlic-fried rice — and, of course, all the Filipino food I've ever grown up with: pancit palabok, adobo chicken, lumpia Shanghai, bangus, and every dessert that folks have grabbed from a Goldilocks bakery on the way over. My mouth is salivating in anticipation. I look around and smile because this is familiar and comforting. Something I've grown up with, easy cultural signifiers I can safely say are part of me. Nothing here is foreign to me; in fact, it's as natural as breathing.

Finally, I find who I've been looking for, my Inay, but I've grown up speaking English to her, so I call her Mom. She embraces me tightly without missing a beat of her sermon to an ate about God's blessing. When she does take a breath, she smiles at me, the child she loves with all her heart. Then she quickly assigns me some work to do, because that's what you do as the adult child of the hosting family. It's your duty to serve your guests, an unsaid rule of hospitality in our culture since time immemorial. Be it rolling more lumpia to be fried or holding your cousin's newborn so she can finally eat or tackling the mountain of dirty dishes to wash; you do your job. It's times like these when people come up to me and say:

"*Mabuhay!* What are you doing for work?"

"*Kuya*, where are the serviettes? We need more."

"*Hay naku*, it's been so long. Let me look at you!"

Those check-ins are fine; they are folks I know and through a genuine smile I respond to their questions or ask them how they are. The conversation is light and airy. However, a new guest to my family's parties comes up to me and asks:

"*Uy, kamusta ka? Ikaw ba yung anak ni Jo? Asan nga pala siya? Gusto ko siyang kamustahin!*"

And the air goes flat, and the moisture vacates my throat. Unintentionally, I dryly say:

"Sorry, can you say that in English? I don't know Tagalog."

There's a slight beat before this guest responds. A tinge of a knowing smile crosses their mouth, not out of judgment, yet with the subtext of: "He's one of those kids." Awkwardly, they repeat what they wanted in English. At that moment, my personal cloud of self-doubt descends on me. It feeds off of that warmth I first felt at the beginning of the party, and as more Filipinxs try to talk to me in Tagalog, outing myself about my non-existent Tagalog — similar to the experience of "coming out" — causes the same knowing smile. And you can't blame them for their responses, because if you were in their shoes, the truth is that their initial assumption about me was correct.

So, as the storm brews within me, I take a break. I allow myself to mindlessly wander through the rooms of people on their islands of calm and joviality. And despite my feelings that I'm a "defective Filipino," I find myself in front of the TV, about to sing karaoke, and a tita hands me a Magic Sing mic to set it up. Through the accepting powers of karaoke, your creed, your political views, or your dubious Filipinx status doesn't matter at all when you agree to sing. When a Filipino party hears karaoke about to begin, all the titos playing poker, the titas at the presentation, and the seemingly untethered children around the house take a moment of pause to briefly listen to the brave voice of the first singer of the evening, kicking off many more hours of singing. We take in those voices and smile.

Chorus (all together now)
My father punctuates the last line with a soft flourish of his hand. The sparkle in his eye keeps glimmering as he makes his way through the rest of the song. I appreciate the beauty of his performance; something I don't see a lot is Filipino men expressing themselves — specifically, old-school Filipino men who have built their lives up with their hands. The lines and scars in the hands of our tatays, lolos, titos, and kuyas (which are also present in the equally fiercely hard-working inays, lolas, titas and ates) articulate the histories of their lives. My father's hands have many, many fine lines as well.

When my father lets his guard down with something like karaoke, those rare moments of softness are so precious. And I hope he knows that softness doesn't mean weakness; it carries flexibility and strength. I wonder if my father knows that he doesn't always have to keep up his stoic façade. At least karaoke is a brief respite from that state of being, crooning like Sinatra, a known "soft man" himself, might I add.

Now the song is over, and an 8-bit logo rudely interrupts the magic of the moment. Tita Darling claps loudly and Tito Charlie nods his head in agreement. My father metaphorically takes off his fedora, and with a small smile of satisfaction, he passes the mic/remote back to me.

"Your turn," he tells me.

Suddenly I'm nervous. My throat is dry, and despite the years of acting training I've had, I can't find any grounding within myself. I ask everyone, "What should I sing?"

"Whatever. Whatever!" Tita Darling encourages me as I scroll through the plethora of artists' names whizzing up the screen in alphabetic order. Then I make a choice.

"Can't Help Falling in Love" by Elvis Presley appears in the middle of the screen imposed on an image of a red rose. I've made a good choice because my father nods his head in approval. My need to please him is met.

As time-lapsed flowers bloom on the screen, and after the terrible MIDI guitar instrumental ends, I take a breath and start to sing.

Verse 3

I don't know when I knew it was hard to ask my father and mother about their lives before Canada. My mother loves talking about what it was like settling down here. I know that my father's first big job in Canada was at a shipyard, which is a lucky one to get when you're first getting started. I know of the many businesses they started and let go of while they raised their family. However, when it comes to their lives in the Philippines, those stories don't flow out of them readily. I only get small springs of information about their before-Canada lives. And the rare times those stories do come up, a recurring lesson keeps interrupting them.

"We grew up from nothing and worked hard to get here for our family. It's all because of our hard work and God's blessing," they say. My mother adds, "We're Canadian now," and "my children are Canadian, so why dwell on the past? What matters is the future."

And that's where it gets complicated. They justifiably wanted their children to thrive on these lands. If the price of reducing my family's hardships was for their children to fully assimilate here, rather than to struggle through full-on discrimination against them, how can I blame them? I am fulfilling what it means to be Canadian: being a healthy, educated, and contributing member of society. And I'm also complicit in not wanting to learn more about my heritage. I've been given the privileges to succeed in the White man's world, so why complicate that fact? However, regardless of all our intentions, the reality is that a price was paid. Something has been lost, and the ability to bring that up, to ask about the past, about tradition, about our cultural roots, seems impossible to do. For both sides. What do you do in a situation when Colonialism, as adept as a showy salesman with fake wares, leaves all of us disconnected? Putting false fears in both me and my parents that prevent us from sharing and talking openly about what has been lost? Instead, we use small talk to skirt what we really want to say. And there is so, so much to say ...

Instrumental Break

During any karaoke, if there is an instrumental break, there is time to catch your breath. Maybe sway to the digital melody. Here is a check-in for ten bars:

Kamusta, how are you doing right now?

Are you enjoying your day?

Do you have trouble talking to your parents?

Do clouds of identity crisis hover over your head?

What is your favourite song to sing at karaoke?

Did you get your own break yet?

What helps ground you?

Has Assimilation stolen something valuable from you?

What have you always wanted to ask someone when you were too afraid to start the conversation?

Did you remember to breathe right now?

Final Chorus

As I sing the last lyric, everyone in the room lets out a little cheer. However, what I care about most is my father's enthusiastic clapping and his quiet "Yup!" to my performance. That little sign of enjoyment makes me blush because even at thirty-two years old, I love getting his approval. As the screen resets back to the karaoke search bar, I ask:

"Who wants to go next?"

Tito Charlie is still thinking over his selection and Tita Darling shyly laughs and says she just wants to watch. When I get to my father, he says,

"Let's do something together."

"What do you have in mind?"

He strokes his chin again, and although he's pretending to not know what we should sing, he's already made his choice. I hand him the remote and he scrolls back to Sinatra's "My Way."

Jokingly, everyone lets out an "Ooooo," referencing the reverence Filipinxs have for Sinatra and his signature song, to the point where no one dares to sing it unless they have the chops to pull it off. Apparently, screwing up "My Way" in the Philippines can be dangerous.

"Let's do it," my father says calmly, but a slight twitch of doubt at the corner of his mouth betrays him. However, he continues to act confidently; after all, today's been a good day for him. He feels brave.

I select the song, and we admire the cinematography of this karaoke video, some generic B-roll video of New York City in the 80s. As the bars disappear, indicating it's time for us to start singing, he points the microphone to me, indicating I should sing the first verse. Right before the last bar is about to disappear, time slows down. Just like my father going into his Sinatra fantasy, I go into my own fantastical scene. The lights on the periphery of my sight start to dim and everyone in the vicinity freezes mid-action. The only ones lit are my father and me. He is frozen as well, his gaze fixed on the microphone. I ask him:

What does being Filipino mean to you?

What do you miss most about the Philippines?

What is the fondest memory you ever had growing up?

Do you ever think about the land of your ancestors?

Can you remember the taste of a mango that was picked straight out of the tree?

Which Filipino ghost story scared you the most as a kid?

What did you worry about when you were five years old? Fifteen years old? Twenty-five years old?

Can you describe what it's like watching Lola, as a young woman, dance at a party?

When you met Mom for the first time, what made your heart swell the most?

When did you decide you wanted to immigrate to Canada?

Is there a moment in Filipino history that ever gave you pause?

Why is it so hard for us to talk about the past?

Are you truly proud of how I'm representing my heritage?

Do you have regrets about how you got to this point?

What is the fantasy that you spin for yourself when you sing karaoke?

What do you think about me? My life, my decisions, my actions?

Who are we in this world of fools?

Time ticks forward once again and the lights brighten back around us. We are all back in the present, and as my vocal cords vibrate, forming the syllables and consonants making up the lyrics of the song, I continue my mental list of questions for my father. They emanate from my brain as psychic waves in the ether. Hoping that my father receives the signal and hears me. To feel my need for him to connect with this desperate transmission.

His turn to take the mic in our father-son duet. As he sings, he also sends out his own psychic signals. However, I can't find the proper channel to get his message. As I scan the channels and strain my hearing, hoping to get a whisper of his transmission, it still comforts me that it exists. Even though there might not be any hope of our messages ever being properly received at our respective stations, they are still valuable medicine for our souls. These signals travel through space, oscillating and dissipating the heavy clouds around me. Karaoke has equalized the atmosphere, calming the storm and giving me hope that I can find the answers to who I am as a Filipinx-Canadian.

In the blink of an eye, the song ends. Everyone claps in appreciation with some added hollers of positive affirmation heard throughout the whole house. My father rubs his thighs and looks down to the ground in embarrassment, but despite his bashfulness, I know he's enjoying the attention. I hand off the microphone to Tito Charlie, who is itching to sing, and I feel my father's hand pat me on the back. A confirmation of a job well done. I feel happy, and my mood is as clear blue as the paradise on the karaoke title screen.

Outro

Singing karaoke with my father and my community goes beyond a bonding moment. It's a way for me — and hopefully other Filipinx cross-cultural children — to acknowledge what is unsaid, what we're scared to share among ourselves as it leaves us vulnerable. And yes, vulnerability is the antithesis to the survival instincts that many Filipinx immigrants have to rely on in order to succeed when they leave the Philippines (i.e., being stoic, protectively silent, and performatively positive). However, those same strategies create barriers for us, the next generation of folks expected to be the stewards of our culture for generations to come. Access to our language, traditions, and histories is at risk of not being carried forward because of the hesitation to share what we really want from and think of each other. We can stand up for ourselves and our immigrant parents in this Western social system, a mess of Colonialism and White Supremacy, which continues to oppress Indigenous and diasporic cultures that also have ancestral wisdom to share.

Now is the time for our Filipino-Canadian community to gather. Not only to celebrate a birthday, a christening, a wake, or a wedding but to share what we deny ourselves. To share the lessons in our Filipinx languages and dialects, the tensions between generations, the unpleasant family truths, the passing on of traditions, and all the stories. We, the children of our hard-working and brave parents, know that we just need to ask; it's our duty to do so. It might take us some time to muster the courage. Maybe after frying hundreds of turon with our mom or pouring glasses of Tanduay for our titos or singing many, many karaoke songs with our papa, maybe after that we can ask our questions out loud.

So, for now, I'll sing my heart out. I'll sway to the digital notes of the karaoke's MIDI track. I'll sing and absorb the ambience of the Filipinx party to get me closer to answering what kind of "Filipinx" person I am until I'm ready to ask those that have come before me for all of the answers. Even if it's not what I expect, I know that moment will be something I'll never forget.

End of Song

Your Score

86

Not Bad!

MARIBETH MANALAYSAY TABANERA

Pagpasok sa Sarili Ko / Coming Into Myself

MABUHAY! MAYAD-AYAD NGA PAD-ABOT! Welcome!

My name is Maribeth Manalaysay Tabanera, also known as Kilusan, pronouns siya/sanda/they/them/theirs/she/her/hers/he/him/his. I am a Tagalog Visayan Filipinx queer non-binary multi-hyphenate educator, artist, and community organizer born and raised on Treaty 1, the original lands and waters of Anishinaabe, Ininiwak, Anishininiwak, Dakota, and Dene peoples, and on the homeland of the Red River Métis Nation. My ancestry on my maternal side is Tagalog from San Roque, Navotas, Manila, Philippines. On my paternal side, my ancestry is Visayan from Tamalagon, Tangalan, Aklan, Philippines. In my youth, I would have introduced myself as Maribeth, a Filipino-Canadian from Winnipeg. The evolution of how I identify is a reflection of my journey toward wholeness, as I continue to heal through intergenerational trauma caused by cisheteronormative white supremacist capitalist imperialist patriarchy, as well as my commitment to reclaim my ancestral strengths and ways of living.

I am a first-generation settler born, raised and still residing in so-called Canada. This context holds me as I continue to ask myself, "Who am I?" and "What is my purpose?" These two questions have come and continue to be at the forefront of my life, but especially during times of great challenge, such as incidents of family conflict, a near-fatal car accident, workplace abuse and exploitation, financial hardships, and the end of valued relationships. Growing up, the message I received from society was that a successful life included finishing school, getting a job, finding a husband, getting married, buying a house, and having children. My model of success growing up was a linear one, and when things went wrong, I would often blame myself for "my problems" and "my shortcomings" and felt powerless in changing my outcomes. The model minority myth manifested in my life through self-inflicted pressure to be perfect, hard-working, overachieving, and non-confrontational. I experienced imposter syndrome and was scared to share my ideas and feelings in school and professional spaces, because I thought they were not valuable in places where I was the minority. Whose voice was telling me I was not enough and not worthy of taking up space and making mistakes? Why did I feel incomplete, despite having achieved so much in my life?

> Internalized oppression — a condition in which an oppressed individual or group come to believe that they are inferior to those in power or who are part of the dominant group   has been identified by various psychological scholars as a salient and possibly the most insidious consequence of oppression.
> — E.J.R. David[1]

I can't pinpoint the exact moment of time I decided to dissolve my internalized oppression. All I can tell you is that my healing toward wholeness and wellness has been one I have longed for in my body for as long as I can remember. I know that when I began to learn about many different histories — the history of the land colonially known as the Philippines; my family's history and migration; and the history of Indigenous peoples on Turtle Island and the Philippines — I realized that it wasn't my fault when I didn't feel well. Colonialism has been used time and again to erase language, culture, family, and histories around the world, causing intergenerational psychological and physical harm to communities. I continue to learn, unlearn, relearn, and question the (mis)education that was passed down to me through informal and formal schooling in hopes of creating and maintaining a state of well-being that is grounded in my ancestral belief systems.

In this personal essay, I will locate myself in relation to the colonial paradigm and discuss my artistic practice as a healing modality and tool to help build solidarity across communities, my methods of breaking the

---

1 E.J.R. David, "Part Two — The Aftermath," in *Brown Skin, White Minds: Filipino -/ American Postcolonial Psychology* (Charlotte, NC: Information Age Publishing, 2013), 51.

cycle of capitalistic productivity, and lastly, the help I have sought from my community and their impact on my well-being. My hope is that by sharing my story, you will be inspired to begin and sustain a state of wellness and groundedness in your unique identity, as well as understand the transformative, liberating, and healing possibilities of art practice and therapy, so you may feel empowered to live your fullest and most expressive life.

Locating Myself

I was born in Winnipeg, Manitoba, in the late 80s. I am the only child of Francisca Manalaysay and Romeo Tabanera. My parents immigrated from the Philippines in 1983 and settled in the North End neighbourhood. For as long as I can remember, I longed to learn the history of my family and the country my parents left. The majority of my relatives stayed in the Philippines. My parents did their best to surround me with a loving community, but I often felt jealous of other Filipinos who had large extended families in the city. I realize now that my family was never able to figure out the sponsorship system and couldn't afford to bring more relatives to Canada. Missing these family bonds in my life made me feel disconnected and isolated. One of my first experiences of cultural loss and identity confusion was my inability to speak Tagalog and Aklanon, my parents' mother tongues. Before I began my Canadian education, I spoke fluent Tagalog. Shortly after I enrolled in elementary school, I began to speak exclusively English, even when my parents would speak to me in their first languages. Today, I cannot communicate in Aklanon, and I can only understand Tagalog and participate in basic conversation. Forgetting my ancestral language was and still is a difficult reality in my life. It has made it challenging for me to connect with my family in the Philippines, which made me feel inadequately Filipinx at times. Today, it's a goal for me to relearn the language of my parents, because I know this will help me further make sense of my identity. It's also important for me to hold space for language to evolve and reflect my unique experience as a queer non-binary Filipinx living in the diaspora. The term *Filipinx* is a new way of identifying those with Filipino/a/x ancestry not rooted in a post-colonial binary identity. Before colonizers came to the Philippines, the Indigenous Tagalog and Aklanon language did not have gendered pronouns and instead used *siya/sanda* — the equivalent of *they* in English. I always wondered why my parents would often mix up she and he, but after learning about the lack of gendered pronouns and that gender fluidity was a part of our culture, it all made sense. Learning about Filipino/a/x pre-colonial ways of living has widened my empathy toward myself and how I show up in the world, but before I get ahead of myself, I want to tell you more about what it was like being raised as a Filipino-Canadian.

Growing up in the 90s, I experienced the world before and after the dawn of the Internet. I was a curious child, and when I would ask my parents questions, they would say, "Check the encyclopedia." One day, I grabbed the *P* book and flipped the pages to learn about the Philippines, only to be disappointed at the few paragraphs in front of me. My main resources for learning about Filipino culture and history were the oral stories my parents would share with me. They did their best to expose me to cultural activities such as food, music, and dance, but my curiosities around my identity were far deeper than what I could find answers for in a textbook. Why did my parents leave the beautiful, tropical archipelago islands for a place where it's freezing cold most of the year? Why, when I asked elders about the history of the Philippines, did they all begin with the colonization of the country by Spain for 300 years and then America for 150 years? Why are Filipinos so proud of their Spanish ancestry? Why do so many Filipinos exaggerate their Spanish ancestry? What were the impacts of colonization on Filipinos? What do my parents mean when they say "colonial mentality"? Was the Philippines always a third world country? Did Filipinos always practise Catholicism? Why were only men given powerful positions in the Catholic Church? Why am I made to feel shame about my sexual desires? What does it mean to be Filipino-Canadian? These are some of the questions I began to ask myself as a young person. I may not have had the exact vocabulary as a child, but these are the beginning curiosities that helped me begin to locate myself.

Colonial mentality is a state of marginal consciousness, which lacks the critical awareness of the forces of domination and oppression that shape attitudes, values, and behaviors in the colonized. This lack of awareness among colonized peoples results in mimicry of the colonizers' attitudes, values, and behavior while their own indigenous values keep subverting and betraying this mimicry.

— Leny Strobel[2]

Colonial mentality and internalized oppression are rampant in the Filipino community. For example, growing up, my elders would say to me, "Stay in the shade and out of the sunlight, so that your skin doesn't become dark." When I visited the Philippines in 2017, I was bombarded with skin-whitening products and ads. After spending a few days on the beaches of Boracay, my cousins had a visceral negative reaction at how "dark" I was. They couldn't understand why I would want to tan and be in the sun. The mainstream beauty standards in the Filipino community to this day continue to uphold and perpetuate colourism, anti-Blackness, and white-centred standards of beauty. This is only a sliver of the way Western life and products are valued more than Filipino ways of living and being.

Filipino history is often summarized by many Filipinos and Filipino Americans in one phrase — "300 hundred years of the convent and 50 years in Hollywood." This is evidence suggesting that many individuals with Filipino heritage may not have a very good understanding of their historical and cultural roots; that they may lack a strong, authentic, and positive Filipino knowledge base that may contribute to developing pride toward their heritage. This limited and inaccurate representation of Filipino history sends the message that nothing existed prior to the arrival of Europeans; that Filipinos owe everything they know, and even their survival, to their European or Western colonizers.

— E.J.R. David[3]

---

2 Leny Mendoza Strobel, introduction to *Coming Full Circle: The Process of Decolonization among Post-1965 Filipino Americans*, 2nd ed. (Santa Rosa, CA: The Center for Babaylan Studies, 2015), xi-xvi.
3 E.J.R. David, "Chapter 2 — The Catholic Convent: Spanish Colonialism," in *Brown Skin, White Minds: Filipino -/ American Postcolonial Psychology* (Charlotte, NC: Information Age Publishing, 2013), 13.

After eighteen years of attending the Canadian public school system, I only began to develop my understanding of colonization while attending university. I learned about the historical genocide of Indigenous people in Canada at the hands of the colonial Canadian government and the Catholic Church. Today, ongoing genocide against Indigenous people is happening through land displacement, the child welfare system, poverty, and the school-to-prison pipeline.

> In order for the settlers to make a place their home, they must destroy and disappear the Indigenous peoples that live there. Indigenous peoples are those who have creation stories, not colonization stories, about how we/they came to be in a particular place — indeed how we/they came to be a place.
> — Eve Tuck and K. Wayne Yang[4]

After learning about the history of Indigenous peoples on Turtle Island, I understood that the dehumanization and genocide of Indigenous groups all around the world has occurred and continues because of settler-colonial projects that seek to extract resources in the name of capitalism. I completed my teacher degree through the University of Winnipeg and Red River College in 2013, and it was at this point that I began to ask questions such as: What is a colonized person? What negative impacts has colonial mentality had on my personal life in terms of how I relate to myself and others? How does one overcome the internalized oppression of colonization? How might I reclaim my true identity and power without the projections of oppressors? What does it mean to be a decolonized Filipinx in so-called Canada? How do non-Indigenous people understand a connection to their original homeland without being on the land? What is my role and responsibility, as a settler on stolen land, to be an educator in a diverse community of learners that includes Indigenous children? How might I, as a leader and educator in the Filipino community, teach our youth about the history of the Philippines and Filipinos in Winnipeg?

---

4 Eve Tuck and K. Wayne Yang, "Decolonization is not a metaphor," *Decolonization: Indigeneity, Education & Society* 1, no. 1 (2012): 6.

As a first-generation settler living on stolen land, I have had to look at how I have benefited from colonization and activate my privilege to dismantle systems of oppression within myself and in my community. Settlers must continually work to decolonize their mentality and take action toward the repatriation of Indigenous land and life. Unlearning internalized oppression is not just mental work, it is emotional, physical, and spiritual work. Throughout my life, I have found joy, expression, and connection through my artistic practice. The relationship with myself and others continues to be cultivated through learning and creating, which has been a powerful healing modality when it comes to self-improvement.

Each One, Teach One

For as long as I can remember, the arts have always been a safe space for me. A place I could practise expressing myself in a creative and fun environment. I loved to mimic dancers on television, teaching my cousins choreography, singing, acting, performing at family parties, drawing, colouring, painting, and making things from scratch. During my time in the public education system, I took every opportunity I could to be part of the arts through classes, clubs, and extracurriculars. My parents recognized my interest and passion for the arts early on, so they encouraged and supported me to explore my curiosities. I remember one day, my mom asked me if I wanted to take up ballet, to which I responded with a quick "No, thank you." I refused the offer because I didn't feel like I would fit in. I had never seen a Filipino ballerina before. I was more interested in hip hop dancing because the music resonated with me. In 1996, my parents enrolled me to dance with Magdaragat Philippines Inc. It was the first place where I received formal dance training in Filipino folk dance, hip hop, ballet, jazz, and improvisation. It became a new source for learning about my culture. I went on to Tec Voc High School, where I trained with Patti Caplette and Sofia Constantini. By the age of seventeen, I was being invited by my friends to professionally choreograph dance numbers for their debuts (Filipino coming-of-age parties). I also began breaking (breakdance) training under B-Boy Rector of Quick Beats Crew and B-Boy Boob Jestser of Dangerous Goods during this time. In 2006, I became a member of Define Movement, a street-style dance crew led by Dammecia Hall. I trained in a variety of dance forms including hip hop, house, dance hall, and vogue. When you learn a dance form, you not only learn movements, but you have the opportunity to learn about the culture, history, and people. The dance styles I gravitated toward were genres born out of the African or Latinx diasporic experience. When I listened to the lyrics of the songs I was dancing to, I felt like my experiences were being mirrored to me. Topics ranged from, but were not limited to, living in poverty, searching for identity and meaning, self-improvement through self-development, and uplifting community through giving back.

As I began to be invited to teach professionally as a young adult, specifically in the styles that I had experience in, one of my greatest fears was participating in cultural appropriation. As a guest in a variety of Black and Latinx diasporic–created dance forms, it was and still is critical for me to know and acknowledge the history of each dance form and to participate in the culture of each dance style. For example, hip hop was born in the Bronx as a cultural movement created by African-American and Latinx-American youth to express themselves, bring about positive opportunities, and create safe spaces in underserved communities through the forms of DJing, MCing, Graffiti, and Breaking. Fifty years later, it continues to serve as a vehicle for transformative learning for marginalized groups all over the world. I resonated with hip hop culture because it was accessible; I felt welcomed and valued, and there I met a diverse range of peers and mentors who had similar life experiences as I did. Many of the street-style dance pioneers and their students are currently still alive and teaching, thus developing relationships with these instructors has been and still is integral to learning how to deliver the cultural knowledge authentically and respectfully. When picking my mentors, I purposely chose teachers who can articulate the lineage of their knowledge. In the summer of 2018, I trained under some of the pioneers of street-style dance forms in New York City. My instructors taught me that being a part of the culture is about family, hard work, perseverance, and dedication. Being a "culture vulture" is not acceptable, and that if one cannot teach the movement without the history, vocabulary, and technical skill, then a more suitable candidate should be hired. Street dance culture has been passed down through generations by oral storytelling and physical demonstration. There are no accredited schools or training centres that a dancer can attend to become a "Hip Hop Certified Teacher." In this sense, street credibility is still an important part of the culture. In order to be regarded as an expert in the styles, there needs to be a demonstrated commitment to the form, its history, and to the culture and liberation of historically marginalized people. Ethical and active participation includes training with elders, competing, organizing, teaching, and advocating for the community. Hip hop artists often quote this African Proverb "Each one, teach one." This motto represents our responsibility to uplift ourselves and our communities through mutual and reciprocal education and solidarity building.

At the beginning of 2022, I felt called to focus my dance practice and work on cultivating the vogue and ballroom scene in Winnipeg. Winnipeg Kiki Ballroom Community is a 2STLGBQIAA+* centred space for the ballroom scene to learn and compete against one another, walking a variety of categories designed to simultaneously epitomize and satirize gender constructs, occupations, and social classes, while also offering an escape from reality. After years of training in Vogue Femme, I asked Matthew "Snoopy" Cuff to mentor me in 2022. My relationship with Snoopy gave me the opportunity to meet and work with Ballroom community members both locally and nationally, as well as offer vogue dance classes and co-organize kiki balls in Winnipeg. I still have much to learn when it comes to the Ballroom Community, and my goal like any of my interests is to be a student for life.

Breaking the Cycle of Capitalistic Productivity

I completed my Bachelors of Education at University of Winnipeg in March 2013 and only a few weeks later started my first full-time position as a teacher. I was an ambitious young professional, with a mission to prove my worthiness and hireability as a permanent teacher. I was also dancing competitively, putting in an excessive amount of rehearsal hours at the expense of rest. On June 1, 2013, I fell asleep while driving my parents' car, hitting a parked vehicle, which caused mine to flip over and crash. I woke up, unbuckled myself, and got out of the car. All I could hear was myself thinking, "How am I going to get to work on Monday?" Why was this the first thing that came to mind? Why wasn't it, "Oh my God, I almost died, but I'm alive"? Looking back, my reaction was due to a mindset that prioritized productivity over personal safety, a reaction caused by internalized colonialism and capitalism. I returned to work on Monday morning and spoke with my then principal. I explained what happened, to which he replied, "Maribeth, you are burning the candle at both ends." It was the first time I had someone tell me that I was a workaholic. That if I kept overextending myself, there would be nothing left. After this event, for the first time in my life, I stepped away from dance and instead focused on learning to slow down and take care of myself. I began to practise yoga and meditation. I realized how poorly I was treating my mind, body, and spirit because I didn't take or value breaks. In 2015, I returned to my dance practice and joined Project Dance Company. The crew became one of the first groups from Winnipeg to represent Canada at the Hip Hop International in San Diego. The following year, I joined B.O.S.S. Dance Team as a dancer and choreographer. I signed my first permanent teaching contract in early 2017.

When the COVID-19 pandemic hit the world in March 2020, I began adapting to the evolving education and arts industries. My most successful strategies to help me cope with the isolation have been honouring rest, slowing down, sitting with my emotions, practising movement and mobility both indoors and outdoors, listening to music, writing, learning new skills, and practising gratitude. I had the opportunity to complete a variety of projects during this pandemic, but this would not have been possible without prioritising my health, as well as my communities. Finding a balance and rhythm between the commitments in one's life is a dynamic dance, but if you practise grounding through cultural and spiritual rituals, mindfulness, humility, and setting boundaries, you will create space to find your own flow and not one controlled by capitalistic productivity. Learning to be still, to be strong, to be at peace with the present moment is an integral part to creating art sustainably. Another critical factor in maintaining a state of wellness for myself is asking for help and connecting with the Filipinx community.

Help Wanted!

In late 2018, after a long-term romantic relationship came to an end, I felt that, for the first time in my life, I was ready to see professional therapists and healers. After speaking with them, I came face to face with many of the questions I had been asking myself around my identity. Up to that point, I would have described myself as an extremely hard-working perfectionist who was afraid of failing. Failing the expectations of parents, failing to be successful at school and my career, and failing to find a partner to spend my life with. We can be our worst critics, but we can also be our most powerful healers. I learned that when we go through traumatic events in our lives, later in life we can revisit younger versions of ourselves to begin processing and healing through the pain. We can begin to equip ourselves with healthy ways of dealing with old trauma being triggered. When I think about the number of racialized friends and their family members I know who access therapy, it's few and far between. The cost of therapy and stigma toward it continue to prevent many Indigenous, Black, and People of Colour (IBPOC) from accessing mental health support. What I have observed in my work with youth is that the discussion around mental health and wellness in IBPOC families is still in developmental stages, with our youth often leading the conversation, and unfortunately in some cases it's completely off the table. Growing up, I would hear elders tell young people to "pray away their problems" or "ask Jesus." I have only begun to examine the trauma I have incurred via the relationships in my life, and my experience growing up in a Filipino Roman Catholic home. One of the most powerful lessons I've learned through therapy is that no one is born with shame; it is taught and internalized.

In 2019, I began to intensely research what other Filipinx/a/os living in the diaspora were doing to reclaim their pre-colonial ways of living. In my search for other Filipinx/a/os with similar curiosities around intersectional identity and decolonization, I came across the term *Filipinx* and found the work of a scholar named Leny Mendoza Strobel. Strobel's work focuses on Filipinx/a/o decolonization; Kapwa psychology and babaylan practice; primary/land-based babaylans in the Philippines; babaylan-inspired practices by Filipinos in the diaspora; and personal narratives on decolonization as a spiritual path. Her work offered a pathway to exploring what it meant for me to decolonize as a Filipinx living in the diaspora, grounded in pre-colonial Filipinx/a/o belief systems. In her book, *A Book of Her Own*, Strobel explains her use of the term "indigenous:"

> I use the term indigenous to refer to the self that has found its place, its home in the world. Emptied of projections of "inferiority," "third world," "undeveloped," "uncivilized," "exotic and primitive," and "modernizing," it is the self capable of conjuring one's place and growing roots through the work of imagination, re-framing history, and re-telling the Filipino story that centers our history of resistance, survival, and re-generation.[5]

After reading Strobel's work and other post-colonial work done by Filipinx/a/os living in the diaspora, I decided to seek out other Filipinx working in the therapeutic industries because I wanted advice from people who had similar lived experiences. Through following #Filipinx on Instagram, I was connected with Heather Rebecca Wilson, a Transformational Coach based in Tongva territory (Los Angeles). I virtually attended her Filipinx Healing Circles, where we co-created a sacred space for Filipinx in the diaspora to connect, express, and release challenges we experienced in the realms of decolonizing our bodies, minds, spirits, and energy. In January 2021, I began to see Dr. Reese Malone, who holds a Masters of Public Health and a Doctorate of Human Sexuality. In April 2021, I redesigned and relaunched my website. The creative process was a cathartic experience for me because I was able to reflect, see, and celebrate the personal and professional growth I have achieved over the past few years. It was also the first time that I publicly shared that I identified now as a queer Filipinx. In the early part of 2022, I participated in my first Kali container with Ate Imee, also known as Mayari Moon. In this virtual class, I was able to remember the martial arts my ancestors would have used to defend themselves from colonizers and enemies. Ate Imee's container created a safe space for diasporic Filipinx around the world to come together to learn and reclaim their ancestral strength. Dr. Malone's

5 Leny Mendoza Strobel, *A Book of Her Own: Words and Images to Honor the Babaylan* (San Francisco, CA: T'Boli, 2005), 182.

therapy sessions, Wilson's healing circles, and Ate Imee's Kali container are places where I have been able to continue to dissolve internalized oppression. Being in relationship with Filipinx/a/o healers and other community members actively reclaiming their pre-colonial identities has been and will continue to be a critical part of my life. I am grateful to have given myself the permission to be vulnerable enough to share my struggles with others, and to be open to practising and internalizing new mental, physical, emotional, and spiritual habits that help me to feel whole and empowered.

Looking Back to Come In

In June 2022, I attended the Fierté Canada Pride Human Rights Conference, where I connected with 2STLGBQIAA+* elders, knowledge keepers, academics, artists, and activists from all over the world. I learned about the history and the current state of my local and broader queer community. It was a life-changing and life-affirming experience. It reminded me we must continue to centre and uplift the voices most marginalized. It reminded me that our collective liberation is bound to the liberation of Indigenous nations and lands. We must protect Indigenous, Black, and People of Colour children and lives. We must remember that gender fluidity is sacred and ancestral. We must continue to build coalitions across generations, locations, and every other intersection. Organize! Mobilize! Educate! Bring your communities into the circle! The time is now and we need everyone committed to creating and cultivating spaces that are safe and inclusive for all.

My healing journey will be lifelong. I believe life is cyclical, and I will continue to circle back to the questions of "Who am I?" and "What is my purpose?" I have only begun to answer my questions around my identity, and that's okay. This work requires patience, research, learning, listening, connecting, and co-creating with the community. It will require us to learn and acknowledge the impact of colonization on our psyche and value systems. But knowing is not enough: we must continually take action in our lives to use our privilege to dismantle all systems of oppression. We are all colonized people, so it is all of our work. I hope we all continue to heal through internalized colonialism and colonial mentality, so we can all live an authentic, empowered, and liberated life. I hope you all find a sense of well-being, are able to fortify your self-confidence in your identity, and remember your ancestral strength. We are the descendants of warriors and healers who have lived and thrived for thousands of years and will continue to do so for a thousand years more.

Coming into myself

You are creation.
You are beautiful.
Your journey is sacred.

You are whole.
You are loved.
Your life matters.

PATRIA RIVERA

LANDING AND ARRIVAL · A map of no return

1 The ugly face of fear

Fear drove us out of our homeland. The constant, nagging fear that on any day, at any hour, some frenzied military soldier would put the whole country on hold, declare a mini-coup, forever shatter the fragile peace we knew under the Marcos dictatorship. Marcos had placed the Philippines under the dragnet of martial rule on September 21, 1972, ostensibly "to keep the peace." Proclamation 1081 suspended civil rights and imposed military authority in the country. The directive effectively barred mass demonstrations and rallies against the regime's inaction to ease poverty in cities and on farms, improve abject working conditions, and end corruption in the government. The military incarcerated labour, farm, and student leaders who led mass protests on the streets of Manila and in other parts of the country. Although the government was ousted from power after two decades, when protest masses and mass rallies in the mid-1980s galvanized effective opposition to the government, the country continued to experience only restive peace.

That was the point at which my husband and I decided we could not live with any more uncertainty. Our four daughters were growing up; we did not want them to suffer and live the rest of their lives knowing the ugly face of fear. We would move to Canada.

2 Six suitcases and a map of no return

Six suitcases. My husband Joe and I decided we needed just six suitcases to emigrate from the Philippines in the summer of 1987. Although staff at the Canadian Embassy in Makati, the financial and commercial hub in Metro Manila, said we could send over household items and furniture free of freightage, we opted to travel light. Our journey would be a clean break. No baggage from the past. Just our clothes, shoes, and some money in the bank to tide us over in the first few months.

We had earlier sold our house so there would be no home to go back to. We were homeless and property-less now. It would be with a certain sense of premonition and irony that 1987 also inaugurated the International Year of Shelter for the Homeless, since we would begin our first day in our adopted country without a home, without any next of kin, and just the shirts on our backs. At the same time, we were heartened that, at the beginning of the year, astronomers at the University of California took first sight of the birth of a galaxy. We had bought one-way tickets only. There was neither a looking back nor a going back.

Six suitcases. One each for me and my husband. One each for our daughters — Jenny, Kim, Isobel, and Rani. Our two older daughters were in their teens, fourteen and thirteen, and our two younger ones, eight and six. How do you leave a past lived for more than thirty years in a suitcase? How do you determine which item or belonging to keep? Or which memento or memorabilia mean the most to you and your family? Our decisions were fraught with risks and uncertainty but were founded on what we knew we wanted most for our family: some peace of mind. A good education for our children. A family life centred on simplicity. Although my husband and I were both gainfully employed and enjoyed thriving careers in Manila, our lives were forever on the brink of the next coup or the next bombing or prey to any and all of the stresses and dislocations that seethed and frothed over the cities and towns, small and big, in our old country.

In January 1987, government forces fired at a group of farmers on their way to Malacañang Palace in Manila to protest the lack of government action on land reform. In June, seventeen civilians suspected to be members of a rebel group were reported to have been killed by army soldiers in Lupao, a town near the foot of the Caraballo Mountains in Nueva Ecija. We chose to follow the map to the Door of No Return, a map that navigated rivers, mountains, and oceans ten thousand miles away from where our home once stood. We left our homeland with its storied 7,641 islands, a cacophony of voices and cultures that spoke in 186 languages (two of them now dead), a diverse flora and fauna, and the uncertain dangers of the Pacific Ring of Fire making it vulnerable to typhoons and earthquakes.

In January 1987, Frobisher Bay, in the Northwest Territories, changed its name to Iqaluit. Iqaluit is now the capital of Nunavut, the newest, largest, and most northerly territory of Canada. On June 30, Canada introduced its one-dollar coin, which locals quickly nicknamed the "Loonie." By early July of that year, we had said our goodbyes to siblings and their children and close relatives and friends. It was like experiencing a death in the family. My parents had died within a year of each other: my father in 1985, my mother in 1986. Joe had lost both his parents years earlier. They had been our anchors. Their loss meant breakage from our roots, our past. We felt like orphans needing to heal. We were saddened but determined, and ready to leave. For good.

3 Landing

On July 31, 1987, we landed in Vancouver, British Columbia, where our immigration papers were stamped at the airport. Earlier, we had asked friends in Toronto to help us find an apartment, but it was suggested we look for a place to live after we'd arrived. Once in Toronto, we stayed at a hotel in Don Mills and spent four days searching, but we were fortunate to find a place right away and settled in a three-bedroom townhouse in the Finch and Leslie area.

The small townhouse on Thorny Vineway in Willowdale overlooked a children's park. It was also close to St. Timothy's Catholic School, where we promptly enrolled our children. At the time of our arrival, the school was in the process of registering new students. It had been a fine, sunny, and breezy summer, so the children did not have a tough time adjusting to life in Toronto.

We planned our move like clockwork: house, school, work, in that order. We came a month early to allow our children to adjust to the weather and to life in a new country. We did not want any surprises. Our goal was to blend in as smoothly as possible. And we did. Our empty apartment soon filled as we went bargain hunting for furniture, kitchen appliances and utensils, fall and winter clothes and boots. Before Zellers and Winners and The Bay, there were the BiWay and Simpson's department stores. We would scan the sales ads in the dailies and got what we needed as the seasons changed.

At school, our youngest, Rani, who had kept mum and just quietly observed her new surroundings, was abruptly hustled into an English as a Second Language (ESL) class. As soon as her teacher heard her speak the next day, however, she was promptly upgraded to the grade one class. "Why didn't you tell me you could speak English?" her teacher asked with concern. "Because you never asked," our tiny tyrant quickly replied.

When we moved to another townhouse a year later, our children responded to the new situation in the best way they could. There was no house help or aunts and uncles around to assist with errands and chores. The kids learned to help with the dishes, the cooking, the laundry, and the house cleanup. Initially, it was challenging. Getting up early to head to school in the middle of winter when they wanted sleep and a warm bed. Doing chores in addition to school work and assignments. Fending for themselves while my husband and I were at work at low-paying jobs.

After two years of struggling with humdrum administrative work because he did not have any vaunted "Canadian experience," my husband decided to go to law school and etch out a new career.

Like most immigrants chasing a dream, we wanted careers we had trained for at university. A job commensurate with our education and work experience. Or if it were not yet achievable because we did not have the requisite Canadian experience, a job just a few notches below what mainstream Canadians would be hired to do. We did not want to think that our skin colour defined us when employers looked at job candidates. We were optimistic that future employers would see beyond what was visible and hear beyond the sounds of our cacophonous and accented voices.

In truth, we were given a modicum of leverage and provided opportunities to vie for employment that typical newcomers would have a challenging time with. I was hired as a telemarketer within two weeks of our landing in Toronto. Since I was still converting dollars into pesos, I felt elated that I was earning eleven dollars when the minimum wage was eight. And when I did find more stable work as a junior reporter for a national religious newspaper, my first real job just two months into my time in the country, I was ecstatic. Of course, I never let on that only four months earlier I had a driver, a secretary, and an office staff three times larger than my then employer.

Early on, the managing editor of a big Toronto newspaper whom I had written to asking for advice on how to get a start as a journalist had generously written back: "Try to get into a local paper first. That is where you will get your Canadian experience." I still thank him to this day, for giving me the time of day to "get real," to get my feet back on the ground. For what was real at that time was immigrant medical doctors selling insurance policies or working as orderlies in hospitals. Or PhD-holders, chemists, and engineers driving taxicabs, Or accountants taking orders for takeout. Or architects sorting merchandise in department stores. Or nurses and pharmacists tending to the elderly as caregivers. You name a service job or a low-income occupation, and there is an immigrant or newcomer in Canada, formerly a professional in their country, ready, able, and more than willing to grab and fill it.

4 First job

Before I went job hunting, I went to the University of Toronto to have my educational achievements evaluated and credentialed. I still have that certificate to this day. A document certifying that my four years of university education in journalism from the University of the Philippines and two years in graduate communication studies from the same university was the equivalent of a bachelor's degree in Canada.

At first, I prepared a concise resumé for prospective employers with my real education and work experience. Soon, I began to realize that requests for interviews were almost non-existent. However, as soon as I downgraded my work experience and education to fulfill the basic education and work experience needed for the job advertised, I had more request-for-interview responses. To get hired, one needed to hide what one was worth. Otherwise, no employer would give me the opportunity to compete for a job. With zero Canadian experience, the best entry to the Canadian job market was to enter at the lowest level of the position one wanted.

With four daughters to raise and Joe having trouble finding a part-time job (even with his extensive education and work experience), I decided to apply as a junior reporter at a Canadian national religious newspaper. Just like my first temp position that gave me unbounded joy, working in journalism again, even at the lowest rung on the ladder, was heaven-sent. To keep me abreast of world events, our managing editor assigned me to rewrite news stories churned out by the hourly news feed from the Catholic News Service based in Washington, DC. Then she began assigning me to cover local news. Six months later, I was upgraded to national news. I interviewed church leaders and church workers — bishops and cardinals, priests and sisters and lay people. And when the news crossed boundaries, even Members of Parliament, business and political leaders, professors and researchers, social and community leaders of every stripe and colour.

My beats and reportorial assignments became my Canadian Education 101. If I needed to draft a story, deep-digging research and interviews became de rigeur. Since our newspaper covered the whole breadth and length of Canada, from east to west as well as the Canadian North, the twelve provinces and territories became a template that opened my eyes to the reality of a nation as vast and as varied as the four seasons and the peoples that lived, struggled, and thrived in it. Even as I wrote stories about the faith life of Canadians, I was also immersed in social justice issues and the struggles of immigrant workers and labourers in the Canadian workplace: from miners and transient service and migrant workers in the Prairies to domestic workers in homes and migrant men and women working in farms, factories, meat- and fish-packing plants, and service industries.

5 Family life

My family settled into a pattern as we tried to establish a new life in Canada. We would find a habitual rhythm to our inchoate and tenuous existence, like the Kellogg's "The best to you each morning" slogan from 1958 that I first encountered when I was nine and in grade three.

This became the lore and legend of our lives:

On weekdays, breakfast-in-a-hurry, and lunch and dinner cobbled from two tins of sardines, some veggies, or a quick casserole.

Also, help with homework, clothes and school snacks prepared for the following day. On Friday nights, laundry and some ironing, if needed. On weekends, off to Knob Hill Farms in Markham to get the cheapest groceries, fruits, and vegetables.

Sundays were reserved for church.

Early on, we taught the girls easy bed-making tricks.

Fluff the pillows.

Take off and tuck in a loose bedsheet.

Tidy up the bedskirt.

Add another sheet and cover the bed with a duvet. Also,

Dust.

Polish.

Scrub,

Sweep.

Mop.

Vacuum.

Clean the bathroom. Understand the basics about laundry and household cleaning chemicals, detergents, air fresheners, and cleaning liquids. In a way, we were mimicking the every-day-as-regular-as-clockwork chores of compatriots whose duty it was to work for, serve, and wait on others. Towel-offering house cleaners in resorts and spas.

Coffee-serving baristas.

Cocktail-serving bartenders.

Stevedores, cooks, helpers, cleaners in cruise ships.

Maids, cleaners, and laundrywomen in hotels. At the end of the school term, our eldest daughter Jenny's English teacher advised: "You should ask your parents to take you to the park or to the CNE. Go somewhere!" Little did the teacher know we only had enough to put food on the table, clothe the kids, or pay for our townhouse rental. But we managed to scrounge enough money to send our two youngest daughters for piano lessons up until they lost interest and began to gravitate increasingly toward school activities. To this day, I have never been to the CNE. My daughters have, with their dad and with their friends. We only went to Canada's Wonderland a few times: once when my youngest sister and her family visited from the United States, and the other times when we were able to get coupons for half the price of admission. I inherited thrift and frugality from my mother. She managed to put her eight children through school as well as numerous cousins and relatives who boarded with us when I was young. She collected odds and ends of clothing and sewed them into new dresses for me and my three sisters. She went to markets to get fresh fish and vegetables to feed our huge household. I knew how to bargain because I accompanied her in her morning forays to the Blumentritt wet market in Manila. No exclusive private schools for us; my father was a product of public schools. Yet we lacked for nothing as we were well fed and clothed within modest means. Our daughters must have sensed our early struggles in Toronto and tried not to demand too much. A trip to BiWay, the cheapest department store at the time, was like a trip to a big mall. It was a cause for celebration. They did not ask for expensive toys or clothes and shoes, just what was necessary to keep warm in the winter months. They did not complain but were grateful to receive hand-me-down coats and boots donated by old friends.

Looking back, I see the years as a blur, with both Joe and I preoccupied with the business of living: children, home, work. There was no time for slacking as every minute counted. Our children grew before our eyes: their wants and needs, emotional and physical, subsumed by the nurture and love we could manage to offer them. Latchkey children — this word I learned from Isobel, our third daughter, who tried to impress us with her immense and fast-growing vocabulary — were children left at home after school while their parents worked two or three jobs. We each held only one job, but they were left on their own when both Joe and I went to work. So, every time we were free from work obligations, we tried to stay at home and be with them.

Still, our children did not have the constant companionship and care of relatives they used to have when we were living in the Philippines. There were no cousins, aunts, and uncles to chat with or visit or give counsel. It was just us, our nuclear family, with a few friends. We did not have a regular social life, let alone go to parties. Christmas and New Year we spent by keeping to ourselves, making do with small presents and simple fare: the familiar chicken adobo, the proverbial pancit guisado, and fried rice. Our goal was to survive and live as self-sufficiently and independently as possible. Home was ten thousand miles away, and early on, we set it in stone to burn our bridges once we set foot in Toronto. "Survive or perish" was our mantra.

6 Workers among us

Although we opted to migrate to another country, my family's decision to leave was no different, or more immediate, than the decision of Filipino emigrant workers who chose to leave because of the political uncertainty and economic turmoil in our homeland. The outflux of workers began as early as the 1960s but became more pronounced in the 1970s, when under then President Marcos's strongman rule, political and economic cronyism and corruption in government drove the average person to further exploitation and abuse. Since civil liberties were suppressed, the rights of workers and farmers to organize and work for reforms were effectively scuttled. Faced with a fast-increasing population, high unemployment, and poor living conditions, and to relieve his government of the need to spend on development projects and social support for the people, Marcos launched a massive labour export program. It began with sailors, then domestic workers — nannies, caregivers, cooks, and cleaners — then migrant workers to fill the lower paid and unskilled sectors in countries in the world with chronic labour shortage.

Before this, the Philippines had already sent doctors, nurses, and allied medical professionals to other countries, in a brain drain that, to this day, robs the country of trained and much-needed professionals. In his book, *Migration Revolution*, Filemon V. Aguilar Jr. sums up the phenomenon: "If Philippine society was ever a cauldron about to boil over, overseas migration has taken the lid off and released the pressure."[1] In 2012, the economic planning ministry reported that the Philippines could not do without the remittances from overseas Filipino workers (OFWs).[2] Even the World Bank agrees that cash sent to the country — about $24 billion, or PHP 1,178 trillion, in 2014 alone — is a "key factor" for the resilience of the Philippines.[3] Remittances from the country's close to two million overseas Filipino workers (1,844,406

---

1 Filemon V. Aguilar Jr., *Migration Revolution: Philippine Nationhood and Class Relations in a Globalized Age* (Manila: Ateneo de Manila Press, 2014).
2 Jodesz Gavilan, "What you need to know about overseas Filipino Workers," *Rappler*, December 5, 2015, updated December 19, 2016, https://www.rappler.com/newsbreak/iq/114549-overseas-filipino-workers-facts-figures
3 Ibid.

OFWs in 2015) have enabled the country to withstand recession amid the economic crises of the previous years.[4]

7 I Just Can't Stop Loving You

In 1987, the world's population reached approximately five billion. A rare earthquake that peaked at 5.0 on the Richter scale on June 11 affected fourteen states in the Midwest of the United States and parts of Canada. At the same time, Supertyphoon Nina hit the Philippines, submerging fourteen fishing villages on the Philippine coast under water, leaving one thousand dead.

We had arrived in Toronto in late July, with the top billboard song "I Just Can't Stop Loving You" by Michael Jackson high-pitched and spilling in from everywhere. The air streamed with purpose when summer meant another life to live. From every corner, a mirror to reflect on. Outside our window, the children's park, though treed, appeared bruised from the dark slits on the windowpanes. *Thorny Vineway*. Did our new street name augur of tomorrows yet to come? Would our life in this new country lead to a path laid with thorns? We were young at the time, and everything looked promising. We were alive in this new country and were no longer afraid, the years in the future distant and to be savoured. We were ready to be every person we chose or wanted to be.

The days shortened in late October, when the sun sank deeper and the leaves fell on the ground: at first, mustard yellow and blood red; later, turning brown, purplish, and ragged. People here called it mid-autumn. At St. Timothy's Church, Joe and I and our children filled the half-sung hymns with thoughts of the past we had left behind. The shade of leaves falling, hung in mid-air, marking our days.

But those early experiences were mere spots in our post-arrival years. They would be subsumed by the tracks in the snow when our first winter came. We would remember the pride in the little fire we stoked three decades later. We knew we could get lost on every road and never find our way. We could run out of a country and never leave it. Memorize the shape of our name and never recognize it. Something so clear could be something so vague. Like

---

4 Ibid.

knowing and not knowing at the same time. Like the day that drowns in the bones. Like the night growing into shadow. Like names echoing many towns, burrowing through stones and fragmentary rocks.

Everywhere was where we wanted to be.

Proximity

ADRIAN DE LEON

Ship Time

in the
salish sea,
our clock glistens
from   *the wake*:
when a blaze breaks the
lavender,   we call her
morning;   a wrestle between
        desperate ray and
oppressive   cloud, we name
their romp   the afternoon; if amber
    blinds the   retina, we bid
    good night   to the sun; if ice seems
to shimmer   in waves as above,
we greet   the night.
the stern churns   a teleology
into birth,   branching timelines
like cedars   evergreening into the shore.
        can we burn   the water's waxy
    leaves into   necessary medicine?
will we breathe   its smoke until our
memory   scars over? or will these
our time   be denied from us until the shoal
        bed becomes   as grainy
    as the dead   of an hourglass?

once,   barangay
glided through
crystal waters
        of the   pasig river,
where reeds
shuddered in *their wake*.
where shanty shores
now stilt, warriors once
waded amidst archi-
pelagic   fish. once,
pasig   churched from
        the same breaths that stretched
        these sails. once,
                before   the stars & stripes,
                we traced   stripes across
                the stars   to steer us
                home.

HARI ALLURI

Oracle Card: Toward Wonder

If you pull this card in diaspora, begin by giving thanks to Anagolay, Goddess of Lost Things, Ancestor of Wandering.

Say: *Magandang umaga, magandang gabi, whether under sun or fog or atmospheric river: Salamat.*

Remember you didn't know how little you loved these mountains here before somebody told you they were also grown from lava: ring of fire kapwa to the island mountains where Siya and you (even if a mixie, monsoon on two sides) connect.

Now you can finally admit, these mountains would be beautiful if they weren't your kapwa. Because they still would be: kapwa.

Send your mind to the edges of our origin, the blade of language holding us. With its incision. Beginning — no longer scraped away. Holding us even after the bone-clean of a meal, bowl-tilt and swipe. Say: *I want that to be my name.*

Now admit, loving Anagolay as you do: *I doubt so much I sometimes feel like wrongness is my only "from."*

Each new re-puncturing, pain and threshold climbing toward surface.
Toward when, in another gender with another name, Siya watched
our bundoks climb and didn't stop them.

Say *portal*, say *tattoo*. When you receive yours, the village your nanay is
from already forgets your name.

Pupri, nkɔ? Birthplace, na so.

You are inflected by all the grammars you've ever been surrounded by. *You*
as in your body. As in you carry them, and they make you porous to more.
You are all reverb.

Apologize to the mountains with the stain inside your voice.
Let the dance floor of it rise the string-tones of an open breeze.

When you hear somebody call for *authentic*, remember your style is so
janky and collage that even your half steps have quarter notes in them:
may every checkpoint except the ones that hold the land itself

turn into a disco ball. And loss

into a wave we surf rather than the oil we plunder. Noisiness in your heels
at the troubled moss of intimate touch.

Let the touch not rancid. Hear me say it
in your ear.
Respond: *May it not become my name.*

Open toward when even the languages we've lost are where we're from.

Now in real, remember: a dragon exoskeleton light in blue, flywheel on the railroad tracks: you were looking for Anagolay then. Thinking about the history of railroad here. Walking-balancing on one track with your eyes both closed.

If the card jokes you what that worship means you take
a sip of sun.

Recall, a day of work when you had to thank every muscle, ligament, tendon, nerve, bone, joint, organ, inch of skin you could think of in the shower after. Just to get through the shower. Make this the practice of giving thanks every time you shower. Say: *Land. Water. Strands. Hands.* All are part of your name.

Here's a story you can't keep quiet — against the voice of your shame itself: when you strip songs
for the delicacy of where you haven't been, you remain
          what holds you.

There's only love,

you've said that before, in the wake of your family's loss.
By blood or chosen. You meant it
because for a little while your faith was not the body of a bee
curled up after sting. Your shame at its kindest says:
          Regardless of my name: I am afraid to tell you
          this: I, always will be.

Here, where there wasn't a word, now there is. But it was also here

before you. In a language before language, and other ones as well. Between

two precipices. Waiting for the obstacle you are, to become more like a
bridge.

"Wonder cuts the keys to doors between the worlds."

To know you would never have written that if it wasn't for our loss.

And also if the homie didn't text you a freestyle that you tried to respond
to, but your phone died. That line was all that remained.

Say this: *I agree that who the poem waited for was not necessarily me. It's
better when Niki sings it. Eric loves her name.*

When you pull the card, these are the conditions:

If mountains are the eyes that make the clouds relax their steps.
If what it takes for mountain-form to be.
If angled off the slightest, this alley at its crouch.
If crow-sex made this valley into city first.
If car-storm breaks, coyotes trot. If bloom
gives way to leaf-turn, fall, whose after-falling purpose (of return) is finally
un-prevented by your hands again this year.
The circles of us widen, even in loss: kapwa.

Kapwa: you must find a branch in water and bring it to speak with the
markings on a cedar.
You must give the branch the name of your demon.
Find a tune by Prince dancing in your head, make up a song with the

demon's name
(do not share the first lines here, do not share their name):

Hopscotch and dream smoke. Trouble-cause and flam.
Even when he's on the run he's never on the lam.

Searching for the rhythm in a phrase makes you forget. Good. What was next was almost quietness. Free of any names.

The card doesn't mean to say that you're not whole (maybe no one is, at least while alive). Only that the image you hold is more like a hologram than a colouring book. Those holograms at the mall in '95 when the food court had ash trays and you thought that getting discounts on fries was halfway to a date.

Let's not get into cricket bats, that's another card. With the pager code for carloads to show up: inflection. Distraction: Hey, *check out this pretty running wall, these birds that cross to the island in the ferry's airstream wake.*

This is more like it: the stutter working river step, the fast-food auntie mentoring a grown-ass child she calls anak, tobacco in its spoken form, the price of smoke-packs at Fraser laundromats. Those types of names.

A city, flayed, can migrate, too: do you believe that now? The closer you look, the less the land seems to move, not unlike a name.

It's clear you want to ask: *If I make an incantation of loss, is it still an incantation.* You want that, careful, to be your name.

Say this: *May I write what I'm calling in. With the ashes I release.*

Believe: *If anyone finds the word that says: "the last migration of touch before departure" — I understand Anagolay will choose them instead of me.*

Good, now the card can tell you: *Curiosity, like love, is older than doubt. Put that in your name.*

In shapeshift is the residue of each previous shape, like the residue of volcano in the island-sand, labyrinth lines of loss, you say, and the card believes you.

Still, you want to lie and say
the blade of language is a shell, and the shell whistling in the sand is a whistle I can hear.

Do not. Instead, invite the land a little closer, as the oceans do.
Because the land is more beautiful
than long-distance phone calls that make us
more beautiful than we are. And loud.

Now loud: *Ingat!*

With the *g* dropping like the word *dropping, aaaaaah* sound elongated.
Good.

Even when your pantry shames from running out of rice: Restoration in the everyday.
If you can, to give Anagolay that, more than just your name.

You must find the cord between you and the rock that calls the phosphorescence, the night of sky and every city light that shuts to give these evergreens their full silhouette of moon. You must not believe that you can ever belong, only that you are here to be with your longing.

When you are, you will quit asking the card to tell you who this is: the one who crosses dimensions, whose bangka is a weather-beaten teeth-grit where the branches crack a smile.

Waves cross over your head from them, engulfing.

It's up to you — Bahala Na   to hold onto Their name.

SHIRLEY CAMIA

To the departed

I'M NOT SURE what to say. I didn't know what to say as I watched you during Mom's funeral, making out with your white girlfriend. Your plainclothes guard stood passively by, in awe like the hundreds of others that had come to pay their respects. Mom's pride was her disgrace, put on full display, as her body was laid out, competing for attention at her own wake. Even I could feel her shame, the heat exposed by the lights that shone on her cold skin.

I cannot blame you alone. But the responsibility that is yours, the weight that we shouldered, you refuse to claim as your own.

How can you be blamed? Taken from your parents at fourteen, transported to a new life and the responsibilities and promises it held. But no one could account for the failures, the line between the two smudged in a foreign land. A new frontier with new rules and new boundaries. No protection but prayer and threats.

Adrift at school, you clung to the wrong crowd. Where book smarts weren't necessary for survival. Where a mastery of English wasn't the golden key. Where you were consoled from racist taunts by traces of power. Where you learned *I*, not the collective *we*. Where the debt of utang na loob was quickly forgotten. By the time you turned eighteen, it was too late. The fork in the road far behind you. The allure of quick cash, the gilded compass, guiding the way.

I can't blame you for that.

I also can't blame you for the whispers of the titos and titas. Their suspicions always raised when the gossip turned to neighbourhood crime.

Did you hear about the robbery at the corner store?

He must've done it.

There was a break-in down the street.
He was there.
What about the shoplifting in the mall?
I think I saw him there that weekend.
Did you see that drug heist in the news?
Of course he was involved.

Mom more concerned with clearing her standing than your feelings. *Tell them it wasn't you.* You, the lone soldier, fighting a losing battle against sharp tongues and their will to see you fall.

No, I can't blame you for that either.

I also can't blame you for the unexplained kindnesses. The crisp, green twenties slipped into our hands like temptation. The silence of unasked questions. Money counted and folded, shoved deep into pockets. Mom extending an open hand, asking for more. Knowing there was more.

> look at her
> mukhang pera
> she only wants my money

Or the flattened pieces of foil stuffed discreetly under parked car tires on Sundays. A substitute for mass. *Who needs school? I'm a ninja,* you bragged, before an escape as deliberate as night.

> they call me fast XXX
> because i never get caught

There are many exceptions.

But I can blame you for other things. Like the bags of "potpourri" Mom would flush down the toilet. Lips firmly pressed as the leaves swam in a synchronized swirl.

> if anyone offers you
> this

don't take it

send them to me

Or the cops she chased away with, *I don't speak English.*

Or how you took me to a casino when I was only ten, when there was no one else to babysit. I sat at the entrance for hours, your friends like hired guards rotating to keep watch. A dinner of chips and Coke followed, with a whispered *Don't tell Mom where we went!* pact sealed with a high-five. I couldn't wait to tell my friends the next day. *Guess where I was last night? A casino! And I came home with poker chips!* Mom scolded you for bringing me home so late, on a school night no less. You laughed as she told you to go to church on Sunday to atone for your sin. *Maging matino ka na,* she said as she chided your back. You, the proud peacock, had already sauntered off, invincible.

You did come to church with us once, as you tried to redeem yourself in the eyes of the lord. Stumbling through devotions you forgot a lifetime ago. Looking for peace in the handshakes of strangers. You said the communion made your stomach hurt — the divine intervention much too hard to swallow. You left before the final hymn was over, vowing never to return.

This was your life, the life Mom pleaded to set straight, but offered no guidance. Not a hug or comforting phrase. *There are things we do not say and things we cannot.* Still, I thought you were so cool, a renegade, and that you'd made it all on your own. A shiny life on the outside, holes in your story filled with fast cars with rumbling engines, little bags of plastic, pagers, then cellphones, tattoos (*Nag tattoo ka na naman?*), serial girlfriends, black leather, and guns.

STEFFI TAD-Y

Islands Along Mount Pleasant

Pockets out of quarters

past Pedal Heads
      & a row of daffodils

you misheard *flawed*
        as *flowered* and filled

what was missing
      in the air with Yes

everywhere
      people flower.

We left an archipelago
       whose elders weather

  heart
attack &
  heat
stroke as
if illness

were a cluster of islands
     we kept crossing.

Water rising
    up to our hips.

Here we live
    in a city that thinks
it can bury the city
    it stands on.

Here we live
    in a city that unroofs
as often as it rains.
Under a glass awning
    we trace patterns
    on our palms.

JELLYN AYUDAN

Roots

IN MANILA, HOME was a two-bedroom apartment that was situated alongside the slums. It was cramped and humble. But my mother always loved to decorate the windows with bright, floral curtains, as if they stood any chance against the dust and pollution. Home was a place where love and laughter resided, but it was no safe haven. I remember a time when it was a place to hide. A dangerous stranger with bloodshot eyes barged through the doors, dismantling three heavy-duty locks in one instant. He was being chased down with a knife by his drinking buddies after a fight over drugs and money. The panicked call from my pregnant mother was one that made me realize how fast I could run home to her.

Although it was a rough neighbourhood that taught me to be distrustful and cautious, I still loved where I lived because I belonged to that city as much as it belonged to me. In the mornings, I navigated the way to the cheapest and the best breakfast spots. Every day after school, I played with the street children in the park that also doubled as a prison enclosure for juvies. If I was ever in a fight with my parents, my grandparents and various family members were only a two-minute walk away. When I wanted to sneak out and buy candy, I knew how to avoid getting caught by the local patrol after the 10:00 p.m. curfew sirens.

Over a decade ago, my father announced that we were moving to Canada. He promised snow angels, ballet lessons, and our own bedrooms. He told us that it was the land of opportunities. It was the first time in my life that I pictured a life beyond the small world that I inhabited, to expand my horizons and seek out adventures beyond books. Every night after dinner, we gathered around a small laptop, typing in *Regina, Saskatchewan* on YouTube just to get a glimpse of what our new life will be like. Thus, at the age of nine, I became so irrevocably in love with a city that I had yet to step my foot on. All I could think of was how I would get to escape heavy rainfalls and trade them for gradual snowfalls.

On October 29, 2009, we arrived in our new home. This home was a two-bedroom apartment that we would share with another family of six. I slept in the living room in a pullout couch next to my sister, while across from us was another pullout couch with another pair of siblings. Since we were all close in age, we would have our own slumber parties every night. In this new city, there was always a surplus of toys and candies. Some days the kids next door would invite us over for a game of street hockey. Other neighbours, like the elderly lady with a golden retriever, would come by to bring us homemade cookies or show us how to make the best hot chocolate. Kids in school were even more welcoming. They talked really fast and always asked if I wanted to play grounders during recess.

After I made countless snowmen and grew bored of the new toys, the novelty of this home soon wore off. I looked around, and I missed my concrete jungle, where the leaves of the mango trees sheltered you from the radiating heat of asphalt coupled with the bare rays of the sun. And no matter how much I wanted the Dutch elm trees to shelter me from the biting cold of harsh Saskatchewan winters, they could not, because even the trees themselves embraced the cold.

The death of my grandmother was not unexpected. We knew that her kidneys were failing. Her chosen healing methods, as far as we knew, were dialysis and divine intervention. Suddenly, life started to change. Both of my parents had to take on multiple jobs to send money back for her medical fees. There were no more family dinners. And it was always "Sorry, anak, wala akong time" or "pagod na ako." My older sister and I were tasked with taking care of our little brothers, making sure that they were fed and that they slept on time. We would be left alone in that house for hours with the TV volume lowered, hoping nobody asks questions.

My parents became tired, and their limited minutes did not account for snow angels nor ballet lessons. My grandmother passed within our first year in Canada. Our last hurried exchange of I love yous over the phone served as a final goodbye. Travelling home was impossible since we lacked the money. It was a miserable time, and I wished so badly to go back.

Over time, I became distant and uprooted from my first home. This new land, however, gave me the chance to see it beyond the failed promises of the ideal life my father initially painted. Canada may not be the place where I was originally planted, but it is now my chosen home that has nourished my growth and allowed me to root and bloom.

On August 25, 2015, when I swore an oath of citizenship to this land, my love and gratitude for this community strengthened. I love how Claude Monet's *en plein air* paintings are nothing compared to the open Saskatchewan skies. I use terms like *double-double* and surprise myself with the numerous ways I can discuss the weather. I know how passionately Canadians take football and hockey games, but I have yet to find my way around them.

Now, I find myself navigating through the world split between two identities with two homes and being okay with that because there's no need to choose. I know now that *home* is not a location you type into a GPS. In many ways, finding home is like the mango or the Dutch elm trees planted around us, they did not choose to be rooted to their land, yet they flourished, adapted to the weather, and continued to grow. And so, I shall too.

ERICA DIONORA

Cutscene

Part I: A Memory

My name comes out like a judgment. The dean reads through his list of graduates, and the video pauses for approximately seven seconds when the letters of my name are splayed across the screen in sans serif.

Mama and Papa stare at the screen, watching my virtual commencement alongside Kuya and me.

"Yan lang?" Papa asks.

Three years of graduate school for seven seconds of screen time. I tell him that we can always play it back once the live event is over. He agrees, so we wait for the end — each one of us sat on the living room couch in our old pyjamas. Then we rewind it, stretch those seven seconds beyond the landscape of time — past and present — until it comes to face with a moment I've lived in for so long. A story. One that Papa laments over and over, it has become a memory that I claim as my own.

ARTICLE XIV

Education

███████ The State shall protect ██ promote ██████████ ████████

██████ and █████████████████ ████████████

████████

█████████ maintain, ██████████ an█ integrated system ██ █████████

█████████ to

███████████████████████████████████████ ████

█████████ limit█ the ██████ right of ████████████ █████████

the underprivileged;

out-of-school

adult citizens, the disabled, and out-of-school youth

They

are

an

additional cost

March 22, 1982

Papa's toe peeks shyly out of the hole on his right shoe. The sole of his left hung with each step like the jaw of a ghost bemoaning its fate.

The security guard standing before the door does not move. "Pasensya na, bawal po kayong pumasuk," he says.

"He's a student," Tita Gigi tells the guard, but he does not meet either of their eyes. Instead, his gaze tracks the sweat pimpling their faces.

It's thirty-three degrees Celsius outside of Iloilo National High School, where all the other students are greeting the day's heat dressed in their Sunday best and eager to get on stage in their caps and gowns.

The security guard shrugs, staring pointedly at Papa's worn shoes and wrinkled beige polo shirt and jeans. "Pasensya na."

Tita Gigi steps forward, face to face with the unyielding guard. "Pasensya?"

Papa puts a hand on Tita Gigi's arm and urges her away from the guard and the school building's entrance, which begins to congest with other graduating students and their parents. He pretends not to notice the iron-pressed clothes and shined shoes of his classmates or the fact that their mothers and fathers are with them as he walks toward the school's quad that he and Tita Gigi passed only moments before. She puts a hand on his shoulder when they reach the sidewalk just past school property.

"Sorry sa sapatos, To." Tita Gigi eyes the worn pair of shoes on Papa's feet and pats him on the back apologetically. Papa shrugs, saying nothing of the shoes that Tita Gigi's husband had lent him. He tells her not to worry, assures her that there is always next time. He tells her that when he graduates university, he will have shoes and clothes, and he will be on stage.

Neither of them believed that.

Part II: A Conversation

My name comes out like a curse.

"Dios ko po, anak! Vancouver?" Mama drops her half-eaten shrimp, and I poke at my cold rice noodles.

The dinner table is surrounded by four chairs occupied with stiff spines and vacant lungs. I am the first to recover my breath, but just barely. "That's where the office is, downtown Vancouver. It will be a good experience for me."

Kuya and Papa are quiet, plates too full to take on any more.

"There are lots of jobs here. You have family here!" Mama reasons, waiting for an explanation or, perhaps, an apology for my wanting to leave. Instead, I tell her that I am tired.

"Iiwan mon na lang ba kami?" Mama asks me.

I swallow a forkful of guilt with my noodles, and the words are caught between my teeth; I pick them carefully.

"The office is in Vancouver," I repeat.

Silence colours in the negative spaces of our conversation.

Mama blinks a staccato rhythm, and her eyes overflow with water, salty, much like the one that stands between her and the home she left behind for this life that I could never seem to love.

ARTICLE XV
The Family

███████ the ██████████ Filipino ████████████████
███████████ strength██ ██████████████████████████
███████████████ is ████████████████████ ███
██████████████
███████████████████████
██████████ a ████████████████ conviction██ ████████
██████████████
██████████ to ████████ care ████████████ ██████
███ for ██ ██████████████ ██ the █ ████████████
█████
████████ family █████████████████
███████████████████████████████████
███████████████████

August 8, 2008

My right foot was first baptized in a puddle of rainwater just outside of Pearson Airport. In my smallness, I thought I would drown, but the waters here are never hungry, only sanctimonious.

Half past noon, Mama, Papa, Kuya, and I finally arrived at a brown-bricked, ten-storey apartment building on the east end of Scarborough, where the night always seemed to come before its time.

I remember the way our voices echoed inside our apartment and how the sounds of bags and boxes being unpacked had bounced around the walls and ceiling like star projections in the dark. We said our grace before meals over spicy ramen noodles, split four ways, but Kuya and I ate most of it. Papa rewashed Styrofoam plates and plastic forks; we slept on beds of flattened cardboards; Mama cried during her nightly prayer when she thought everyone had fallen asleep; and I counted the minutes down until daybreak.

The next sunrise did not come for another few years.

ANGELO SANTOS

Boxes

1.

They are almost the size of kitchen ranges, these boxes made of corrugated cardboard and sealed with packing tape, overstuffed with items like canned corned beef, Vienna sausage, bagged potato chips, and foil-wrapped chocolate bars. We bring them with us every time we fly back to the Philippines; they are our silent stowaways. In the days leading up to our flight out, they sit next to large suitcases in our living room, top flaps agape, as my parents debate in Tagalog about what should go in next:

— Kasya kaya dito ang isang spiral ham?
— Spiral ham? Yung nabibili sa Costco?
— Oo. Yung naka-vacuum pack.
— (*rummages through box*) Kung mga limang pounds ang timbang kasya siguro.
— (*pause*) Kailangan bang naka-ice pack?
— Hindi na, cured yan! Ganong katagal ba flight natin?
— Mga labing-anim na oras, straight flight tayo. Sana naman hindi ma-delay o magka-problema ang flight natin.
— (*pause*) Pwede bang idagdag yung ham para isa bawat isang pamilya?
— Pwedeng pwede. Magkakasya pa dito ang isa, doon sa isang kahon kasya pa siguro mga tatlo.
— O sige, dagdagan natin! Para masaya sa Noche Buena!
— (*chuckling*) Magugustuhan nila yan, imported kasi!

Once each box is filled just shy of bursting, my dad weighs it on a bathroom scale to ensure that it doesn't exceed the airline's allowance for checked baggage. Some boxes are so large that they cannot be balanced on a single scale, making it necessary to use two scales, one placed underneath each side of the box — far enough under for the weight to register properly, but not so far that the box obscures the window for the scale's dial. After the weighing, my dad closes each box and applies a generous amount of tape to secure the flaps and reinforce the corners. The last step is for my dad to write, in his trademark fine printing, my maternal grandmother's name and address — *LUCY CRUZ, 93 BLUMENTRITT ST., SAN JUAN, METRO MANILA, PHILIPPINES 1500* — on the outside of the box, to protect against accidental loss.

These boxes are balikbayan boxes, staples of any returning Filipino's luggage, whose chief objectives are to maximize storage capacity and to minimize weight. From a design perspective, ergonomics and convenience are clear afterthoughts: the boxes are unwieldy despite measures like lashing with rope to facilitate handling. Lugging them around the airport is Olympic-level difficult. Removing one of these boxes from the baggage carousel is always a two-person affair: my dad has to pull the box from the conveyor belt while I steady the baggage cart below, such is the transfer of force when the box hits the cart.

Once we arrive at my grandmother's house in Manila, the boxes are hauled up a narrow flight of wooden stairs to a frigid air-conditioned room in which my extended family are gathered, eager to see this trip's bounty, each family member wondering whether their individual request has been remembered. A utility knife slices open each box, an ad hoc caesarean, and one by one, the contents are removed:

ANSBERT (my cousin). Tita, nakapagdala ka ba ng KitKat?

MOM. Siyempre naman, kasi kabilin bilinan mo yan.

ANSBERT, *chewing*. Mmmm. Talagang ibang iba ang lasa ng mga chocolate na dala ninyo kaysa sa nabibili dito! Fresh na fresh. Salamat, Tita! Kaya ikaw ang paborito kong Tita!

DAD, *from across the room.* Pakilagay na muna ninyo itong mga ham sa ref! May instructions yan kung papano lutuin. Siguradong magugustuhan ninyo yan, tunay na tunay na ham yan!

Every time we go back, my extended family celebrates this doling out of pasalubong, gifts from the other side of the world. Like seventeenth-century seafarers, my family has returned from our voyage from afar with plunder, plunder to divide among our landlubbing financiers. Of course, in the case of my family, no actual money is contributed by our parents; rather, the cost borne by my grandparents, my aunts, and my uncles is my parents' absence, a cost that incurs a debt that is compounded every passing year, a debt that is paid back over time in monthly remittances and regular phone calls, a debt for which these small gifts serve as mere tokens. Each time we leave the Philippines, there is an unspoken question: *after you leave, will you remember us?*

2.

My parents emigrated from the Philippines in their twenties, shortly after I was born, in search of a better life and greater opportunity. For them, each trip back is a family reunion and a repatriation, a return to the place where their parents and siblings live, the place in the world where they will always feel at ease and in their element. Every time we are in the Philippines, we spend an inordinate amount of time being driven in mammoth-sized SUVs through standstill traffic to and from the houses of relatives serving large, sumptuous meals. Growing up, I thought that these vacations were nothing more than a carnival of gluttony and self-indulgence, until I got older and realized that these weeks we were spending with my relatives were my parents' attempt to make up for lost time, to cram all of those missed birthday parties and celebratory dinners and Christmastime festivities into one hard binge, a family-time bonanza.

3.

There is a phrase in Tagalog, *utang na loob*, which translates literally to "a debt of the inside," although there is something lost in translation here, as the phrase references a concept that goes deeper than regular, run-of-the-mill debt, and the inside being referred to here is the inside of a person — namely, the person who owes the debt. The phrase refers to a debt that is immeasurably large, unquantifiable, and almost unpayable, a debt that is owed from something deep within the inner self of the debtor, perhaps something from within the debtor's very soul. It is a phrase that has no real analogue in the English language. I have seen it translated sometimes as "debt of gratitude," although this isn't quite the same.

4.

Most years we visit the Philippines, we make it a point to travel to Cabanatuan, the place where my dad was born, a more rural part of the Philippines compared to Manila, where my mom grew up. Depending on traffic, it takes about three or four hours to drive there from my grandmother's house. Rice fields flank the roads leading there; carabaos dot the horizon. The main roadway is a narrow two-laner, with one lane in each direction and no median barriers, and so it feels perilous for us to overtake slow-moving traffic, which we are often forced to do because of the proliferation of tricycles and other slower means of local transport.

Shortly after arriving in Cabanatuan one year, my dad announces that we are going to visit "The Doctor," the person who, he explains, paid for all five years of his tuition at the University of Santo Tomas, an act of generosity that laid the foundation for my dad to be able to pursue a lifelong career as a pharmacist. The Doctor turns out to be a wiry Filipino man with a closely cropped head of white hair who lives in a large house at the end of a dusty road. After being introduced, I notice that The Doctor often repeats himself and sometimes appears to forget what he is talking about. Still, my dad engages him in respectful conversation as if nothing were wrong and asks him about their shared past, which prompts The Doctor to respond genially. After listening to them for a while, I get the sense that The Doctor has only a vague recollection of who my dad is. Despite this, I can tell that it is important to my dad that we have come here, and that he pays his respects.

5.

A few years after I graduate from university, my maternal grandmother and three of my mom's sisters and their immediate families all come to visit us in Canada. It is the largest planned gathering of my extended family outside of Asia; in total, there are fifteen of them, enough for a rugby team. For my mom, my dad, my sisters, and me, it is our opportunity to finally reciprocate the hospitality that has been extended to us each time we return to the Philippines. Some family members stay with my parents at their modest two-storey home, and others stay at my newly constructed townhouse nearby. After a day of getting settled in, we drive everyone to many of the usual Ontario tourist traps (Niagara Falls, the CN Tower, and SkyDome), then we rent two boat-sized vans and drive down to the States, where we visit New York City and Atlantic City (my grandmother is fond of casinos). For these few weeks, we all keep close quarters: when we aren't crammed into the tiny seats of those rented vans, we are crammed into small three-star hotel rooms, or else we are back in Oakville where we are crammed into either my house or my parents' house, both of which have been converted into makeshift hostels for a few weeks, always abuzz with activity. It all reminds me of our trips to the Philippines; the cast is the same, only the backdrop has changed.

One afternoon at my parents' house, while the rest of the family is getting ready to leave for one of our planned outings, I catch one of my aunts looking at the view from my parents' living room window. Turning to face me, she says, "Look, there are no people walking in the streets here — life is so lonely in Canada!" I remember feeling a sudden urge to tell her that this is an unfair comparison because my parents' house is located in a quiet suburban neighbourhood and that this is far from how all Canadians live, but then I pause and realize that she is specifically referring to *my parents'* experience of Canadian life, which *is* lonely, at least compared to the life they had in the Philippines. In that moment, I see clearly the life that my parents left behind: a life of company and bustle, of noisy mealtimes and street food vendors, of TV shows and movies in which they got all the jokes, of pouring rain and city-wide flooding, of near-constant close proximity with family members, of a language and a culture of which they were in full command. It is the world that I always get a taste of when I visit the Philippines, the world I am getting a taste of again as my extended family spends time with us here. This is the life that my parents have to steel themselves to abandon in order to be able to provide for us and for everyone else that matters to them. Such is the plight and the irony of all transglobal economic migrants: sometimes, the best way to show your love is to leave.

6.

Once, I have to lift a balikbayan box by myself. The box has fallen off the baggage cart that I am in charge of pushing, likely because I was too hasty in loading it onto the cart at the carousel. The box hits the floor with a muffled thud. My dad has gone ahead with our passports and declaration forms to line up at the customs area, followed by my mom and sisters, all of whom are eager to exit the airport and see our extended family gathered like groupies just outside the concourse doors. I struggle to lift the box for several minutes, with little success. After a while, I discover that I can raise the box a few inches off the ground if I wedge a foot underneath it and kick while stabilizing the box on either side with my hands. This, I realize, allows me to lift the box just high enough to plant the edge onto the cart's platform, and from there, with a strong heave, I can push the rest of the box onto the cart — *voila!* Once the box is secure on the cart, I walk briskly to catch up with my family at the customs area, where I know I will find them, waiting in line for me.

LEON AUREUS

Just My Imagination

WHILE SHE WASHES the breakfast dishes, Delia thinks about what to do with the drafty windows in the bedroom where Mama and Papa are going to stay when they arrive in two months. It will be the middle of November by then, with winter right on their doorstep. Even the fall months here feel colder than any "winter" she'd ever experienced in Naga, so she plans on buying cellophane tape and plastic sheets for the windows and more warm blankets (they are on sale right now at Bargain Harolds) so her parents won't do a U-turn and immediately decide to go back to the Philippines after the first cold gust of wind off the lake hits them.

She momentarily considers delaying their arrival to the summertime so the cold shock won't be so extreme but immediately dismisses the thought. Enough time has passed. Three years. And now the immigration paperwork is approved, the plane tickets reserved, and they will be reunited in two months. Papa will walk Jun-Jun to school and help him with his studies, Mama will cook sotanghon, and gulay natong, and Bikol express (and all the foods she is craving in her mother's signature style), and they will both babysit Joy so she can work full-time to help Junior with the ever-growing expenses for the very small two-bedroom semi-detached house they have just bought in the east end of Toronto.

Two months! It seems like a dream. A happy dream that could almost make her laugh, shout, cry for joy. The first three years here in Canada have been so lonely. Of course, she has her young family and they are her world, and Junior's Ma and several of his brothers and sisters are also here in Toronto with them, but beyond her second cousin Odette, there isn't anyone here for her, with her. No one to share and confide how difficult it is to settle into a new country, to build a new home from scratch.

When they first arrived in Toronto with their two children — four-year-old son Jun-Jun and ten-month-old daughter Joy — they stayed with Junior's sister (and her very *makulit* three year-old son) in a small one-bedroom apartment in St. James Town. All their worldly belongings were stacked in one corner of that sparsely furnished fifteenth-floor unit. The kids slept with Delia on a small pullout bed while Junior slept on the parquet wood floor.

In the rare quiet moments of those early days, when her husband was out papering the city with his resumés and the kids were napping while their meagre savings melted away, she would sit on the cement and rust balcony, look out over the city, and allow herself to cry a little, despair a little, wondering if they had made the right decision.

At the time, Junior was making good money in the Philippines. His family owned and operated a printing press and a small newspaper in Manila, but with all the *gulo* happening, with Marcos declaring Martial Law, everything was starting to look so unstable. When Junior, Manny, the newspaper's city editor, and other several writers were taken in for questioning with no explanation other than "public security" following the bombings at the candidates' debate, the decision was made. They were going to Toronto to start a new life with greater opportunity — for themselves, for their children.

Speaking of which, where is that boy?

"Jun-Junnn! It's already eight o'clock! If you don't hurry up you're going to be late again!"

No response. *Hay naku*, that boy always has his head in the clouds, always daydreaming! Only two weeks into grade one and she has already received three late notices from the school office. He is very bright and imaginative but that often results in a glacial pace as he observes the world around him and comes up with all sorts of stories, both real and fantastic. She also guesses that the feet dragging is due to the awkwardness of still trying to fit in at school.

She still remembers accompanying him on his first day. When they introduced him to his new class and he was asked to tell everyone what his name was, he enthusiastically replied, "Jun-Jun!" and was welcomed by the many giggles and quizzical looks from his new schoolmates. Her stomach tightened as she saw him recoil a little bit at their innocent but not so encouraging response.

"You're in Canada now, anak," she told him as they walked home that day. "In Canada, you're no longer Jun-Jun, your *real* name is Joseph."

He looked down at the pavement, contemplating this new reality suddenly presented to him.

"If you want, we can call you Joe?" she said, trying to be helpful and also break the silence.

After a few quiet seconds, he looked up.

"It's okay, Mama. I like Joseph better than Joe. I will be Joseph now," he said with a faint hint of sadness.

He was always proud of the fact that he shared the same name as his Lolo and his Papa, but she could also see the distant mourning in his eyes for the person he once was, for the life they were leaving behind. She held his hand a little tighter and joined him in that feeling as they stepped forward into this new life together, carrying a *Star Wars* backpack and a little bit of hope for the future.

"JOSEPH! FINISH BRUSHING your teeth and come down now! I still have to bring your sister to Tita Lucy's and you're going to make me late for work! *Naku*, this boy, hurry up!"

No reply. What is he doing up there? She puts the last of the cereal bowls in the dish rack (Cap'n Crunch is on sale at Bargain Harolds — remember to pick up three boxes), hurriedly dries her hands, looks over to check that Joy is securely in her booster chair and finishing up the last of her apple slices at the kitchen table, then walks over to the bottom of the stairs leading to the second floor.

"Sst! Where are you now! Come on, you don't want Mrs. Sanderson to call you to the office again!"

Still no answer. The silence is slightly uncomfortable as sunlight shines onto the narrow stairway with faux-wood-panelled walls on either side of it. Glimmers of dust dance in the sunbeam lighting the stairs, which are covered with a dark burnt orange shag carpet left by the previous owners.

Her mind races, shifting from irritation at the thought that he may have crawled back into bed and gone back to sleep, to panic that he might have somehow injured himself.

"Jun-Jun? Don't make me come up there!"

Glancing over to confirm that Joy's still okay, she quickly goes up the stairs, making sure to stomp loudly enough so her son understands the gravity of the situation he's putting himself in by dawdling like this.

Above the upstairs landing, there's a big poster of *The Thirty-Nine Presidents of the United States of America*, featuring portraits from George Washington all the way to Jimmy Carter. Another remnant, a curiosity from the previous residents that she just hasn't had the time or energy to replace yet. The blank stares of these white-wigged white men, most of them unknown to her, are a disconcerting welcome at the top of the stairs that she's been meaning to get rid of since day one. But when you have house payments, and grocery bills, and hydro bills, and a two-year-old and a six-year-old, and a (feels like) hundred-year-old Chevy Nova, and a second language to wrestle with, and a new job as a sales associate in a downtown furniture shop, and a tired, sometimes cranky, husband who works alternating day and night shifts at the city sewage plant,

and,

and,

and,

some things you just have to let slip.

But she'll make sure to change it before Mama arrives to save herself from any commentary. She can already hear her:

"Hay, Delia. Why do you leave this ugly painting up here? It's so panget! And don't you remember what the Americanos did to our country?"

Her Mama isn't a fan of the Americans, or the Japanese, or simply the Second World War that took her first husband. She met her second husband (Delia's Papa), who was also a widower, a year after the war. In addition to the two sons and one daughter her Mama had from her first marriage, they had three more boys and two girls. She was the youngest and, no one would argue, the favourite. Mama and Papa could hardly speak when she told them of her plans to immigrate to Canada. She could hardly believe it herself. So they barely spoke about it until it was time to go and they suddenly found an ocean and a continent between them.

UPSTAIRS, TO THE left of the landing, is the bathroom and the kids' bedroom. Strangely, it doesn't look like Jun-Jun is in either room. She quickly checks under his small twin bed and Joy's crib just to make sure he's not hiding. Jun-Jun has decorated the teal-blue walls of the room with stickers of the Superfriends and pictures he's drawn of G-Force, the Flintstones, and a handful of sci-fi and fantasy beings of his own creation. As she enters the bathroom, a light breeze blows in from the partly open window that looks out into the backyard. The faucet is still slightly running, and his toothbrush is oddly on the counter instead of being returned to the toothbrush holder. She rinses the toothbrush that still has toothpaste residue on it before returning it to the holder and tightening the faucet.

What's going on here?

"Anak, come on. This isn't funny. Come out now. We don't have time for this."

She crosses over the small landing to their bedroom. The drawn curtains have made the room slightly darker and her eyes have to adjust a bit as she scans the room. It's so quiet that at first it also appears to be empty. But then she sees it. Really you couldn't miss it, and she's startled just a little bit by the sight.

There's a small mound in the middle of their bed. It doesn't move, but it's about the size of a six-year-old boy. It's comical and creepy at the same time. Curled up under a forest green woollen blanket, he looks like a small creature or maybe more like a hill, like one of those green rolling hills you often see back home. This one though, a lone solitary hill.

"*Hay naku*, Jun-Jun, you scared me. Come out from under there!"

He doesn't move. Impatient to make sure he's okay and also because they're running even later now, she pulls the blanket off. He's curled up in a ball — thankfully he looks uninjured and is breathing. He's covering his ears with his hands, his eyes are tightly shut, and he's frozen like a statue — well, not quite; she notices he's shaking.

"Oh my God, what's going on? Are you okay?"

He whimpers then mumbles something.

"Is it gone?"

"What are you talking about? What's gone?"

Slightly unnerved, Delia sits on the bed beside her son and scans the room for whatever he might be talking about. A squirrel? A cat? Oh, please don't be a raccoon or a mouse.

"Smmk!"

"What?"

"Like a cloud!"

"What!?"

"Smoke, smoke. Mama, a grey cloud!" he says, eyes still tightly shut. She checks his forehead for any trace of a fever. The poor boy looks pale and afraid. It looks like he's seen a —

The thought is interrupted by seeing the time on the bedside alarm clock and her concern for her other child who's been left alone for far too long now downstairs. She chooses to be practical and irritated rather than be carried away by this flight of imagination. Fighting back the urge to get angry, she pulls him up and into her arms.

"Oh my God, Jun-Jun. It's nothing. There's nothing here. Open your eyes. Look around. Mama's here and you're safe, *na*. Look. Come on, we have to go. Your sister is alone by herself downstairs."

The boy is warm and perspiring in her arms as he cautiously opens his eyes and looks around. She feels the tension relax in his body as he rests his chin on her shoulder, still cautiously scanning the room.

It's that imagination of his again, she figures. He spooked himself. Like when he said the Child Catcher from the movie *Chitty Chitty Bang Bang* was creeping around the back alley. Or when King Kong was peeking in through the basement window. Or when the ghost lady from *Fiddler on the Roof* —

"It came in from the window, Mama! While I was brushing my teeth. At first it was just some grey smoke, then it started getting bigger, like a cloud, then it started taking the shape of a face and it was looking at me and coming toward me and — and I ran and it followed me! And its mouth was moving! It was saying something!"

A chill runs through her, but she shrugs it off with the practicality of the fact that he is definitely going to be late for school *again*, and she can't afford to be late for the job she just started two weeks ago. Now Joy is crying downstairs.

"Okay, that's enough."

"But Mama, it was really —"

"*Tama na*, Jun-Jun! That's enough stories from you. Your imagination, *talaga*! I'm going to tell your Papa about this when he gets home and you're not going to have TV or comic books for a week! Let's go!"

"I don't want to go."

"Jun-Jun!"

"I don't want to!"

"Okay fine, you can stay here with the ghost."

She gets up and pretends to go. Jun-Jun's face crumples, tears glistening on his cheeks, and she immediately regrets the mean impulse brought on by her own stress and disquiet. She rushes back to the bed and embraces him, his warm tears dampening her shirt.

If her father were here right now, he would surely be angry with her. He served in the military during the war and was notorious for being incredibly strict and disciplined. However, when it came to his *apo*, his "Little Jeprox," he melted like butter in the sun and showed a fanciful side that no one ever knew existed. He had a soft spot for Jun-Jun and was the one that encouraged the boy's flights of fancy in their earliest stages.

While seated on the *kudkuran ng niyog* — the coconut grating bench — he would have Jun-Jun ride behind him on their magical horse, Silver, and they would travel to faraway lands in search of a magical *anting-anting*. "Heigh ho Silver!" they would yell in unison, over the sound of grating that doubled as hoofbeats. Sometimes, in the early morning, he would take the boy for walks by the river and tell him stories of the *duendes* that watched them from the trees.

She remembers how tightly they embraced one another at the departure gate and how his eyes shone with sadness and his voice wavered as he tried to comfort the boy clinging to his neck. Delia feels her cheeks warmly flush and she holds her son a little tighter. She can almost hear her father's voice now, hanging alongside the specks of dust, dancing on the sunbeam.

"*We will see each other again, anak. Do not worry, okay? You have to be brave, anak. Lolo loves you, okay? Your Lolo loves you.*"

Two months. They'll all be together again soon. Things will get better. Things will be easier.

"I'm sorry, anak. That was not kind of me. Mama's just tired and in a hurry, okay? Look around. Whatever was here is gone and I would never let it hurt you. Mama and Papa are here for you and your sister and we will always protect you. And remember, soon your Lolo and Lola will be here too! Now, can you be a brave big brother and come with me so we can take care of your sister?"

"Okay, Mama. I will."

THE REST OF the morning is pretty uneventful. Thankfully, Joy is still secure in her booster chair, and after two cups of milk and several chocolate chip cookies, both children are placated. By the time they do the drop-off at the babysitter's and finally arrive at the schoolyard, Jun-Jun is carefree and at ease as if nothing even happened this morning. He stops and turns to her as he reaches the front doors of the school.

"Love you!"

She smiles and waves back, watching him skip down the hall and around the corner. Finding herself standing alone in the empty schoolyard, she suddenly feels very alone. The unease of what her son said he saw creeps back into her thoughts. Did he really see something? What was it? Who was it?

"*Tama na*, Delia. Stop scaring yourself. Now it's just my imagination. It's nothing," she reassures herself.

On the slow, rumbling streetcar ride to work, she says a few Hail Marys and Our Fathers to calm her disquiet.

She also reminds herself to buy the wool blankets and cereal at Bargain Harolds after work.

AT DINNER, JUNIOR is tired from his first day shift after three consecutive nights at the water filtration plant, and they continue their debate about making the move to Mississauga in a few years. They can sell this house and get a much bigger one for less money, she tells him. Everyone can have their own room and they'll have a big yard for the kids to play in. He argues that the suburb is barely a city, mostly just farmland, joking that he doesn't want cows for neighbours. Jun-Jun excitedly talks about what he wants to be for Halloween, either Luke Skywalker or Bruce Lee. The latter, he decides, might be too cold for trick-or-treating if he goes *Enter the Dragon* shirtless with red claw marks on his body. In the midst of all the chatter, Joy happily enjoys the evening's pork adobo and ginisang monggo with rice.

Not wanting to dim the warm glow that surrounds the family dinner table, Delia opts to stay quiet about the morning's excitement and the ensuing unease that followed her around for the rest of the day.

Grey smoke ... turning into a face ... following me ... saying something.

It's Jun-Jun's and my own overactive imagination. It's my excitement, my anxiousness to see Mama and Papa again soon. That's all. Don't spend any more time giving thought to it, giving life to it.

It was saying something.

"Everything okay?" Junior sees the tension on her face.

"Yeah, we were just late again this morning. Was late for work. But it's okay *na*."

She offers him a vague smile that she hardly believes herself, pushing away the doubt and fear by busying herself with the kids' bath time, with the preparations for tomorrow's lunches, with the taking down of the *Presidents* poster, with the washing of the new blankets she bought for her Mama and Papa. With the busy-ness of making this new life a better one.

THE HARSH, METALLIC ringing cuts through the blackness and immediately fills Delia with dread. The dimly lit plastic flip numbers on the alarm clock read 02:51. She's frozen in place as the urgent ringing continues but can only lie there and wait for Junior to groggily shuffle out of bed to answer the phone downstairs. She can't, doesn't want to. It's a wrong number. It's not connected with anything. She frantically fights back a torrent of irrational fears. It couldn't be. It's not. No-No-No. She can hear Junior walking down the stairs. Please God. It's nothing. The ringing stops, he's picked up the phone. Please don't let it be. His voice sounds tired and distant. Who is he talking to? No. It's not. Hail Mary full of Grace ...

"What!?!"

That's all she hears. All she needs to hear. It's the shock, the pain, the sadness in it. Her husband's voice slices through the air right into her heart and everything goes cold.

THERE'S A SOFT knock at the door come in it's Jun-Jun what time is it what day is it the doctor said these meds would help ease the pain why why his heart I've stopped crying the tickets were refunded exchanged must of been the excitement how many days have passed Mama doesn't think she can go without him why no one coming I have to get myself together for Papa for the flight Junior says he can manage with the kids his sisters will help we can't afford to all go why it was only just two more months why there's no reason why he was old they said don't worry about it his heart my job will be there when I get back there's not enough money I have to return those blankets I can't bear to —

"Mama?"

She can't do this right now. So tired. Sad. Hopeless.

You have to be brave, anak.

She takes a deep breath and braces herself. Be strong for your son.

"Yes? Jun-Jun? Come in."

He stands by the bed. Hesitant. Holding a piece of paper in his hand.

"It's okay, come here, sit beside me. What do you have there?"

"I ... I made this for Lolo. Can you please bring it to him for me?"

It's a drawing in crayon of the Philippine flag. At the top he's written "PHILIPPPINES" and just below the flag is a man, a boy, and a silvery-white horse. In the careful scrawl of a six-year-old, it's signed: "I love you I will miss you always Lolo. Jun-Jun."

"It's beautiful, anak. Thank you."

He moves closer into her and settles into her embrace. They sit in silence. He smells like Johnson & Johnson baby shampoo and sunlight. She feels better with him here.

"Mama?"

"Yes?"

"He said ... he said he was sorry. He told me to be brave. And that we have to take care of each other now."

"We will, anak. We will."

KAY COSTALES

If I Talked to Death

For Lolo Pete, who passed away on November 4, 2021.
You nearly made it to eighty-three and that's amazing. I wish we had more time together.

WHEN LOLO PASSES, it is in the middle bits of autumn, cold like a meal left exposed and untouched. The hunger to reunite scoops the belly empty, preparing the body for food. We won't get a taste of what we crave. All we have is aching unfulfillment.

It's been a long time since we shared a meal, sat at a table together with plates filled with something in thick sauce paired with jasmine rice. It's been a long time since we were together. It's important that we remember it with satisfied stomachs near bursting at the seams with the results of old family recipes.

Before we know that it's goodbye, we prepare the home for his coming.

ONE NIGHT, WE'RE on the phone with him, trying to use video to communicate and settle the plans for his arrival. He and I wouldn't understand each other with only words to speak. Language is a wall between us, almost as divisive as the land and ocean that force us to live on opposite sides of the world. The video cuts in and out like the rise and fall of waves. The static on the audio is as frequent as regular inhales and exhales, sharp as a needle point pressed to the eardrum.

It's frustrating to try to make plans like this. He can't hear and can't see on his side. On ours, the image is pixelated, boxes and blurs, indistinct colours on a dark background. The volume goes up and up, the screech of poor connection and unstable communication.

Wave and smile, say hello again and again. Say *love you* and *miss you* and try not to weep when you're hoping it was heard. It's hard to know what manages to reach across the space. Already, we squeeze ourselves into the small overlap when both sides of the world are awake but weary. Sun rises at the ancestral home and sets in the migrant's new nest.

"Will you be there?" I ask. "We'll be waiting."

"What?" Lolo says. "Huh?"

"They can't hear," my mom explains.

"Can you ask?" I feel guilty making the request, but I don't know how to learn the language. We found a book the last time we landed on home soil, trying to turn the text into lessons. Reading the pages and notes and explanations led to a feeling of being and feeling overwhelmed, buried alive in what I don't know. I know I should learn but I don't think we have the time to catch up. I am lagging behind by decades.

My mom repeats the question in a translation.

"*Oh!*" they say in sudden understanding.

It's defeat for me, a blow to the belly that knocks the air out of my lungs. I try to smile, try not to look like it hurts. There's no blood, no cuts or bruises, only the injury that comes from tripping on the steps to the front door only to find out I don't have the key to get inside.

What we understand is limited in scope. I can catch a few here and there, like scooping up fish with my bare hands. We lean in toward the camera like it will help us translate better. When I catch myself, I look at my mom and laugh.

Most of the time, I whisper to beg for a translation, to ask what was said and what I can say back.

I know that on the other side, he's smiling. It doesn't matter what we say. There's love here and it doesn't need to be spoken. In the end, we say our goodbyes. I shuffle away until the next time, embarrassed by my limitations. I am the young one, the one with all the years to come. I should be putting in more work, but I don't know where to start.

Guilt puts my tongue in chains. It shackles me to the ground and tells me that there's no point.

At least we're planning to have them fly to be with us and see them all again.

It's a rush to get to that day, trying not to glance at the hourglass with its sand spilling from the abundance at the top to pile below.

"It's okay," my mom says. "You can still learn."

I'm embarrassed that it's easier to speak French than it is to understand my family's native language. I hope I can better carry a conversation when I'm immersed in our history and culture again, whenever that may be. Maybe I'll feel less like an outsider the more I'm in the homeland, where I almost look like I belong.

Lolo will be with us here this time, flying through the skies for the first time to spend however much time is allowed before he's on the next journey.

DURING THE MONTHS that Lolo will be with us, it will be his ninetieth birthday. He would hit the miracle of becoming a nonagenarian. We want a big party in his honour, something to celebrate the man who raised four children in a house built on joy. There were cracks in the floor and stains on the walls, it got too warm inside during the hottest season of the year, but it always smelled like food and music played every morning.

We get a record player solely in anticipation of his arrival. It's an unfamiliar place to him despite its long since established position as our home. I imagine him leaning over to listen, closing his eyes and smiling as he enjoys the songs. It's his favourite pop band, the one whose albums he blasted at full volume to ensure he could hear them.

He'll love it. We know he will. At first, he might be confused.

Why would you buy that? he might wonder.

It could turn a strange place into a safe one.

I have a new house with rooms to spare. It's the first big space that our family knows in the years since leaving the last in the countryside. It was my idea for all of us to stay here during his visit so we can be close and make the most of however many days would be allowed.

A room is ready for him. A soft bed with pillows and a window that offers a view of open fields and a suggestion of the cityscape. I hope he will be impressed. My parents left their roots to build a life like this.

The house is stocked with Philippine products, brands that he would find in his own kitchen. We plan out every dinner that we'll make during his stay, things that would be new to him and recipes that Lola would make for him too. Clothes are ordered and delivered to prepare him for the winter months. It might be his only opportunity to experience snow for the first time.

He knows of it through pictures and videos, through television shows and films.

Christmas decorations are on display on the first of September when there's still heat and golden sunshine. The leaves are still green without a tinge of orange and brown. It's hardly at all like we're approaching the cold season and slipping into holidays. That's what it's like in the malls back home though. They paint the country in red and green and silver and gold, play music on the speakers, and blast air conditioning to get the right chill.

"Will he like it?" I ask my mom. I feel like I'm four years old and I've crafted a little papier mâché with my hands. I want to present it with a flourish, cross my fingers behind my back, and offer a toothy grin.

"Of course," she says, like it's nothing.

Her eyes are on the photos dug out of storage, a box of film that was developed before I was even born. She keeps them with me now for safekeeping. I guard them like a dragon with its treasure, hoarding it like an archeologist has gifted me with pieces of the past. I will be the museum to all our memories even if I don't understand what happened in them.

"Maybe he won't be homesick," I say.

"He'll be happy to be here."

"With me?"

My voice is small and trembling, and I am, once again, like a child. My grandparents didn't know me when I was a baby, didn't get a chance to cradle me in their arms as they crooned lullabies.

"That's all he wants."

We miss each other and feel the hollowness in the gaps of time. I want to offer him more than the comfort of this new home we built and furnished and filled.

IT'S EARLY MORNING for us, late in the evening for them. We have the sun and they have the dark sky, the moon and stars hidden behind a layer of the city's exhalation. The phone rings with the ominous music of a funeral and we dread having to pick up. My Tito is there when we answer, and he looks tired. He says his hellos and speaks to my mom — his sister — before sharing the reason for his call.

Lolo isn't coming. He's too sick to make the journey.

The news comes packaged in heartache, shared on the phone again with crackling sound and blurry video.

When the camera turns on Lolo, he's all smiles and laughter like there isn't any aching. He's lasted longer than anyone's ever expected and his whole life is a miracle of survival.

"Sorry, sorry," he says. "Doctor says no."

The Christmas tree is up behind him. There are garlands on the wall decorated with shining ornaments and flowers from the market. They curl around the frames like arms over shoulders, holding on to pictures taken in different parts of the world where his children and grandchildren have travelled. I imagine him looking at them like windows, arms crossed as he examines them with pride.

I want to tell my Lolo that I only know the world the way I do because of the love he offered my mother that she passed on to me. Our family heirloom is of raising children in a house that might not be fancy but one that's filled with a variety of nourishment that goes in the belly and the heart. His legacy is his teachings, the example of love he offered.

He speaks in Tagalog and I can't keep up. If I follow the chatter, I can find my way back home. My mom holds my hand as we sit together. I have to turn my eyes away every now and then to compose myself.

Lolo looks older than he did the last time. More wrinkles around his eyes and mouth. His cheeks sag lower and I want to scoop his face in my hands and touch my forehead to his. Lola isn't on camera but she's talking to him and they're joking with each other again. He laughs and her hand is visible for a moment as she swats at him. They're a funny pair, both hard of hearing these days and both still in love. It's so unlike my father's family. The relationship between his parents was sliced apart years before I was born. Love does not exist as echoing laughter in their home, not like it does where my mother grew up. I prefer the noisy evidence of affection.

"When can we go?" I ask.

I am thinking of our work schedules and the cost of plane tickets. I am thinking about the sacrifices necessary to take time away from my normal life. I am thinking about the numbers in my bank account and if it's enough to get there and back and to make all the time in the middle worthwhile.

Lolo's on camera again and he's confused for a moment like he has forgotten he was on a call. My cousin holds the phone and points the lens in his direction. You can hear her laughter, muffled as she tries to stay calm. He squints his eyes and then they brighten, like he's happy to see us.

His birthday is weeks away and we're trying to organize something to celebrate it .

Most of the grandchildren are young adults now. All his children except my mom are with him. What can we do for such a milestone? We're thinking of an abundance of food the family has grown over the years, offering more than what was possible in his youth.

He continues to speak in Tagalog and he's trying to talk to me. I catch a few words, but the meaning slips between my fingers. He's talking about the next time I come to visit. He wants to show me more of the neighbourhood and the secrets between the buildings. I remember that it doesn't have any of the refinement of what I'm used to. The colours are more vibrant while other things are muted. Despite being within the same world, his experience in it is vastly different and he seems to want to show me how. He seems to want to ensure that I don't miss out on the beautiful things I wouldn't have noticed without his aid. I like that he wants to share pieces of his life with me and I imagine that knowing such details enables me to fit with the family.

I'M PREPARING A package to send back home for his birthday. I can fit my whole body into the balikbayan box if I curl into a ball. It fills up: from clothes to candies to little knick-knacks that I want to share with him. There are Bits of Canada — syrup in maple-leaf-shaped bottles, a keychain of raccoons, a snow globe with the Toronto skyline. Tourist-y things that make me laugh and I hope he likes them as much as the Toronto Raptors hat we brought him before. We have a call with him and my mom translates again. The package is on its way.

"Can we have a party?" I ask.

They don't seem to know how that's going to work.

Dinner here, breakfast there. We'll plan to have it around the same time so it's like we're eating together. He thinks it's funny and laughs all the way through the conversation. We'll cook the same things and set our tables like it's a fancy occasion. We can dress up and decorate our homes. It will be like having a party despite being so far apart.

It isn't entirely for Lolo, but he doesn't know what he wants. He looks amused as my mom and her brother discuss the options. I don't speak much, relying on them to sort out the details.

By the end of the call, Lolo is asleep in his chair. His head lolls to the side and it makes me laugh. During the short length of time that I visited him, he loved his naps. He only wakes as we're saying goodbyes, then he jolts into alertness. There's a strange shadow on his shoulder that resembles a hand. It falls behind him as he leans forward, opening his eyes as big as he can to stay awake.

I wave to him and he waves back. Every time I interact with him, I feel less like an adult and more like the child I wish I was when we met. There's a significant portion of my life that he would have made better. He was always there, just far away.

IT'S THE NIGHT before the planned party when I'm woken from my sleep by a whisper.

The words are impossible to decipher. They're so light I feel them against my face like I'm standing at the window instead of in bed. My eyes meet the blank wall, searching the surface for some sign that I'm not alone.

I reach for my phone and check the time.

Only eleven o'clock at night. Too early for my partner to come to bed. I barely get an hour of rest before waking. My heart beats violently, as if it might shatter my rib cage to get free. If there's something in the room with me, I can't find it. Shadows move across the walls as a car and its lights pass down the street and shine through the window. I follow them like they hold a clue.

I am not superstitious. I don't believe in folk tales and horror stories.

We do hang a rosary in the car. We have one crucifix in our home. Every

Sunday, we say we ought to go to Church. We take the day off when it's a religious holiday. But we do not worship as much as we would if we were in our homeland.

My mom is not superstitious. She does not pass on the myths of the Philippines to her children like they're history to be studied and reasons for wariness. The only time she speaks of them is in passing, treating them like side notes in her memories. Still, she talks about monsters that prey on the weak — the old and the young, the sleeping, the vulnerable — like we ought to be careful in case they're real.

Mumble apologies when you walk by a mound of dirt. Avoid being entirely in the dark. Listen for sounds that aren't natural, the clicking that gets quieter and quieter as the monster gets closer. Worry about the dead coming back and not only to say a proper goodbye.

Ghost sightings there are as common as a raccoon in Toronto. Your loved ones might linger in this world before passing to the next. That's why we hold on to religion, why we say our prayers to God and keep him in our hearts. It doesn't mean that one might encounter malevolence. It could be nothing, a spirit waiting to move on, wanting to spend a little longer with their loved ones. I open my messages and check my calls, waiting to see if my mom has tried to contact me.

If she wants to alert me with news that Lolo is gone.

But there's nothing. He must be okay.

All I have are the shadows in the night, the lights of passing cars, and the sound of my heart pounding. I lie back down and go to sleep again. In the morning, we will prepare for our little party spanning two sides of the world at the same time.

WE HAVE A guest before we finish setting the table. The rice is in its pot, still bubbling as it cooks. The porcelain plates shudder where they sit, the spoon and fork beside them rattling like wind chimes. A breeze drifts in and lifts the scent of the stews from the serving bowls.

It looks like we are about to host a grand affair, a party of dozens of people rather than a handful. A tablet is already positioned on a tripod, facing the table in preparation of tonight's event. It will be so late for us, nearly eleven o'clock in the night, the same time that I woke from sleep the night before. But back home, it will be close to noon.

A door opens, one we can't see from the kitchen and dining area.

I stare in the direction of the noise, waiting to see what might enter, if anything at all.

"Should we pray?" I ask.

My mom doesn't find it funny. Her face shows concern. Nothing has appeared, not yet, so she shakes her head. I press my hands together anyway, the act more meaningful than anything I could say.

Still, nothing emerges, so we carry on with our preparation.

Minutes later, when we've moved on from the worries, a shadow sweeps into the room. The figure is a black veil of a being. It moves to the table, tracing circles onto the plates with its hands.

I drop the glass I am holding, and it comes crashing to the floor. The sound of its shattering alerts our guest. It doesn't say a word, but something speaks to me of its name. Of what it is.

Death is an expected guest, but He arrives without a flourish. He did send a warning; I understand that now. No eyes on His face, no mouth to offer explanation. Just a silhouette pressing against fabric, a smooth surface. He turns to us and inclines His head.

Is it an apology? It feels like one.

He doesn't take a seat. Death does not rest. He has a duty, and we may fear Him, but we must also acknowledge the necessity of His existence in tandem with God. He moves around the room, inspecting the work we've done like it's up to Him to decide if it's good. A hand drifts over the table and settings, causing the cutlery to move slightly.

I want to laugh that this is our guest, though not the one we meant to honour.

Slowly, He swings over to me. The hem of His cloak brushes against my legs as He gets close. I hold my breath, wondering what the interest in me might be. But soon, He moves away, going close to my mother. She has a knife in her hand and she grips it tight, as if she might fend herself against this ghostly entity. For a moment, it seems like they're staring at each other in the face.

Then Death is gone.

"What is that?" I ask. "Why —"

My mom rushes over to the tablet and sets up the video call, immediately trying to connect with her family. Her brother answers only with his voice, no image available

"Ate, Tatay isn't doing well," my Tito says.

The rest of it, I don't really understand. They switch to Tagalog and it all blurs together for me from there. I slide my fingers into my hair, twisting and tugging on it in frustration. My mom turns away, shutting off the video and hiding her face. The hard part about being far from family is that we can't be there at a moment's notice. There's no reason to rush. Even if we left this second, we would be a day too late.

She ends the call and stands there in silence. I inhale deeply and exhale slowly, still positioned where I dropped the glass. Fragments surround me on the floor and I'm almost too afraid to move. We don't need another cause for worry.

"What happened?" I ask.

"Tatay is in the hospital."

DEATH STANDS AT the window when I wake in the middle of the night. It's a miracle that I managed to fall asleep with the stress ravaging my body like a tornado in a dense neighbourhood. I stop breathing the moment I feel His presence. It takes another moment to find the ability again.

"Who are you here for?" I ask.

Again, I am alone. My partner must still be in his office, working away on something urgent. It's dedication that I've always admired, but I curse it now, wishing he was here beside me to give me strength in the presence of this faceless fiend.

"The old man ought to rest for we have a long journey ahead."

At first, I don't understand the words. Once they hit me, tears fill my eyes. In less than a second, I am weeping. I miss him already, like an old teddy bear ripped from my arms. The only strength I have, I use to hold myself together. My mom is here in the guest room, unable to find her way home after meeting this being.

He stands in silence as if willing to be patient. This might be kindness, some compassion I didn't expect. Then again, Death has to come at some time. He has kept a distance from Lolo longer than expected. Maybe that's generosity and I should be more grateful.

The question twists around my tongue. I can't find it in myself to ask if He waited, if He allowed us to have these moments of excitement and joy over this milestone. Is Lolo dead now? Is he dying? I don't think I can afford the time for the funeral. I don't think I can manage to keep myself composed on a plane for an entire day, if I'm lucky enough to get a non-stop flight.

Hatred cuts into me. That's how I see it, the violence of the emotion. I do not hate Death, who is here out of duty, who comes to warn me of the loss. We are not friends nor enemies. We are nothing to each other except beings who exist for a purpose. I roll out of the bed onto clumsy feet. Sleep is still a blanket on me and I shake myself to wake up, trying to have full consciousness so I can speak to my mom.

To tell her what Death has come to say.

"Is he gone?" I ask Him as I pass.

"Soon."

"Could I —"

"No, it would be too late."

I nod and then I'm heading down the hall, looking for my mom. I knock on the door before coming in. She's still more asleep than awake. She doesn't notice Death standing right behind me, not at first, but when she does, she cries out in horror.

None of us needs to clarify who has been called to their final journey. She sees the tear tracks on my cheeks. I lean my face into her palm. Again, I'm like a child around my elders, hoping for their wisdom and comfort to get me through the worst.

"There is no time to say goodbye. He sleeps," Death says.

Still, my mom releases my face to find her phone. She's about to call her brother when, suddenly, his name is on her screen. There's a rush of Tagalog and a loud reminder that we can't be there in the final moments of Lolo's life. We are too far, so distant that it's like we're in another world.

I am still so full of hate that I direct now to the ocean and sky. I hate the masses of land that separate us. I am on my knees before Death and He does not have eyes to meet mine.

"I wrote a letter. I was going to send it with the gifts, but I forgot to include it in the box," I say.

He doesn't say a word. It's not a refusal; I take it as an opportunity. My mom remains on the phone while I run back to my room. An envelope sits on my desk. Cursive lettering graces the back: *Lolo*. I wrote this for him weeks ago, starting it when I was emotional and taking my time in choosing my words.

Death turns His head, then tilts it, suggesting curiosity. It cannot be strange for loved ones to make requests. He should not be surprised and I don't think He is. I know the superstitions. I know I didn't believe them before, but now I'm hoping there's truth to it all. If there is, it will take forty days to cross the Earth and reach the Sky. He'll remain with us in a way, a ghost in our world.

"Take this letter. Give it to him at the end of the journey once he's caught his breath," I plead, as though they're only taking a walk. A scenic route where he'll see the best of the landmarks that we always wanted to show him, that money and time never allowed.

I don't want to touch Death. I don't want to pass something from my hands to His. I place the envelope on the table, push it toward Him. But Death leaves the envelope untouched. He won't reach for it. "Please."

"He won't carry anything from this world," Death says.

I pick it up and force it into His hands. It feels as though I am touching stone and smoke at the same time. Only the palms are tangible.

He releases the letter as if it would disappear if it's no longer in His grasp. It doesn't though. It finds the air and floats briefly like a feather. I grab it. He turns away from me, leaving me standing in my bedroom. I follow as Death climbs down the stairs to the front door, slow-moving but steady.

He leaves footsteps on the pathway, His own and another. As if Lolo walks with Him, the two of them side by side like a pair of travellers. The trail leads away and away and they're so far gone, I cannot see a shadow or silhouette.

"They are half a day ahead of us," my mother reminds me.

"We're so far away," I say. She lifts up her phone to show the screen. She is still on the call with her brother. He points his camera at Lolo, eyes closed in the hospital bed. We can't be there in his final moments. It's only through a screen that we see him fading, his chest rising once more before falling for the last time. And then there's stillness and he's gone. He was back home, but here too. Here with us as though he asked Death for a goodbye when he had a sliver of himself in this world.

The front door stays open.

To go home now, to be there for the funeral, would cost thousands of dollars and several days. We cannot fly across the world for a day of services. We cannot spend money when it would be easier to send it home and let them handle it. I lean against my mother, looking out at the empty space in front of my home. It feels like a foreign place at this moment, like I'm not where I should be and where I belong.

There is a dining table set for a party. When I turn around and look toward it, I think I see Lolo sitting there. The silhouette matches the hunched figure I've seen on the phone, the tired old man who wants to nap during the day. Is this all I can have of him now? Forty days where he may drift around until it's time for the final farewell.

He made it to ninety. He fought on.

"Happy birthday, Lolo."

It's all I manage to say.

I want to weep over the distance between us now, the stretch of ocean and land that means I can never catch up with him on his journey.

Made In Canada

HARI ALLURI

The Problem Is I Actually Love Mountains

SO MUCH SO, I've memorized roundabout routes to work (and back from the grocery store at sunset) to give me better glimpses. Which is why it vexes that my nemesis is Dumakulem: capital letters and everything, Guardian of the Mountains.

And it's not like I don't believe in what he stands for, it's just that we're both in love with the Goddess of Lost Things. We both know her as Anagolay, though siya has other names.

You'd think I'd be on his side, you know, cuz I'm like against fracking or whatever and because my love for tunnels is less about my hatred of my nemesis than my leap of breath at the light on the other side, the temporary feeling of suspension that doesn't make sense but somehow accompanies — for me at least — being inside a vehicle or a train in a tunnel, especially one that runs through a mountain.

So, now I try to think of tunnels as a form of winning. But, I try not to think of mining as some kind of victory over him. For wider reasons, but selfishly because I'm not a miner and I'd want the help of a guardian of mountains if I were going to be on the inside of a canary shaft with only a helmet between me and the depths of time. There are musics whose origin is this. And I come from a people who terraced mountains to grow rice. Whose cousins offered their arrows to the mountain who granted them safe passage.

Meanwhile, I wasn't even brave enough to be part of the exploring party of kids that entered the culvert down by my childhood home, emerged an hour later on the other side of a field and over the next street. Well, I entered and went a few crawls in, got my cheers of them to echo, and turned around. I mean, when I describe standing in the Cave Rock chamber, just up the hill from where I used to race before migration, it *should* be in third person. As you can tell by now, I am a poor nemesis for the Guardian of Mountains. But I stay his willing if unworthy opponent. Because I'm still in love with Anagolay.

The other problem is I get it. I mean, if I were a Deity of What's Lost, I'd want a lover who was the kind of person who isn't losing things *con-stant-ly*. I mean sure, mountains face the carving years from water & wind (which is a form of loss but not a form of harm, you know?). And sure, there's never quite a final resting shape. Still, it's not quite like they *lose so much as have* parts of themselves *taken*.

So, yes, I get that siya is into being with someone steady. If I were me (and I know I am), I might say: as a mountain. And, while I feel Dumakulem's real struggle, what with all the tunnelling going on these days, the mines and the fracking (which, yes, I admit, I'm not that into) there's a part of me that appreciates his attention being divided between loving Anagolay and having his own set of nemeses to contend with.

His attention being divided allows me more time to lip sync to The Goddess of Lost Things. I just can't sing. Despite my karaoke lineage. Even in the hopes Anagolay might leave Dumakulem for me. Never mind that she's got to be proper polyamorous, maybe more so than anyone else. Because the world is so full of large and tiny losses in every given moment — and takings siya must attend as well — Anagolay's busy all time long. Maybe too busy to notice my overtures, but hopefully also too busy to notice how often I lose things. And, omg, I lose things and temporarily misplace them almost as often as anyone buys anything solid that came out of a mountain (I say *solid* to avoid dealing with *power* and skip to the next part: it doesn't work).

I do love crystals. At least there's that, so when I buy crystals I'm taking a little shot at Dumakulem. I don't know how the crystals feel about it, first of all the whole extraction thing, the people who belong to them, and then the whole complex of the journey from mountain to final purchase thing, with each attendant extraction on the way, then finally the whole me using them to take shots at my nemesis thing, but that's just how it is: if you're a crystal and in my apartment, you're a soldier in the battle I'm waging against the Guardian of Mountains.

Or is it that I'm inviting Dumakulem into my home with every crystal? By caring for them: inviting him to do his work right here in my living room, writing his little crystal odes to the Deity of What's Lost. Each one of them, dammit, cradled, turning. In my actual lover's hands. Caressed by Mahal's tattoos: story touching story. Catching, reflecting, prisming each angle of light, basking in their wonderstruck attention. Mahal, who might — how can I blame them — be in love with both: Guardian of Mountains and Goddess of Lost Things.

RACHEL EVANGELINE CHIONG

Desidido

Desidido's sweater smelled like
bay leaves buried in its wrinkles
Receipts tucked into soft pockets
crinkling like fresh rice paper

Desidido's apron smelled like
canola oil caressing its corners
Brown grease staining its white ocean
clustered like continents adrift

At her restaurant, while the winter wind howled
customers hung their coats on hooks that glistened like polished trophies

On weeknights, Desidido sat behind the bar,
shrouded in a cavern of licorice-coloured bottles
The ends of her lips like a beckoning finger
curled into a smile

On weekends, Desidido sat behind the mixer,
watching bands come and go like passing clouds
Their melodies like a blossoming lily
unfurled into a song

At her restaurant, while the winter wind howled,
Ate and Kuya held hands across a counter that shimmered like a mirror

On weeknights, Desidido stood beside the tables,
healing break-up pains with halo-halo
The heartache like a bruised knee
soothed into a sob

On weekends, Desidido stood beside the fryer,
lumpia laughing in a golden bubble bath,
Her Tagalog playing tag-a-long until it burst and
belted into a joke

At her restaurant, while the winter wind howled,
she kindled a dream in the hearth that flickered like a star

Desidido's apron smelled like
A salty spray an ocean away
mixed with muggy daydreams
in a warmer country

Desidido's sweater smelled like
camia kisses and fresh pine,
fixed with a steaming Milo,
on a windy day

KARLA COMANDA

arrival

(calgary international airport)

o canada
i didn't come to take ownership
of anything (except the clothes
i have on my carabao back (and
maybe the ones in my overweight
luggage)) because i don't belong
to this glacial hell you call
winter & i don't understand how
your airports can be so deceptive,
fooling me that your sun
is just as good as the one i left
behind.
can i call
you mine
except my blood isn't rooted
here — you iced it over so now
it can't circulate around my sun,
crippling me from returning
to coconut rays. i have no choice
but to stay here
so perhaps i should start calling you
our home and na[]ive land

ARIEL DE LA CRUZ

in little manila

little manila is the smell of smoke
clouds crafted by working hands that billow
with traces of lechon and isaw
is the sound of cackling titas
carrying rustling no frills bags
while waiting for the bus
the same bus that brought me home
from that mostly white, all-girls catholic school
that I commuted to for an hour each day for a better education
the same bus where my classmate turned to me saying
"*this* is where all the nannies get off"
the same bus where I learned
that another word for kadiri is nanny
is mother
is ate
is lola
here, debt is another word for living
is the way she tries to shove more gulay into my bag
when I tell her to keep the change on the sidewalk
little manila is the sound of an empty tip jar
because a tip is an impossibility
and a missing paycheque is just a thursday
but I've learned that a missing paycheque is also a promise
is tinola from your neighbour when the bills are too tight
is a protest at the bathurst-wilson parkette

is the feeling of makibaka in the air
is knowing that you are always beholden
that another word for beholden is ingat
ingat is the last word you say to each other
before leaving little manila

DEANN LOUISE C. NARDO

Mimosa pudica

Have you ever heard of the plant
Mimosa pudica?
It has compound leaves that fold inward
      and droop when touched or shaken
Like hands touching in prayer.
It is defending itself from possible harm,
From grazing animals who could eat it
      by disappearing into the greenery.
Have you heard of it?

As a kid, I would spend hours just sitting by a patch,
      touching them, waiting for them to reopen.
No matter how harsh or how gentle I touch,
They always hide.
It's called *Makahiya* in my language,
The shy plant. Others even call it the shame plant.
So, imagine a little plant that when touched,
      hides inside its own reassuring hug.

diaspora thrives in memory

The first time I rode a plane, I was ten. It was a long ride, the food was
meh and I missed everyone
I had left behind. At the same time, I loved being in the sky, floating with
the clouds.

It was thrilling, like I was doing something naughty, naughty like defying the laws of gravity.

Close

Open

The first time I set foot in Canada was at the Toronto Pearson Airport. I stepped out

of the automatic double-doors and into the December chill. My tender, tropical cheeks felt like they were sliced by the white wind

Close

Open

The first time I had stretchy, melted cheese was at Pizza Hut. I was always amazed by the commercials back home. We only had salty queso, and when I finally had that first pizza here, I couldn't stop giggling because the stretchy cheese just kept going on and on and on and

Close

Open

The first time I was called a racial slur was at a bus stop, by two little white boys. They were my neighbours, brothers, aged five and seven. They used a word that didn't even represent my nationality. I so badly wanted to correct their mistake. They told me to go back where I came from.

Close

Close

The first time my father took me shopping was at Value Village. I had no winter clothes to speak of, so we went through the coats section. I could choose by era, by style, by level of wear and tear. I could mix and match a ski jacket with a baseball cap, or a fancy velvet coat with a toque. I've never had this many options before!

Close

Open

My first day of school in Canada was in a small elementary school in Ontario called St. Bernards. It was winter. I was wearing the stuff I bought at Value Village with my dad. I was wearing a pageboy cap and an ankle-length brown wool jacket. I looked straight out of the Great Depression.

   Close

   Open

The first time I saw what my half-sister looked like was when my dad was at work. My mama and I were cleaning a closet when she found a shoebox, hidden on a high shelf. It was full of letters and photos of people I had never seen before. There was a photo of a little girl who looked vaguely familiar, familial even.

Close

Close

The first time I saw my father beg with tears in his eyes was in the middle of the night. My mama was sleeping beside me on the bottom bunk and he crept beside her. He was crying and begging as quietly as he could. I was facing the wall and closed my eyes tighter, not wanting to give myself away. She didn't respond. He sulked out of the room. I wanted so badly to call out to him.

Close

Close

Close

The first time I lived in a house with anyone but my family was with a bunch of strangers in a

giant house. We cooked and ate meals together. They helped my mama find a job. They had a basement full of clothes and stuff, like a mini–Value Village I could shop in!

   Close

   Open

The first time I cried on the phone was when I called my dad on a payphone in this giant house. I cried and told him I loved him and missed him. I didn't understand why he couldn't come pick us up, we were in the same town. And we just got there.

Close

Close

The first time I saw snow — it was through giant windows of my aunt's house, like a live-action large screen TV. I only ever saw it in cartoons, like the episode where Bugs Bunny met the Abominable Snowman. I had to go outside to taste it to believe it.

Close

Open

The first snowman my brother and I ever made was with my dad. Although he was a civil engineer back home, he had no idea how to construct one. So, improvising, he took out a big bag of recycling filled with bottles of Coke, boxes for waffles and pizza, and said, *"Just pack around it!"* The snow wasn't packy enough, but we made it happen. I put my green scarf around the snowman's thick neck and stepped back with my brother. He looked like Jabba the Hutt. So, when my classmates asked if I wanted to build a snowman during recess at school one day, I asked them, *"Where do I get the recycling bag?"*

Close

Open

There's always a first time for everything, right?

There were experiments run by Dr. Monica Gagliano, an evolutionary ecologist from the
University of Western Australia. They made a swing that held a potted *Mimosa pudica* and they would drop the plant unexpectedly. Pull, drop. Pull, drop. Pull, drop. The first and second time, they always close. After they find out that the same move does not hurt them, they stay open.

Like the *Mimosa pudica,* diaspora thrives in memory.
I close
I close

&
I transform
My experiences, my traumas, my emotions, My memories
By learning, processing, and sharing.
Sometimes it takes more work,
Sometimes I hold my leaves
      touching in prayer a little longer
Sometimes I hug myself a little tighter
Sometimes I remind myself that I've defied gravity before.

I am cautious
And I learn
And I remember.
To stay open
I won't remain a closed, shy plant forever
I won't remain a shame plant forever
I stay open
Open
          Open
               Open

CAROLYN FE

I clearly remember

I clearly remember
Over fifty-five years ago
The day you welcomed me to your circle.
I clearly remember
We were children then
The laughter, the staring and standing back.
I clearly remember
Walking into the classroom
The slow-motion turnaround
The eyes wide open, mouths aghast
The bullies giggling and whispering
How the room suddenly smelled stinky
Like shit, they say.

In the lunchroom sitting alone with my Tupperware of adobo and rice and
spoon and fork
Backs turned toward me
Scraps of peanut butter and jelly sandwiches, ham and cheese and iceberg
lettuce
Flying past me, some even hitting my face
Staining my dress.
My favourite dress that reminded me of home, so colourful and bright in
its rich patterns.
Stained.
I clearly remember my first crush

Oh he was a handsome blue-eyed blond
Taking my breath away every time he passed by.
When one day he finally noticed me
Him smiling, looking straight at me
My world no longer lonely
My world no longer pushed aside
My world of hope Dashed
When he tripped
Me
I, falling flat on my tummy
Knocking the wind out of me
My hands breaking the fall, knees and palms scraped on the schoolyard's
icy gravel
My favourite dress soiled. Ruined. Forever hidden in the back of my
closet.
As a reminder.
And again
Left alone.
I clearly remember
The laughter, the pointing, the staring and standing back
Walking into the classroom
The slow-motion turnaround
Eyes wide open, mouths aghast
The bullies giggling
I jumped right back to my feet
From the thumbtacks they left for me to sit on
My chair
Smudged with mud.
I clearly remember
Saying to myself
Welcome to your new life
You will have to fend for yourself
To stand up on your own
To keep holding your head high no matter what

All this …
Until today
As you run toward me
Bright-eyed
Arms wide open
I can only surmise your smile under your mask
That only old friends can be
Until today
When I put my hand out
To stop you from coming closer
Because
I clearly remember
You.

MARC PEREZ

Bones are Seeds

for Benson Flores

But now the stark dignity of
entrance — Still, the profound change
has come upon them: rooted, they
grip down and begin to awaken
— William Carlos Williams

The island greets me with satin clouds and light rain, parting as
the ferry docks at the cove. Rough as the precipice, my mind
careens to the chimes of a concertina: and my heart begins to
grieve, "Here he is, the man without love, country, or soul —
forgotten, abandoned, buried with no tomb." *But now the stark*
dignity of

remembrance. Tracing the ebb of history, I turn each pebble and seashell,
awashed in time and polished with seaside
reflections: *Your breath is home,* a shelter amidst the plague.
The coastal forest is a testament to your banished footprints,
a welcoming totem to your life's *entrance — Still, the profound change*
arrives in the form of a deer
traversing slopes of wild berries and fern to bid farewell. For
now, I use the North Shore mountains as your headstones and
the sakura blossoms for candles, while I pray and offer a song of

loss and rebirth. My feet, too, are planted in a land that is not my own; and the tide *has come upon them — uprooted, they*

find themselves in hostile shores like driftwood carried by turbulent currents. Unable to return, we learn and adapt to numbing rain and snow. They do not know where we come from bones are also seeds — even in barren landscapes, untended, we flower. They can cast us in a crevice, nameless, yet we continue to survive, thrive *grip down and begin to awaken.*

RAFAEL PALMA

Lunch box

It is steaming when placed inside,
stir-fried beans with
a palette of onions and garlic,
sauced with soy, packaged
in a treasured ware, for you.
To eat and take home,
or forget later.

Before putting it in the glass bowl
with a suctioned plastic lid,
my hands guide each
stir of the ladle in the pan,
rearranging them carefully.
Each vegetable and pinch of seasoning
carefully cast in its rightful place.

As they bubble and steam,
announcing their conclusion.
It is received by the senses,
like directors in the front row,
the nose guiding the tongue,
who inspects with a small teaspoon,
checking for minor adjustments.

Now the dish is set,
clutched in the branded, suctioned container,
put inside a tote bag,
sealed, and secured.
I hurry to drive it to you, knowing full well
you have eaten nothing
but a bagel for breakfast.

For one afternoon,
a pumpkin soup.
In a late-night turn,
fried tofu with hoisin sauce.
For this last one,
using a rectangular Tupperware,
with a sky-blue elastic band
fastened in the lid,
with two matching clasps
on each long side

I cooked bean sprouts,
cabbage, and carrots,
julienned roughly, all bundled
in a dumpling wrapper, then fried.
All neatly placed like freshly processed logs,
golden brown, crisp, and perfect.

I hurried off with a borrowed car,
with a warm closed container
on the passenger seat.
Hoping that I get there in time,
so that on the first bite,
the wrapper,
fried to perfection,
would echo with a loud crunch.

Every dish was an offering.
Instead of a letter bringing a confession,
I hoped that each meal,
each ingredient cooked carefully,
conveyed something that resembles warmth.
As you opened the lid, the message rose,
steam and smell in congregation,
melted and reduced over time.

Hoping each bite
is just as filling
as every time I filled a lunch box
and brought it to you.

Yet those lunches,
skipped by sleeping in,
were not enough to fill you.
Wishing my food
could never let you forget
you missed them.
Foolish of me, to think that a few meals
would be enough.

What you gave back to me
as gratuity is a compromise.
Saying you've held
your end of the deal,
pushing forward:
being friends, as a settlement.

This isn't what I gave you.
Not in the same components,
not in the same delivery,
nor is it in the containers

you've collected over time.
Not in the transparent plastic rectangle
with matching clasps.
Not in the glass bowl
with a suctioned lid.
Not in the partitioned plastic red bottom,
with a clear top cover.

In the dim of the backyard,
I am sitting on a lawn chair,
exhausted, craving a cigarette.
Wanting any other kind of high,
than my addiction to food,
or to you.

OPM

Another familiar, blueprint, romantic song
plays in the background, and a drunken
man, sombrely sings along. Somehow, in
this instance — gathered with no specific
agenda, with friends from four-hour-trip
cities, barely legal, or just weaning from
the joys of childhood — we are happy.
These are the better times.

As we try to sing songs
for the sake of nostalgia,
singing in a language born far from here,
framing our lungs for the stress under.
We — for now — get back into dancing,
flailing our arms and pushing out

our legs to step back into reality.
The crushed adulthood. The dealt
problem of bills and living.

RANI RIVERA

All Violet

I used to think
verandahs were a construct for contentment
instead I'm here
extrapolating on the reversal of repute,
50 years from now,
Jilly's on Queen and Broadview
will receive from future Torontologists
on a pretentious but never watched
literary newsmagazine
vis-à-vis a red-flamed editrix
having settled herself appropriately
in a brown leather club chair
kissing faux mahogany shelving
hiding a deficiency of real gilt-edged books
but still standing and making do
with a room full of interns.

It's enough for a person to say
they've done it,
acquired national opinion rights
on the precise amount of cheese
and study needed
for poutine and Stendhal.

Charming the dress socks off
the resident poetry-loving investment banker
just enough to reward me a fat cheque
and another 500-print run.
Ingratiate myself to book club admin groupies
by owing a big thanks
to incest, milliners, and Sioux Lookout.
Warrant a cropped likeness
of my insulated, too-big-for-my-snow-pants head
drawn beside a weekly column
in the Arts section of one of the dailies.
Make a dark chocolate–munching émigré of distinction
fall off his chair in round-bellied laughter
at yet another awards dinner.

Forget what CC and soda taste like
on a budget.

Take in a mangy stray and call her Maurice
Show her off at the Jazz Festival
and be extra careful she doesn't get stepped on.
Write a poem about love, jazz, and Maurice, and how she's
so cute, I could eat her.

Night and Day

I'm getting off the 501 streetcar
and stomping my big, black boots into the sidewalk.
Surprisingly, my posture is perfect,
unburdened by a knapsack full of poems
and one vintage men's Burberry trench coat.

I'm heading home on Queen West
in an asymmetrically zippered coat
and a Northbound Leather shopping bag in tow.
Carrying war wounds and forgotten accessories.
Feeling confident, cocky even, assured.

Even after it occurs to me I've never even considered
daylight before.
Relegated mornings to that dead air
occupied by
waiting for coffee to be made for you
while Cole Porter sings the blues away.

Sends your lover away.

Mornings are anoxic and pure,
full of phatic lovers and shared baths.

I'm seated at a new dining table
you salvaged from the street
and my bottom is cozy on a once-white chair
but now a sunburnt polypropylene
and showing that sickly pallor of disease.
I'm trying to believe that I will remember this night
as a pleasant evening of tea and innocuous banter.

Blocking out
that after pushing aside
our worn Cohen vs. Dylan debate
I ask to use your bathroom
and find a tin cup of makeup brushes by the sink.
A full set.
Professional even.

There's a loofah sponge in the shower
and I'm livid.

Angry that my mother never warned me
to stay away from
men in leather pants
who wear metallic nail polish
better than I ever can.
From men who tell you:
you smell like bamboo and freshly cut grass.
From men who trek all the way to Scarborough
to find tiny D-rings to make your four-inch stiletto boots
look couture.

I'm getting off the 501 streetcar,
feeling confident,
cocky even, dammit
assured.

A Dereliction of Line

All I see now
are tuck shops full of ginsengs
the preliminary "g" pronounced hard
and false by a friend who thought
me fearless.
Announcing gutturally it's time
to clear the detritus
too many hours have passed
tableside over a paltry purchase
she's spent and the lights are giving way.

One red
two black

starts a lazy exquisite corpse,
lying unfinished in a haze
of the recognizable smoke and scent
of hard-topped construction cut
with digestives and filler.
Inclined to rush out
with trusted PIN codes and
newly acquired phone numbers.
Quashing old allegiances
and established sponsorships of
rehabilitated behaviour.

AILEEN SANTIAGO

Phantom Pains

On a hot day in March
I said goodbye to my left foot
And promised I would write
And send word by air mail
My right foot stepped into
The cold waiting on the other side
And steeled itself for
the hard work
To validate the goodbye
My right foot
Bore my weight as I planted
Posts to rest on
It hopped from North York to Scarborough
To Markham and back again
While I sweated, cried, and grunted
I always admired
My right foot
It teetered at times
And wavered at the knee
Yet still stood strong
I felt proud
And others smiled
because my right foot
fit nicely
Into its winter boot

And summer sneaker
But when I finally took time
To look behind me
At an old quiet ache
I was surprised to find
My left foot
Had actually followed
And had been there
All along

HARI ALLURI, SOL DIANA & CARLO SAYO

Offering for Eric

Dedicated to the memory of Eric Cardeno, a.k.a. DJ Wundrkut

In the stillness of departure
A stone's throw from unravelling into dust
I reflect on two things:
1. Are you truly gone?
2. What is in the name, Wundrkut, but a manifesto about where
   we've been, and where we are trying to go?

Wundrkut;
To Wundr, as in, to dream. To imagine a world better than this.
And to Kut, as in, to scratch. To chop, like our ancestors swinging bolos
back in the day
beating back conquistadors.

Wundrkut, is the name of someone who knows he's champion.
Looking life straight in the eye,
Hit it with a 1, 2 when he's on the 1, 2's
Best check your P's and Q's.
Mic check, 1, 2
Check hook when the record scratch
Uppercut when the beat breaks —

You know it's Wundrkut
When he makes his mark like he's here to stay

And make your mark, you did.
If there's 1, 2 things you know how to do
It's to do it well and to do it wondrous.
We — We broadcasted your face over the Queensborough Bridge
Knowing that somewhere, someone would be chin-lifted into recognizing
that opening salvo blast of a smile that burst... for miles on end
And if not that: then the Sacred Spirit Ink engraved into your skin like
ancestral patchwork.

A resounding no, no, no you are not gone.
Look at how you brought us together today.
Look at how we wear W's on our chests like emblems.
Look at Kaya and Tala and this whole new generation of Filipinx
scratching in your honour.

What is in a name? But a commitment toward forever?
The way we forever chant "Wundrkut forever,"
When we Kut through all else sometimes all we're left with is Wundr;

Dreams and divine visions, the process of constructing a better tomorrow.
Constructing forever.
What is in the name, Wundrkut, but 1, 2 love letters to the people
Scratched into our hearts,

Reminding us
Reminding us,

Reminding us what is possible.

Tattoos on your fingers, scorpions and stars
old as our children's names in sky
when we search for you. When we ask why
you left, the answer plays in dark
behind your pogi smile, the cross-fade spark
your hands put into records. We scry
in dreams, in tawas, in every city nook our eyes
can grasp. You're part of the music now, the bars
you looped are your return. Scratch that
now part: you've always been the music. Your reach,
thanks to your humility, wider than we could know. Wider
since you got called home Memories of you unfurl
in stories we tell at your altar on the beach,
in dreams, the moth that follows me, in spider-
webs of sound. Wonder cuts the keys to doors between the worlds.

There is no time to match Pantone colour swatches
No time to obsess over which typeface
Just make sure people know your face
        Height. Weight. Age.
        Detailed description —

It's not about the kerning
Between the letters M to the I
To the S S I
N ...
Fuck. me.

Could this really be?

        Take a moment
        Wipe a tear

Then back to work
It's not about the kerning

Check the margins

Make the layout clear
Cut nothing off — keep what's essential
Now Save. Print. Check the margins.

We checked the margins
Walked the water's edges
Of this queen's borough and beyond
Your queen's army mobilized for days 'til dawn

We had to let the world know.

… In the moments   when doubt whispers
That you didn't do enough
Know that we did everything we could
And if asked to find the strength
To do more,   we would.

Reminding us,
Reminding us

Reminding me when we were two introverts
just driving in a car
Conversations didn't travel far
But together in silence we contemplate our craft
Beyond windows grey cityscapes blur past

These moments, once fleeting
Now precious memories
Now, never, not for granted

We drove the town
Examined wood and stone
Stood at the foot of metal giants
Asking what it meant to hold space of our own

Memories of you unfurl

There were few words to speak
Break beats were your speech
Only after did we witness the breadth of your reach
Blessed with the sign of the cross-fader, preach
Preach about the old school techniques that you teach
To the new,
        You knew the importance of embracing the next generation
Fostered care to peers and pupils
You kept good vibes on heavy rotation

Memories of you unfurl,
Reminding us, Reminding us.

When we spoke of settlement, of community
You provided the soundtrack
After all, what are we?
But products of   cuts and scratches
Survival stories walking immigrant paths
carved before us in wood and stone
Markings beneath our skin
Cultural remixes spin
Lost in the diaspora
In wonder for a place of our own.

Wundr kuts the keys to doors between the worlds
Reminding us,   what is possible.

PRIMROSE MADAYAG KNAZAN

Where Are You From?

A GRANDFATHERLY WHITE *male busker plays familiar folk tunes on a guitar or ukulele outside of a grocery store. He nods and smiles, saying "Thank you" as passersby drop coins or bills into his open case. (This part of the scene can take place as the audience enters.)*

A Filipinx woman in her late thirties walks out of the store. She wears business attire with high-end shoes and a designer purse slung over her shoulder. She holds two bags of groceries in reusable bags. The grocery bags are not heavy, but she is tired and cranky, having left a full day of work to buy a few items for dinner that night. After a long day at the office, the bags feel as if they are holding ten-pound weights.

The Busker assesses the woman and sees the designer purse and shoes. He smiles at her and nods. She nods back, smiling politely. She attempts to pass by him, trying to avoid further engagement. He steps in front of her.

BUSKER. Good evening, Ma'am.
She is instantly annoyed at having been called ma'am.
WOMAN. Evening.
BUSKER. Are you having a good one?
She purses her lips and lets out an exasperated sigh.
WOMAN. As best as can be expected.
BUSKER. That's all that we could ask for, eh? If you don't mind me asking, *where are you from?*
The Woman drops the smile.
WOMAN. *(to audience)*
This happens all the time. I'm asked "Where are you from?" Strangers,

co-workers, friends. I take the words at face value, "I want to know where you're from" as in "Where were you born?"

(to Busker)

I'm from Winnipeg.

BUSKER. No, no. Where are you *really* from?

WOMAN. *(to audience)*

There it is. The question isn't "Where are you from?" The question *really* is, "Why do you look like you don't belong here?"

(to Busker)

I'm from *Winnipeg*. I was born here.

BUSKER. No, no, no. You're from the Philippines, right?

WOMAN. *(to audience)*

Respect your elders. All Filipino children are taught, respect your elders.

(to Busker)

My *parents* came from the Philippines.

BUSKER. Ahh, I knew it! *Mabuhay! Kamusta ka!*

WOMAN. *(to audience)*

I think that means "Welcome"? "How are you"? Why would you say that to a stranger *leaving* a store? "Welcome. How are you."

I was born here. I was raised here. I barely know Filipino. I know the import-ant things such as the swear words and "*Salamat*" for "Thank you." My parents spoke to me in Tagalog when I was very, very young, but once I started kindergarten, the language dissipated into the English ether.

(looks at Busker)

I'm not sure what he's expecting me to say. Does he actually want to know how I'm doing or does he want some sort of validation, a pat on the head for saying the funny words correctly?

(to Busker)

Um, okay.

BUSKER. All right! I love pancit and lumpia!

WOMAN. *(to audience)*

Once someone finds out I'm Filipino, why do they feel the need to tell me they like traditional Filipino food? When someone tells me they're Jewish, I don't start talking about matzah ball soup. When someone says they're Métis, I don't yell out "Bannock!" When someone says they're British, I feel no need to bring up Bangers and Mash.

Why not start a real conversation?

(turning to the Busker)

Why couldn't you have said something along the lines of —

BUSKER. *(puts down the guitar)*

Ahh, you're Filipino? I had a Filipino co-worker at my last job. He brought pancit and lumpia to our work potluck. They tasted amazing. Can you recommend a Filipino restaurant?

She smiles at him genuinely.

The Busker picks up the guitar and the eager look on his face returns.

The Woman sighs and drops her smile.

WOMAN. *(to audience)*

But no, I have to respond to the shouting of random Filipino dishes.

(to Busker)

That's … nice.

Where are *you* from?

BUSKER. *(proudly)* Nova Scotia.

WOMAN. Ahh … *(thinking of a Nova Scotian dish)* The Donair.

BUSKER. That's right! I love Donair!

WOMAN. *(to audience)*

He says where he's from so proudly because he is never asked The Question. He answers with pride because that's the place where he was born and the place where he grew up. No doubts. No questions. Everyone believes him the first time he answers.

I'm rarely given the privilege of being believed.

She puts down the grocery bags.

A few weeks ago at work, all of the managers were introduced to the new Director of our unit. We started off great but as I walked him back to his office …

The Woman shakes hands with her new Director.

DIRECTOR. Great to meet you, and thank you for making me feel so welcome. By the way, where are you from?

WOMAN. Winnipeg, sir.

DIRECTOR. Oh, sorry, that's not what I meant. Where are you from
   originally?

WOMAN. *(smiling politely)*

I was born in Winnipeg.

Sir.

The Woman picks up the grocery bags and steps away.

(to audience)

But what else could I do? What could I say?

She closes her eyes.

I needed to be home. I needed to be with my family.

The Woman puts down the bags.

I have two sons, five and ten years old. They're mestizo, Eastern European
   and Filipino, the perfect fusion of my husband and me in every way. I
   looked at my five-year-old as he played with his toy cars. I see my dark
   hair and his father's straight nose, my almond eyes and his father's
   eyelids. I needed to know.

(to five-year-old)

Jamie, come here.

Jamie stands in front of her. She takes his hand.

WOMAN. Have you ever been asked the question, "Where are you from?"

The boy nods.

She takes a breath.

WOMAN. What do you say?

JAMIE. I'm from Canada.

She smiles and touches his face.

WOMAN. That's right, honey. You're from Canada, born in the same
   hospital where I was born, in Winnipeg, Manitoba, Canada. Can you
   do me a favour and get your brother?

JAMIE. Okay.

(calling out) Gerald! Mommy wants you!

He runs out.

Gerald enters sulkily.

GERALD. I'm in the middle of a game.

WOMAN. I just have a quick question, honey.

Have you ever been asked the question, "Where are you from?"

Gerald shrugs.

WOMAN. How do you answer?

GERALD. *(shrugging)* I dunno.

WOMAN. *(sterner)* Gerald, how do you answer the question, "Where are you from?"

She takes his hand.

You can tell me.

GERALD. The Philippines.

WOMAN. What?! The Philippines? Why do you say the Philippines?

GERALD. *(stepping back)*

Because that's what they want to know.

WOMAN. Why do you say you're from the Philippines? You were born here. *I* was born here. My parents have been here over forty years. Daddy was born here. His parents were born here! *Their* parents were born here! And one of their parents was born in Poland. You are not from the Philippines!

GERALD. I'm sorry, Mommy. I'm sorry.

WOMAN. No, honey! I'm sorry for yelling.

She hugs him.

GERALD. I thought that's what it means.

She pulls away and looks at him.

WOMAN. That's not what it means.

I'm so sorry. I'm not mad at you.

She looks down at their hands.

I'm not mad at you.

She lets go and Gerald walks away.

I'm not mad at you.

She looks up at the audience, scanning the people in front of her.

She turns and glares at the Busker with seething anger.

WOMAN. I'm mad at *them.*

She directs her anger at the Busker, circling him.

I'm mad that my ten-year-old has been asked the question enough times to know that it doesn't matter that he's half-white or that he's second-generation Canadian.

I'm mad that he knows he is viewed as an outsider.

I'm mad because those words mean one thing when you are white and another thing when you are brown.

She turns to the audience.

Where. Are. You. From.

She turns to the Busker, picking up her bags, turning to leave.

BUSKER. *(jovial)* Since you're Filipino, I wanted to play you something.

The Busker starts to play the chords to "Bahay Kubo," a children's song from the Philippines. He sings "Da da, da da" for the melody. He keeps playing the same verse over and over again (three chords).

The Woman turns to him slowly and is taken aback as she hears the song. She listens for a moment. Her anger trickles out of her as she stares at him.

WOMAN. *(to audience but looking at Busker)*

"Bahay Kubo ..." It's a song from the Philippines. My mother used to sing it to me. She had a beautiful voice.

(singing along with the melody) Bahay Kubo, kahit munti ...

It means Little House ... And a garden. It's about a little house and the vegetables that grow in the garden. I remember singing the song with her. I remember speaking the same language.

(singing along with the melody) Bahay Kubo, kahit munti ...

She closes her eyes for a moment.

My mother died two years ago. I would give anything to hear her sing to me again.

She circles him, her eyes fixated on him as she speaks.

If I wasn't so wound up from the stupid, ignorant, racist question he used to get my attention, I probably would've given him a loonie, a toonie, maybe all the money in my purse for a memory I hadn't thought of in years, maybe decades.

How did he learn this song? Who taught him the melody? A friend? A lover?

(singing along with the melody) Bahay Kubo, kahit munti ...

We bought Gerald a ukulele last year for his birthday. After three days, he never touched it again. If this man could teach Gerald the song, I would give him money. I would give him my jewellery. I would tell him about the fantastic Donair place in St. Vital. I would do anything to share this song with my children so that someday they can share the song with their children.

(singing along with the melody) Bahay Kubo, kahit munti ...

Why? Why did you have to ask me those words? Why couldn't you just say —

BUSKER. *(stops playing, speaking politely)*

Excuse me, Miss, I am so sorry to disturb you. I'm just curious, are you Filipino? You don't have to answer, of course, but if you are Filipino, and even if you're not, I have a song that I think you'd enjoy.

The Busker starts playing an exaggerated version of "Bahay Kubo" again, badly singing the lyrics of the song.

She steps back into her original position. Defeated.

WOMAN. *(to Busker, angrily)* HEY!

He stops playing.

Next time, if you want to know someone's ethnicity, you should just ask. Racist asshole.

The Woman walks away in frustration.

The Busker is confused, oblivious to her anger. He shrugs it off.

He nods and smiles at an unseen person passing by.

BUSKER. Hey! Where are you from?

Jamaica? Hey mon! I love doubles and beef patties!

The Busker starts to play a set of syncopated reggae chords.

He smiles as the unseen person drops money into his case.

Yeah! Thank you, mon! We be jammin'!

He continues to play the song.

Lights fade out.

Where. Are. You. From. was commissioned by Royal Manitoba Theatre Centre and produced as part of *Tiny Plays, Big Ideas*, a virtual festival featuring four short plays exploring the theme of human rights. The original creative production team included Audrey Dwyer as dramaturge, Hazel Venzon as director, and starred Rochelle Kives & Rob Patterson.

JIM AGAPITO

Punk As F*ck

I was asked to speak at the FAB 5 conference for the Manitoba Teachers' Society. The conference is geared toward teachers in their first five years of teaching. It was fitting — they were starting their careers as teachers and I was starting my career in radio. The following is my keynote address and what I came up with.

MY NAME IS Jim Agapito.

I'm a Filipino-Canadian from the north end of Winnipeg. I spent the early part of my life living in a duplex with my entire family. I had two grandmas, two grandpas, five uncles, five aunts, three cousins, one brother, and a mom and dad all living in one home. To this day, I eat fast. Why? Cause if I ever wanted seconds from a meal, I had to make sure I could beat everyone, cause kids always ate first.

My aunts listen to pop and my uncles listen to rap — but there was always one uncle, my Tito Bong, who was into rock. He was the coolest. I don't know what it's like in other cultures, but Filipinos always have this wild and crazy party uncle. Mine was my Tito Bong.

So why am I mentioning this? Well, it has a lot to do with my personality and my unique perspective on life. My talk today is about diversity. I promise I'm gonna go the hella long way around about it. But I promise you'll get a kick out of it.

I went to a private Polish Catholic School for Filipinos. I know that sounds crazy, but it's true. I know what you're thinking. We teach in public schools. What the hell does this have to do with us? Well, the truth is, it has to do with diversity.

How many people here went to Holy Ghost School? I went to school back when they still gave the student the strap. Now I never got the strap. I did, however, have nuns smack the hell out of my hand when I was being bad.

It's not something I completely understood, and it's also something that never bothered me. Now I'm not saying it's something I approve of, but I guess it's something my parents were used to in the old country, so they had no problem with it. Yikes! (The truth is the nuns loved me.)

But I was one of those hyperactive little kids that was always goofing around. The truth is, I would be diagnosed with ADHD. How many people here teach young hyper children? Here's my advice to you: give them a lot of love.

My poor mother, Yolanda, once asked the doctor to give my older brother Mark and I meds to chill us out. The truth is, after one day of being on meds, my mom said we weren't the bundles of joy (or intensity) she was used to, so she just let us act like bundles of energy trapped in a jar with the lid slightly off. So amazing.

Growing up in school, all the kids played basketball. I don't know what it's like in other cultures, but playing basketball is one rite-of-passage thing Filipino kids did. It's one of those things that your family watched you play, that you watched during playoff time, and that your titos and titas, meaning aunts and uncles, told you you stunk at if you were no good.

My mom was super protective of both my brother and me growing up. When we moved out of the north end and into the Maples, basketball was the one thing I was allowed to do. You see, my mom, like so many Filipino moms during that time, was hyper protective of her children. If Yolanda couldn't see me playing ball in front of the house with my older brother, I wasn't going out. My mom was always worried something was gonna happen to her little Jimmy Boy.

For a long time, my best friend in the neighbourhood was white. This was a super big deal for me. For the first seven years of my life, I was surrounded by Filipinos. No diversity there. Being friends with Derek gave me little glimpses into what it was like not to be Filipino. One of my best memories was surprising Derek with the kind of breakfast we Filipinos ate. It is composed of eggs, beef, or longanisa (which is Filipino cured sausage) and rice.

Filipino breakfasts are huge. You always feel a little bit of carb shock. So seeing Derek having nothing but cereal in the morning was super weird. He was always stoked to come over and have breakfast with us. I was always excited to have cereal when I could. It wasn't until years later that I learned why this is a thing.

Traditionally, Filipinos don't put cold things in their stomachs first thing in the morning. My mom convinced herself that I hated cold cereal. Truth be told, it's because she never let me have it.

At age ten, these were the first inklings that I might be different from other people.

For example, Filipinos love sugar. Sugar is in everything. Heck, even our spaghetti, which I detest and nearly gets me thrown out of the culture, is on the sweet side. Why? Because of colonialism. Here's a quick history lesson. The Spanish colonized us. Then the Americans. The Americans decided to take our sugar, refine it, and, after decades of buying it from us, said they didn't want it anymore. Instead, they flooded the market with it, and then, when we got desperate, they got big business to come and buy it from us cheaply. Oh yeah, and because we had so much of it around, we would use it in everything.

And that's my first lesson on diversity for y'all. I don't know what it's like now for you teachers. You've got the Internet, so kids probably Google stuff all the time. But for a wide-eyed, ten-year-old Filipino, I never realized that we were different. This was what my family ate, so I thought that this was what everyone else ate.

When I discovered that they didn't, I tripped out. It led me to more questions. Questions I asked my mom. Questions she had no answer for.

It wasn't until I went to another private school in grade nine that I really discovered that I was different.

I went to an all-boys Catholic school on the opposite side of town. It was so far that it was a two-hour bus ride back and forth. There were so many weird new things for me to get used to — not only was I not around girls, but kids were coming to school in BMWs and, sometimes, even their own cars!

I came from a working-class family. My dad worked nights for CN. He always made sure to drop me every morning at school. Up until grade ten, my dad drove an '81 Ford Mustang. It was a shit box. It was covered in Urban Camo, meaning it was partly rusted out. On the very rare occasion when my mom would drive me, I came in a '81 Caprice station wagon! Yes, it had the fake wood panelling on it!

Some of the rich white kids made fun of me. It is the first time I experienced racism. They used to say awful things like, "Your parents couldn't clean enough rooms for a new car?" or "Did the nursing gig not pay enough for a new car?" It used to bum me out. It also got me into a lot of fights.

Now we Filipinos love food. We have an obsession with food and making sure we always have enough. What some of you call dinner, we call an appetizer. More on this later.

When you're in the cafeteria and all your friends are buying lunches and stuff, you feel a little awkward carrying around a giant-assed piece of Tupperware with yesterday's leftovers. Some of it was delicious food that my parents prepared that we didn't want to go to waste. But imagine taking that out and some kid saying, "What the fuck is that?"

I felt sad that my mom carefully double packed something that I thought was a piece of heaven, but what others said smelled and looked funny.

That gave me a horrible complex. That's when I begged my mom to buy me pizza pops and crappy sandwiches. I just wanted to fit in more. And boy did it suck.

I think my parents sensed something was up. They could tell that I was awkwardly asking to get dropped off closer to the school bell. So they did the unimaginable. They let me blast the most profane gangsta rap you could imagine rolling up.

And I mean real gangster shit. Like, I was playing Wu-Tang Clan's *Enter the 36 Chambers* and Ol' Dirty Bastard's "Brooklyn Zoo." It was the bomb, and it wasn't like I was coming in quiet. My parents let me blast it as loud as I could.

My parents didn't want me to feel different. They wanted me to fit in, and that truly led to a bunch of issues I have now.

For starters, my parents never forced me to learn the language. Other than the swears, I didn't know much. I could kinda fake understanding based on inflection, but really, I never spoke it at all. Which also kinda sucked cause you know family members were judging you when they stared, smiled at you, and talked in Tagalog.

Secondly, I was never forced to eat Filipino food. I am allergic to seafood. Imagine growing up in a Filipino household where fish and shellfish were in everything. My family, to this day, has a hard time believing that a Filipino can have allergies to those staples. It's come to a point where they've tested my "hate for it" by putting trace amounts into everything. The moment my lip gets swollen or my eyes start closing is when they believe something is changing with young Jimmy Boy. But it didn't stop them. It's only recently that they've started taking this seriously.

The only thing we could agree on was fried chicken. Yup, Filipinos love fried chicken. It might be one of the most Filipino things about me. It came to the point where the only way my family could get me to come to the gathering was by ordering a big bucket of love. That love continues today and it's even inspired me to get a fried chicken tattoo on my leg.

So why am I telling you this? Well, issues regarding food made me the odd one out of the family. They started to ask me questions like, "What kind of Filipino are you? Food is so important in our culture and you don't want to eat?"

Now remember how I went to an all-boys Catholic private school? Most of my friends were Filipino; most of the kids from grade school transitioned there. My other classmates? Well, they were from all over, but a majority were white, and a majority played hockey, And remember how I told you that we played basketball? Well, I have news for you. I completely suck at it, but I still played because I wanted to be a part of something.

If you weren't a jock playing either basketball, hockey, football, or volleyball, chances are you weren't considered cool. I didn't do any of those things, but I discovered something no one else was doing. Punk rock.

Keep in mind, my Tito Bong was a banger. He schooled me in so many hair metal ways. His favourite pastime was blasting heavy metal and vacuuming the house. He would crank up Maiden, the Scorpions, AC/DC, and Metallica so loud that it would rumble the house.

Sometimes our neighbour would knock on our door and ask if we could turn down the music. My uncle, sporting his jean vest and mullet, would tell him no and continue to clean the house.

I remember when he had to babysit both my brother and me. I was about nine at the time. Metallica was playing at the old Winnipeg Stadium. It's where the Silver City is now at Polo Park. We weren't going in. It was summer and my Tito Bong decided to park his car across the street in the parking lot. He bought my brother Mark and me two Slurpees. We proceeded to sit on two lawn chairs while he stood up and rocked out in the parking lot.

You have no idea what kind of influence that had on me. Here was a guy who was rocking out without a care in the world and not taking it from anyone. That's amazing. Blew my nine-year-old mind. I thought he was the coolest.

So, remember how it took me an hour to get home? I had to transfer onto another bus downtown. In the dead of winter, I had to get warm, because Winnipeg is so freaking cold. There was a record store downtown called Music City. I would go in there to warm up. But downstairs there was this creepy alternative place called the Cellar. This place used to frighten me. In fact, I was always scared of the loud music and characters coming out of there. But I was intrigued. To me, it felt like the porn area of a video store. One day, I looked in. One of the guys in the store noticed me. "Young man, is there something I can interest you in?" he asked. I looked at him and said, "Ugh." Keep in mind that this guy had a vest covered in spikes. He gestured to invite me in. I started looking around. The music that was playing on the PA was punk. I've never heard this kind of music before. I was pretty blown away because it didn't make sense to me. Nor could I understand how anyone would even like this music. But it was exciting!

In the background was a videotape of music vids playing on VHS. It was Rancid, one of the most pivotal punk bands of the 90s. They fused punk and ska. I thought, "This is amazing!"

The weird dude that I thought was creepy based on his appearance was super cool. He wasn't the intimidating person I thought him to be. His name was Andy. He's now a schoolteacher. But at the time, he played in the Horribles, one of Winnipeg's most legendary bands.

I wanted to put on headphones to check out some music. There were a whole bunch of records in the player and I went to the first one. Just as I was putting the headphone on, Andy stopped me. He said, "Young man, you don't want to listen to that. You want to listen to this." And the best part is, the band was local. They were political punk rockers called Propagandhi. The song I listened to was called "… And We Thought Nation States Were a Bad Idea." It's become an anthem in my young teen life. It was the beginning of an awakening for me.

Since I had no money, Andy hooked me up with cassette tape dubs and sampler CDs.

One day, he gave me a flyer to an all-ages show. It was like five bucks and I thought this was super rad. The only problem was, who would go and check this out with me? And that's when I decided to play the songs for my Filipino friends at school. Their automatic reaction was, "What is this? Is this like some angry white music? Don't you like hip hop?".

Of course I loved hip hop, but this was something different and new. This had an energy to it I'd never experienced before, and this newfound love for punk now made people question how Filipino I was for not keeping to the status quo.

You also have to remember that the Internet wasn't a thing back in 1996. You couldn't just go Google a topic or a musical band. You had to seek stuff out by physically doing it.

So here I was with stuff I cared about and no one to share it with. It was sad. I pretty much spent a good year feeling like a loner. And that's when things started to go wrong. Eventually, I would leave private school. Things just weren't working out. I chose to leave.

Now I'm not knocking the private school. That experience taught me a lot of things. But going to public school completely changed my life.

For starters, I met people from all different walks of life. And there were girls, so many girls! The awkwardness I felt talking to girls went away the moment Nicole asked me if I wanted to have lunch with her and her friends. That was rad.

And remember my best childhood friend that lived across the street? Yup, I was now going to school with Derek. The best part was, he was into punk just like me. I was beginning to meet new people who were into the same things I was, and school became fun. And I was acquiring an identity.

There was no class system here. It wasn't a place where the jocks ruled. You had everyone — jocks, geeks, freaks, theatre kids, punks, kids from all walks of life. There was racism, but it wasn't as bad as before. And the teachers in public school were super cool to me.

When I went to private school, a couple of teachers picked on me for being different. One teacher always made sure to pronounce my last name wrong. So many people in class would laugh and mimic it. To this day it pisses me off when someone purposefully gets my name wrong. I have PTSD from it.

Another teacher made sure to make fun of the stuff I was into. Here I was, a kid in high school listening to the best music on Earth. And he made fun of me for not understanding why I'd write an entire essay on Minor Threat and being "straight edge." If you don't know what straight edge means, it means to abstain from drugs and alcohol. It was rebelling against the cultural norm. It was punk as fuck. It was cool to be different. Although I didn't identify as straight edge, taking a stance on being different in society meant a lot to me.

That started this me-against-the-world attitude that took me a long time to shake. If no one understood me, screw it, I would just rebel. So I had a really hard time talking to teachers. Academically, I was pretty sound. Attitude-wise, I was a lot of trouble.

It wasn't until one public school teacher called me on my shit. They didn't treat me like a child, but like an adult. That started a dialogue. They were willing to listen to me. This taught me that you can trust people and give them a chance.

It made high school a lot better. I felt accepted for who I was. People come from all walks of life, in all sorts of shapes and sizes. That's when I decided to seek out more people like me. That's when music became a big part of my life.

For me, wearing a band T-shirt was a gigantic cultural badge saying, "This is what I'm about." That was what was cool about the punk scene — it was usually made up of outcasts. People from very diverse backgrounds who weren't accepted into "normal society." It didn't matter if you were straight, gay, Muslim, Christian, black, brown, or white. You just had to be a good person and like the music and the message.

Punk got me into vegetarianism, putting me inherently at odds with Filipino culture, which is pretty meat-heavy. Remember the local band Propagandhi that I was slightly obsessed with? Well, let me tell you something about that band. That band taught me a lot about politics and vegetarianism.

It was my eighteenth birthday, and I had just graduated from high school. To celebrate, my lola bought a KFC feast with all the fixins'. She looked at me and said "k'ain na," making a gesture with her hand to put food in my mouth.

I turned to her and said, "Lola, I'm a vegetarian now. I don't eat meat."

She looked at me confused. "There's fried chicken there. Go eat some before it gets cold."

"No, Lola, I'm a vegetarian, no more meat for me."

My mom looked at her and said a couple of words in Tagalog.

"If you don't like my food, you don't eat," my lola said. I could almost see the steam rising from her head.

Lola was already angry with me because I didn't eat a lot of Filipino food and this just angered her even more. For the next ten years, she tried to entice me with fried chicken, but I held my ground.

So how does Propagandhi play into this? Imagine being a seventeen-year-old watching animals being slaughtered on a constant video loop before entering the concert venue. Yes, that was a thing at punk shows growing up. That alone traumatized me enough to not touch meat for a decade.

But imagine being part of a culture that doesn't accept your lifestyle choices. My lola nearly threw me out of the family. My parents thought it would be something I'd grow out of quickly, but they were wrong.

I was officially the outcast of the family.

I ended up moving to Ontario. I studied journalism. I also got way more into drinking and drugs, which drained my already limited income.

I loved alcohol. I loved it so much that I pretty much drank daily. That led to many bad decisions.

Alcohol is something that turns me into a "sailor on shore leave." Trust me, it's not pretty.

Today, I stay away from it.

My mom was hyper religious growing up. She rarely drank. However, around Christmastime, she would drink some awful sparkling champagne called Baby Duck. She'd get extra funny as the night progressed, belting out Christmas carols or dancing around with some yuletide flair.

Now let's fast forward to my mid-twenties. After several years away at college, I wanted to bond with my mom. Before I left home at nineteen, my mom was strict and a stickler for rules.

Keep in mind these rules were self-inflicted "decency" ones. That meant no drinking.

Well that was about to change. When I went away to college, I became a heavy drinker, amongst other things. When I returned home, I introduced my mom to red wine.

My mom can keep it under control, something I can't do. My drinking led to other bad things, like drugs, which I'd rather not get into.

At my lowest point, I was buying a loaf of bread and going to the college cafeteria to make condiment sandwiches. Sandwiches made of relish, ketchup, and mustard, packed between two slices of white bread. Appetizing, huh? It got to a point where I lost nearly thirty pounds due to bad nutrition. My college professor expressed concern, my friends said I was turning grey, and a nurse friend was convinced that I had scurvy. It wasn't a pretty picture.

Luckily, Christina, a close friend I knew from Winnipeg, started inviting me over for dinner with her family whenever she could. She always made sure I took something home with me.

Kids can have a lot of pride. The home situation isn't great or maybe the family is too poor to afford food. And no one likes charity. I certainly didn't. But the fact that my professor would bring me extra sandwiches, and that Christina would invite me over for dinner on a semi-regular basis, saved my life.

I know that many of you carry extra granola bars and go out of your pocket to help people in need. Keep doing that — little gestures can affect the way someone thinks about life.

For the next five years, I honed my craft as a storyteller. I travelled the world with bands, documenting their lives and shenanigans for terrible pay.

Until a bombshell hit me. My Uncle John got cancer.

My Uncle John was Ukrainian. My auntie Linda, or Dada, as I call her, married a Ukrainian man. Filipinos have a thing where we adopt people in our lives into our family. Since my grandpa died when I was eleven, Uncle John kinda became like my grandpa because he was the same age my grandpa would have been.

Dada and John had no children. He made sure to teach me some of the Ukrainian traditions he thought would be important, like what's done around Christmas and Easter. It came to a point where Karpaty's, a Ukrainian deli in the north end, knew me and always had an order ready for my Uncle John.

My aunt died of cancer when I was nineteen. Since my parents didn't have a lot of money, she wanted to make sure I could go to college, because she said I had a gift for storytelling. This is why I decided to study journalism.

Uncle John was very close to my dad and mom. When he got sick, my dad took early retirement to help care for him, even though John was too stubborn to ask for help. That's just how my family rolls.

When I found out about Uncle John, I packed up my life in Toronto and headed home.

The next couple of months became anchorless. I moved in with some buds, and I started working a job in a telemarketing firm.

One day my friend brought home this gigantic American Film Institute desk reference book. It was about eight hundred pages long. I just devoured it, reading it in between stints of caring for my uncle and working. It became a Bible for me.

One day, in 2005, I mustered up the courage to email a producer at the National Film Board of Canada. He responded, and we met. I told him I had a documentary idea.

The idea was to follow my wrestling-obsessed friend to meet wrestling icon Vince McMahon. He already had a history of getting pictures with wrestlers and this would be the "pièce de résistance," so to speak.

He proceeded to tell me that I didn't know what I was doing. At the end of the meeting, I said, "I don't care if you believe I can do it or not, I'm still doing it." Remember, I've got this me-against-the-world attitude. The punk world, which was my community, was so used to being DIY that I just expected people to say no if I ever asked for help.

As I walked out the door, he said, "Listen, this world is hard. You need to learn certain things about it. But if you show up on Monday, maybe there's something you can learn." And that became Monday, and Tuesday, and soon every day for about eight months.

Finally, a diversity initiative emerged to train ten filmmakers across Canada to make their first documentary feature through the National Film Board of Canada. It was highly competitive. I ended up being one of the ten chosen out of eight hundred applicants.

My parents thought that I was wasting time. They didn't understand why I was devoting all my time to filmmaking. They wanted me to do something practical like become a nurse or go back to school.

Then, two days before I was set to leave for Montréal for a week to start workshopping my film, my dad called me and said I had to go see Uncle John right away, because he didn't have much time left.

My Uncle John shooed me away from being by his side all the time. "You're a young man, Jim," he said. "You gotta live your life."

I spent the evening with him in palliative care. He was not completely lucid because of all the pain meds he was on, but he gave me one of the most encouraging speeches ever.

My family may not have understood what I was doing, but he did. He told me that in life, people are always going to be against you. They will always bring you down. They will say that you're living a fantasy and bring up all sorts of reasons why you can't do it. They are going to say you will fail because of race, age, or social class. But here's the thing. You're a fighter. You always have been. So when you start your career making films and telling stories, you're going to be great. He said he was proud of me.

Uncle John died the next morning.

My dad asked me what I wanted to do. Should they have the funeral now, or should they wait for me to get back?

I didn't want my Uncle John to come back from the grave and haunt me. So I went to Montréal and started my career as a documentary filmmaker.

During that time, I met Métis filmmaker Ervin Chartrand, who remains a close friend. We both wanted to tell stories about people who didn't have a voice, especially kids.

That's where this project came along.

It was called "Live/Life from 95."

It was a co-production between the Winnipeg Arts Council and CBC Manitoba. Here's the art council's description of the project:

The WITH ART program matches artists with community groups to collaborate on art projects that explore ideas and issues and give voice to community. The filmmakers worked with the youth of the Immigrant and Refugee Community Organization of Manitoba to create a hip hop video and a documentary of the process.

IRCOM, located at 95 Ellen Street in downtown Winnipeg, is a transitional housing complex and delivers social and recreation programs to newly arrived refugees and immigrants to Canada. Over 250 new immigrants from Afghanistan, Bangladesh, Burma, Burundi, Congo, Ethiopia, Eritrea, Iraq, Iran, Korea, Liberia, Nigeria, the Philippines, Russia, Rwanda, Sierra Leone, Somalia and Sudan live at IRCOM and access their programs — over half of whom are under the age of 18. Navigating their new environment is challenging and some youth become vulnerable to gang-related activities. The goal was to offer opportunities for more productive activities and creative growth.

The artists, Jim Agapito and Ervin Chartrand, worked with the youth over an extended period and together developed a project that reflected an artistic style and content that was relevant to the youth. The filmmakers brought in Wab Kinew and Dammecia Hall who mentored the youth in hip hop writing and dance as well as other professional artists and craftspeople to create a high quality rap video and documentary of the process. The youth were able to decide what they wanted to communicate and in what fashion, making it a unique and personal, as well as a universal, expression of life in a new land.

This was filmed in 2007. One of the kids is Jamshaid Wahabi. The other is Dagmawit Fekede. We wanted to run an after-school filmmaking program. At this point, I had made a lot of music videos for some big-name clients across Canada. Lots of my work was featured on MuchMusic at the time.

Ervin had just come off of making a music video for our good friend Wab Kinew, the current leader of the Manitoba NDP. Wab was a rapper and wanted to teach the youth how to rap.

Newcomer gangs around the Immigrant and Refugee Centre of Manitoba, or IRCOM, were at war with Aboriginal gangs. As a former gangster, Ervin knew bridging his culture with the newcomer could help bring better understanding.

Here are two extreme opposites. Dagmawit was a girl who wanted to make a better future after leaving poverty in Africa. Jamshaid's father was killed in the war in Afghanistan. He was ostracized at school for not being able to speak the language well. He joined the African Mafia gang.

In the end, we were able to make the music video, and the kids were able to watch the video screened at the Mayor's Luncheon for the Arts. The city also played their video and documentary during moonlight movies at the Cube, which meant so much to these kids.

Dagmawit went on to get a full scholarship to Ryerson University. She studied journalism and went into the world of publishing. That was a success! She told me that our program taught her the possibilities of storytelling.

Jamshaid Wahabi was shot and killed outside the Citizen nightclub in November 2019. For years, Jamshaid tried to steer himself in the right. Every time he got out of jail, he asked if he could put me as a reference for jobs he was applying for. I said yes.

It just goes to show what kind of impact you can have on someone. While I'm not a teacher per se, I taught these kids. I have no idea what it's like to be a refugee, but I know what it's like to be poor and to struggle. I had a bond with these kids, so much so that they trusted me years later to help guide them with their futures. That's an example of the difference you can make in your students' lives.

While I was helping these kids with their lives, my own life was out of control. My addictions were getting the better of me. Because of drugs and alcohol, I put on a lot of weight. I had lost all connection to my family and my culture. I was in freefall. That's when I got into boxing and met Roland Vandal. He was a person affected by addictions and trauma. I made a documentary on him at the time that I was sorting out my own trauma and addictions.

His parents were alcoholics. He had been sexually abused by a boxing coach. His brother also abused him. He turned to gang life.

He had lived an extremely hard life. But you know who he thanked to get him to the other side? His school principal, Mr. Bodding.

Roland now spends his time giving back to the community. He's on the board of the Red Road Lodge, a shelter for men in downtown Winnipeg. He's running two foster homes and teaches boxing to many at-risk youth and champions at Stingers Boxing Club. I've been helping him with that for many years.

Roland got me clean and sober. After I finished shooting the documentary, I binged and ended up in the hospital. Roland convinced me to go to rehab and straighten my life out. As of this year I've been six years clean and sober.

But I'll say this: I've had a strange relationship with alcohol and drugs. I ended up in the hospital and my doctor told me to stop, or my body would start shutting down. Plus, it was bad for my mental health. I was a mess for a while. I was a high-functioning alcoholic and drug addict.

Lots of it stemmed from feeling like an outsider. I joined the punk rock / music scene because I wanted "family." For a long time, that puts you at odds with your culture. I felt like I wasn't "Filipino" enough for my family and Filipino friends. In reality, they always accepted me. It's something that I got over and I'm glad I can have a conversation about this now with my mom.

In my experience, Filipino culture doesn't talk about addictions or mental health issues, but they should. My family might not want to ever talk about it, but they know it's there and they've come to terms with it, and that's put my heart at ease.

So that's the road that led me to this podium today.

When people hear that I am a filmmaker, they say, "That's great! As a person of colour, you get so many opportunities presented to you and you're killing it." It feels like a backhanded compliment. I want people to understand that, despite my race and background, my work is just as good as anyone else's.

Yes, I want to give voices to many diverse cultures and people. But that entire argument fuelled the "me-against-the-world" argument. I was so convinced that I had to fit in that I forgot what it's like to be a Filipino living in Canada.

Because no matter how much I try to fit in, all I have to do is look in the mirror and see that I'm not like everyone else. I'm Filipino. I am BIPOC. I forgot the very essence of what it was to be BIPOC. My voice in the community matters. That disconnect to my culture fucked me up. I was constantly trying to be just Canadian. But I'm a Filipino-Canadian.

The road back to my Filipino culture has been the journey I've been on since I got sober.

My first stop was trying to understand what bakla (roughly translated into English as "gay") culture was through my friend, the talented photographer Ally Gonzalo.

Growing up, friends and family members from my community made fun of baklas. As a straight man, I wanted to educate myself about being a gay Filipino in a homophobic and racist society.

As a storyteller, my agenda is to give voice to people from diverse backgrounds. This was perfect. I knew a lot of people in my community would be prejudiced toward this film. Some would cite their religious beliefs, while others wouldn't want to talk about anything to do with sex.

Some of the people featured in this project were coming out to their families and friends for the first time. And what this project helped me do was start a path to discovering my own culture and identity.

At this time, I was teaching film at the University of Manitoba. I was an instructor. The fact that I was teaching filmmaking at a university blew my mind. I had been at the job for a decade. But when the pandemic hit, I lost my job and was forced to find work elsewhere.

That's where CBC came into play. Although I've made many documentaries for them in the past, I've never been a journalist working in the news department. I was also in a medium that was new to me: radio.

I had long been struggling with the fact that my lola, or grandma, called me a bad Filipino. Now, not only are Filipinos digging the show, but people from all backgrounds are telling me how much they relate to it. It's starting a dialogue, which means a lot, because I know I was the unlikeliest person to wave the flag of Filipino culture.

Recovering Filipino has had over a million listeners on CBC Radio One. It's been downloaded around the world thousands of times. It's the first time a Filipino host is hosting a show on Filipino culture on Canada's public broadcaster. It's brought my family and I closer, and it's made people from other cultures want to ask questions they might have been afraid to ask, both about Filipinos and their own cultures.

We live in a world where things have become so black and white, but it doesn't have to be that way. My podcast is a way to encourage people to embrace differences. It's also offering audiences — especially younger Filipino-Canadians, who may feel disconnected from their heritage — a history lesson.

And it's exactly what you teachers do for so many students. You give them important lessons. You get the opportunity to mould the minds of young people everywhere.

They'll spend more time with you than most people in their lives. So do me a huge favour: please teach your students how to empathize with people who are different from them — different for whatever reason.

I applaud all of you. You have one of the hardest jobs out there, but it's also, I think, the most rewarding. Thank you.

JENNILEE AUSTRIA-BONIFACIO

Seven Steps to Reuniting with Your Teenage Daughter

WELCOME TO THIS self-help guide for mothers reuniting with their teenage daughters!

My name is Ginette, and as a sixteen-year-old daughter of a Filipina caregiver in Canada, I'm definitely an expert in this subject. When I was three, Ma left me in Malolos, Bulacan and worked in Hong Kong and Taiwan before ending up in Waterloo, Ontario, where she finally sponsored me to be with her.

If you're wondering what to do when you finally reunite with your teenage daughter after thirteen years apart, let me show you in seven easy steps. There are multiple choice exercises in each section to test your knowledge. Don't forget to check your answers at the end!

Step One: Do Not Tell Me I'm Fat

When you met me in the airport, I was about to hug you for the first time in thirteen years, but you held me at arm's length and looked me up and down. "Oh my gulay! What happened?" you exclaimed, pinching my belly. "You're so fat!"

I could have said many things back: Why did you dye your hair an unnatural shade of black? Why do your eyebrows look like they were drawn on with cheap markers? Why are your lips so wrinkled and thin?

But instead, I just looked away with tears in my eyes as you led me toward the airport exit, shaking your head in disappointment.

Please select something else that you could have said to welcome me:

a. "You're finally here! How was your flight?"

b. "I'm so happy you're here! I love you so much!"

c. "You look so grown-up now! We have so much catching up to do!"

d. "I'm so proud of you for flying across the world all by yourself!"

e. All of the above.

After we got to your little house with the cupboards stocked with weird Canadian things like kale chips (chips made of salad?!?) and gluten-free cookies (what the heck is gluten?!?), I excitedly unzipped my carry-on to show you that I'd filled an entire suitcase with my favourite snack: boxes and boxes of Hello Panda.

"Look, Ma!" I exclaimed. "I brought the whole sari-sari store with me!"

You looked horrified. Zipping up my suitcase, you declared, "If I let you eat this Filipino junk, you'll get even fatter."

"I wasn't going to eat them all at once," I protested. "I didn't know if they sold Hello Panda in Canada and I —"

You shoved my suitcase into your closet. "No more snacks," you said, narrowing your eyes. I could feel you judging everything about me, from my thin black hair to my greasy brown face to my zit-covered cheeks to my soft stomach that spilled over my leggings. "Since you like this Hello Panda junk so much, you know what I'll call you? Panda."

My eyes filled with tears, and I wanted to argue that you could call me Ginette or Ginnie or Gin-Gin or Gigi but never-not-ever *Panda*, but before I could say anything, you pulled out your phone and video-called Mama-Lola in Bulacan.

Mama-Lola's old face filled up the screen and crinkled into a smile. "Is Gin-Gin there? How was her flight?"

I jostled for the camera. "Mama-Lola! It was so long and scary and —"

"Baby ko! How are you?"

"Ohmygosh, February in Canada is sooo cold and —"

You pushed me aside. "What did you do to my little girl? She's so much fatter than I was at her age!"

Mama-Lola laughed, showing the gaps in her teeth. "Hay naku, Gina! You were probably malnourished from your tired yayas. Remember how all of your nannies hated you? They said you were so maarte. I remember when the last one quit, she yelled, 'That Gina is the most dramatic girl I've ever seen!'"

"I wasn't maarte — I was opinionated!"

"That's the same thing, no?"

I tried to grab the phone but you held me back.

"Mama, I can't believe you let Ginette get this fat. You spoiled her!"

Before I could tell Mama-Lola how much I missed her, you hung up the phone.

Step Two: Accept That I Have Two Mothers

I was used to the kind of parent who always told me that I was special. Mama-Lola filled my world with a warm, unconditional love.

You were the exact opposite.

"Aren't you going to give me a house tour?" I asked, trying to lighten the mood.

"Don't fall down the stairs," you replied flatly. "You can't break any bones because you don't have your health card yet."

I thought you were joking, so I tried to hug you. "I love you too, Ma."

You backed away. "You smell like airplane. Go shower."

You went upstairs to your room and left me standing in the hallway alone. I didn't know where the shower was.

At this moment, there are so many other things you could have said. Please pick the best one:

    a.   "Thank you for the hug! I've been wanting to hug you for so long!"

    b.   "Let me show you around so you'll feel at home."

    c.   "Shower later! We have so much to talk about!"

    d.   "Let's call Mama-Lola again so you can actually talk to her."

    e.   All of the above.

After you left to work abroad, Mama-Lola put your graduation picture up in our bedroom and told me that I could talk to you whenever I wanted. But since I was just a three-year-old, that didn't make any sense to me. Why would I want to talk to a piece of paper when I could just turn around and talk to Mama-Lola instead?

We shared a bed up until the morning I left for Canada.

In Waterloo, as I lay in my strange new bedroom, I missed her body next to me, the smell of freshly cooked rice on her clothes, her warm breath in my hair as she snored. I missed how she would let me wear her loose cotton dusters to bed after I had a growth spurt and none of my clothes fit me anymore. I missed the way she made me a bedtime glass of Milo mixed with filtered hot water and extra powdered milk, just the way I liked it.

I missed everything about her.

She was my mother and grandmother rolled into one: Mama and Lola.

You were just a stranger.

Step Three: Do Not Constantly Tell Me I'm Lazy

During our first days together, you yelled at me all of the time. I left my clothes on the floor, my hair in the bathtub, my dishes in the sink, my bed unmade. At Mama-Lola's house, we always had maids to clean up after me. I never realized how messy I could be. "Linis, linis, linis! Clean up, clean up, clean up!" you'd yell.

I tried to make my bed, but since your Canadian blankets were so unbelievably thick, I had the hardest time folding them properly. Mama-Lola only used a cotton blanket that was so thin that it was practically tissue paper — nothing compared to these huge, heavy quilts that you bought at some local Mennonite market. Maybe you forgot. But you didn't have to yell at me and say, "Even a Mennonite baby could fold this better than you!"

"I don't even know what a Mennonite is!" I cried.

I could feel myself getting sad, and so I thought of one place that could cheer me up. "Can we go to the mall?" I suggested.

You kept doing the dishes. "Too busy. Working double shifts today."

I didn't want to stay alone in your freezing, empty house. "Can I come?" I asked.

You kissed your teeth. "While I'm gone, you can clean. Clean your room, the bathroom, and the kitchen. And when you're done, do it all over again because you didn't do it right the first time."

"But I don't know how to clean," I protested.

You angrily dropped a pan into the sink, splashing cooking oil and soapy water everywhere. "I just bought you the latest iPhone, didn't I? Look it up on YouTube!"

I wanted to make you proud of me, but I was so jet-lagged that, the minute you left, I fell asleep on the couch. I didn't wake up until you came home fifteen hours later.

You were so mad.

"Anak ng demonyo! Ang tamad mo! Hayop ka!"

"Ma?" I asked, rubbing my eyes. "You're home already?"

"It's already ten thirty!" you yelled, throwing your cracked imitation Louis Vuitton purse onto the floor. "You slept all day while I worked back-to-back caregiving and cleaning shifts so I can support you? You're so lazy! You really are a panda!"

"But Ma, I'm still jet-lagged, and my head really hurts, and —"

"Your head hurts? You didn't do anything but sleep all day and you're complaining that your head hurts?"

There are a few things you could have said instead of yelling at me. Please select the best option:

a. "That's true, there's a thirteen-hour time difference between Waterloo and the Philippines right now. No wonder you're jet-lagged! Here's some headache medicine."

b. "It's been so long since we've seen each other. Let's catch up; that's more important than cleaning."

c. "I didn't mean to yell at you. I just had a hard day at work. I'm so sorry."

d. "When you feel better, we'll clean together, and I'll show you how to do everything."

e. All of the above.

Ma, I really wanted to tell you about my boyfriend because I was feeling lost without him. All I could think about was how, on the day I was leaving, Janno showed up right as the driver loaded my suitcases into the van. He held my hand up until the last minute, saying, "Promise, Ginette! Promise you'll sponsor me so we can be together forever!" I sobbed so loudly that the annoyed driver yelled at Janno to go away before he ran him over.

I felt like half of my heart was missing and my entire world was falling apart

I wished I could've talked to you about finding my one true love and feeling lost without him. But instead, you pulled me off the couch and made me scrub your bathtub with a dented box of Arm & Hammer baking soda and your dirty old toothbrush.

Step Four: Understand That Going to a New School Is Difficult

It was a cold February morning when you brought me to school for the first time. I was shaking uncontrollably, but you thought it was because it was cold.

"It's only minus eight, Panda! Don't be so maarte!" you said, propelling me up the school steps.

You didn't even realize that I was shaking because I was so nervous for the English and math assessment — the most important test I had ever taken in my life.

When it was over, the guidance counsellor told us that I would be placed in grade ten.

My eyes welled up as I realized that I wouldn't be in grade eleven like I was back home. "Sir, are you sure?" I asked, watching him stuff my results into an envelope as you took the package with a strange look in your eyes.

I thought you were going to stand up for me, but instead, you just left the room, storming out into the empty hallway. "All of those years of private school, and this is the best you could do?" you demanded, your brown face turning bright red. "Ang tamad mo talaga, Panda! So lazy!"

When you saw that I was about to cry, you told me that you were late for work and left me standing in the hallway.

My first class was physical education. I was stunned when I looked at my batchmates: all long hair and long legs and long arms and perfect white skin and perfect white teeth. They looked like models while I looked like the short Filipino janitor mopping up sweat outside the change room who muttered to me, "Hoy Ineng — your batchmates are six-foot Russian and Ukrainian girls. Ehh, you'll be lucky if they even let you play." I stood at the far edge of the volleyball court and tried to be invisible.

But when the ball sailed across the gymnasium and came right toward me, one of the gorgeous blondes went rushing for it with her arm outstretched. She crashed into me, scraping the floor. "Oww, my elbow! OhmyGodwhatthehell!" Her hair was the colour of gold, and her skin was so pale it looked like she had never seen the sun. I had never been touched by someone so beautiful.

The gym teacher ran over. "Speak up when you're going for the ball!" he yelled at me. "Ya gotta call it! Say 'mine'! You can do that, can't you?"

"Sir, the new girl can't even speak English!" the blonde cried, rubbing her elbow.

I wanted to shout, "Yes I can!" but the words were frozen in my mouth. Back in Malolos, the teachers used to tell me I was good at English. But here in Waterloo, where I was already ugly and fat, suddenly, I was stupid, too.

I darted out of the gym and texted the only person I knew in this whole country:

Ma, I don't like my new school.

I didn't have to wait long for a reply.

Just study hard and don't be a crybaby, Panda.

I grabbed my things, threw myself through the school doors, and ran back to your house. When you finally came home, instead of asking, "How was your first day?" you saw me playing on my phone and demanded, "Why aren't you doing your homework?"

"I don't have any," I said, glad that I wasn't lying.

You snatched a slipper off the floor and threw it in my direction, narrowly missing my thigh. "Wow, Panda, you really are the most useless girl in all of Waterloo! Of course you have homework — you just started school!"

"I promise, I don't have any!" I cried.

Your face softened for a minute before it reverted back to its usual pinched state. "Then clean the bathtub again. You did a bad job earlier." You turned to tackle the pile of dishes that I had left all over the counter so that you could have the space to angrily chop a mountain of vegetables for pinakbet.

As I squatted barefoot in the tub with that soggy box of baking soda and your disgusting old toothbrush again, I thought of the text messages that you could have sent to me when I wrote, "Ma, I don't like my new school."

Here are some options for you to pick from:

a. "I know it's hard, but just do your best. I'm proud of you for trying."
b. "Everything will get better in time. Let's talk."
c. "I know change is hard. How can I make it easier for you?"
d. "What happened? Give me the name of the teacher I have to talk to."
e. All of the above.

Step Five: Do Not Dismiss My Depression and Anxiety

The next morning, I woke up as you came into my room to put my laundry away. Wrapped up in my thick Mennonite blankets, I confessed, "Ma, I feel sad all of the time. I don't want to go to school. I miss being back home. I don't even want to get out of bed anymore. I'm depressed and I have anxiety."

You yanked the quilts away and barked two words at me: "Get dressed."

We drove and drove until we reached a strange warehouse area in the middle of nowhere. I thought we were going shopping. But instead, you brought me to a weird basement church located below a knock-off designer furniture depot and shoved me into a room with a big, cluttered desk. A Filipino pastor came in, groaning and clutching his lower back as he sat across from me.

Rather than leave us alone to talk, you stood behind me with your hand firmly on my shoulder like you were trying to stop me from running away. "She says she's got depression and anxiety," you blurted out, as if I'd made it up just to make you mad.

"You can't be depressed," the pastor said, shaking his finger at me. He had a patchy moustache and he wore too much gel for the few dyed black hairs left on his head. His glasses were dirty with fingerprints, and his breath smelled like patis. "Do you know how difficult it was for your mother to bring you to Waterloo? How hard she worked to satisfy the caregiver program requirements, deal with the demands of her employers, and complete all of the tests and paperwork just to bring you here?"

You stood behind me and sniffed so quietly that I couldn't tell if you were getting emotional or if you just had allergies.

"But Pastor, I'm sad. I miss home. I don't want to get out of bed."

"But you're in Canada now."

"And I'm depressed."

"But you're reunited with your mother."

"Yes, and I'm depressed."

"And you say you have anxiety, too? How did you get that?" He looked at me like I'd caught a disease.

"I think it was triggered by culture shock."

"Ha?" He looked up at you and you let out a dramatic sigh.

"Pastor, she spends all of her time on her phone. That's where she learned how to talk like this." Squeezing my thick shoulder, you added, "She won't even lose weight."

The pastor's eyes lit up as he looked me up and down. "Your weight! Yes! This is why you're stricken with these diseases. As your pastor, I recommend that you pray to our Lord Jesus Christ before each meal. Pray that you will eat less and exercise more."

"I think I need a real counsellor," I muttered.

"This will end your depression and anxiety in Jesus's name," he declared. "Amen?"

"Amen," you said together.

THAT NIGHT, YOU turned on your karaoke machine to sing "May Bukas Pa" on repeat. It sounded like you were trying to be a Pinay Adele, but all your notes were flat. Maybe by singing it over and over, you were trying to tell me to have hope, that there would be a brighter tomorrow, that God would help me with my suffering — or maybe you were just practising your high notes. Either way, I didn't care. You couldn't even hear me crying because you were so damn loud. I put on the noise-cancelling headphones you'd given me and sobbed myself to sleep.

After being told that the answer to my depression and anxiety was portion control, exercise, and Jesus, I wasn't in the mood to hear you sing. At that moment, I really needed you to talk to me. Here are some things you could have said:

a. "These are some good solutions, but they're part of many things that you may need to feel better. Let's brainstorm some other strategies you might like to try."

b. "What are the things that make you sad in Waterloo? What do you miss about Malolos? Let's talk about it."

c. "I love you no matter what and I'm glad that you talked to me about your depression and anxiety. Tell me how I can help."

d. "Let's find you a professional counsellor."

e. All of the above.

Step Six: Do Not Take Away My Wi-Fi

As the days went by, I was spending less time talking to you and more time on my new Canadian phone. I was talking to Mama-Lola, calling her constantly so that I could feel like she was still part of my life. And after nine thirty (when you said I had to go to sleep even though it's almost impossible for any teenager to sleep at that time), I was talking to Janno.

When I called him on Valentine's Day, he kept asking when his plane ticket would be coming so we could finally be together again. "Ginette, where is it? I keep checking my email but it's not there. What's taking so long?" Janno demanded, the hurt in his voice piercing my heart.

"I don't have any money yet," I said, my voice a whisper so you wouldn't hear. "I'm not allowed to get a job. Mama said I need to focus on school first."

I could hear Janno slamming a door and storming outside, the sounds of the Malolos morning traffic almost drowning him out. "You don't care about us! If you keep disappointing me, I'm going to cheat on you, I swear. The girls at school keep asking me if I'm single now that you're gone. You can't expect me to wait forever!"

"But I thought you loved me!"

"Love has a time limit," he said. "I can only take so much long distance. I'll tell the girls that I'm still your boyfriend, but only if you send over my sponsorship papers and my plane ticket."

"But you know I can't do that!" I cried. I dropped my phone and clamped my mouth with my hands, but it was too late.

You burst into my room and started yelling.

"You're on the phone again? It's past bedtime! See, this is why you say you're depressed and can't get out of bed — because you're staying up so late!" You grabbed my phone, and I began babbling about love and heart break and sponsorships and money, but you couldn't understand a thing I said.

"Why do you always think you can cry and just get your way? Grow up, Panda!"

"But I'm — I'm —"

"Maldita! Bruha!" You stuffed my phone into your pocket. "I shouldn't have given you this. You'll get it back when I say you can."

"But I don't even want the phone!" I cried.

"You don't?" you sneered. "Is it because I bought you a new laptop, too? Then I'll take away your Internet. When you start going to bed at a better time, I'll give you the password. Like I keep telling you, when I was your age, I went to bed at nine thirty so I could wake up at five thirty every morning to study before school. I was a top student. When you get on this schedule, you'll get your phone and Internet back. Now go to bed!"

You went to your room.

I couldn't stop crying. I knew that I had to let Janno know what you'd done, or else he would think I was ignoring him and he would cheat on me on Valentine's Day and stop loving me forever, but I was too hysterical to explain. All I could do was burst into tears and yell, "I hate you, I hate you, I hate you!"

Honestly, I didn't mean it, but I just needed to scream. When I calmed down, I knocked on your door to apologize.

You never came out.

If you'd just opened your door, there were so many things you could have said to me. Please pick the best option:

a. "Was there a good reason why you were on your phone past bedtime?"
b. "Did something bad happen? Do you want to talk about it?"
c. "Rest is important for your health. What's a reasonable time for you to turn off your phone and sleep?"
d. "It's normal for you to miss your friends and family. It was hard for me when I first left home, too. Do you want to hear about my experience? It might help you with yours."
e. All of the above.

Step Seven: Don't Tell Me I'm Not as Perfect as You Are

When you take away your daughter's phone and Internet, thereby cutting off all her ties to her old life, her depression will probably get worse.

There are many things that you should not do at this time. Which do you think is most important?

a. Do not insist on continuing to call her "Panda" to remind her that she's fat and lazy.
b. Do not point out everything she needs to clean whenever she actually works up the will to leave her bedroom.
c. Do not call her school to tell them that she's a spoiled brat and that's why she's missing classes.
d. Do not call your friends and complain so loudly that she constantly hears you say that she's a disappointment to you.
e. All of the above.

When you had a day off, you finally took me out of the house. You drove to the Toronto Premium Outlets in Halton Hills. You said that we weren't going there to buy anything, and that it was just a way for me to get out of the house, but you didn't have to get mad at me every time I touched something.

"That's expensive! Put it back!"

"Mama, I'm just feeling the fabric. What's Tencel? It's so soft."

"You don't need that!"

"I didn't say I needed it. I just want to look at it."

I flipped over the price tag and we both gasped. "Things in Canada are so expensive!" we said at the exact same time, in the exact same way.

I looked at you and you looked at me. And we both smiled the exact same smile.

Together, we blew through the Tory Burch, Burberry, and Kate Spade outlet stores, dramatically gasping and laughing as we found more and more preposterously priced things that we would never buy.

It would have been a good day.

But when I got hungry, you said that we had to go back home to get

"But Mama, can't we just get some pizza?" I begged. "I don't want to go home yet. There's still so many more stores. I think the cheaper ones are on the side we haven't seen yet!"

"No, we have to go home. We have leftover tempeh and kale salad, remember?"

"But Waterloo is forty-five minutes away. And Mama, I want pizza."

"What, you don't like my healthy food? You want to get diabetes? Gout? Cholesterol? Ahh, I know — you want high blood? Grabe, I knew it! You want high blood so you can die early like your Lolo and your Papa did!"

"No, I just want to stay here and —" I stopped talking as my tears began to fall.

"You're going to throw a tantrum? You want to be like that kid?" You pointed your lips at a Filipina mother being attacked by her vicious little son at the Roots outlet store. She was trying to put a sweater on him, but he kept slapping her face and screaming. With her bruised cheeks and downturned eyes, the mother looked too exhausted to react.

"He was probably raised in Canada," you said, kissing your teeth. "No manners! Walang respeto!"

"Maybe he's just trying to figure out how to make his mama listen to him," I said, watching the boy throw himself onto the floor and kick his feet against the store windows as she desperately tried to zip up a red hoodie with a Canadian flag sewn across the chest. "What if he can't talk yet?"

"No excuses for bad behaviour. He's too big to not talk. Such a brat. It's not like how it was when I was younger. We knew how to obey our elders!"

I stopped on the other side of the store windows that shuddered with every blow.

"Is that why you left me with Mama-Lola, even though she told you to stay in the Philippines with me?" I blurted out. "Didn't you disobey her when she said that you shouldn't let me grow up without a parent?"

"My Papa and my husband both died in the year you were born. I was the only one left to support you and your Mama-Lola. What was I supposed to do?"

"I don't know, maybe listen to her and not leave?"

"You don't know anything about my options at the time."

"You wouldn't know the right option even if it was written out in front of you," I snapped back.

Grabbing me by the wrist, you pulled me away from the little boy who kicked his mama away again and again, screaming like the Canadian sweater burned his skin.

And when we got home, I shut myself into my room for the rest of the afternoon to write out these seven simple steps.

I need help, Ma. And I think you need help, too.

This self-help guide is over, but I want you to know that there is actually one step that, if you'd followed it before any of the others, Steps One to Seven would not have been necessary at all. Now doesn't that sound nice?

Step Zero: Don't Leave Me Behind

When I was a toddler and you decided to work abroad, did you know that it would be thirteen years until we saw each other again? I built my entire life without you. I had Mama-Lola, my kasambahay, my teachers, my boyfriend. I had so many people who made me feel loved and special. I know you wish that I was different, but honestly, I wish that you were different, too.

Now that I'm here, you're constantly disappointed that I didn't turn out more like you. But how could I do that when I don't know who you are? I know that you've worked hard to bring me here, to give me a nice house and a good school and the latest gadgets, but none of that means anything when I feel like you don't really hear what I have to say.

Now you've reached the end of Seven Steps to Reuniting with Your Teenage Daughter. In case you haven't figured it out already, the answer to every single exercise is e) All of the above. If you didn't circle e) every single time, read this guide again and again until you do. When you show me that you got a perfect score, I'll be proud to announce that you're truly ready to start building a relationship with your teenage daughter who ...

a. Wants to apologize and start all over again to build a better relationship with you.
b. Wants to spend more time with you to get to know your past and who you are.
c. Wants the Internet password and her phone back please please please.
d. Wants to post this online to help the millions of other Filipino parents and kids who are struggling just like us.
e. All of the above.

CHRISTINE AÑONUEVO

roots & routes

AS A CHILD born and raised in the Okanagan Valley, being Filipina felt very much like a performance. My parents would spend hours practising in the basement before dancing the tinikling at a community event. My mother is an excellent seamstress, which ensured that my sister and I were fashioned into handmade terno dresses before trekking down Main Street, waving to people in the annual Peachfest parade. Other instances of performing that come to mind include a stunning black-and-white photo of my Tita Chita, my father's eldest sister, participating in a Filipino fashion show in the west end of Vancouver in the late 1960s. It's a photo of her in a beautiful, hand-embroidered dress with elegant butterfly sleeves with her hair upswept, effortlessly holding a fan adorned with sampaguita flowers. These sorts of events shaped my earliest knowing of what it means to be Filipina. There were other material objects in the house I grew up in that gestured to me, reminding me of a motherland far away. There was the capiz shell chandelier in the southwest corner; a teak carabao figure whose horn I broke and fixed with Elmer's glue; baníg mats; baskets and hats made from bamboo, tilog grasses, and rattan.

I think about being Filipina as a tenderness rooted in one's tongue. My family and I did not live in an urban centre where Filipino foods were readily available at Asian stores. I remember my father bringing a box of mangoes home from Overwaitea, sniffing and smelling each one as if he had won the lottery. He tried taking the mango seeds and planting them in the backyard, but to his disappointment, nothing came up. To this day, my father still saves the tops of pineapples and plants them in the backyard. He never loses faith or hope that maybe one day the fruit of his childhood might make an appearance. While no tropical fruit trees exist in my parents' backyard, two Italian plum trees have been bearing fruit my entire life. For over four decades, my father has picked the plums and shared them with whoever came to visit. My mother dehydrates the fruit and makes plum chutney or plum fruit leather to give away to friends and family. I like to keep the seeds from the plums in a little jar by my writing desk. Those stone fruit seeds keep me grounded and connected to the place I was born, to the longevity of my father's ability to grow food, and are a reminder that seeds germinate nostalgia and connection. The seeds also represent the generative nature of my father's hands and heart in taking care of a small space that, year after year, continues to bear kamatis, upo, kalabasa, ampalaya, bawang, and many kinds of flowers. Only now do I reflect on how challenging it must have been for him to leave his home during Martial Law and to be uprooted from familiar food, tastes, and climates.

My tongue does not twist easily around Tagalog. My mother's first language is Pangasinan. My father's first language is Tagalog. My first language is English. My parents speak Tagalog at home but wanted me to be rooted in English. While I wish they had spoken one of their mother tongues to me while growing up, in this day and age you can take classes online. For most of the two-year pandemic, my Wednesday nights have been spent learning verb tenses, ligatures, monosyllabic roots, and those confusing markers ang/ng with other Filipinx in the diaspora searching for the sounds that connect them to the empty parts of themselves. Language is an expression of a world view, a way to share thoughts, feelings, and ideas. Part of me has always felt that something was missing because of this inability to convey myself in the sonics of language that surrounded me during my formative years. My mother's language is still largely inaccessible to me, although I did Google how to say "I love you" (Inaro taka). I have a son, a stepson, and two nieces, who mostly speak English. I try to teach them the Tagalog words that I know and search for age-appropriate bilingual books for them. I want them to learn more about the Philippines, the diversity of the islands, the many languages and dialects, the folklore, the colonial history, and of course, the food. I didn't learn anything, as there were no classes in primary, secondary, or post-secondary school about the Philippines. I don't begrudge my parents for wanting me to adapt and assimilate into the mainstream. They were learning themselves how to find their way as new arrivants. But losing that connection and relationship with my roots and habitually not seeing myself reflected in media, pop culture, literature, and textbooks had an impact on how I view myself in relation to others. Sometimes I was the only racialized person in a classroom, or in a piano or dance recital. This had a detrimental effect on my self-esteem causing stress, anxiety, and feelings of being an imposter. I try to find examples of pop culture, books, and movies with Filipino characters so that my nieces, son, and stepson can feel validated and proud of who they are.

My mother was one of the first Filipina women in Penticton in the 1960s. She worked at the Penticton Regional Hospital for over thirty years. Beyond her labour, she is an active volunteer, a lover of birds and orchids, a talented seamstress, and an avid reader. As a child, I have memories of my mother exchanging leche flan and lumpia for whole salmon from her friend on the Penticton Indian Reserve. On a recent trip back to Penticton, my mother and I visited the Penticton Library and Museum. The permanent collection at the museum has changed over the last few years, highlighting more Sylix, Okanagan, and Penticton Indian Band histories, languages, stories, and culture. My mother lamented the passing of her friend who used to give her salmon but saw her spirit in these initiatives to highlight more Sylix, Okanagan, and Penticton Indian Band ways of knowing and being.

When I was in junior high school, the book that made me dream about being a writer was a novel called *Slash* by Jeannette Armstrong. It is a powerful novel about the political realities of First Nations' ongoing struggle for recognition of rights and land claims. It was a story set in a place that I was connected to and published on the Penticton Indian Reserve. It was a novel that opened me up to learning and unlearning what I know. This novel and author taught me about the power of literature and made me aware of systemic issues that are at the forefront of contemporary current events in so-called Canada.

My youngest son is First Nations (Witsuwit'en, Gitxsan, Ts'msyen) and Filipino. He likes to call himself *Indipino*, a combination of the words Indigenous and Filipino. He attends a trilingual elementary school (English, Gitxsanimx, French), although English and French are the predominant languages, and he is learning how to read. As a mother, I try to infuse daily life with Tagalog words that I know and recipes passed down from my mother and father. I often wonder what life is like for him, navigating different world views and ways of knowing and being. I think back to my own childhood and formative years of existing in the interstitial spaces of unbelonging. Not quite Filipino enough due to my inability to converse in Tagalog, and never quite Western enough, despite a lifetime of "Oh, you speak English so well!" microaggressions.

I reside in Northern BC with my family and circle back to Penticton as often as I can to visit my aging parents, despite the fourteen-hour car drive. My father turned seventy-seven this year and my mother is in her early eighties. I try to time our visits to coincide with the blossoming of the plum flowers and when the stone fruit is falling off the branches. Climate change, wildfire threats, and inclement weather have become a reality that impacts our planned road trips. Each time I visit, I return to the place that moulded me, and my kinship roles shapeshift from daughter to caregiver, to mother, to Tita, to Ate, and back again to daughter. Three generations eating food from the backyard, conversing in English and stitched-together Tagalog, and spiralling through the histories of our memories of one another. I am nostalgic for the smell of ponderosa pine trees in the thick of the summer heat. I feel grateful for the time my parents, my sister, my nieces, my son, and my stepson can spend together as we braid time and geography: past, present, and future existing in each other's iterative and shared moments.

ISABELA PALANCA AUREUS

Finding Home

"BA'T MAPAIT 'TONG orange juice?" is my first thought as I sip my drink, served cool by the flight attendant. I drink this on the last leg of our family's trip to Toronto. It's Good Friday, April 2, 1999, and we're flying to our new home in Canada to be reunited with Papa. I miss the sweet hit of sugar and my tongue looks for the undissolved crystals of Eight O'Clock orange juice that aren't in this thick and pulpy beverage with a slightly bitter finish. Eight O'Clock was one of the tastes of our old home that I didn't realize I'd be leaving behind. I've been anticipating this day, this new home, for the last four years. I have said my goodbyes to the homes, family, and friends we left behind in San Juan and then in San Mateo. Mom and I have purged, packed, and unpacked for two major home moves in the last two years and this third one is the biggest yet. I can't wait to settle in. I wonder what home here and now will look like for the six of us. When we arrive in Toronto to the apartment that's waiting to be furnished, we discover that Papa has thought to put Sunny Delight in the fridge. It is sweet and tastes new and yet also familiar.

For our first Canadian breakfast the next day, there's something called kielbasa that he's sliced up and pan-fried, along with sunny side up eggs that had brown shells and some bagels warmed in the oven. It will be some time before we get our red Betty Crocker toaster oven, but we're not impatient. I'm excited to have an oven and look forward to making all the dishes I read about in the books I got from Tita Ditse in the States. Homemade cookies and coconut macaroons need an oven. Lasagna was only ever served at parties in houses that had working ovens or ranges. Maybe I'd even be able to make lasagna myself now. Our new Canadian breakfast doesn't seem too dissimilar to the ones we used to have, back in San Juan or — for the last two years before we moved to Toronto — in San Mateo, Isabela. Papa isn't too surprised that we drink coffee with our breakfast. Mom probably told him I did. That Jade and I do now. We're fourteen and fifteen, and we've been drinking milky, sugared coffee since we started high school two years ago in Isabela. Coffee's on the menu here for the four of us, except for the sips my little sisters, Bea and Tiny, the youngest in our family, will sneak even as they are teased, "*Huwag muna, hindi kayo tatangkad.*" I make the coffee in a Proctor Silex coffee maker, not too different from the one at Mama and Lolo's house in San Mateo. I won't need a lesson in how to use it.

Our first morning, we're awake at five thirty, incredibly jet-lagged and excited. We're sitting on the bare dark wood floor of our fourth-floor apartment at Park Vista Drive. There is a table and some stackable chairs in the dining area of the apartment. Our balcony faces out to the street and right at our sightline there's a big pine tree with a raccoon curled up in sleep. Papa goes out there to smoke and there's an ashtray on this small, round wooden table that I'll later figure out is a spool for cable or telephone wire. Years later, I'll fantasize about decorating a whole room around this spool, making a Guitar-brand matchbox bed with postage stamps blown up to poster size. I'll make everything human scale but cozy like it's for a little Disney mouse who's decorated its home in the walls of the house with found objects. My sisters and I are watching *Breakfast Television* while eating this new breakfast. I'm getting used to how to watch news TV here, suddenly caring about temperature and all the new numbers that factor into how we'll be dressing these days. Back home, *Alas Singko Y Medya* was on at breakfast in the same way MTB was on at lunch and TV *Patrol* was on at dinner, just in the background. I never used to have to check the TV for the weather before I went out. Now I do. Flurries, wind chill, feels like minus five. We have to care about that stuff now.

There's a Filipino store not too far from our apartment. It's three blocks north of Park Vista Drive, past Halsey, Chapman, and then Gower, on the west side of Dawes. It's on the same side of the street as the library where Mom will borrow *Shirley Temple* movies on VHS and where we will all get library cards, even Tiny who will write her name on a library card "Maritnee." I'm orienting myself to the way people give directions here. Eventually, I'll step into my new skill of learning and giving directions, or maybe as my Lolo will later say about me, it's because I'm never lost like his Tatang, "*di ka naliligaw kahit saan magawi.*" We're lucky to be living not too far from the Filipino store and have these tastes available to us within a short walk. We find out they have longanisa in Canada, twelve pieces of frozen sausage on a Styrofoam tray. It's only the sweet, red kind and it will be a few more years before I easily find Vigan (sounds like vegan but is definitely pork not vegan) and Lucban longanisa here. None of the garlicky Ilocano pork longanisa flavour that transports me to the yellow kitchen on Rizal Street or even to the early mornings in San Juan, when someone from the province came south with longanisa, frying it up for breakfast, the first task of their visit. Nothing like that, at least not for a while. No matter, we buy the longanisa, cooking a twelve-pack to split among the six of us, together again after two years apart. We can't forget the little bowls of Datu Puti white vinegar, seasoned with a little bit of cracked pepper. Oh yeah, Papa, we picked up eating with sawsawan at Mama and Lolo's house while we waited for our landing papers.

Nana Leony and Tata Ernie's shelves and freezers are stocked well. At Palma Food Mart, besides finding what becomes Mom's first job in Toronto, Mom and I will also find sardinas in cans, six-packs of pan de sal, Sky Flakes, and Sunflower Crackers. I'll miss the merienda of Nissin Butter Coconut biscuits and my younger sisters sometimes think about Iced Gems, V-Cut, and Cupp Keyk. We see they have kornik and we grab some of that to snack on with balsamic vinegar, Italo and not quite Iloco, but it will do, and we'll later learn it can stand in for mango sawsawan. We're a little homesick so we stock up — frozen daing na bangus, frozen siopao, frozen hopia, frozen malunggay, frozen sili leaves. Mom even brings home frozen dugo and frozen papait. She never used to make dinuguan and papaitan, but here she learns to make these dishes and we learn to crave them.

"*Mahal ng* Filipino groceries," we think as we can't help but convert dollars to pesos when we shop for our new favourites. We're buying flavoured Century Tuna for snacks, newly excited for tastes we would have ignored or taken for granted in the days and months before our big move. For a while, we are making and eating a cassava cake almost every week, thrilled that we can make our own kakanin with canned coconut milk. We don't have to work too hard to squeeze milk from kinayod na niyog and it's easy enough to cut open a bag of frozen grated cassava that's been QC'ed for export. You rarely find hard hairy bits of the tuber mixed in.

We still eat rice, cooked in the *kaldero* we packed in one of our ten *alis bayan* boxes. We were allowed twelve each on our departure and I had carefully documented the contents of each box. In the back of my Papemelroti brown paper diary, past the calendar pages where I recorded everyone's birthdays to remember to send birthday cards, I had written out an inventory of what we were bringing. Mostly, details about our thickest, heaviest clothes in preparation for the Canadian cold. There are five bulky comforters packed in there too — cotton fabric, polyester-cotton fill — a present to us that Lolo, Mama, and I made together in the weeks leading up to our departure. And because we were warned that everything was expensive, we came with *dahon ng* laurel, sewing kits, and a couple packets of safety pins ("*Dahil walang aspili sa* Canada."). There are no toys in the mix; eight-year-old Tiny said goodbye to her Barbies — leaving them as a goodbye present to our cousin Ien in San Mateo — and the three of us older girls had already left our toys in our old bedroom for our cousins Mishi, Sara, and Sammy in San Juan when we moved to the province two years before. There aren't many books; they would be too heavy anyway, so I had donated some to our school library as gifts, while the majority would stay at Mama and Lolo's house. A shiny new kaldero came with us because it is *the* pot for cooking rice. Is it steel? I assume it is and write that down too, in case Canadian Customs and Immigration officers ask us. (I am responsible for knowing what we packed and being able to answer correctly and truthfully.) When we arrive, nothing is confiscated. I don't think they even ask about our luggage, just whether we speak some English.

With the kaldero in play, my sisters and I can fight over whose turn it is again to *saing*. There is too much choice available on TV and no one wants to miss a thing with the few minutes it takes to cook rice. In those early days in our new home, we're distracted by episodes of *Full House* on TBS that we've never seen before, and we frequently crisp the bottom of a few pots of rice. It's no big deal — Mom and I don't mind tutong anyway. Once, in an attempt to rescue the rice, someone rushed to take the kaldero off the heat but then let it rest without a trivet on the laminate countertop. It left a three-inch burn that would be there until we move out of Park Vista.

We have three kinds of oil to cook with at home. Two are familiar: vegetable oil for breakfast food frying and *pang-guisa* for easy stir-fries. But olive oil is new to me. It smells light and clean, and I'm thrilled at the novelty of having a different kind of oil to cook with. I'm careful not to leave it on high heat, saving it for Canadian cooking.

We notice how easy it is to cook pasta here. Look at all the different noodles — rotini, penne, macaroni, bucatini, farfalle! We still buy mostly spaghetti, but sometimes we pick up fettuccine and I handily make an alfredo with Campbell's cream of mushroom soup, which is a pantry helper we also use to make seafood pasta. (Throw in some tuna flakes drained of the water or oil.) If we can make the effort, we bake tuna casserole in the brown glass Vision cookware we found in the giveaway section of our building's laundry room. We use that cookware for many years until we learn that it can shatter from exposure to high heat.

The smells of Filipino food linger longer in the apartment. To keep the smell down, we take to baking our longanisa over frying them so that we can use less oil. On Sundays, when we go to St. Catherine of Sienna on the Danforth, we probably bring the smells of our breakfast on our coats. When I cook Canadian food, I don't find the smell sticks as much. We learn to light candles throughout the house to help keep us smelling fresher and less like *ulam*. I wonder if we carry these smells to school with us.

During our first winter in Canada, I learn how to make vegetable soup. Asparagus is readily available here. It's tender, succulent, and each stalk looks fresh and crisp. I make a variation of the sopas we used to eat at school for merienda. I sauté asparagus and carrot with onion in olive oil, adding some vegetable stock, salt and pepper, and some herbs, then some 2 percent milk at the end for a lighter version of the soup pictured on the Knorr Cream of Asparagus packets we used to buy back home. I'm proud of my soup and I make it a couple more times for practice before I volunteer to contribute it as the starter for our first Canadian Christmas dinner. This year, we're going to celebrate with our extended family at the building next door where Papa's cousin Uncle Sean, his girlfriend Auntie Yolly, and their daughter, our little

cousin Julie, live. I make a concoction of Sunny D, peach juice, and Sprite —
a mocktail we invented that Papa says is good. I'm excited when Christmas
lets me showcase my cooking prowess, whereas Thanksgiving didn't because
we decided to order KFC. We ate fried chicken, coleslaw, macaroni, and gravy
with rice when we gathered at the little house on Denton Avenue where
Papa's sister, Tita Ann, her husband Tito Chris, and their young daughter,
our cousin Tina, lived.

In September 1999, Mom leaves Palma Food Mart. The job has let her
earn some pocket money. It doesn't add much but she shouldn't need to
work; Papa works at an animation studio at 401 Richmond. At Palma, Mom
works from nine to three. when she spies the school bus coming down from
Our Lady of Fatima on St. Clair. Bea and Tiny are latchkey kids for a few
minutes every day from the time they get off the bus to when Mom gets home
after a fifteen-minute walk. Palma is convenient for picking up ulam when
we don't feel like cooking, and it keeps Mom occupied while we are all at
school. On the referral of a new friend and armed with a resumé I typed on
Tita Ann's electronic word processor at the Denton house, Mom lands a job
at the Department of Chemistry, University of Toronto. She starts a career in
academic administration that gets her dreaming about our future education
at U of T, now that she has benefits and can get our tuition covered. It's a
given that we will all apply when the time comes. There's no doubt in Papa's
mind about it, so he is slightly offended when my grade eleven General Religion teacher suggests they encourage me to pursue post-secondary learning.
"*Siyempre*, you're going."

Mom gets me a casual job too. I feel productive being able to work and
go to school. After class at Notre Dame, I take the Bloor train westbound
to Spadina, then take the 519 streetcar to get off at Willcocks and walk to
the Lash Miller Chemical Lab. Mom usually has a snack waiting for me,
either leftovers from an occasional splurge at the food truck or more often a
selection of extra sandwiches from a catered faculty event or grad students'
lunch. My favourite is a tuna sandwich with avocado and alfalfa sprouts. I
love the crunch of alfalfa and the soft cream of avocado. There's a way to eat
avocado without adding sugar and milk! Mom's manager comments that it's
good I don't eat fast food and my mom contributes that I only eat fast food

once a month. It's a new rule I've given myself after too many McDonald's lunches after Sunday mass at Our Lady of Fatima or Burger King meals from the BK at Shoppers World Danforth. Not to mention how the dryer's been shrinking everyone's clothes lately.

I help with large mailings for the Faculty of Chemistry a couple of days a week after class at Notre Dame Catholic Secondary School and I imagine myself going to school here someday soon. When I return a few years later, I am already knowledgeable of the food trucks along St. George Street. I have had the occasional hot dog or sausage from the cart in front of Robarts Library. And I know I can be squared for those longer days on campus with lunch and a *kallong* if I split smoky beef ho fan or spicy ma po tofu on rice from the maroon truck in front of the Sid Smith building. In my second year of university, I pick up the habit of drinking sugary and milky orange pekoe tea during my evening shifts from six to nine in the basement of 21 King's College Circle. The other student tele-fundraisers and our supervisor teach me it's a good alternative to coffee. Free from the staff kitchen, the milky tea in a U of T mug, labelled with my name in Sharpie, goes well with sweet Timbits on those late and dark autumn and winter evenings we work to get pledges, raising funds for scholarships, bursaries, and capital projects at the university. I look forward to graduating.

IT'S 2005 AND I'm in my third year at U of T, but I've taken time off because I am having a hard time and I feel like I am going to fail out of school. I ask Mom to come with me to speak to the registrar, and then I discuss my options with her. I take a semester off, then come back in the summer and work hard to catch up. We live with Mom at Overbank Towers in Scarborough. Papa let us have Park Vista for a bit while he bounced around, then he moved back to the old apartment for a bit. These days, he lives northeast of us at a house on Kennedy. He's staying in someone's basement. It's easier if we make plans outside of the apartments, but sometimes we go see him and he cooks. The only dish I really remember him cooking is this chicken and potato stew that is yellow like curry but is coloured and flavoured by Dijon mustard. I eat it and tell him it tastes interesting. Sometimes we might meet him for a movie, or he bikes to Old Navy in the same plaza at Eglinton Town

Centre where I work part-time, and I use my discount to get him some St. Patrick's Day shirts. He meets up with us for phở at the next plaza over on Eglinton and Warden and talks about the first year we are apart. It was the year before he landed in Toronto for a visit with Tita Ann, when he tried to make it in Vancouver, living with my mom's Diego cousins, aunt, and uncle in Richmond. I know he couldn't find animation work in Vancouver, so he made his way back to Toronto. Eating Vietnamese food reminds him of his time working in Ho Chi Minh the year before he moved to Canada and two years before we are reunited.

My sisters and I are careful with our words when we say goodbye at Kennedy Station. It's hard on him and he gets sad if we say, "Get home safe." It sets him off and he says things like, "Home is where you and your mother are." We don't know how to answer, so we try to avoid the subject of Mom or home. We part ways when he takes the 43 Kennedy north to the basement apartment and we take the short, mostly walkable bus trip home, travelling west on the 34 Eglinton.

When I walk home from Kennedy Station, I usually make a stop at Soon Lee Supermarket on the southeast corner of Kennedy and Eglinton. It's where I pick up Lee Kum Kee sauces and other Asian groceries. My sisters and I help Mom cook. We learn to make pad thai, black bean sauced chicken or fish, teriyaki anything, and ma po tofu. On Sundays, after church at Maria Goretti, the four of us hit the No Frills on the northeast corner of Kennedy and Eglinton with Mom. It's there we pick up groceries — just what's on the list, Mom's on a budget. We make sure we pick up our new flatbread of choice for homemade pizza.

Mom's still at U of T, she's at 21 King's College Circle now, working as the Circulations and Advertising Manager for the *Bulletin*. She and I usually leave for school and work together. On the westbound train to St. George Station, we catch seats for the morning commute, long enough for a nap before my first class, while Mom closes her eyes and prays a rosary. We walk to the station to be on the platform before eight in the morning, which means everyone with an early morning has to move fast. We take turns in our one shower and quickly eat an early breakfast at home at the crowded pine IKEA kitchen table that doubles as extra counter space. Morning coffee is ready in our programmable coffee maker as long as someone presses the button the night before. Everyone drinks it these days, milky and sugary. Breakfast might be rice, a fried egg, and some other breakfast protein like ham, Mom's salmon fritters with patis dip, or Tomé sardines. Sometimes there's Vienna sausage, but I can't eat those anymore, not after babysitting Noelle, my best friend Mia's toddler, through a bad bout of a stomach bug and catching it from her afterward. Just like the coordinated way we get ready in the morning, there's more choreography to follow throughout our day, especially when we get back home. We fall in step and do our parts: defrost the protein for the day, saing in the rice cooker (remember to press the button), chop up the vegetables, cook the ulam, set the table, pray, eat, clear the table, wash the dishes, sweep up the kitchen and the dining room, wipe down the counters, program the coffee machine, close the kitchen, open it up if we're snacking while watching movies rented from Blockbuster or whatever show we're following on the WB channel.

Money's a little tight, so that Christmas, I'm in class three days a week, working retail two weekdays and the whole weekend. For extra cash, I pick up some Saturday night shifts at a club on Richmond Street, doing coat check with my best friend Mia. I keep it up for a few weeks just for the season since they need an extra girl. Every bit helps and I remind myself I won't need to keep up this frantic dance for long. On Saturday nights after a full day working at Yorkdale, I head back east to get home, drink a coffee, get ready for an evening shift at the club, drink another coffee before working four hours checking coats. I catch a ride with Mia to be home at three thirty, sleep 'til seven, wake up and grab a coffee and some breakfast, pack a lunch then help Mom sing at Maria Goretti. I leave after the final blessing, take two buses on Eglinton west and then a northbound train to make it for my ten thirty shift at Yorkdale, and I'm home by eight thirty or nine to eat dinner and wind down before the week starts again. It's tiring but I know when I graduate things will change. I'll sleep again and home will really be where I rest my head.

The next year, our family moves to the west end of Toronto to a house at McRoberts and Rogers Road. From this home, we're only one bus ride away from Yorkdale Mall where I still work part-time. Papa lives in the Philippines now. I'm one year away from graduating and I'm happy not to share Jade's room when she moves out to the east end of Toronto and I move back home after a few months living with the family I babysit for nearby on Glenholme.

Mom buys that McRoberts house with her brother Tito Manong, his wife Tita Blanca, and our cousin Ace. Bea and Tiny make the long commute east to Notre Dame. There's been at least one Palanca girl every year there for the last eight years and it ends with Tiny, who will graduate high school in 2009. Here in the west end, Tita B, Tito, and Mom mostly shop at B Trust. Tita Jack drives everyone. Eight years on from when we first arrived in Canada, there is more choice for what to buy. Plus, we eat inabraw and pinakbet more frequently these days with Tito and Tita in the kitchen.

In the last few years, cousins arrive to be reunited with their moms and are now living in the west end too, just nearby at Tita Jing's house on Glencairn and then later, the condo at Marlee. We find ourselves watching movies on demand in our basement as long as our schedules permit. A bunch of us have school and more of us have to work part-time jobs too. We order pizza and chicken wings, and we talk about how we used to eat Tito Raul's lechon manok. We say we'll all drink together too, but the cases of beers and coolers we buy gather dust, stacked by the washing machine. We're (almost) all together again; it's just the Julians, the youngest five cousins, who are left back home. Being together like this brings me back to summers at the house on Rizal Street, when my sisters and I have made the bus trip up from Manila and Ces, Tata, Ien, and Lex have been picked up from Bayombong to join Ace, Theo, Coco, and Weewong in San Mateo. It's nice to hang when we can make time, and these days, my weekends aren't as frantic as they used to be.

In the early days of living at McRoberts, we enjoy having Angel's Bakery within a five-minute walk from us. Picking up the crusty loaves of bread they bake fresh reminds me of the times I used to walk two minutes out of our gate and buy fresh baked pan de sal. The thin brown bag had "*Sampung piso, tostado*" written on it and was warmed by the bread inside. We make room for dessert all the time at McRoberts, and having our extended family around makes it feel like there's always something to celebrate, and it's fun to commemorate these days. One time we even come home with a white cake iced with a greeting of "Happy Wednesday."

"*Ana sida tayo? Ada ipagatang yo?*" It is a good habit we pick up calling the home phone to check in with any of the parents if anything else is needed for dinner that night. If one comes home early enough, the offer to stop off for a quick shop is appreciated. I'm always curious about what's for dinner and what to leave room for later in the day. What will I kallong when I come home from my closing shift at Yorkdale? Ace and I coordinate catching the 47 or the 29 if we're both working late. It's nice to have a brother to walk with when you have to do the dark walk home. Those times, I don't have to use the TTC Request Stop on the 161 to get off a block before the designated stop. Despite the *baon* available from the kitchen at home, there are options at the Yorkdale food court that I just can't pass up. There are discounted, end of day cucumber and avocado rolls at the Sushi and Bubble Tea kiosk close to Little Burgundy, where Ace works, and I still like a sweet milky tea, so I pick up hot taro milk tea with bubbles if I need the sugar rush. I eat a little bit of dinner when I get home.

On Sundays, after morning mass at St. Matthew, we might pick up freshly made cod fritters and some pasteis de natas on the walk home. Maybe that dessert is not quite the leche flan we know, the Portuguese flan is lighter and barely requires chewing. We have small treats from outside, but more frequently we eat what's cooked at home. "*May ulam na. Isu pay.*" Sometimes we can convince the parents to have pizza with us. Often though, Tito and Tita would rather cook. There's always food at home.

In 2008, it's just Mom, Bea, Tiny, and me at the McRoberts house. We shuffle rooms after Tito, Tita, and Ace move out to a triplex on Winston Park Boulevard. I help Mom with the house. I travel for work, and it's a whirlwind few weeks, setting up and striking down booths at trade shows, spending hours on my feet showing samples, making contacts, and taking orders. I live out of suitcases for trips to Edmonton, New York, Atlanta, Dallas, and Florida, but I'm done. In early spring, I quit my first job out of university, two months shy of a full year, but I feel overworked and underappreciated and very tired from my three-hour commute every day from the west end all the way east and north to the office and showroom at Pharmacy and Steeles. I pick up some retail shifts at Yorkdale and I look for a new job. Mama and Lolo are visiting from the Philippines to celebrate their fiftieth anniversary with us and they tell me the home improvement store that's opening just up the street from home is hiring. Mom is proud of my work at Kapisanan where I volunteer and I'm board chair and she tells me to keep volunteering. I'm happy to be doing this work and invite my sisters to volunteer with me and get connected to our culture and learn from other Filipino-Canadian youths we meet through the Centre and its community partner, Carlos Bulosan Theatre. Mom's only happy for us to be occupied, and anyway, she's confident I will find the right job soon. After a month of working retail again, I find myself interviewing for a copywriter position at a small advertising agency. Mom scores me that interview after she mentions my job search to someone who's placing an ad with her at the *Bulletin*. I start my new job in late spring and soon the four of us are moving to new choreography as we bump around that house, working, living, studying, not knowing the dance is about to change again.

That summer, I'm volunteering and associate producing a Toronto Fringe show out of Kapisanan called *Baggage* and I get to know one of the actors, Leon. I think he's serious because he always has his shoulders squared and I've only seen him in dramatic roles, until he plays a drag queen in this show and I take his dress home from rehearsal to get Mama's help fixing a ripped seam. He makes jokes about turon and ad libs a line about it in the play. We talk and I promise to make it for the closing night party. My sisters are volunteering with the show too and Bea helps me roll the plantain Mom buys for me because I have a migraine that morning. The show closes, cast and crew party, and the turon gets served. The weekend after, Leon sends me a message on Facebook with the subject line, "Sheetrock in Suburbia," to tell me about his time visiting with his parents in Mississauga and to ask me out.

We make plans; we go on dates. I like him. I start to stay out more. He lives in the Annex, so I'm there a lot to hang out, eat sushi late at night at New Generation, have beer and wings at Paupers, and on weekends, brunch at Dooney's. He jokes that he probably threw a jacket at me at the Fifth when I used to work coat check. I am in love, and I am home less and less. Sometimes I remember to call, often I don't. On weekdays, I take a cab home early in the mornings to catch breakfast with my mom and make lunch before I get ready for work. I get in arguments with Mom and my sisters for not being home and for not remembering to call. Eventually, I get better at calling again or maybe Mom just knows I'm only ever at work or I'm safe with Leon so we don't have to fight about it anymore. I don't check in as much.

I feel at home in Leon's red-walled apartment on Bloor Street. I get to know the little kitchen and find things in it even he never realized were there, like the crisper drawer in the fridge, or the baking trays stored in the warming drawer. I cook. One day, we both crave nilagang baka and we buy the wrong cut of beef. It takes five hours to tenderize the meat and we are starving when it finally is fit to eat. I move in the next summer and I get better at making meals on the one good burner in that kitchen. We shop for our ingredients at Oriental Harvest and the Metro on Bloor and I make adobo and pinakbet for a dinner party we have with friends at home. I make pasta with mussels when my best friend Mia comes over and we joke that it's the most muscles we've seen on the workout bench that doubles as our coffee and dinner table. I learn to cook lobster tails so they don't curl up into a ball and I make a levelled-up seafood pasta for one of my first New Year's Eves with Leon.

IT'S 2022 AND Leon and I live in the east end of Toronto, where we have been living for the last twelve years. We're a bit far from his family who are in Mississauga and Burlington, but we see them often. My sisters live in Rexdale and in the west end of Toronto. Mom lives five minutes away from us with Tito Manny, now that they've made their home in Toronto after some years in Baltimore.

Leon does most of our grocery shopping these days, taking the risk of being indoors with other people while we ride out the pandemic. He works from home mostly as well. I am on maternity leave, and I stay home with our baby, Anders Noel. Then Leon and I alternate kindergarten drop-offs and pick-ups for our older son, Leon Victor. We also trade off cooking for our family. Some of the things I make these days are lasagna, guinisang munggo, a slow cooker pork or chicken stew with tomato, cumin, star anise, cinnamon, dates, and root vegetables, pork chops, nilaga, baked oat fingers for baby-led weaning, vegetable soup, lumpiang Shanghai, roast beef with gravy, tofu kare kare with almond butter, my own version of Cantonese chow mein, and chili. Leon makes palabok, adobo, spaghetti, mushroom risotto, steaks, roast chicken, macaroni and cheese, and breakfasts of hot dog, sunny side up eggs, and rice. I can make my own versions of longanisa, one sweetened with maple syrup and another loaded with minced garlic. We leave dim sum, fancy pizza, Mediterranean, and Middle Eastern food to the experts. We attempt to make sushi. We work together to bake and decorate our son's fourth birthday cake, his request of "a black-and-white cake with pink icing and rainbow cheerios, and monsters on it." We make a home together.

GEMMA DERPO DALAYOAN

First Few Years in Winnipeg, Manitoba, as Immigrants Climbing the Educational Ladders in Canada

I WAS A mother of five young children when my husband Tony, an engineer, left for a job in Brazil in 1972. Our combined income was not enough to sustain and provide for our growing family. Raising the family in our town of Paniqui, Tarlac was a lonely existence for me and my children during those years. Tony was never able to visit us during those four and a half years, but it was a price we had to pay for our family's future.

Amid this loneliness came a letter from Tony in February 1976, telling us that he had applied for our family to come to Canada. The news was followed by hectic preparations for our immigration papers, which involved my frequent trips to the city of Manila.

Then one Saturday night, after feeding supper to our children, the phone rang. With my heart pounding, I picked up the phone. It was Tony, who said, "Ma, you should go to the Canadian Embassy to pick up your visas."

I jumped with joy as I thought of our family getting reunited and our children seeing their father for the first time in many years.

With my parents, siblings, and my in-laws around to send us off, we boarded the plane, our children wearing beautiful and well-tailored suits sewn by our neighbour. My father gave me a long necklace with a medallion of the Virgin Mary dangling from the chain. I knew that he and Mama had mixed emotions seeing me go abroad, yet they did not say a word. Mama was also quiet, just holding my hands as if comforting me as she noticed my mixed emotions of apprehension and sadness. I hugged them tightly. Maybe they heard the strong pounding of my heart due to my anxiety at leaving them and the country of my birth.

On October 12, 1976, we landed in Vancouver after a fourteen-hour flight from Manila. After a two-hour wait, we were on our way to Winnipeg.

The children were quiet on the plane when I finally heard the flight attendant announce: "We're landing in Winnipeg in twenty minutes." As the plane descended, overwhelming joy and amazement engulfed me as I looked outside the plane's window. Below was a vast expanse of land, sparsely spread houses, and neatly planted trees along the roadside. I saw two rivers joined like a fork. Later, I would find out this place was called the Forks, now a tourist spot. I breathed in the fresh air coming from the gaps of the window. My heart beat faster in anticipation of seeing my husband, whom our children and I missed so much. He had arrived in Winnipeg in February and was there to welcome us with his relatives and friends. Tony's cousins, Pacita Hidalgo and Demetria Nanali, were among those at the airport to meet us.

Tony had found work at Dominion Tanner and, after five months, became a machinist with Canadian Pacific Railway (CPR). I knew his salary would not be enough to sustain us and decided I needed to find a job soon to augment our income.

Back in the Philippines, I was a scholar at the University of the East, graduated with a Bachelor of Education in 1962, and earned a Bachelor of Arts, majoring in English, in 1975 at the Central Institute of Technology in Paniqui. When we arrived, however, I had no knowledge of the settlement processes and services of the immigration department of the Manitoba government, and I didn't know how to apply for jobs that matched my qualifications. I did not have a computer and did not attend orientation sessions given by the Canadian Embassy. I was solely dependent on relatives and friends to give us information on how we could successfully integrate in Manitoban society.

With my husband's low salary, I needed to work somewhere, though, and my friend Sylvia suggested that I apply for work as a garment worker. I had never touched an industrial machine before. But thinking of our survival needs and five children to feed, I applied at one of the sewing factories downtown. I was hired immediately; however, before noon I was already tired. I perspired as I pulled the heavy coats, which needed to be inserted flat, close to the needle, before I stepped on the sewing machine's pedal. At one point I felt so dizzy I threw up.

I told Tony I could not bear to be a garment worker. He agreed for me to stay home. I rested for a week. However, I was worried that Tony could not afford to single-handedly support all of us. Sylvia accompanied me again to Tan Jay on Notre Dame St., where I became a sewer of skirts. I found myself again struggling as I tried to sew even the simplest item correctly, such as the hem of a skirt. Unknown to me, I was being observed by a supervisor, who stood behind me. She approached and said, "You are not really a garment worker. I know you used to be a teacher, and I could easily detect it in the way you behaved." I wondered why she had said that. I found out later that some of the workers were gossiping and fighting among themselves. I refrained from getting involved.

One of the workers approached me, taunting me to talk to a Spanish-speaking co-worker to prove that I had been a teacher. So, I did.

"Como está usted?" I asked my fellow worker.

She replied, "Muy bien."

"Cuantas hijos o hijas tienes?"

"Dos hijas e dos hijos," she answered.

I said, "Muchas gracias." After that simple conversation we became fast friends.

In my letters, I never told my late father that I was a garment worker, or how we were adjusting to the challenges and difficulties as new immigrants. We knew that it was just a matter of time before we would know more about living in Canada, and that eventually we would be successful. We were already in a land of opportunity, a country that respects people regardless of their religious, economic, political, and social backgrounds.

A month after our arrival, I was surprised to find out that I was pregnant, but I continued to work. In wintertime, I would go home with achy muscles, so I told Tony that I wanted to quit as a garment worker.

This decision to quit proved to be a turning point in my life.

My husband had found a townhouse on 521 Magnus Avenue in front of William Whyte School, and we moved into the three-bedroom house in December 1976.

With five children and pregnant with our youngest, Jonato, I trembled at night every time I heard noises of drunk people in front of our house. Tony worked on night shifts, so I was the only adult left to attend to our children.

I continued to work as a garment worker at Tan Jay on Notre Dame when, one slippery day, heavy with a child, I slipped and fell while walking on the pavement going to the Eaton Place shopping centre. I was with Ludy, a co-worker and friend at Tan Jay, who helped me to get up. I got scared that I might have a miscarriage because that night, my lower back ached. Fortunately, the pain vanished the following morning.

Days went by, and on July 10, 1977, I delivered a baby boy, our youngest and sixth child. We named him Jonato, with the first syllable "Jo" taken from the first name of my father, Jose, and the last syllables "nato" from my father-in-law's name, Fortunato.

I again suffered loneliness at the hospital as I received no visitors, while my roommate, a Black woman, had lots of visitors. It was during these pangs of loneliness that my thoughts hearkened back to my hometown of Casiguran, Sorsogon, as I pined for my parents and wished that they could come to see our new baby.

After three days, my roommate left. Before leaving, she gave me the white flower vase with a single rose in it. I was so embarrassed; however, I accepted it. Maybe she felt sorry for me for not having at least a rose by my bedside.

In our conversations, I discovered that my roommate was a co-teacher of a Filipina — Lolita Oandasan — who was one of the first few teachers who had arrived in Winnipeg in 1965. Both taught at Polson Elementary School in East Kildonan.

I phoned Lolita later and she recruited me to be a member of the Manitoba Association of Filipino Teachers Inc. (MAFTI), an organization she had founded. Lolita encouraged me to attend MAFTI meetings and to have my credentials certified.

I was truly fortunate to be certified by just taking six credits hours of reading courses at the University of Manitoba during the summer of 1977.

I became active and committed to MAFTI, eventually becoming its president for three terms. My involvement with MAFTI honed my leadership skills, from meeting dignitaries to being invited as a panelist in conferences and giving presentations on methodologies in teaching English as a Second Language.

Our townhouse on 521 Magnus Avenue was right across from William Whyte School. I was naïve about the school system here in Winnipeg. Our friends told me that the children should get to know the culture here in Manitoba first before being sent to school. They should be taken out for field trips, to the malls, and driven around the city; in short, exposed to the Canadian environment. So, we kept our children at home 'til December.

In January, the principal of Strathcona School visited a friend of his who was our neighbour. He saw our three boys — Antonio Jr. and the identical twins, Fernando and Hernando — playing outside in the snow on our front yard. He asked them why they were not in school. They could not give an answer, so the principal went to his friend's house to inquire further. She told him we had five children not yet enrolled. The following morning, our neighbour came to convince me and Tony to enrol our children at Strathcona School on Burrows Street, which was four blocks away from our house. The principal phoned me too. Thus, I registered them the following day. Maria Estela, our four-year-old youngest daughter, became a nursery student. Maria Carmelita, our eldest daughter, became a grade four student. Antonio Jr. was in grade three. The twins, Fernando and Hernando, were grade one students.

Maria Carmelita, upon arrival from school, would tell me how she would drag Estela to walk faster to keep her from the cold, but being so small, she had mincing steps. Maybe her jacket was not warm enough too. Now I shudder at the thought of my youngest daughter suffering from those cold winters. We could not afford to buy them very thick coats of decent quality. I was not aware that there were agencies that could have helped us provide good clothing for our children. Our children studied at Strathcona School for the rest of the year.

Maria Carmelita turned nine years old in March of 1977; however, at an early age, she was a tremendous help in looking after her siblings. She would hang washed clothes in the backyard and wash the dishes. The twins were featured in a film by their teacher, Mrs. Pajonk, as aliens visiting Strathcona School. At the time, the Winnipeg School Division still had the film program. Tony and I were very appreciative of the twins' teachers, Mrs. Pajonk and Ms.

Rockwell, for the opportunity they had given to Fernando and Hernando. Our sons' portrayals as aliens in the film boosted their self-esteem, and they felt very welcomed. Also, the experience of being in a film must have inspired Fernando to take up filmmaking as a hobby. Aside from being a teacher, he now owns Blue Water Buffalo Productions and has made documentaries, one of which, *Manila Road*, won third prize in the Winnipeg Film Festival.

A month after giving birth to Jonato in July, an opportunity came in the form of a flyer in our mailbox. It said William Whyte was looking for a community teacher's assistant. William Whyte is a community school in the core area bounded by Salter and Powers streets.

I applied for the job.

In a room close to the kitchen, I faced a serious-looking panel of interviewers led by Mrs. Zimmerman, the vice-principal. One of the questions asked was, "If you're hired, would you transfer your children to our school?" I quickly responded, "Of course, because it's closer, and besides, we just live right across the street from this school." I was told to remain in my seat for a while, and Mrs. Zimmerman and members of the panel went to a separate room. My heart leaped with joy when she came out and announced, "You did well, Gemma. You are hired as a teacher's assistant, and you will start on Monday."

Living on Magnus Avenue from 1976 to 1983 was a blessing for us newly arrived immigrants. We enjoyed the privilege of living right across from the school. Having no fence, the school was open for children to wade in the wading pool, skate on the skating rink, play baseball in the schoolyard, and slide and swing on the playground equipment.

As well, a summer program was offered and was supervised by then community coordinator Anna Tynes and an area social worker, Greg Selinger. Greg later became the premier of Manitoba from 2009 to 2016.

One day, sporting a T-shirt and his hair in a ponytail, Greg knocked at our door and said, "Anna mentioned you to me to help us request from the school board to reinstate the Summer Enrichment Program, which has been cut back. Could you help us present a brief to the school board?"

I hesitated; I thought it would be a conflict of interest because, at the time, I was already working as a teacher's assistant at William Whyte. However,

Anna Tynes told me that I was also a parent of six children studying at William Whyte School. I relented, and on one evening, along with other William Whyte parents, I presented the brief to the trustees of the Winnipeg School Division and other parents in the audience. After I finished, the board did not raise any questions. Consequently, a motion was passed to reinstate the program. Our children benefited from this program as we did not have a car at that time. They joined field trips and other excursions that exposed them to diverse cultural experiences.

While in William Whyte, our children were highly active both academically and physically. Fernando became a fast track athlete and, at the end of grade six, got the highest academic award. Hernando won first prize in an art contest, so did Maria Estela. Antonio Jr. also became an outstanding basketball player. Jonato was a nursery student, and his teacher, Mrs. Sinclair, praised him for his exceptionally good vocabulary. He said to her one day, "Oh, the bubbles disappeared." She could not believe he knew the word "disappeared." His English was very formal as we did not use baby talk with him, but we spoke to him in adult language.

During the day, Tony babysat Jonato before he worked on night shifts at Canadian National Railway (CNR). When Tony slept, he would let Jonato lie face down on his tummy, holding him tightly so he would not fall. He taught Jonato nursery rhymes. On weekends, I also read nursery rhymes to our toddler. Before Jonato turned four, he had already memorized twenty poems. Tony would ask him to recite poems in front of his friends and relatives. They were so delighted, they would give Jonato a dollar for each poem recited.

During the late 70s, there were two Filipino TV programs in Winnipeg. One of them was hosted by Dante Buenaventura, founder of the Magdaragat Dance Troupe. Dante invited our children to join his group, and all of them except the eldest, Maria Carmelita, became members. Their being members of Magdaragat boosted their self-esteem and leadership skills.

Despite being certified as a teacher, I continued working as a teacher's assistant (TA) at William Whyte School 'til 1979. During this period, my friend Cory Juan, who was also a teacher's assistant at John M. King School, suggested that we both get our Bachelor of Education degrees from the University of Manitoba as part-time students.

When a vacancy occurred at John M. King School in May, Mr. Patterson, the principal, asked Cory to phone me to apply as a teacher's assistant. I thought the compliment that I had given Mr. Patterson when I met him previously impressed him, so he remembered me. I had told him that his school had well-behaved students and that the school was clean. Mr. Patterson hired me immediately as an English as a Second Language (ESL) teacher's assistant. (ESL is now called English as an Additional Language or EAL in one classroom.) However, he made the arrangement for me to be a substitute teacher.

The influx of immigrants from Southeast Asia propelled the opening of ESL classes in schools, especially in the Winnipeg School Division. Between 1979 and 1981, not many teachers trained to be ESL teachers, so school divisions were caught by surprise. Most of the students in 1979 came from southeast countries as refugees.

Although I had been a high school English teacher in the Philippines, I was not confident about teaching elementary ESL students. To be more efficient and effective as a teacher, I spent the entire day on Saturdays researching ESL methodologies at the Department of Education.

When the teacher I was substituting for moved out of the province, I was assigned to be a term teacher in 1981.

"I am now a teacher," I whispered happily and confidently as I opened my classroom door. A surge of pride filled me. But my happiness was tinted with pain and sorrow that night, when my eyes welled with tears as I remembered my Papa and Mama. I imagined myself on the phone saying to my father, "Papa, your dreams for me have been realized. I am now a teacher here in Canada! I did what you had always been telling me to do: to try my best and to work hard."

Being a permanent teacher spurred me to obtain more career opportunities and subsequently improve our economic lives in Canada. I became a three-time president of a prestigious association in Manitoba, the Manitoba Filipino Teacher's Association (MAFTI), where I currently still serve as adviser. I completed my Bachelor of Education at the University of Manitoba in 1983 and went on to get a Master of Education in 1990, again as a part-time student.

In 1994, I was appointed vice-principal of Victoria Albert School. A decade later, in 2004, I retired after serving as vice-principal in two more schools:

Sisler High School and Shaughnessy Park School in the Winnipeg School Division. I devoted my retirement years to serving the community in various associations, most particularly MAFTI. In 2019, I received the University of Manitoba Alumni Award for community service.

I have written four books: *First Filipino Immigrants in Manitoba*, published by the Manitoba Filipino Writers' Guild in 1997; *Understanding Filipino Seniors in Manitoba, Their Immigration, Settlement, Adjustment*, published by the Knights of Rizal in 2010; *gemma: The Bud*, a book of poetry (2020); and *Grammatically Yours, Gemma* (2021).

In my moments of reflection, I thank the Lord for giving me and our family a chance to be here in Canada, truly the "Land of Opportunity."

YVES LAMSON

Reliquary

THESE WORDS THAT you're reading, though flat on the page, are in fact in the shape of a time capsule. The things herein are tucked away for the future generations to see and hold a snapshot of the past, what it was like to live in my time, in this skin, with these experiences. What they do with these words, the memories shaped like the objects they're tied to, is up to them. I can only hope that they hold them with as much care as I have for the cultural inheritances left to me.

SEE THIS LOW seat made of wood, rectangular in shape. Its colour faded to deep grey like stone, signalling the strength imbued in the wood from years of use and love. Hold it in your hands. Now set it down. Sit. Feel the grain of the wood; the grooves are deep and filled with story. Notice how sturdy and level it is? The square, squat legs were salvaged from a sofa and fixed to a thick plank of teak.

My mother had trouble standing in the shower when she was heavy with me. To help her, my father built this seat, a place to sit while she showered. Mom never learned to swim so she never enjoyed tub bathing, and my father understood this.

After my birth, the seat found a new purpose as a stepping stool in the kitchen. Sometimes I'd sit on it and watch her cook or chat on the phone to her sister.

When I was five, we moved from the house in Scarborough to a farm in Stouffville. When we had settled in and my mom found time for baking again, my father transformed the relic into a kudkuran for her. He added a tail, forged from blackened steel and imported from the homeland, to one of its width-ends. I can still see my mother straddling the small beast, scraping out meat from inside coconut shells to make budbod to sprinkle on kutsinta and maja blanca.

SEE ME IN this photo, with rounded edges and checkered matte finish. The words "Winter — 1983" scrawled in my mother's cursive on the back.

I'm sitting in a snowbank, cradled by my mother. My mittened hands warm in red acrylic, I'm clutching a pale orange shovel in my left hand, raising it to the falling flakes, my lips curled into a howl. My snowsuit is blue, sinking into the sea of white fractals. See my mother, bundled up in a snowsuit, her hair in a bob cut. She's smiling at my father, winking behind the camera, her arm wrapped around me.

What was she thinking in those moments? Was she thinking how far she's come? Was she thinking about my future? Or was the present too urgent and fast? What did this sampaguita from Banca-Banca, the barrio named after the boats that carried our seafaring ancestors through the archipelago, know of snow and cold before she came? Had she heard no two snowflakes were the same? Did she wonder what I would come to know of this land?

HOLD THIS BROWN paper towel roll, white paper cut to triangles, rubber bands, and a sando. Ordinary things made extraordinary. Trust me. I'm telling you stories.

My parents were frugal. They often avoided purchases from department stores and instead hunted for sales at Bargain Harolds, BiWay, and Goodwill. All the while, those on the outside, looking in, labelled me spoiled. My parents poured their all into me, spending little on themselves. I had every He-Man I could wish for. I had monogrammed Yves Saint Laurent print bedsheets I thought were made special for me. I attended private schools. Still, I remember times when it had to be explained that we could not go get a new action figure or visit a drive-thru for a Happy Meal. Sometimes I'd complain, with petulance, and my dad would warn me, "Don't dabog." Two words said sternly, with threat looming behind them.

In these times between paydays, my father would rely on his storytelling to entertain me. These moments came to be my favourite — soft vignettes filled with narrative and play. He'd tell me about the boys getting circumcised by the river, how they'd jump into the water after the slice and stitch. He was one of them. He'd tell me about flying a kite with his older brother in low winds, how he'd make my uncle run with the spool in a futile attempt to leverage the kite into the sky. When it was clear the winds were insufficient for flight, he'd throw his hands up and yell, "You take it home!" stomping away in frustration. He'd tell me about the time he was dared to jump on the back of a carabao on his way to school, and how he rode the water buffalo for a few seconds before it threw him off. He'd tell me of the old man who let him take guava fruit from his tree, but drew the line when my father, a troublemaker, began cutting limbs from it trying to find the perfect Y shape to fashion a slingshot. He'd tell me about his older sister, my quiet and reserved tita, dunking his bullies' heads in the fetid street canal water outside their home in Cabanatuan.

He'd tell me about magic, monsters, history, and lore. His stories made me believe he was magic himself, that he could make anything, and make anything happen.

"Do you believe in magic?" he asked, as he cut up paper into triangles. With both his hands, he swept the triangles into a neat pile on the colourful baníg on the floor of our bedroom. Gathering all the small triangles into his hand, closing his fist tight, he handed me the cardboard tube, the sando pulled taut like a drumskin over one end, held in place by rubber bands. "Hold," he said, his hands cupped around mine as he poured the triangles in. Then he reached for his night shift flashlight on the dresser. Flicking it on, he put it under the clothed, closed end. Leaning over, his open eye spying into the tube, twisting it clockwise then counterclockwise. "Look," he said, tilting the tube to me. I peered in, one eye squinted as he had demonstrated. I saw a kaleidoscope of colours and shapes powered by imagination and my belief in him.

SEE THIS PHOTO of a library, tall shelves packed with books, small chairs and long desks between the resting tomes and novels. The children are sitting quietly in the chairs as the librarian, Ms. Heinz, hands out worksheets. I am six years old, wild curls, uncomfortable but sure. This is a class for gifted children, a supplementary portion of the school day where students nominated by their teachers and deemed exceptional through a series of tests were asked to participate.

Peek over my shoulder, I'm holding a worksheet. There are questions on it, asking us to write any answer we like. The first question reads: "What do you wish to be when you grow up?" I write, "A helicopter." The second question reads: "What is the name of your hometown?" I write, "Stoveville." The third question reads: "What city is your school in?" I write, "Scarboro." The fourth question reads: "What province do we live in?" I write, "Ontairio." The fifth question reads: "What was your favourite part of the summer? Write four full sentences or more." I proceed to write the bare minimum, purposely misspelling every word I can. I would continue to do this through the next few days until I was unceremoniously removed from the gifted program.

I did this because my friends treated me differently on the ball court at recess when gifted classes started. I did this because I already felt distant from all of the city kids, who had friendships with each other outside of school. I did this because I did not want to be in the different class. I already felt different.

SEE — NO, HOLD — this bylaw book for the township of Whitchurch-Stouffville. Feel its weight in your hands and leaf through its pages. See the annotations written in the margins? That's my father's handwriting. My father went to war with my hometown in '89. It started with a series of impotent siege attempts by our NIMBY neighbour, Terrence. Terrence was constantly harassing my father, calling him to meet on our joined driveway after work. He was jealous that my father had so many friends. Or maybe it wasn't green that shaded his heart, but something whiter, like prejudice. Each weekend, my father's friends would come over to the farm, hang out, drink all through the hot summer days, and reminisce about their lives back home. Sometimes — often — one of them would pass out in the tall grass, only to be woken by the chill of nightfall and high hum of mosquitos. At night, they'd tell stories in Tagalog around a fire, sharing food and drink and laughter. They'd talk about how much a night outdoors, by a fire, with the murmur and cooing of nesting hens settling in for the night, reminded them of their villages back home.

To accommodate larger animals like pigs and goats, my father decided to build an extension to the existing barn. With the help of his friends, it was finished in a handful of weekends.

A few days later, I saw my father speaking to Terry at our gate. I watched from our kitchen window before deciding to move outside, curious as to what was happening.

"Hi, Yves," he said, before continuing with my father. "That barn extension looks like shit. All cobbled together with wood and rusted roofing tin. You're decreasing the value of my property! You see how I keep my yard? It's beautiful and manicured. Look at our rose garden! Look at our grass! Then you look at your property. It's all tall grass, weeds, and junk cars."

"You see junk, Terry. I see things I can use to fix my car. You see tall grass and weeds. I see places for our hens to lay eggs and for our chicks to hide from hawks. I like what I see. If you don't, don't look over here." Terry walked away in frustration, throwing his hands in the air and cursing.

A few days later, a letter arrived from the township by courier. It was an order to attend a meeting. Terry had called the township to report my father, claiming that the barn extension was in violation of the bylaws.

At the meeting with bylaw officers and other officials of my hometown, my father sat and listened as they began reading off alleged violations from a book. Before they could finish, my father asked, "What are those books, and where did you get them?" They told him the books contained the town's bylaws and that he could purchase one from the township. Dad stood up and said, "Then this meeting is over until I get one of those books."

He left the township offices, tome in hand, walking back to the car where Mom and I waited. Hopping in the passenger seat, pulling the car door shut, he said, "I'll get these fuckers. You'll see." His brazen, devilish smile was broad, appearing closer and larger in the car's side-view mirror as I looked on from the back seat.

Days passed and each day he read the bylaw book as passionately as a seminary student would a Bible. He combed each passage for some hidden meaning, searching for an interpretation of the words that would allow him to find peace. Eventually, he found a path forward.

Our five acres are zoned agricultural while the flanking properties are zoned residential. This difference, along with a permit, allowed for the addition of our barn, which still stands today.

Over our gate I watched Dad put on a clinic. "I could've fucked you over, Terry," Dad said. "That pool you just put in? It can't be on the eastern side of your yard according to the bylaws. It's too close to my property line. That's a violation. There's also no fence around it with a locking gate to prevent my chickens from drowning if they crossed into your yard," he said wryly. "That's another violation. Also, that addition to your barn you put on a few years ago? That makes it too tall according to the bylaws. Another violation. I could've said something to the township and you'd have to fill that pool and tear down your barn, but I didn't. Why take away joy? That's not what life is about " He turned to me. "Life is about not getting fucked over, son."

SEE THIS PHOTO, snapped vertically. This was taken before I was born. The solo figure in the photo is my mother. She's standing high atop the Scarborough Bluffs, her back to the water and sky. The trees at both her sides, their limbs touching above her. She's smiling, her body quarter turned to the camera, hands hanging at her side. She's wearing a simple dress of dark red. The heel of her forward foot is raised slightly, pulling the hem just above her knee. My mother is beautiful and strong.

Pull back. The photo is in the centre of the Bristol board, hand-drawn lines emanating from it with important dates and facts from her history.

This was an assignment from grade nine. We were asked to give a personal history of a hero in our family. I chose her.

She was the first of her family to leave the Philippines for Canada. She bought the home that provided her siblings with a roof over their heads and a starting point for the next phase of their lives.

She was the one who, as a result of a severe asthma attack, lived in a coma for weeks. I remember a Thanksgiving years ago when my mother sat around a table with her nieces. My cousins were young mothers then, discussing the rearing of children and the uncertainties that they felt. They were looking to her for advice. She told them about her time in stasis, how dark and lonely it was. There was only one constant in that time, the thought that I was still young and needed her. That was the invisible tether that had led her back to me. She said that each of them, too, had that bond with their children. All they needed was to remember that. Mothers are the ones who make the Fates genuflect, make them change their plans. She forced them to bend for me.

For months the assignment hung on the wall of my history class. After the semester ended and we returned from Christmas break, I went to Mr. Gallagher's class to retrieve it.

"I told all the students on the first day that anything left behind at the beginning of winter break would be thrown out," he said unapologetically while at the blackboard, scrawling something for incoming students to read. This had been my favourite picture of my mother, the only print I had. The negative developed and lost years ago.

In a moment of desperation, I ran out to check the school dumpsters. It was never possible that it would still be there, but I had to try. I never found it.

How could this man look at this photo, read the history of this woman, know the hardships she experienced, then shrug and throw it out?

HERE, TIE ONE end of this thick, knotted rigging rope around your waist. I'll help you. My father taught me good knots. Feel its coarseness and see the twisted natural fibre it's comprised of. Dad purchased this at a garage sale. On the farm we've used it for many purposes: to saddle break our spirited hackney, Bagga, that I rode. To tow cars we cannibalized for parts to the back of our property. To lead trees away from the house to fell them safely. To anchor myself to Dad.

In the winter of '97, there was an awful windstorm that pulled sheets of roofing tin off of the barn, rolling them about the yard like loose-leaf. Some sections of tin clung to the roof by a few sturdy nails, and the wind turned them over like book pages, slamming them back down with eerie finality. A winter storm was coming, and my father and I rushed to repair things before the burying blizzard arrived. The side of the roof stood at a sixty-degree angle with a height of eleven feet. Having collected all the sections of tin, we waited for the winds to die down. The quickest and only way to secure the sheets to the roof was for one of us to hang over its edge. I was the lighter of us two, so we determined it should be me. Out of this rope, my father wove a harness to slip my legs into. The other end he criss-crossed around his torso, his body an anchor for me in case I fell. Coiling the slack around his arms, he was the hoist to bring me back up.

Swinging my legs over the peak, nails in my pocket and hammer in one hand, I slowly made my way down. Between lulls in the bluster, we worked like this, and when the work was done, he hoisted me back up over the peak. We lay there on the roof, looking at the grey sky, panting with exhaustion as the snow started to fall.

NOW, SEE THIS pendant. Careful. Don't drop it. A delicate gold crucifix, with four small diamonds stacked on top of each other, two additional diamonds flanking the second from the top.

"My mother gave it to me when I started high school, and it's time for you to have it. I've worn it all the days since then, only taking it off a few times," Mom said as she gave it to me in the days leading up to my first day of high school. This pendant is an heirloom, its true meaning hiding behind an entire belief system. As a child, my father worked this pendant into stories he told me before bed. He'd look at my mother, gesturing to her pendant, and tell me that the diamonds came from the sea. As a young adult, when pensive or stressed, I used to put it in my mouth. I could taste the soothing salt of the Pacific.

When I was in university, I began writing a story about my mother. I was under pressure to write the centrepiece for a portfolio that would be used as part of my application to enter creative writing as a major. Only one hundred students had been selected to enrol in the introductory class. From those one hundred, only twenty would proceed to the major. My work to this point had been experimental and awful. I was a nascent trying to harness fire. Out of fear and what felt like a last-ditch effort, I instinctively turned to the stories that I had heard as a child. I was unknowingly writing what would become the beginnings of my first book. It was a short story titled "Water Whisperer." Priscila Uppal, our professor, had us pair off to discuss our stories.

I was working with a young man named Dan, who always wore a wool beanie. We talked about sentence structure, dialogue, and pacing. We talked about imagery, authorial intent, and character motivations. We talked about motif, metaphor, and anachronism. We talked about symbols. And as our time drew to a close, he hesitated to tell me something.

"What is it, man? Just spit it out."

"Well, I see you're wearing a cross," he said, gesturing to my pendant. "I don't want to offend you."

"I wear it for my own reasons, not because I'm religious. My religion is more Ctrl-X, Ctrl-V," I said.

What I went on to explain is that I was raised Roman Catholic, but I was never a fervent believer whose hands burned when I prayed. Through my life, sharing stories with others, I've found beliefs outside of Catholicism that mesh better with my core — my very own cut-and-paste religion is still a work in progress.

He nodded, saying, "Gotcha. I understand." But he didn't actually understand me, and that wasn't his fault. I was doing what I always did back then. I said something clever to put him off the scent so that I wouldn't have to show him how uncertain and uncomfortable I was with reaching back into my history for stories. I felt shame doing that, felt that I had no right to these stories. I only knew them third-hand, and maybe I was not Filipino enough to wield them. I was bifurcated; though I held the stories close to my heart, I felt removed from them because I did not think that they belonged to me. It's taken me years to feel that they are a part of me, that their value and inherent strength make up a large part of who I am.

Too often in youth I shied away from putting my heritage at the forefront of my writing and identity. The stories were important to me, but in that way that keepsakes from childhood are — never meant to be played with, just stored away for sentiment's sake. Having never seen anyone like me or the things I knew of being Filipino portrayed in mass media, I was afraid I'd be made fun of. Though it's true Canada is a mosaic of cultures, there was always a deep-seated longing in me to belong. I also did not feel Filipino enough to take up the mantle of storyteller. I assumed that someone who spoke the language fluently, someone who lived in the Philippines, was surely better positioned and more knowledgeable than me. But also, who was I to write Canadian fiction, when much of the Canadiana I read at the post-secondary level was written by white men and women? I was of both, yet belonged to neither — how could I have a voice in either land?

If I told Dan that as a child I used to wander the forest behind my home while imagining the motivations the aswang might have for eating babies in utero, what would he think? If I told him the stones in the pendant came from the sea, how they were once made of one stone and came to be lodged in my great-grandmother's spine, what would he say? If I told him about tikbalang and Mariang Makiling, and Berberoka, and kapre, and dwende, and manananggal — if I told him all the stories that hid behind the broad symbol that hung from my chain, then he'd see me in a way I wasn't yet able to see myself.

Dan only saw the symbol, the cross, not how the minerals break invisible white light, revealing an entire spectrum of colours. He could not see the refracted shades of light my heart swam in behind the half-inch pendant. This was my fault, not his.

HOLD THIS BLUE book in your hands. See the figures on the cover, four women in water, sampaguitas in their hair. Flip it over. This is the first of my books, and this particular copy is the first of all the physical copies — the prototype, the proof. I can tell this one from the thousands out there because the blurb on the back is left-aligned, not fill-justified. I made this. I wrote this. But I wasn't alone in doing so — I could not have created this in a vacuum. The women within those pages, though embellished and modified, are the women of my family. I am descended from an ancestral lineage of warrior women, healers with infinite care, patience, and wisdom. I have their fire in my chest and their stories under my tongue.

There is a spike on my wall back home in Stouffville driven into the wall, deep in the stud. It used to be a push pin that held up rejection letters like participation ribbons for my failed attempts at finding a publisher to print my book. Over time the collection outgrew the push pin. Those letters were boulders set in my path, another obstacle preventing me from telling the stories I loved. I buried them, repurposed them, turned them into stepping stones toward self-publishing.

This book reminds me that dreams and wishes do nothing neatly tucked under the mattress or locked away in a drawer. It reminds me that every year is the year of the long shot, that a failure earned is better than one handed to me. This book is a symbol, a touchstone, a turning point. This book is a key that opened up my life. This book is a love letter.

THESE OBJECTS AND photographs I've shared, they remind me who I am and where I've been. These treasures are landmarks, constellations, points of reference that help me see the path forward through the unmapped landscape ahead.

I hold them close.

I take them with me.

Forward.

REMILYN "FELIX" POLICARPIO

Over the Grave and Back Again

February 8, 2022

Venancio Faundo, my grandfather, passed away on January 26, 2022. I began thinking and writing about this entry during his funeral. He was eighty years old, with an infectious laugh. Venancio will be remembered as a Knight of Rizal and a Knight of Columbus, a handyman, an electrician, a spiritual soul, and an award-winning gardener.

To be totally transparent, my writing is going to focus on death. However, I would like to stress that I want to focus on the macabre in order to recognize how it affects our lives. This fascination is nothing new. It would have, probably, been the case regardless of my current circumstance. It is odd to be back in my parents' home after so long. My visit was due to my maternal grandfather's passing. The trip had been planned and then moved upward due to his worsening condition. Now, death is something at the forefront of my thoughts more commonly than most. Perhaps this had to do with its constant presence in my life.

My grandfather's daughter, my Ninang Winavee, or Wing, died in 2004. I knew that something terrible had happened to her in the past, as I was growing up. There was a vertical divot in the back of her neck, something I scarcely saw as it had been usually hidden under her long brown-black hair. It was a scar leftover from a tumor. The procedure had left her unable to turn her head. This was a specifically tragic thing, as she was once an archer. Now unable to move her neck, the bow and arrows stayed in the backyard, never to fly again.

This had occurred before I could remember. She had always been that way in my mind, and that disease lived in the past where it couldn't hurt us.

Ninang Winavee was one of my best friends. One of my favourite places to be was sitting with her and watching her play video games. She would let me run around in these worlds all I wanted, aimlessly. She could see the joy in my silly ways and would encourage me. We would watch anime together or play with toys. She would often get McDonald's Happy Meals, even as an adult. A collection of these (particularly the *Mulan* set, of which she was particularly fond) sat in her closet on some shelves.

This closet was built by my grandfather. There was a light inside of it, and to me it seemed like a magical place. All of her little effects and her clothes. Toys I wasn't allowed to touch. Of course, my little imagination ran wild, as imaginations often do.

Unfortunately, the past often comes back to haunt us. One night, she had gotten up for a glass of water. My grandmother found her on the floor of her bedroom. She was hospitalized immediately. Ninang Wing had been in the choir — they came to her room and would sing her songs. I would sit with her sometimes, hoping that maybe she would be awake and aware to see me. Regardless, the hospital waiting room was where we would do homework and play on our Game Boys. The gloom was interspaced by moments of levity.

Papa Ven would often give us pocket change. Two of my three siblings and I would get snacks from the vending machine, the fourth far too little for anything of that sort. The whirring of machinery was interspersed by Hillsong and the family supporting one another. It was there we would pray, as well as in church.

When she passed, I met Death. I had seen it before, of course. On the television, and in stories, but mostly in nature. This, of course, now strikes me as unsurprising as death and nature are often hand in hand. It was usually manifested in smaller creatures. Goldfish in an aquarium at Papa's house, for example. I had experienced the dirge of the toilet bowl flushing for not one, but at least four "Goldies," one of which notoriously too large for The Flush. This Goldy had taken up its post-mortem residence in the freezer, where even at my grandfather's passing, my mother joked it could still be there among the leftovers.

Of course, with meeting Death, you also come in contact with Death

Aversion. Something that, once I was given a name for it much later in life, I was able to identify everywhere. There is the way that people react to it in more obvious ways, like using euphemisms. Cameras panning away in movies or TV shows, the way some even refuse to acknowledge its existence.

This aversion can be found in myself as well. Then, part of it was a lack of understanding. At Ninang Wing's wake, I was convinced I had heard snoring. That maybe, possibly, the doctors had made a mistake and she wasn't dead. She had one foot in the grave for months, after all. I grew used to holding her hand, trying not to be caught in the horror of the situation. Instead, focusing on when her hair would grow back instead of about how they shaved her head, those wavy locks I knew shorn away. Trying not to think about how much weight she lost, or about the hole in her neck that they made for the tube that had pumped food directly into her stomach. No, it was time to think about how nice it would be to hear her voice again, about how I would love to see her sit up again, or even open her eyes.

On her passing, we built a bear. To be more specific, two bears — twins. A matching pair of them, one to go with her, and the other to stay with my grandmother, Mama Winnie. They were both named Angel. Equipped with the suitable fixings, of course. This included more traditional things — the golden wings, a white gown, and a shining halo. We also insisted on a pair of binoculars so that she could see us from heaven. The most wonderful and most personal touch was the little voice box. When squeezed, the little brown bear would speak in our little voices.

"We love you, Ninang!"

She looked, if anything, more alive in the casket. The desairologist, the funeral cosmetologist, had done their job well. This is something I would later learn is not the norm. As a person of colour, a bad final makeup job can leave the deceased looking like an entirely different person.

And so, convinced that necromancy was real, I ran into my mother's arms and told her that Ninang must be sleeping. Of course, this was a child's fantasy. Mom cried, holding me and explaining to me. I continued to do what I had gotten used to doing: holding her hand, kneeling by the casket in my dress, feeling her fingers for the last time.

It was a frigid coldness that would sit in my heart.

Reality hit when they interred the body. The grave had been dug, and one by one my family members placed a flower on the vault. After the prayers, the body began to lower into the grave. As it did, my uncle and my father stood on two sides of the hole. My siblings and I were called to their side. One by one, we were lifted up over Ninang's body. The flowers, placed atop the cross made with the pallbearer's gloves, sat on the case. She was being lowered into the cold ground, and for a moment, I was above it.

I now know that this is a Filipino tradition. At my age, it was actually rather late for me to partake in it. Usually, the practice is reserved for toddlers or babies. It is believed that passing the children over the grave will encourage a good visit from their deceased loved one. This was something that I had, perhaps, fallen for. I remember being convinced that I could feel her angel tucking me into bed at night, even sleeping on one side of the bed to make room. Once, at recess, I told my teacher that her spirit felt "like starlight."

When telling people about this memory, sometimes they react with horror. The idea of being suspended over a coffin is so viscerally abhorrent to them, that it's really all they can do. In fact, while conversing with the parents of the children I educate, I was told in some families they wouldn't even bring children to funerals. It is understandable how the idea of confronting your loved one's grave directly could be traumatizing. However, I see it as a gift. It was a way to participate — being lifted up that way was always fun. More profoundly, it was a way to say goodbye. In a way, I was there until the very end. Being suspended in the air over her, I looked down and said my final farewells.

It is a powerful metaphor as well. The remaining adults of the family physically carry the children over the tragedy. The arms of the strong, the ties of the living, allow us to look at death and know we will always have a place in the cycle created. For the deceased, it is a promise that we will always be remembered. For the living, it is a promise that the adults will be strong and persevere.

Growing up, I continued my dance with the macabre. Obviously, part of it had to manifest in a Hot Topic scene kid way. My Chemical Romance blared in headphones on the swings. Teenagehood came and went, but I kept my grim examinations. If it had anything to do with ghosts, ghouls, vampires, or Halloween, I was all over it. This would bloom into a desire to be a Death

Counsellor, maybe even a Death Doula, and a need to be Death Positive. To face it, prepare for it, and embrace Death as a part of Life.

A funeral was what brought me to my family in California. Through my great-grandmother Pura's death, I learned about my heritage. Apparently, she had owned a bra factory and made sure to hire women to help her local community. I met relatives I hadn't seen since my infancy. They took one look at me and knew I was Queer. The Pedagats welcomed me with open arms and waited for me to be comfortable enough to tell them about my identity. We lit up the town, going to a gay bar for the first time with my titos and tita. I came into my adolescence in the shadow of grief. The feeling of community was incredible.

By this time, I had been to quite a few funerals. These included my Tito Martin, another victim of cancer. He, too, joined the ancestors very young. His wife's father had passed away right before this loss, in the same year. He was my Ninong Umby, a lover of music. This was the first wake I played my violin at. The song was "Yellow" by Coldplay. My father and I stood in a little alcove, practising until the last second in the funeral home. I remember being a mess, hands shaking, sweating, convinced the notes were sour. Years later, I would be assured that nobody noticed.

After I moved away, I attended my first funeral via virtual means. It was the death of a sweet old lady. Our family made friends with her at a local dog park. Her husband would build picnic tables for people to sit at, painting them the most wonderful colours. This included a Pride bench, and I greatly appreciated it. My youngest sister would lie on one of them with a gigantic Great Dane. I would play ocarina for Carol and her husband while our dogs all played together. I said goodbye to her through a screen, not knowing that the practice would become widespread in a number of years.

This continues into adulthood. I was always fascinated by encyclopedias and their scientific illustrations. In my artistic ambitions, bones are a regular subject of mine. Although they're usually connected with death, they're only created by living things. Bones are the scaffold, minerals given energy and structure by a beating heart.

When I graduated from high school, my journeys brought me from Mississauga to Ottawa. I was hours away, alone for most of the year. This was something that I had, admittedly, craved. It was difficult to express myself at times, especially when I decided to make my gender transition.

The distance was something I believed I needed. In Ottawa, I accomplished a lot. Over the years I educated many children, began my hormone therapy, and came into my own. It was not without a price, of course. When the pandemic hit, my routines changed very little. My health had always been on the poorer side. An injury left me using a cane, and I had already been making trips to the hospital for multiple other reasons. Growing up, I had been so used to being surrounded by family and found myself isolated from them. Of course, this was a decision I had made on my own. Unfortunately, I didn't call as much as I should have, but I made sure to visit during the holidays.

My marriage was in 2018. My wife and I are in a long-distance relationship. We were a couple of artists and authors that found inspiration in one another. Nights were spent on voice calls, streaming video games and shows, and serving as one another's muse. Our friends played together from around the globe for Dungeons and Dragons and other creative writing activities.

I spent the Christmas of 2019 with my wife's family in Oregon. It was my first time not spending the holidays with my clan. It was bittersweet to be away from everyone. I promised that I would spend the next Christmas with my family. After all, I had just seen them that November.

Yet another death pulled me from Ottawa back to my hometown. Isabelita delos Reyes, known to me as Ninang Abing, was my grandfather's oldest sister. She was Ninang Tina's mother. Her husband, Gabriel "Gaby" delos Reyes, had died in 2017. The priest had made him seem like a pious man, which was confusing and a little laughable. Ninang Tina and my mother knew the source of the misunderstanding. Tito Gaby hadn't been to church in years, but he had driven his wife to church every weekend nonetheless. Perhaps the priest had wrongly assumed that he also attended mass. This would later drive my mother to write my grandfather's eulogy herself.

While sitting in a suit I tried to feel confident in, Ninang Tina recounted her mother's life. I learned that Ninang Abing was the first of us to set foot on Canadian soil. She immigrated in the wave of Filipina nurses in the 70s. With the promise of a job, she boarded a plane with a cardboard suitcase and the clothes on her back. Ninang Abing asked the secretary at the hospital that hired her for a list of all of the Filipino people that worked there.

She went down the list, calling numbers in her hotel room until she found a place to stay. Of course, this would never be allowed in this day and age. At an event for death, I learned about her life. As I grow older, it seems to be that way. Another thing that I'm rapidly learning is that I regret not asking them more questions while they were alive.

During my holiday in Oregon, it was a wonderful time. My wife is white, and I got to experience some things that I never had before. It's a little defined by the delicious mystery that is casseroles, something I have a warm, gooey, soft spot in my heart for now.

We walked around the small town. The days were spent making art, heading to vintage stores, and getting to know my in-laws. A number of treasures came to light in our adventures. These included some old folk song books, old cookbooks, and even a first-edition *Monster Manual*. Although this holiday was not all perfect, it was wonderful.

The promise I had made, unfortunately, would not be one that I would be able to keep. Ninang Abing's funeral would be the final time I saw my Papa Ven in the flesh. We hugged one another, and he helped me into the car. Of course, I had no idea I'd never hear his voice in person again.

I was meant to visit that Christmas. The high prices of train tickets left me stranded again, but I promised to visit in the new year once I had my booster. That was a long process, but the kindness of one of the mothers I worked for made sure it happened. She had even paid for me to Uber to the Jabapalooza event in time. I had known Papa Ven wasn't doing well, but I planned to be there in a week. The date for the trip was to be the thirty-first.

I called him for a video chat. I had known he had been deteriorating. I was prepared for the end of his life, but it was made clear to me that his mind was going as well. The older of my younger sisters was there with him, along with my Ninang Arlyn and Ninong Ev. Ninong and Ninang lived with him, along with their three children.

Laurie, my sister, held the phone up for him to see my face. Without his glasses, he seemed bewildered. His features were much more weary, and the physical change was something I had prepared myself for. What made the other shoe drop was how my sister explained who I was and where I lived. She spoke as if to an infant — slowly, tenderly.

I had wanted to ask him about the upo he grew on a trellis in the backyard. The huge, green, sausage-shaped bottle gourds that he was so proud of. I had shown him one of my pieces last year — a bound carabao skull with mango branches tangled in its horns. When I had asked my grandparents about what to paint from our homeland, they had both told me about the beasts of burden. He knew I wanted to paint the things he grew. I told him about my aspiring art career and how he inspired me. It seemed to please him as much as it could.

I spent most of the call comforting my grandmother. I found myself reliant on the skills my fascination with the morbid had taught me — Death Positivity. As his condition worsened, it crept nearer and nearer. It was decided on the twenty-sixth I should be there for the next day.

That night, I had a dream about Papa Ven. It was mostly a journey. Part of the trip was with my father. But we had separate paths to get to where we were going, even though we were headed to the same place. I walk up to a strip mall. The Asian kind, with medicinal herbs, restaurants, and gift shops. Coming into the food court, I see my Ninang Wing sitting and talking with her friends. Papa Ven is standing there to greet me. He's wearing a red-collared shirt and khaki slacks. His white newsboy cap is on his head, dark eyes sparkling behind his glasses. He's much taller in the dream than he is in reality. Perhaps it's because I'm remembering him as when I was a child — when he seemed as tall as the trees he planted. We exchange a few words, hugging one another before sitting down to eat.

Upon waking, I called his house that morning. He was asleep, but I was able to tell Mama Winnie about my dream. She cried over the phone, the sobs carrying over miles. The vision had comforted her, and as I expressed the guilt of my absence, she insisted she understood. Because of the pandemic, I had to stay away for my safety and their own. My parents, whom I would have stayed with, ended up catching the disease over the holidays. To her, hearing my voice was enough to make us feel together. Internalizing that, we supported one another before bidding farewell.

Buying the train tickets was over the phone as well. A minute or two after that was finalized, I got another call. When I answered, my mother Myra's distraught voice came over the line.

Papa Ven was dead.

She was clearly beside herself and needed her own time. I reassured her that I would be fine on my own. Shortly after, I received another call from Laurie. She was clearly in tears, calling me *Ate* over the line. With a cool voice I explained that I already knew. Also needing her own time to process, I thanked her for calling. When I told my wife, Jessa, she and her family ordered flowers for my grandmother from Oregon.

For better or worse, I was in my element. The funeral didn't intimidate me as much as the overwhelming task of packing everything in a night. My father, Fred, told me over the phone that he knows I'm strong, and that once I came home I'll be taken care of. That any past disagreements were under the bridge, and what was important was that we could support one another.

I was able to make my early train. I was wearing Ninang Wing's red Mabuhay Bowling League letterman jacket. I spent most of the six-hour trip either napping or staring out the window. By some stroke of luck, the same day that I left Ottawa was the same day the Truckers Protest moved in. This emergency would lengthen my visit but would be chalked up as another one of my grandfather's miracles. I wouldn't be downtown in the middle of the crisis.

Planning for the funeral was a busy and stressful time. I wanted to make the collages for Papa's wake. Being a mixed-media artist, I had more than enough experience cutting out paper. Stacks and stacks of photo albums sat in bags by my side. My mom was planning on taking photos of the photos, but my inner perfectionist denied this vehemently. Instead, we got to work scanning the pictures. Although my mother helped me at first, she had plenty of her own work to do.

My favourite picture had to be one of him "piloting." He had never flown a plane himself, but he was in the navy as his first job, working on the wires. His last job would be making the wires for Bombardier. His career was bookended by flight. The original view through the plane's window was the hangar wall. This was carefully cut out and replaced with a sunset from Hagonoy, his hometown.

In the end, it took me four days. The photos were used for the memorial slideshow, and I had my pick to create my art pieces. There were over three hundred pictures of my grandfather that I recorded in the end. It was a magical journey, flipping through page after page. I sat for hours, carefully removing and replacing photographs after digitizing them. Another one of my favourites had to be the second black-and-white photo we recorded. My grandfather stood in a line with his navy friends, grinning ear to ear and all in drag. Beautiful dresses, headdresses, and smiles so bright. Apparently, it had been a contest of sorts to boost morale. It certainly worked on me.

Like the historian I fancy myself as, I peeled back each layer. I had found myself afraid that perhaps I did not know my grandfather very well. And it was true, while there were things I discovered, I also was reminded of things that I had always known. When my friends asked about him, I was able to recount many stories. Humorous, inspiring, and human. How cranky a cat Ronin had been, how happy Papa would be to pet him again. About the MacGyver-style, upcycled playscapes he made not only for my siblings and me, but also for my cousins.

I did not know he was a Knight of Rizal until his death. Due to my own research, I knew about Jose Rizal. This sparked a pride in me, as I had also aspired to be like him. A renaissance man, soft-spoken, powerful with words. Papa Ven and I shared the same insatiable thirst for knowledge, and the same endless wonder for the world and people around us. We would go camping, and Papa would take a fancy to a particular wildflower and simply take it home, planting it and being able to coax it to thrive.

My memory flits to how he had once grown corn. Although the fruit was mostly harvested by birds, it hits me now how poetic it was to have both indigenous plants along with the ones he had brought along with him. There were so many wonderful things that he cultivated. One of his final wishes was to see his two cherry trees bear fruit again. With the climate changing, they hadn't flowered in a number of years. My childhood was spent out back, with a metal hook Papa built. He would use it to bend the boughs down to us, filling our little buckets with white and black cherries. The halo-halo my grandmother made would cool us from the heat of the sun. Whenever that shaved ice touches my tongue, I'm transported to those days.

When Ninang Wing died, we planted a blue spruce. In 2004, it was a sapling. In 2022, I'm able to stand in its shade. There's a chair there, along with a stone engraved with a prayer for her. When I visited in 2019, I had to search for it. It lies under the long branches now. I expressed a desire to plant another, for Papa, once the winter thawed. Instead, Ninong insisted on focusing on the trees that were already there. This, of course, is fine with me.

The first thing I did when I saw my grandfather in his casket was take his hand. This, from my observations, seems to be something few people venture to do. I understand the stigma a corpse faces, but I know that I remember them as people. I looked him over the desairologist did a great job, matching his skin tone well enough. His lips could have used a little more colour, but that was more of a nitpick than anything. He had been in the morgue for quite a bit longer than most, due to the strain of the pandemic. It was most apparent on his hands, how the skin had dried. When I saw a stray hair on his nose, I reached in and removed it in the same way he would before a photo I'd be in as a child. As the person most comfortable, I felt it was best.

I was also the one that placed his rosary in his hands. My grandmother gave me the beads and asked me to break them. This is the custom when you bury a body with a rosary. Looking at the Knights of Columbus emblem it bore, I considered my own decolonization process as the chain gave way in my hands. I gently weaved it with his fingers, respectfully, reminded I have both indigenous Filipino and colonizer roots.

One of Ninong's favourite pictures featured my grandfather in front of his white cherry tree, the delicate blossoms filling the background. He sat with a satisfied and sage smile on his face. Happy, with his yellow flannel and garden chair. The image was on the front of the memorial fliers we had made. The subtitle was "A Life Well Lived," something that I have to agree with. He went out on his own terms, which is something very few can say.

PAPA, LIKE HIS daughter before him, would be buried with a stuffed bear. This was a gift from my younger cousins. Instead of being of the Build-A sort, it was the Bear of Caring kind. This served as a link for me to the children, who were shocked to hear that I, too, grew up watching them stare darkness in the face with their stomachs.

His funeral was the one I was most involved in. Laurie had made a large oil painting of him for the occasion. It was so fresh, it was still wet, and we needed to clean the fingerprints of curious little fingers. I found myself comforting my relatives, thankful for the robust end-of-life vocabulary I had been collecting. My paternal grandfather, Papa Art, came to pay his respects. I made sure to sit with him. I told him about this project, how I wanted to return to my roots, and how I wanted to learn Tagalog. I lost my chance with Papa Ven, and I wouldn't waste my time with my remaining grandparents.

I was asked to perform, and I thought about the last time I played at a funeral. This went much better, with my sister at my side. She sang with me at the wake, with me on ukulele. "Any Dream Will Do" was the first song; Papa was a fan of musicals and our family was fond of *Joseph and the Amazing Technicolor Dreamcoat*. The second was "Power of Your Love," which the youngest in my family, Sydney, soloed. This song was special — Mama Winnie's favourite, and also one that was played at Ninang Wing's funeral. It would be eternally short the last two lines, the emotions overcoming her. At this moment, my brother Jacob and Laurie joined us at the piano.

Laurie held Sydney as she cried. Jacob pulled the mic away from them and looked at me. Immediately delegating the situation, he helped me manage my sheet music for the next song. Any of the hang-ups we had in the past simply melted away. Even though I had been distant from my brother, we shared a real tender moment that I felt changed our relationship forever. All of this healing was in the face of our darkest hours. Although it was a sentiment I often thought about, I felt it extremely viscerally on that day.

The funeral was spent reconnecting with family and friends we hadn't seen in years. There was laughter mingling with the music and sobs. A reunion, tinted with the knowledge that all our time is short. A final gift from my grandfather, who, from his casket, reminded us of our own mortality. "As you are, I once was. As I am, you one day will be." Looking over the slide-show, I was reminded of the friends and family he had lost that he would be joining, and that I, one day, would join in the future. Now was the time for the living.

After the performance, Jacob and I insisted on being there for the closing of his casket. This, unfortunately, would have to serve as our "Over the Grave" ceremony. There was a certain reverence in how the funeral directors produced a silver device that fitted over some mechanisms on the coffin. Turning this rodlike key, the body sank down into its box. I was unaware he was on a raised platform at all, but it was convenient for viewing. He lay almost above its walls when displayed and sank down into it before the lid was closed.

The next day, before the burial, my siblings and I dug Ninang Wing's grave out from underneath the snow. Laurie's fiancée, Gavin, used an ice scraper from his car. All our hands cleared the snow so we could remember her in the moment as well. I placed flowers on her grave, and an extra one on Papa's casket in her name.

We were unable to have the children jump over Papa's grave. The winter meant that heavy equipment was going to be used, and policies dictated we had to watch from the road. Despite this, I had discussed the meaning of it to my relatives and how thankful I was that it had lived on with me. My father and I watched at the roadside as the huge vault sunk into the ground. Our car was the last, remaining at the cemetery until the backhoe started to bury him.

I was, once again, thankful to be there until the very last moment. This time, I found myself even more grateful for those around me that were still here.

Epilogue
August 2, 2022

I return to my writing after a trip into the forest. There is so much I would like to say, but I only have five hundred words and I am known to ramble. Right after my grandfather's funeral, we went through his belongings with my grandmother. His old workshop was home to all his tools and a photo of his parents and siblings with him as a child. We talked about memories and examined his old coin collection. I pocketed one with Joze Rizal on it, and my mother confided we were related to Marcelo del Pilar. While going through his possessions, I picked up a book called *Hagonoy: A Shared History*. Opening it up, I found a passage about traditional toys and I read his name. It turns out my grandfather had helped to write the book and he had never told us.

In his voice, I read that he believed his grandchildren had never played with traditional toys. What he did not know was that I had just been given one by a friend. It made me feel close to him. A new quest began to attain more copies of the book to give to the rest of the family.

It has taken quite a bit longer to get to this than I would have liked, as I've started a new job. Delightfully, I now work at the Ottawa Haunted Walk. This, of course, aligns with my Death Witch sensibilities. Being paid to wear the cloak and tell ghost stories is a dream I've always had. Now, I'm the Official Lorekeeper. This title has extended from being the Family Historian to being a Professional Storyteller. I find myself flourishing. My crafts will haunt the gift shop until a guest invites them into their home. I ran a booth in a market, peddling charms and collages of my own design.

I could feel myself remembering this summer fondly in the future. Connected to time in ways previously unimaginable, broadening my horizons. To be truthful, my heart is usually heavy with self-loathing. These past few months have lifted some of that burden from my soul. I've begun to internalize the idea that the knowledge I possess is a Gift. Not everyone has the stomach, patience, or resources to build such a robust spiritual vocabulary, especially about Death.

Kaleidoscope 2022 was so eventful I could write an entire book about the experience. This was a spiritual gathering in a wonderful place called Raven's Knoll and in fact was my first time attending. A journalist had come to my little stall in the woods, and I had returned after some shenanigans that are a detour too long for these pages. He had requested a pendulum with skulls and other death imagery. I laughed and said he had come to the right place; of all the shops, he wandered into the domain of a Deathling.

Our conversation swiftly turned into an interview. He asked me about what it meant to be a Death Witch. I answered, "My goal is to help the community when a living person is taking the journey to become an ancestor." We spoke about many things, and I was more than happy to explain. He was curious about me — not only for real life but also for some creative writing he wished to do.

I began recounting stories of the week and my life — he took out his phone and began to record. I confided that my father had at first been confused and disgusted with my desire to be a Death Counsellor. By the end of my experiences with Papa Ven's funeral, he pulled me aside and told me he had asked about the funeral home's hiring process in an implied approval. This included me counselling a recently diagnosed cancer patient, explaining how space and time works, and my views on the universe.

The last words he recorded were, "Death is not the end. It is a transition."

Live and die well, friends.

ALMA SALAZAR RETUTA, MD

My Journey as a doctor in Canada

MY HUSBAND AND I were originally doctors of veterinary medicine. This was post-2000s. We got married, settled in Baguio City in Northern Philippines, had five kids. My husband put up a farm and a clinic and pet shop. I went back to school at age thirty-five to become a doctor of medicine.

After passing the boards, I started neurology residency training at Saint Luke's Medical Center in Metro Manila, but being away from my family took its toll, and I did not finish my residency. I then went into internal medicine at Saint Louis University in Baguio and completed my residency.

We had a good life plan. I would have a clinic. My husband and I would continue our pet shop and veterinary clinic and farm. Our kids would go into vet med, medicine, or engineering, and we would all live happily ever after. That was our fairy-tale dream. Not in a million years did I ever plan or even imagine going abroad. I didn't want to raise my kids abroad as I was afraid that they would lose the Filipino values that we took so much pain to instill in them.

Then one day, I was on post-call (from overnight duty) during residency training, and an attending physician reprimanded me for something that was not my fault. I felt very embarrassed, upset, and aggrieved. At that vulnerable moment, my sister-in-law, who is also my best friend, asked if I wanted to go to Canada with her family. I said yes, and here we are!

We came to Calgary in June 2011. We wore multiple layers to save luggage space. We wore winter jackets, snow pants, scarves, bonnets, and gloves, in June! Then we noticed that most people were wearing shorts and tank tops, and as we got out of the airport, we found out that it was summer in Canada.

On this fateful day, I met my first friend in Canada and inadvertently found my first job. She was a Filipino-Canadian woman who was offering credit cards to passengers at the airport. I asked her if her company had any job openings and was hired on the spot, along with my eldest daughter. On our first day of Canadian work experience, we earned fifteen dollars an hour with an additional fifty cents for every credit card application we were able to get. I worked there for about four months, then moved on to work as an at-home call centre agent for TELUS for almost five years.

Since I worked from home, I had time to work a second job as a clinic aide and study for the many exams I needed to take to be licensed and recognized as a doctor here. I worked at least fourteen hours every day, seven days a week.

In the meantime, my husband worked as a window cleaner, then as a warehouse associate and forklift operator, then as an Internet and TV technician. He even had a short stint as a security officer. Now he works as a community support worker for adults with disabilities.

To practise medicine in Canada, one must pass at least four very expensive exams, take a language test (IELTS) and another qualifying exam every year, then undergo residency training for two to five years. To get accepted into residency training, one would have to get matched to a training program.

There are two pathways to a residency: one for Canadian graduates and one for international medical graduates (IMG). However, for every ten to twenty slots for Canadian graduates, there is only one or even none for IMGs. And for every one slot for IMGs, there are about 2500 to 3000 applicants, all of whom are specialists in their own right in the countries where they come from.

To complicate matters, many Canadian-born citizens who could not get into medical schools in Canada go abroad — Australia, England, or Jamaica, for example — to study medicine there. When they come back, they compete with the other IMGs as they are also considered international medical graduates. They are favoured over those of us who have come as immigrants because of the loyalty they show by coming back to serve their country. Thus, for a fifty-plus-year-old woman, this competition was proving to be not in my favour. For some reason, even if I thought I did very well in my exams and interviews, attended masses in ten churches, prayed to all the saints, and asked for "signs," I did not get matched.

After four years, I stopped applying for residency and concentrated on just being a good clinical assistant, which has been my job for six years now. I am basically a decently paid, supervised physician in three hospitals in Calgary. I function in the same way as a doctor, admitting patients to the hospital, managing them in the units, going on twenty-four-hour and sixteen-hour calls, making prescriptions, discharging patients, doing the necessary paperwork, interacting with patients and their families, collaborating with other doctors and the multidisciplinary team, and occasionally performing minor procedures like a bone marrow biopsy or paracentesis. It is a very demanding and difficult job but a really fulfilling one with less responsibility than a fully licensed physician. I am indeed fortunate for being able to practise my profession in Canada.

Our first ten years here just whizzed by so swiftly. Through those years, I helped support four nephews and nieces, who also now have good, independent lives. My kids have almost all graduated from universities and found careers. My husband has found his retirement job, which is not too physically demanding and which he enjoys very much.

When describing the life that we left behind, I remember mostly the good things: that the temperature in Baguio is about sixteen degrees all year round except during Christmas when it falls to five to eight degrees; it is the cleanest and greenest city in the Philippines; food is cheap and really great; people are friendly; patients loved me. Life was peachy. When people hear this, they ask, "Then why did you come here?" to which I give the cliché answer: "For the kids."

When our children and I talk about it, I tell them, well, we thought it was the best decision at the time. But really, there must have been reasons other than the kids that pushed us to make that ultimate decision to leave everything behind and take a risk somewhere else. Then I realize that we tend to forget the crimes, that one of my kids' classmate's father was kidnapped in broad daylight in the middle of a public place, the "padulas" that we were forced to give to the BIR lady despite our business's immaculate books and documents, the heavy hours-long traffic, the many issues that we only remember whenever we went to visit.

Since we left the Philippines, many things have changed. Many Christmases have been missed. Many loved ones have passed. It could be sad, and sometimes lonely, and we always yearn for "home." But I had a realization the first time we went for a vacation. As we got back here and entered Vancouver airport, I suddenly relaxed, released all tension, and thought, "Thank God, we're finally home." That was the first time I realized that this — Canada — is home.

FIRST WINTER

by Lorina Mapa

January 1992.
Pointe-Claire, Québec.

...for a total of 40 centimetres by midnight. And that's Montréal CHOM weather. Now for some "Tom Sawyer"...

R R R N G!

This town sure does love Rush.

Hello?

Hi Babe, how's it going?

Good! I finished all the kitchen stuff. And for dinner we're having adobo.

Well, I'm headed to the metro now. A lot of snow fell so maybe I'll just take a cab from the train station.

What? No why? I'll pick you up as usual.

I'm worried about the conditions. Did the snow removal guy come?

Yeah. Besides, I have to practise driving in the snow sometime.

Okay, but you should start getting ready now.

Now? It's only a ten minute drive

Well, just make sure you give yourself PLENTY OF TIME.

I'll be fine!

Much later...

Eeep! I forgot to shovel the path.

Oh man! The car!

C-c-cold...

I wonder why his ancestors chose To settle here?

SCRAPE o SCRAPE SCRAPE

Oh my gosh, I'm so late! He'll be freezing!

VRRM

RRRR

FFF

??

Looks like you need digging out, Miss!

I--I thought The snow removal cleared our driveway...

Yeah, but The street plow just came by. Let me get my shovel.

MONICA BATAC

Sisters in Practice: A Readers Theatre Script

Performed on November 7, 2022, at Nakai Theatre's twenty-four-hour challenge cabaret / share-back in Lefty's Well, Whitehorse Yukon.

I, Monica, introduce the performance as a creative experiment with research interviews with Filipina practitioners in the Yukon, then we begin with these words from Filipina-American writer Barbara Jane Reyes:

MONICA. "This soothsaying, this hollering me
This lyric-making me, now a dazzling we —
IRA. "We howl, we witness, we testify
We stand firm, and you cannot break us
GWYNETH. "We are raw nerves, and we are fire. We rise
And in writing, we restore our lives."

Characters
Narrator
Monica — Social work researcher
Ira — Bachelor of Social Work student
Gwyneth — Social service practitioner

NARRATOR. Tonight, we centre kwentuhan, Filipino-specific ways of storytelling, conversations between Monica, Ira, and Gwyneth: intentional relationships nurtured across space and over time. Tonight, we weave their stories together.

Repeating a line from Barbara Jane Reyes, "this lyric-making me, now a dazzling we" — may we learn more about their journeys: on how they, how we, how Filipinos come to call the Yukon our home.

NARRATOR. Scene 1: Introducing ourselves.

MONICA. I call them my sisters in practice: we are Filipinas in Canada working in the social services sector, with shared commitments to work and support fellow Filipinos, our kababayans, wherever we may be.

GWYNETH. I'm Gwyneth Williams, full name Gwyneth Iola Villoria Williams. I was born and I grew up in the United States in Washington, DC. My father's from Wales and my mother is from the Philippines. From my mother's side, we originate from Nueva Ecija, and the predominant Indigenous groups there are the Aeta. After studying in the UK, I worked abroad in many places, including Sri Lanka, the Philippines, and the U.S. I then moved to Canada with my partner.

IRA. I'm Ira. I've basically lived here all my life. I was born in the Philippines and migrated to the Yukon in 2006 with my parents and have lived here ever since. And certainly, while I've had my temptations of leaving and going off to the bigger cities, it's really a special place to live.

MONICA. "The Yukon is a special place to live," she tells me. And Gwyneth, no longer seduced by some of the world's biggest cities, chose to visit here, then chose to stay.

I am intrigued. Most of my life, I've stayed within a one-hour radius of Toronto. And so, with these budding friendships and a research travel grant in tow, I board two planes to land here in early February. To visit them in person.

NARRATOR. Scene 2: What brought us here?

IRA. For my family, it's similar to a lot of immigrant stories: that search for a better life.

MONICA. A common refrain: if you want a better life, you come to Canada.

GWYNETH. But in Toronto, we couldn't find meaningful work. We knew we had a couple of friends who had moved out to the Yukon, so we decided in April 2016 to drive out there. We were originally thinking we'd spend just the summer visiting —

NARRATOR. Six years later, they're still here.

IRA. I've really dug deep into understanding my immigration story and what makes me *me*.

GWYNETH. I've done some study and self-learning too.

IRA. I reflect back on my life, coming here when the Filipino population was little to none. Seeing the community grow and blossom, recalling the challenges that I faced, my parents faced, coming to rural Northern Canada …

NARRATOR. Please, continue …

IRA. I really admire how our Filipino community here has remained resilient. If you think about it, I mean, you're moving from a country where it's very collectivist and you're around people all the time.

NARRATOR. Plus, it's really hot in the Philippines —

IRA. And then coming to a place like the Yukon, where it's winter eight-plus months of the year —

NARRATOR. So cold.

MONICA. So VERY cold.

IRA. Where there's a new language, new culture, new society, new customs.

GWYNETH. Filipinos are the most resilient humans — I mean, I know I'm biased [*laughs*]. But there's a humungous population of Filipinos here in the Yukon. Such a harsh cold environment and yet they thrive.

NARRATOR. My God, it's incredible.

GWYNETH. It's incredible! I had no idea. I was just going out to the Yukon to check it out. It's the Wild West here. Especially Dawson City, Trondek Hwechin territory. You really feel it, it's one of the most famous places for the gold rush, and you still feel that really …

NARRATOR. [*Sing-song*]

GWYNETH. Freedom.

NARRATOR. [*Ends sing-song*]

GWYNETH. Like, you can do anything! You have to know how to connect with people to thrive and grow. And that's what Filipinos know how to do.

ALL. That's what we know how to do.

NARRATOR. Scene 3: Filipinos in the Yukon.

IRA. I would describe the community as very colourful and vibrant. We now have a Filipino restaurant and store, people are really trying to stand their ground and establish themselves here. Similar to what's happening across Canada, employment-wise, many are in the fast-food industry, housekeeping, the medical field as well.

I'm not going to say it's very rare to see Filipinos in leadership positions, I think that's changing. I'm sure you've heard, our first-ever Filipino MLA was recently elected ...

NARRATOR. Yvonne Clarke.

IRA. And we have a Filipina city councillor ...

NARRATOR. Jocelyn Curteanu.

MONICA. I meet them in my first few days here.

IRA. I think people are trying to make those strides. But it's very common that for the first five-plus years, Filipinos are remaining in the jobs they originally come here for, they get a little bit more comfortable, and then they might work up into a higher position.

The Filipino community: it's small but growing, and I'm excited to see what's to come.

MONICA. Witnessing the changes with my own eyes ...

NARRATOR. It's incredible.

GWYNETH. My first experience in the Yukon with the Filipino community was in this tiny place of Dawson City. And I met incredible Filipinos. I first met Filipinas working at the daycare. Incredible loving humans, my God. And then through my youth work with Trondek Hwechin, through the youth centre, I got to know all the youth, the Filipino youth of Dawson City, and got to know their stories, too: how they made it out here and how they're liking it.

And then when I moved to Whitehorse, oh my gosh, I had no idea.

NARRATOR. Totoo, I had no idea too!

GWYNETH. It's a thriving community. Every winter, all the Filipino houses in Whitehorse, folks do them up for a Christmas lights competition. You can do a little toodle around, and you know it's a Filipino house because it's got the incredible lantern, what's it called again? I forgot ...

NARRATOR, IRA, MONICA: Parol?

GWYNETH. Parol, yes, parol. And then we've got, they have this epic party that everyone wants in on. All my Indigenous friends were like, what's this party, this Filipino Christmas party? And I was like, oh, you come with me, we'll check it out.

　　And there's karaoke! Oh! That was another thing about Dawson City. The first time: there was an uncle, there was a tito there who regularly would have karaoke nights, which is so fabulous, especially in the winter months when you need community, you need some fun. They just thrive.

　　It just feels good. I've travelled and lived in so many places, I'm fairly comfortable with coming and going.

ALL. Making a life wherever it is.

GWYNETH. I think that's really my Filipino-ness. It's so heartwarming to see that my community is doing the same here and they're thriving.

IRA. We're out here, we're thriving.

NARRATOR. End scene. Thank you everyone!

KAWIKA GUILLERMO

Untouchable, Or, The Most Filipino Story You'll Ever Read

BACK WHEN HE was young and gave a shit, apologies bounced off his tongue and sentiment beckoned from every hi and hug. Now it's 2021, he's thirty-six, and everyone comes to his party just to get pissed out of their fucking minds. He urks whenever he hears that word, *community*.

They revel; he lolls in the gardens sussing out the suspended snow. The way it hangs in the garden, as if atmosphere can sleep. Samantha, his agent, rented the house; perhaps the visitors believe he owns it. He lets them believe it. He is a performer, you know. YouTuber, blogger, tweeter-twit. The anti-intellectual video essayist who rails against hipsters, bobos, and academics. He thought he'd be cancelled by now. And he does get cancelled, every week at least. But the offers keep coming.

Marites, his frequent collaborator and confidante, calls him untouchable. (They both know how untouchable can refer to the caste outside caste — or the Noli — but neither points this out.) Why was he untouchable? Why was he the one chosen? He ponders this from the chilly winter-quiet garden. He was raised in Oahu, had lived in South Korea, and arrived in Canada with a traveller's sense of language as something that designates a place. And when a place believes it's bigger than it is, it turns into a bubble, an empty bubble that floats away. He, pinprick, could not help but pop.

He calls Samantha as he creeps closer to the frosted windows of the rented house (he checks: not fake frost, real frost). The phone in his ear protects him from having to go inside or from appearing creepy as he spies on his guests.

He met Samantha just a year before, after she saw his YouTube show, "The

M-3" — a name that referred to his own Filipino, Chinese, and mixed white background with three Ms: Mango, Mongol, Mongrel. The byline: "The M-3 features three-second sketches. Some are about colonialism. Some are dick jokes." He spoke to Samantha's sharp, blue-rimmed glasses through his tablet screen, and their first conversation went like this:

I thought you'd be much more …

Crazy? Suicidal? Insulting?

Younger.

He liked that she didn't even say hello.

I've been watching your video essays. I wouldn't call them sketches if I were you. Sketches make people think of comedy, not colonialism.

Colonialism is comedy. Or is comedy colonialism? Hmm. That's a sketch.

He had expected nothing from the meeting, and he told her as much, not with words but with rigid artistry. When making his sketches — and *sketches* they were — he had to be totally free. His method was no thinking, no planning (what Samantha later translated as his "biteable" style). He drew from life (an "about me" vibe). He would not hold back (a "chunky" attitude).

I have no inhibition whatsoever, he told her. I am a child. He heard her breathe, so he spoke for her: And being of the community, representing the things I represent, this could get me in trouble.

She offered him a contract. The next day, he posted a sketch featuring various positions of unprotected sex while he, the receiver, groaned in pleasure: Records in sales! Call my agent, she'll set you up! They accept non-union performers! Twenty percent royalty on international markets! Here's a chance to showcase your skills!

Despite The M-3's verbatim quotes from her agency-speak, Samantha somehow got the show a six-figure contract for an hour-long episode for wide distribution on home streaming services.

Did you ever see those blips? he asks Samantha as he wipes his breath from the glass. He had, eventually, stopped calling them sketches. But not because of her.

The ones with the dog?

The dog? I don't think we mean the same thing.

I'm very protective of my time.

That interview you set up. The DJ called my rise meteoric. Bugged the shit outta me. Meteors must stay away from planets. They are as much burning beauty as they are total devastation.

She clacks on a keyboard. As he expects, or as he hopes, she's translating his nonsense into a systemic edit, hacking his words to pieces, running it through a mill. In the end, she'll have a shiny plank to help build his image.

The premiere starts in ten minutes, she reminds him. Aren't you going to make a speech?

I'm not actually inside the house right now.

You'll need your community behind you. You know that.

This all just feels so set up. Wouldn't they know what's going on?

I think people just want to be seen. She goes over the concept again: The audience must be aware that the show isn't really about *you*, that you're just playing a toxic Filipino man. You're just poking fun at your own background, not shaming it.

The self-hating buffoon.

Exactly.

An important fiction.

Well, okay then. She was never one to say goodbye either.

He pretends to stay on the phone, peering at his community through the frosted window. He hates the idea of a party in his name. Guests saying congratulations, sipping wine in his direction. Smiling. The celebration is Samantha's event all over: at a house he's never been in, with appetizers from a Filipino restaurant he's never dined in. She knows the stakes, having seen the community feedback. He opts to stay ignorant about the market, the culture, the vibes. But he does know that of the thousands of fan emails he's received since starting his YouTube channel, not one was from a Filipino.

He finds creative stimuli through the glass: cans of beer and glasses of wine and black hoodie jackets that are all identical besides the logo above the left nipple. Perhaps none of his guests saw his series on Vancouver. It began with three-second blips about Vancouver racisms: Cringe Racism, Watered-Down Racism, LuLu Racism, Prime Ministerial Brown-Face Racism, Bottom-Shelf Racism, Under-the-Table Racism, Japandroids Racism, Over-Prescribed Racism, Self-Care Racism. The videos' popularity at millions of views each led to more: Vancouver, the Land of False Creek and Even Falser People; Vancouver, Our Only Identity Is We're Not America; Vancouver, Where You Never Know Just How Much Rat Poo You're Getting with Your Morning Granola.

Inside, the circle of people grows in circumference. Soon it will turn into an oval, then curve into the kitchen, and droop into the hall. None will leave the circle, however. Do they trust so well in its powerful chismis? Are they so afraid to turn their backs?

Sketch idea: the circle widens until it droops through the front door. People squeeze in and someone who drives a Tesla slips into the fireplace.

He sees Marites in the circle and remembers one of the many reasons he doesn't drink: Chinese red face. Rosy cheeks give away mixed blood, then lack of knowledge, then inability to speak Tagalog, then a forbidden disgust for Christmas kitsch.

Marites spots him. She has the look of an erotic intellectual, a Sontag or an Arendt, though she is only a sessional film lecturer at the nearby hilltop university. She performed at her best for over a decade before she realized that the department would never promote her. They had her labour, her ideas, her art. Why would they pay more for it? Since this fact dawned upon her, her blood pressure dropped significantly, while her resentment grew like an oil spill.

Marites leaves the circle, probably to find him. He sees his own reflection in the window (creep-ass!) and walks back into the garden.

Of course they talk about him. And why not? He talks about them ruefully, in public, in sketches, in subtweets. The Filipinos, in their enclosures, he once said. Or maybe it was that series of blips he made about Filipinos being not-quite-Asian: Filipinos, the Mexicans of Asia; Filipinos, the Street Market Asians; Filipinos, the Off-Brand Asians. By the time Samantha encouraged him to ease off with the "challenging content," he got away with one more: Filipinos, the deluded, the diluted, and the dead.

The further he paces into the garden, the more the house looks like a mansion. Like many Vancouver properties, someone probably bought it as an investment to rent out to up-and-comers like himself. An aspirational happiness loan.

Above the roof, the moon takes the rough shape of an axe poised to drop.

He imagines another sketch: spirits live on the moon and can hear all the unheard things. When a tree falls in a forest, they can hear it. When someone whispers a prayer to their palms, they can hear it. When someone offs themselves without a note, they can hear their last words. They can't do anything about it.

In the garden of dead rose bushes, he feels the dread cold.

And here comes Marites, bringing him a glass of Diet Coke with loads of fizz. Her fingers graze the snow from the bushes as she approaches.

I thought this was your party?

I'm in character. Eccentric artist hides in the garden.

In negative five-degree weather.

Is it that cold?

Marites isn't half, like him, but they both have scummy cheaters for fathers. When they first met, encountering time and again at readings and celebrations, their detachment from their cultures attached them to each other. Marites told him that you can't be anti-colonial and still believe in white Jesus. He didn't quite agree, yet the provocation struck ground between them, a place where they could play with the soggy dirt.

Most of his videos began as a joke between them, and sketch ideas flowed with the wine. They could intuit where the bubbles were and jab at them freely. It made the work raw, funny — couch humour flung to the touch screen. Their conversations about white Jesus led to his first sketch to go beyond three seconds: Gum. He plays a Filipino Catholic priest, a padre, who tells a young woman, Marites, that pre-marital sex will make her feel like a chewed-up piece of gum. She says she will definitely not have sex, but she still likes gum, because it tastes like semen.

Marites's eyes settle on the empty field near the parking lot. You know what new snow always reminds me of? she says. A skating rink after hours, when the Zamboni slowly smooths out the ice, leaving everything flat, not necessarily to make it slippery or sleek again, but to erase the evidence of scraps and scrapes. Like no one has ever touched it, ever.

A Zamboni?

Right. You've never been to a hockey game. She looks at her phone. Aren't you going to watch your premiere? Make a speech or something?

Not really.

You worked hard for this.

I worked less than a year for this. How long has Michael been making short films? How many Canada Council grants are represented in that house? Yet, I, the shitty YouTuber, gets the big deal.

You're right. They probably think you're a self-loathing narcissist. Oh no! So awful. Get over it. Anyone who holds fast to their integrity inevitably has ruptures. Doesn't matter what institution, family, or community they're in.

Her words just drip into the snow.

You're sulking. You've got a sulking presence.

This was a shit idea. Filipinos will hate us more than anyone.

Well, first you gotta stop referring to us and them. We are Filipino, aren't we?

Man, they'll do us in for sure.

This party was Samantha's idea, right? What did she expect?

I don't know. She believes in my work, so I don't get it. Why throw us to the wolves on the day of the premiere?

She gives him a look. Like a Sontag-Arendt smoker. Have you ever heard of an *agent* being cancelled? Or a talent agency? Or a book publisher? If anything happens, they'll just fire you and look all the better for it. Nobody cancels the institutions that made us, not if they still want to be made.

And what about you? Do you think they won't come for you?

You think I can't disavow you in a second?

A sketch: this absurd fucking conversation, but just now Marites exhales a cloud of smoke and his phone-camera catches it crawling into the snow.

THROUGH THE WINDOW, he watches his streaming special begin. The title card on the fifty-four-inch mounted television states:

The M-3 Show Presents
The Most Filipino Streaming Special You'll Ever Watch

Scene 1, he's on stage in various thrown-together wigs:

Define a Filipino: a person who's being all extra about being Filipino.
Define a Filipino: a mixed-race sell out who doesn't look or act Filipino at all.
Define a Filipino: do you mean Filipina, Filipinx, Pinoy, Pinay, Pilipino …
Define a Filipino: wait, what's a Filipino?
Define a Filipino: who in God's name was Philip anyway and why are we all named after him?

Already, someone's got their hand on Marites's shoulder. What? He wants to scream at them. *What?*

He retreats back to the garden where the steady sound of his boots crushing snow reminds him of his mother crunching garlic. No, that couldn't have been his mother. She rarely cooked anything but American frozen foods. Alas.

Cackles from inside the house. Not from the living room, where his special plays to a leaned-back audience, but from the kitchen, where a new circle has begun to form. What are they laughing at? The hors d'oeuvres? Is the lumpia Shanghai too thick? Can they tell he only moderately likes Filipino food based on his menu choices? Do they think the dinuguan is overselling it, with its dark blood and cartilage brew?

Another title card darkens the living room: Act Two, Losing Sight.

Someone cracks a joke. More jokes bounce around the room, none of it from the television. More guests leave to join the circle in the kitchen. More snark. More laughter. None of it near the TV.

Yup, he says to himself. There it is.

He looks up and sees the sky open from its sea of clouds. Stars like little torches like the end.

BY ACT 3 of his premiere, the kitchen circle has widened through the living room and spilled outside, where a head-shaven spoken word artist freestyles over the television's low volume. Smart phones rise, each with the face of the poet who speaks with a relaxed, surferesque drawl. His words coil through each listener:

The St. Louis Fair is where they made me, imagination.
Of the dog-eater Filipino.
Got nothin to do with me.

Sketch idea: an Igorot and an Ilocano at the St. Louis World's Fair escape their enclosures and find each other near the Native American exhibit. They run away together, north.

I ain't no zoo animal.
I'm Rizal, I'm Bonifacio,
I'm Gabriela, I'm Bulosan

The Igorot and the Ilocano decide that they will never be like the well-fed, subservient ones who wait in line for the dangled carrots of sympathy.

a new history, new religion

They run, and run, until they make it to Canada, true north. They live with Indigenous communities, the only ones who accept them. They huddle together and wait for the day the rest of us learn to bite better than we jump.

we plant our flag for the next generation

His ears overdose on the sounds of high-pitched whistles and applause. Someone has turned their camera around, and he sees his own face on it. More phones aim toward him. Finally, silence, as they wait for him to speak.

You're an inspiration, he tells the poet. I mean, you inspire me. Literally, just now!

Inspiration? Inspiration to do what? To go on the Internet and spread fuckin' bullshit?

Oh!!!

Yeah, that's right you walk away! Fucking *zoo animal*!

Somehow, amid the laughter and finger pointing, he had the idea for his first how-to sketch: how to beat a motherfucker to death with his own Japanese-made thermos.

HE CIRCLES THE empty field bordering the parking lot, lulled by the crunch of his own pacing. His feet glide in ever-tighter circles, a clean wipe of every edge.

Noelani materializes in her usual bedraggled sweats and oversized hoodie. Yo.

Hey. It must be hard being my cousin right now.

What you think? Ever since you moved out here, you always been a fuckin' dick head. You think I ain't used to your bullshit?

He watches the sky, wondering if that portal to nothing will open again.

What Apobakit always say? So what? Bodda you?

Fuck it, I'd give it all away to be ten pounds thinner anyway. Can you tell them to beat me so bad I can't eat for a month? Aim for the stomach? Maybe the mouth, just to be sure?

Psshh, ever since you started blogging, it never been a secret: you the guy who hates himself. Everyone got these bubbles of self-doubt. You just let them grow, leave them alone long enough they turn to, like, a fuckin' Nietzschean abyss.

He points out the smudges of vinegar on her brown jacket.

Fuck man, I can't see a thing. Your eyes must got really dilated out here.

It is dark. Relatively.

Man, so, why won't you, like, do something with what you got? Honestly?

Like what? Pull up a flag? Come, see the next Maria Clara Marie Sue!

How's this for a story, right? Remember when you first moved out to live with us, after a year bein' without a home, and you *hated* the snow? But one day I come home from work and you've gone out and shovelled the curb around the whole apartment building. Then you're doing it every fucking morning. Why? Cuz you got thanked, right? And who thanked you? The titas, the workers who spent all day in hospitals and cafés and the last thing they needed was shovelling sidewalks. You set your alarm, got off your ass, and shovelled. And come March, you all bitchin' to me, Noelani, cousin! There's no more snow! What'll I do now?!

He remembers holding the shovel, the weakness in his arms. The women, all two heads shorter than him, the oil on their face yellow from the lamp-post light.

You write that story down. That one's hot!

I can't. That's not me.

Bitch-ass, it fucking happened *to you*!

I mean, it's not *in* me.

Cuz, you may not see it, but I got a Glock to your head right now. And by Glock, I mean a tweet. You think anyone who knows you doesn't got a fuck-ton of evidence of all the stupid shit you done? Like you remember that night, two months ago? The last time you drank?

Oh no. That was —

— DO NOT say it was an accident, or a misinterpretation. You asshole. You better than that.

He picks up his Diet Coke from the ground. Heavier than before, its edges frosted with ice.

So what. I gotta do what?

Show us some love, that's all. And you know, grow the fuck up. Quit being a fuckin' man-child, shit. I don't know.

And if I don't?

Then I'll feel real bad for your mom.

He drinks from the fizz and notices steam coming from his nose in bits of smoky pebbles. He follows them up, up to the pulsing stars. Another sketch idea comes.

In an eternal village, people begin to disappear. First one or two, then dozens, then hundreds. The villagers realize something must be happening back on Earth: someone has found a way to resurrect people, to kidnap souls from heaven and imprison them in their former bodies.

In the end, there are only a couple hundred villagers left, the ones whose bodies back on Earth were cremated upon their death. They're more alone now, but they don't worry. Their kin will soon return home.

JOSÉ ROMELO LAGMAN

A Day in the Life of a Meatpacker

February 9, 2001
Toronto

5:00 a.m.
Under a heavy winter blanket, Pepe stirs to the vibration of his digital watch. He presses a button on its side to stop the alarm. He disables an analog alarm clock on a high shelf by his bed that serves as his backup in case he oversleeps. God forbid that it goes off because its shrill mechanical bell is loud enough to wake up his roommates and everyone in the adjacent rooms.

He sits up and yawns. In the dim light, he sees his three roommates sleeping in their bunk beds, gently snoring. They're all in their mid-twenties, all doing odd jobs. Though he arrived in Canada as a landed immigrant and the others arrived as refugees from Central America, he has bonded with them. He's the most recent renter in this rooming house on Palmerston Boulevard near Bloor Street. He pays three hundred dollars a month for a bunk bed and access to a shared bathroom and kitchen.

He climbs down and pours himself coffee from a thermos. It's Nescafé instant, nothing fancy, but it has enough warmth and caffeine to jolt him awake. Boiling water and making coffee the night before saves him a few minutes in the morning.

He walks to the bathroom to piss, wash his face, and brush his teeth. He gets dressed, puts on his winter boots and jacket, then toque, scarf, and gloves. He grabs his backpack, goes downstairs, and he's out the door.

Toronto is bone chillingly cold in the middle of winter. The forecast is minus fifteen Celsius and minus twenty-something with the wind chill. The two-block walk to the streetcar stop on Harbord Street seems to take forever. The uneven mounds of dirty snow along the icy sidewalks present an unwelcome obstacle course.

He doesn't see a patch of black ice; he loses his balance but quickly regains it. He grins to himself, remembering that he has managed to avoid slipping since he learned to skate at the Toronto City Hall public rink. He bought the cheapest pair of skates at Canadian Tire as a Christmas gift to himself and spent the weekends learning to skate. Hopefully he'll soon be good enough to play shinny hockey, but for now his primary goal is to reach the streetcar stop on time. If he misses it, he'll have to wait fifteen minutes for the next one and he'll be late for work.

5:24 a.m.
Pepe is waiting alone at the streetcar stop as the 511 tram approaches, right on time. He steps forward as the doors chime open. He gets on and settles in the single seat opposite the middle doors.

Three other passengers are on the streetcar, all brown like him, all staring blankly ahead, probably wondering why they traded the forever-summer of their tropical lands for this bleak winter.

The street lights streak by the wide windows as the red tram rolls south on Bathurst Street. A few more sleepy souls get on at the following stops, none showing enthusiasm for their ungodly work hours.

5:40 a.m.
Pepe gets off on Niagara Street, one stop south of King Street. He trudges along a couple of blocks and arrives at the meat-packing plant. Looking from the outside, this three-storey industrial building looks like any other Victorian-era warehouse that is common along the rail corridor in Toronto. Except that its windows have been bricked over and its roof and walls thickly insulated.

Adjacent to it is a similar building where the hogs are slaughtered — six thousand a day — and the dressed carcasses are transported to the meat-packing plant via a covered conveyor bridge twenty feet above the ground. The owners call the slaughterhouse an abattoir; the French word does not provoke the same aversion as its English counterpart.

A slaughterhouse has existed at this site for over a century. Toronto loves its pork; in fact, one of the city's nicknames is Hogtown. And Pepe is one of hundreds of immigrants who work here to keep the pork traditions alive.

5:50 a.m.
Pepe joins the lineup by the entrance. He shows his ID to security and walks through the revolving steel door.

He rushes to the men's lockers; every minute counts. He opens his locker, retrieves his blue hard hat and insulated steel-toe slip-free waterproof boots, and deposits his winter boots, jacket, toque, scarf, and gloves. He sits on a long bench and slips on the specialized boots. They were supplied by the plant; their cost was deducted from his first two paycheques.

He stands and stretches. He doesn't have to piss but he goes to the toilet anyway and waits for a free urinal. The first thing he learned here was that it's a pain to get a pee break outside break time, so he goes to piss at every break.

He washes his hands and joins the rest of the men as they exit the lockers.

Most of the workers make a side trip to the cafeteria; it's a wide hall with twenty long tables. Pepe leaves his backpack at the Filipino table, beside the Latino table. The four tables closest to the microwave machines are designated as the Portuguese tables. The next four are the East European tables. The others are for Africans, South Asians, Caribbeans, Chinese, and the farthest one is for Muslims. Yes, there are several Muslim workers in this pork meat–packing plant. Good jobs are hard to come by; Allah will understand.

Pepe returns to the corridor, which it is covered with non-slip rubber mats. The mats are interrupted by a shallow, sanitizing boot-bath that smells of lemony disinfectant.

He joins another lineup. Everyone picks their time card from the wall rack, inserts it on the bundy clock, then returns it to the rack. The location of this bundy clock is a source of debate among the workers as they realize that the several minutes from the entrance to the boot-bath are unpaid.

On the side of the next corridor are hangers of freshly laundered thick white butcher coats; he grabs a medium and wears it over his thick flannel jacket. Next to the coats are dispensers of plastic aprons, rubber gloves, hair nets, and face masks. He puts them on and saves extra gloves and masks in his coat pocket.

Everyone enters through the work area doors and heads to their assigned stations.

6:00 a.m.

The buzzer sounds. Work day officially starts.

The work area is impressively massive. It's a series of cutting and trimming stations that process the whole carcass into standard retail cuts that are then forwarded to packing stations. There are hook chains, conveyor belts, elevated chutes, industrial bone saws, lots of knives, and knife sharpeners. There are large stainless steel bins for various cuts and discarded trimmings, transported by forklifts driven on the aisles between stations.

Pepe waits by his station. From where he stands, he sees the carcasses entering the queue at the far end of the work area. They move through mechanical cutting stations and the resulting primal cuts are directed to different chutes. His task is to wait for the pork legs to emerge from the chute in front of him, grab each one, and throw it into one of three bins: small, medium, large. Each leg weighs between eight and twelve kilos.

He's been assigned to this station for a month. One of the supervisors saw him at another station, he commented on his broad shoulders and transferred him here. A supervisor walks by every hour and gives him a thumbs-up. Pepe is not certain who's who as all of them are masked, but their white hard hats distinguish them as supervisors.

The bins in front of him are supposed to be replaced by forklift operators when they're over three-fourths full, and the operators have been mostly diligent about it. Only twice had he needed to push the big red STOP LINE button suspended from the ceiling near him. And when he did, the whole line stops until the overflowing bins are replaced with empty ones, amid much yelling and name-calling from the stressed-out supervisors.

Pepe watches the pork legs slide to him from the chute; they remind him of Christmas ham and Iberian jamón. Some people say workers at meat-packing plants become vegetarians after witnessing how meat is processed. But not him. To fend off boredom, he imagines new ways to cook the pork leg as he grips and tosses it. Maybe deep-fry it whole — crispy pierna, instead of crispy pata? Braised it for a few hours — pierna tim, instead of pata tim?

Before his two months at this plant, he worked as a shelf stocker at a supermarket, then as an assistant at a retirement home. Working at the supermarket was okay, but it was minimum wage and he hardly got full shifts. The retirement home paid more, but it was particularly, extremely difficult work. On some days he changed soiled adult diapers, on others he was subjected to racist rants from the very residents he was assisting. And then there was that one day when a creepy old man kept grabbing his crotch through his loose scrub uniform as Pepe was feeding him. He offered Pepe five dollars to cop a feel. Five dollars? That's not even one hundred and fifty pesos, not enough for a movie and snack at Jollibee back home.

But at the same retirement home, there was one old widow who was kind to him, Doña Juana from Argentina. Initially Doña Juana was indifferent to him. One day he greeted her in Spanish, and since then, she had been friendly toward him. When he finished early with the other residents, he brought her tea and listened to her stories of her childhood in Buenos Aires. She loved to tell stories of *sus años felices* — her happy years.

One morning Pepe was pulled aside and told that Doña Juana had died in her sleep. The Filipina nurse attending to her knew the lady was fond of him so she let him say goodbye. He saw her serene face; he leaned into her and whispered.

"Adiós, Doña Juana. Que en paz descanse usted. Que le reúna usted con su esposo, su familia, y todos sus amigos de la infancia." (Goodbye, Doña Juana. May you rest in peace. May you be reunited with your husband, your family and all your childhood friends.)

The nurse patted Pepe's shoulder as he walked away from the deathbed.

"Pepe, ibinulong mo ba sa yumao 'yung mga problema mo?" (Pepe, did you whisper your problems to the deceased?)

"Huh? Naku, hindi. Nagpaalam lang ako sa kanya." (Oh, no. I only said my farewell.)

He left that job when a friend told him about this meat-packing plant: they pay five dollars above the Ontario minimum wage, and full shifts and overtime are the norm.

8:00 a.m.

The buzzer sounds. First morning break.

Five more pork legs exit the chute. He throws them into the bins. He stretches his shoulders and arms and walks through the work station doors.

He discards his gloves, apron, and mask. He keeps his hair net and hard hat. He returns to the corridor, steps on the boot-bath, and heads toward the cafeteria.

The Portuguese tables are the busiest, the immigrants from Madeira and the Azores making up the largest ethnic group among the workers, including the supervisors and managers. They get first dibs on the microwaves to warm up their snacks.

The East Europeans are Serbians, Croatians, Albanians, Romanians, Ukrainians, and Russians, almost all men, almost all taller than six feet. Instead of snacking, they smoke and drink their coffee on the outdoor patio.

Pepe exchanges high-fives with the kababayans at the Filipino table. Most of them are recent immigrants like him. They open their bags and put their merienda in the middle for sharing: pan de sal with Cheez Whiz, ensaymada, hopia, turon. Pepe takes out his thermos and pours himself coffee. He chews on granola bars and dried fruit.

The table beside them is sharing their snacks too. Several Salvadorans, Chileans, Venezuelans, Mexicans, and Dominicans. Lupita, a morena from Mexico City, sits near Pepe. She takes a sip of his coffee and tells him it's not strong enough.

Behind them are the tables for Blacks, Indians, Islanders, and Chinese. The Muslim brothers at the end, mostly Pakistanis and Bangladeshis, keep among themselves, trying to safeguard their already compromised state of grace. Interspersed among all tables are the few white Canadians who sit wherever they want.

Though the tables are not officially reserved for any ethnic group, the workers converge along shared origin or language. Newcomers see this on their first day and gravitate toward their tribe of choice. The food and drinks on the tables reflect the diversity of the workers in this plant.

PEPE CHECKS HIS watch; it's 8:10 a.m. He stands and heads to the toilet inside the men's lockers. There are six urinals; the first four are already occupied. The sixth has its usual pisser, Vladimir the Serb, who is always at that urinal. He opens the high window above it and he smokes while he pisses. He stands there for a while until his cigarette is finished, oblivious to the lineup behind him. There is no smoking inside the building but he persists; the others are either scared of him or simply don't care.

Pepe checks his watch. With just a minute to spare, he walks to the fifth urinal and pisses.

Vladimir looks over to him.

"You Asians, you have small dicks."

Pepe keeps his eyes on the wall.

"We have bigger brains though."

"If that's true, why are we both working in this hell hole."

Pepe laughs. He doesn't have a witty reply to that one. He finishes up and walks to the sink.

"See ya, Vlad. Don't forget to wash your hands."

"See ya, man."

Everyone here is "man," "mate," "buddy," or "friend." Except among tablemates, no one really asks for names. With the high turnover among workers, people don't invest personal time in getting to know others.

Still, the Filipino guys know Vladimir because of his smoking habit at the urinals. They even nicknamed him "Supot" after one of them inadvertently saw his uncircumcised penis while pissing beside him.

Pepe makes his way back to the work area and puts on a new apron, face mask, and gloves.

8:20 a.m.

The buzzer sounds. Work restarts.

Pepe has a couple of minutes free as the pig parts make their way through the line. But soon enough, the pork legs race their way toward him, one every four to six seconds, sometimes faster.

Where he is, this is the first stage. It's physical and mechanical work. They're all men here, and he's one of the few Asians. The output from here goes to the second stage where they perform deboning and precise cutting and trimming by hand. The company offers a course on butchery techniques; it teaches the industry standard to prepare bacon, ribs, shoulders, loin, ham, and other retail cuts.

The output from the second stage goes to different packing lines on the third and final stage. There are different sizes of plastic bags and carton boxes. Some cuts are packed with absorbent pads. Each bag is electronically weighed and labelled before going into a box, which is likewise labelled and then carried onto a pallet. A full pallet is wrapped with industrial-strength stretch wrap and moved by forklift to a holding area before it is loaded to a refrigerated truck.

The only parts of the carcass that go straight from the first to the third stage are the head, trotters, and tail. They are accumulated in a special bin and are shipped, together with the bones and trimmings from the second stage, to another plant in Brampton, northwest of Toronto. That plant produces hot dogs, among other things.

From start to finish, the pork meat travels through the three sterile stages, all maintained at minus four degrees Celsius. All stages are scrubbed clean, power washed, and sterilized every evening.

When Pepe was hired, he started at the third stage. He picked up the boxes from the end of the packing line conveyor belt and stacked them on a pallet. It was grunt work, but he didn't have to wear aprons, hair nets, and face masks, so it wasn't all bad. The mostly Portuguese guys he worked with even had a boom box playing MuchMusic dance CDs.

Lupita and most of the women work at the second stage. Those who complete and pass the butchery course are paid a slightly higher hourly rate. At the first stage, the men who were trained to operate the industrial bone saws also enjoy extra pay to compensate for the risk of serious injury.

10:20 a.m.

The buzzer sounds. Second morning break.

Pepe again waits until the last pork leg exits from the chute.

He exits the work area, discards the hygiene kit, returns to the cafeteria, and sits down at the Filipino table. He takes his thermos and slides his chair toward Lupita on the neighbouring Latino table. She takes the thermos from him and pours coffee on the cap.

"¿Ya está frío?" (Is it already cold?)

Lupita takes a sip and passes it to Pepe.

"No, está bien." (No, it's all right.)

Buboy, a chatty thirtysomething Manileño, teases him across the table.

"Hoy, Pepe, sinagot ka na ba ng Mexicana?" (Hey, Pepe, has the Mexican agreed to be your girlfriend?)

Pepe grins and brushes off Buboy's comment.

"¿Qué te dijo tu paisano, Pepe?" (What did your countryman say, Pepe?)

Pepe puts his arm on her shoulders.

"Es nada, no le hagas caso." (It's nothing, don't pay attention to him.)

Buboy doesn't give up. He picks a turon with a napkin. He slides his chair closer to the couple and offers the turon to Lupita. She readily accepts and bites it. The flaky wrapper and sweet fried banana hit the spot.

Buboy tries to make small talk with Lupita.

"Turon. Turon de … Turon de banana. Hoy, Pepe, ano sa kastila'yung saging?" (Turon. Turon made of … Turon made of banana. Hey, Pepe, how do you say banana in Spanish?)

"Plátano. Turrón de plátano."

Lupita takes another bite and gives the rest to Pepe while licking her lips and fingertips.

"Es riquísimo." (It's really good.)

Pepe sees Remedios looking at him. She's one of two Filipinas in their group.

He smiles at her.

"Remedios, binata pa pala itong si Alvaro na taga-Venezuela. Gusto mo ba na ipakilala kita?" (Remedios, Alvaro from Venezuela is still single, would you like me to introduce you?)

Remedios furtively glances at the handsome Alvaro. She giggles with Consolación, the other Filipina. Buboy slides back to his seat and rejoins the ladies.

"O ano, Remedios, Consolación, guapo si Alvaro, 'di ba?" (So what do you think, Remedios, Consolación, Alvaro's handsome, no?)

From the Latino table, the Venezuelan turns to them and smiles.

"Oye, escuché mi nombre y la palabra 'guapo.' ¿Ustedes hablan de mí?" (Hey, I heard my name and the word "guapo." Are you talking about me?) Pepe replies as the ladies giggle even more.

"Alvaro, eres soltero, ¿no? Pues, tengo dos amigas solteras aquí, Remedios y Consolación." (Alvaro, you are single, right? Well, I have two single lady friends here, Remedios and Consolación.)

Alvaro waves at the ladies. Pepe encourages him to join them.

"Platica con ellas, ándale." (Chat with them, go ahead.)

Alvaro takes the vacant seat across the ladies and tries to break the ice, albeit haltingly, in English. Remedios insists on being called Remy, and Consolación asks him to call her Siony. Buboy tries to join the chat, but Alvaro is focused on the two Filipinas.

PEPE CHECKS HIS watch; it's 10:30 a.m. He stands and tells Lupita he'll see her at lunch.

At the toilets, Vladimir is at his usual spot, but fortunately the first urinal is free so Pepe doesn't have to stand beside the Serb and inhale his cigarette smoke.

He washes his hands and makes his way back.

10:40 a.m.

The buzzer sounds. Work restarts.

Pepe stands at his station. Someone pats his shoulder. He turns toward the masked guy beside him. The guy temporarily lowers his mask and smiles. It's Alvaro.

"Pepe, ¿de verdad son solteras?" (Pepe, are they really single?)

"¿Remedios y Consolación? Sí, son solteras. ¿Te gusta una de ellas?" (Remedios and Consolación? Yes, they're both single. Do you like any of them?)

"Pues sí, de hecho las dos me gustan." (Well, yes. In fact I like both of them.)

The first pork leg exits the chute and Pepe prods Alvaro to go to his own station.

"Hablamos luego. A trabajar." (We'll talk later. Time to work.)

Pepe's mind wanders as he does his task. It would be great if either Remedios or Consolación ends up dating and even marrying Alvaro. Imagine the beautiful babies.

Both ladies are in their early thirties, same as Alvaro. They were all here by the time Pepe started. They were sitting at the same tables but those tables never intersected until Pepe arrived and began chatting with Lupita. She initially viewed him as a novelty as she had never met a Filipino before, but they hit it off.

Being a good Catholic boy, Pepe invited Lupita to attend mass at St. Michael's Cathedral downtown. She loved how old that church was but told Pepe that they have churches in Mexico that are five hundred years old. He told her that they have centuries-old churches in the Philippines too, though a lot of them have been damaged by war, earthquakes, and volcanoes.

One Sunday after mass, Pepe and Lupita took the subway north and he brought her to Sampaguita, one of the oldest Filipino restaurants in Toronto. They had pancit and crispy pata. And even though it was already autumn, Pepe ordered one halo-halo and they shared it; she finished most of it, she especially loved the red and green nata de coco.

Lupita is living with a spinster aunt. She's hoping to move out and find her own place and eventually find a better job that matches her skills. She was a grade school teacher in Mexico City. Her aunt sponsored her to come as her personal caregiver with the understanding that she'd find her luck once she was here. It's a story not unlike that of many Filipinos in Canada.

Remedios and Consolación were sales ladies at ShoeMart in Manila. They are taller than average and are quite easy on the eyes. They also started out as caregivers. Buboy hangs out with them on weekends; there's a karaoke bar on St. Clair Avenue West that they frequent on Saturday evenings. Pepe thought that Buboy was pursuing one of the ladies, though he wasn't sure which one.

12:40 p.m.
The buzzer sounds. Lunch break.

Pepe chats with Alvaro on their way back to the cafeteria. He suggests that he should get to know each one of the Filipinas first before making up his mind who to pursue, if at all.

Pepe opens his backpack, retrieves a Tupperware box, and walks to the microwaves. All ten of them are being used by the Portuguese. He waits in line. Lupita joins him with her own lunch box and rubs Pepe's back.

"¿Qué hay para comer?" (What's for lunch?)

"Arroz blanco con pedacitos de Spam. No he tenido tiempo para cocinar algo." (White rice with slices of Spam. I didn't have time to cook anything.)

Lupita makes a face. She doesn't like Spam.

"La próxima vez me avisas y te cocino algo." (Next time, tell me so I can cook something for you.)

"Gracias, mi Lupita." (Thanks, Lupita.)

After heating their food, Pepe pulls Lupita's chair and they both sit at the Filipino table, her hand resting on his thigh. Upon seeing Pepe's Spam, Buboy offers him catsup packets. Pepe accepts and squeezes them on his lunch. He notices the McDonald's branding.

"Nagnakaw ka ba ng catsup sa McDo?" (Did you steal catsup from McDonald's?)

Remedios interjects before Buboy could respond.

"Iyan pa? Pati asukal, asin, paminta. At napkin, sangkaterbang napkin ang inuuwi niyan galing McDo." (He's the one to do it. He steals sugar, salt, and pepper packets. And napkins too, he brings home loads of napkins from McDonald's.)

"Sobra ka naman. Masigasig na pagtitipid 'yan." (You're exaggerating. That's resourceful frugality.)

The other Filipinos chuckle at Buboy's defense of himself. Pepe translates this for Lupita and she laughs, saying that Mexicans bring home condiments from McDonald's too.

After finishing his lunch, Pepe takes out his thermos and pours the remaining coffee on the cap. It's already lukewarm. Lupita takes the cap and volunteers to heat it up in the microwave.

Buboy nods at Pepe and points to Lupita with his lips.

"Pepe, kayo na ba? Obvious naman e." (Pepe, are you two officially a couple? It's already obvious.)

"Masaya kami sa isa't isa." (We're happy with each other.)

"At bakit naman hindi Pinay ang niligawan mo?" (And why didn't you pursue a Filipina?)

Remedios and Consolación join in and insist that Pepe answer the question. Pepe grins at the three, then replies to the ladies.

"Sa totoo lang, akala ko kasi nililigawan na kayo ni Buboy kaya hindi na ako nakisawsaw." (The truth is, I thought Buboy was already pursuing you so I didn't bother to get involved.)

Remedios, sitting beside Pepe, leans and pinches him on the arm and admonishes him in a low voice. He pretends to recoil at the pain.

"Naku, Pepe, hindi kami talu niyang ni Buboy. Hindi mo ba alam!" (Oh Pepe, Buboy and us, we're like sisters. Didn't you know?)

Buboy's eyes open wide on realizing that Remedios has just outed him. He opens his mouth but is speechless. He dismisses her with a wave and tells Pepe to ignore her.

Lupita returns with the reheated coffee and gives it to Pepe. He sips it while reassuring Buboy.

"Ano ba naman, Buboy? Taong 2001 na, okay lang kung kapwa mo lalaki ang gusto mo. Anong pakialam ng ibang tao?" (What's the matter, Buboy? It's 2001, it's okay if you fancy guys. Who cares what other people think?)

Buboy looks at Pepe, then at Remedios and Consolación.

Remedios offers Buboy the peace sign.

"Peace na tayo?" (So all is forgiven?)

Buboy's scowl slowly turns into a smile and he gives a high-five to Remedios, then Consolación. And finally to Pepe. And to Lupita.

"Espera, espera, ¿qué pasa?" (Wait, wait, what's happening?)

Pepe whispers to Lupita that Buboy just came out.

Lupita's jaw drops and she raises her hands to her face. She stands up and walks to where Buboy sits and hugs him from behind. And in her limited English she cheers on Buboy.

"We are happy for you."

Buboy smiles, takes Lupita's hands, and thanks her.

From the other table, Alvaro turns toward them and asks what the excitement is all about. Lupita tells him.

"Es que Buboy acaba de salir del closet." (Buboy just came out of the closet.)

Alvaro also stands and pats Buboy's shoulder.

"Muy bien, Buboy, muy bien." (Very good, Buboy, well done.)

Buboy awkwardly thanks Alvaro but raises his hands in protest.

"Stop, that's it. Please don't tell anyone else or the whole cafeteria may start a pride parade for me."

PEPE CHECKS HIS watch; it's 1:10 p.m. He packs up his Tupperware and thermos, then he squeezes Lupita's hand before getting on his feet. He goes to the lockers.

Vladimir is at his usual spot, and there's a haze of cigarette smoke enveloping him.

Pepe takes the first urinal and yells at the tall Serb.

"Open the window, Vlad, the cigarette smoke stinks!"

The haze quickly dissipates as soon as the window is opened.

1:20 p.m.

Pepe stretches and burps as he stands at his station. The supervisor walks by and gives him a thumbs-up.

Last week, during a lull in processing, the supervisor stood beside him for a quick chat. He told Pepe that he could stay in this station as long as he wanted. Or he could take a forklift operation training course or take the bone sawing course. Both of those positions pay a higher rate. Pepe told him he'd think about the forklift course. The supervisor, a native of the Azores, also commented that he spoke excellent English for an Oriental. It's the first time that he's been called an Oriental. He let it pass; he was called worse things at the retirement home.

Pepe now thinks about the forklift course. If he completes that, he can work at other warehouses, maybe even at construction sites. That would be good and reliable money.

Driving the forklift in this plant is probably the least physically taxing of all the jobs here. The operators are not on their feet the whole day like him, they don't risk losing fingers or hands to the bone saw, they're not in danger of getting cut by knives, and it's unlikely they will suffer from repetitive movement injuries. They just have to be cautious in transporting bins and not crashing into corners or other forklifts as they navigate about the plant.

NOT HALF AN hour passes when Pepe hears an alarm much louder than the buzzer. He sees red lights flashing in the ceiling and walls, followed by an automated announcement:

"SAFETY ALERT! PLEASE REMAIN CALM AND EVACUATE THE BUILDING NOW!"

The line is stopped and they evacuate quickly. They walk out with their aprons, masks, and gloves all the way to the parking lot inside the building compound. Based on an earlier experience, Pepe guessed that this may be another nitrogen leak. It happened in his first month, when they were herded and kept here for thirty minutes while the building interior was flushed with fresh air and retested for toxicity.

Pepe walks through the crowd and finds the workers from the second stage. He sees Lupita huddling with Buboy, Remedios, and Consolación. He and Alvaro wait with them. It is cold, maybe minus ten degrees Celsius. It's worse when the wind blows. After fifteen minutes, they are led to the cafeteria for further waiting. They sit at their tables and in hushed tones the workers confirm it's another nitrogen leak. Liquid nitrogen is used to refrigerate the building. It has neither colour nor odour and is extremely cold. It can cause serious physical injury and even death without warning. If the building did not have an advanced warning system, they'd all be dead by now.

Pepe holds Lupita's hand as he checks his watch. It's 2:20 p.m. He wonders if they will have to work overtime to make up for the delay.

The safety manager and the union representative enter the cafeteria. The manager stands on a stool and announces that the safety of the work stations has been re-established and that work will resume in ten minutes.

Pepe goes for one last piss and hand wash. He returns to his station with fresh gloves, a fresh mask, and a fresh apron.

2:30 p.m.
The buzzer sounds. Work restarts.

Pepe sorts the pork legs abandoned earlier at his station and tosses each into the appropriate bin. The supervisor walks by and gives him a thumbs-up.

He's still thinking of the nitrogen leak. The danger is real. One day the warning system may malfunction and the colourless and odourless gas could flow through the building and put everyone to permanent deep sleep. At least it'll be quick.

If he and Lupita are to move forward, he needs to be more ambitious and work toward his and their next level. The forklift course is looking more promising now; it's a stepping stone to a better job in construction. That has its own work hazards, but at least not with nitrogen.

4:00 p.m.
The buzzer sounds. Work ends.

He waits for the remaining pork legs to arrive and tosses them to the bins. He looks up toward the beginning of the line; there are no more carcasses in the queue.

He and Alvaro head out and they stamp their time cards. The timestamp indicates at least an hour of overtime.

Pepe sees Lupita gathering her lunch bag at the cafeteria. He hugs and kisses her. She smiles and tells him she'll wait for him outside.

He gathers his backpack. He's about to walk out when the union representative asks for a few minutes with him. Carlos is from Chile, and he's a bit older than Pepe. He fled Santiago with his parents when he was a kid; his activist parents would have been imprisoned by the dictator Augusto Pinochet had they not escaped. He hung out with Carlos in his first month here; they both worked at the third stage together, stacking boxes on pallets. Then Carlos was recruited to be a union representative for the United Food and Commercial Workers, then he became very busy after that.

"¿Podemos platicar en el vestuario? Tengo prisa, Lupita me espera." (Can we chat in the lockers? I'm in a rush, Lupita is waiting for me.)

Carlos walks with Pepe and sits beside him as he changes his boots.

"Pepe, ¿has pensado en ser representante de la UFCW? Como viste esta tarde, necesitamos más representación en las decisiones sobre la seguridad para esta planta. Necesitamos personas como tú, especialmente tú que andas en ambos círculos de los filipinos e hispanos." (Pepe, have you thought about being a representative of the UFCW? As you've seen today, we need more representation in the safety decisions for this plant. We need people like you, especially you who form part of both Filipino and Hispanic circles.)

"Gracias mi amigo, pero no he pensado en eso. No creo que me quede aquí por largo plazo." (Thank you my friend, but I haven't thought about it. I don't think I'll be here for the long term.)

Pepe stands and closes his locker. Carlos walks with him to the exit.

"Nunca hemos tenido un representante filipino. Vas a hacer un gran servicio para tu comunidad si aceptas la posición." (We've never had a Filipino representative. You'll be doing a great service for your community if you accept the position.)

Carlos places his hand on Pepe's shoulder.

"Piénsalo, mi amigo. Seguiremos los pasos de César Chávez y Larry Itliong." (Think about it, my friend. We'll be following the footsteps of César Chávez and Larry Itliong.)

Pepe smiles. Larry Itliong was the legendary Filipino labour leader who fought for Filipino farm workers in California from the 1930s to the 1970s. To walk in his footsteps is something he never even dares to think of. He's only an ordinary guy trying to survive in this new land. But life is more than a paycheque. Maybe he can do more.

He sees Lupita waiting outside the door with Remedios, Consolación, Buboy, and Alvaro. Snow is falling heavily, so they all have their hoods up.

"Bueno, Carlitos, vamos a ver. Tengo que consultar a la jefa." (All right, Carlitos, we'll see. I'll run it by the girlfriend.)

Pepe and Carlos part ways with an abrazo.

He exits through the revolving door and takes Lupita's hand. They follow Remedios and Consolación as they cling on to Buboy's arms for support. Alvaro walks alongside them and points to the slippery spots to avoid.

He had always dreamt of snow since he was a kid, but now that he's here, winter is simply another challenge in an already long list of challenges in an immigrant's life. Still, he revels in how picturesque everything looks when covered with freshly fallen snow. Even this trashy alleyway they're trudging on looks like a postcard.

Pepe fondly watches the gleeful reaction of his friends to the wintry scene. He pulls Lupita closer to him, she who holds his hand and warms his heart.

GRACE SANCHEZ MACCALL

Wild West

THE RHYTHMIC CLACKS of tiles being shuffled for mahjong, now in its sixth hour of play, rumbled on along with the adults' continuous chatter. My titos' stories got more colourful and the volume louder with the passing time and the growing pile of empty beer bottles until, finally, when they got too loud and raunchy, my mom said, "Hoy, bastos," and shushed them quiet, a command met with raucous laughter.

We can hear them from the basement, where we are attempting back bends and splits inspired by Nadia Comaneci's perfect ten. The boys opted for a Starsky and Hutch shoot out, hiding behind the washer and dryer, suitcases, empty boxes, and paint cans in our otherwise stark, cemented indoor playground. We were told to stay inside and avoid other kids because Mom said the neighbourhood kids are "salbahe" and have no manners. "Can you believe it, I heard a boy talking back to his parents," she said.

Our house is a gathering place for Filipinos each Sunday. My cousins, the ones born in Canada who cannot speak Tagalog, were part of the regulars plus the Inocente family who Dad met when he first arrived alone in Calgary in 1971 to work for an oil and gas company. We live closest to St. Mary's, so everyone just ends up here. There is always somebody new these days — from Winnipeg, from Toronto, from the Philippines — and when they find the Catholic Church, they find us. I'm not even sure who my real relatives are because everyone at the house is a Tito or a Tita whether they are my real Uncles and Aunties or not.

The adults call each other Doctor and Attorney when they get together for these events even though we all know that Dr. Santos mops the floor at Foothills Hospital and Attorney Villalobos is a security guard downtown.

Dr. Santos saved my brother's life, Mom said. My brother was holding his side in pain in his room one day and Doc took one look at him all bloated and feverish and drove him to Emerg. The next Sunday, instead of the usual batch of garlicky pork adobo, we made Doc's favourite: a fish relleno that took forever to prepare. I had to remove the fine fish bones from the flesh so my mother could mix the sliver-free concoction with onions, potatoes, peas, and raisins, then stuff it back in the skin and sew it up to the fish shape it once was.

At the Stampede that summer, we lined up for free pancakes even though Dad objected. "We are not beggars," he scolded. I thought everyone looked strange wearing gingham shirts, denim vests, and cowboy hats and greeting each other with a "Yahoo!" My dad usually wears suits to work, but during the Stampede when the "greatest outdoor show on Earth" is on for ten days, he wears blue jeans and cowboy shirts just like every single person in the city. I didn't want to be a cowboy. I wanted to wear my moccasins instead of boots. Also, I had a vest with fringes so I wanted to dress more like the girl in Sister Dolores's book of Western pioneers — "Indian child," it said on the photo. I even have the same long black hair that I wore in two braids.

I like this girl Pauline in my class who also has long black hair that she sometimes wears in braids. She doesn't seem interested in school at all but she is the best in art class. I saw her drawing of an eagle in flight that she drew from her imagination, not copied from a book even, and I wish I could draw like that. Pauline is the only other girl in my grade who is different, an outsider like me, and I am always disappointed when she doesn't come to class, which is most of the time. "Find another reading partner," Sister Dolores would snap on her way to the office to call Pauline's parents. When she is in class, she's usually very quiet, looking down with her curtain of bangs covering her eyes, while she doodles in her notebook. Or else she's looking out the window absentmindedly, touching her long braid draped over her left collarbone, hand over hand as if slowly climbing an infinite rope. I once asked Pauline what shampoo she uses to get her hair so shiny. "My mom rubs special berries on my hair," she said. My mom only buys the $1.44 sale shampoos from Woolco even though my sister and I keep asking her to buy the fruity herbal essence kind. I asked Pauline what kind of berries her mom uses and where I could find them but she was quiet and gazing outside again. Later, on the playground, she told me she will ask her mom if I can come pick berries next spring and that made me happy. I have not been invited to any of my classmates' houses before.

It snowed in October and Mom went into a panic because I swear to God her worst fear is us freezing outside in the winter. We discovered that my hand-me-down coat was too small, so the following Saturday, we went downtown to the Bay to buy a new one. Dad didn't want to drive us because of all the construction. "Too many one-ways now and there is no place to park. It's faster for you to take the Number Seven bus," he said. We were about to enter the store from the doors on Eighth Avenue when I saw someone who I thought was Pauline. I ran to her but it was a different girl who had the same long shiny black hair almost to her waist. She was with an adult, maybe her dad or grandfather, and they were leaning on the windows of a store that had a display of cowboy boots and leather saddles. The grandpa smiled at me in the same friendly way my titos did with their flushed red cheeks and sleepy eyes when all our good TV shows were finished and we'd say good night to them. I opened my mouth to say hi but Mom called me to hurry up. As I was holding the heavy glass department store doors open, another woman rudely shoved past us like she didn't even see us, her tense grip pulling her two kids closer as she warned them in a voice loud enough for everyone to hear: "Stay away from those drunks on Eighth Avenue Mall."

I LIKE IT when the other families come to the house a little earlier on weekends. When the adults are busy in the kitchen, the men smoking, laughing, and telling stories and the moms frying lumpia or stirring pancit noodles, they send us kids to set up their mahjong table in the living room. I double fold a flannel blanket and smooth it out as a tablecloth while my sister takes the mahjong suitcase and carefully scatters the tiles on top. None of us kids know the rules of the game. All we know is that the adults stack the tiles face down and build walls in front of them, two layers tall, then take turns drawing tiles that they then hide from each other's sight. They also discard an unwanted tile to the centre before the next person can draw. I think the game is about matching patterns, flowers, bamboo sticks, dots, or Chinese characters, and yelling "pong," "kong," or "chow," and pretending to have tiles that you don't have so other players will discard the ones you really need to win the game.

We make up our own games. We stack the tiles into tall structures, building towers like the kind we see sprouting in the city centre, then knocking them down to hear that clacking sound as the tiles hit each other. Another game is to tumble and swirl the pile of tiles in the middle the way the adults do, then instead of building walls, we stand the tiles on their ends just a little bit apart to make a curvy snake pattern that weaves on the surface of the table. We'd play rock paper scissors to decide who would get to push the first tile, then, breathless with anticipation, we watch the lucky winner gently push the front one to start the magical scene of the wall of tiles falling one by one like dominoes.

LEAH RANADA

Foragers

THE TIKI TORCHES are Papa's idea even though he hates everything capricious. "Iris has never been to Boracay," he says by way of explanation, and I barely stop myself from saying, "Neither have we." The flames make the hot June evening hotter. The hedges around Iris's small backyard crackle in the sweltering air.

"She looks like Cate Blanchett," Paulo says.

I glare at my older brother until he realizes how weird he is, gushing about Papa's new girlfriend. But the night has started out weird anyway. I showed up at Iris's townhouse, four on the dot, finding Paulo practising card tricks in the living room, our father staking torches in the backyard. Iris was still at work. When she arrived, it seemed like she knew something was up — my father had provided just enough hints to intrigue — but she had not anticipated the presence of his children in her home. Her smile was wide and stiff when Papa introduced us, his voice booming with pride. I excused myself to the kitchen, *her* kitchen, and busied myself mincing herbs on the marble countertop, picking up any bits that strayed from the chopping board. Paulo bowed and started performing card tricks. Iris relaxed. She laughed throatily, her smooth, wintry face alight when a coin disappeared in Paulo's hands and he plucked it from behind her ear. "I'm speechless. Can you do it again?"

The bay window overlooking the backyard frames Papa and Iris perfectly. A torch at each end of the table, pearly white tablecloth and serviettes, on which Papa has set Iris's Noritake's dining set and crystal wine glasses. I have picked the bottle of rosé sitting in an ice bucket near the tall clear vase of sunflowers. The blooms face the aquamarine bar of Jericho Beach beyond the hedge. They are working on my first course: arugula salad with oranges, pomegranate seeds, and goat cheese.

My father puts down his fork whenever Iris speaks. They met a month ago at a health and wellness convention where Papa was selling an herbal supplement that improves everything from hair follicles to the digestive tract. Since Mama kicked him out two years ago, we have lost count of the odd jobs. It is easier to track the short-term girlfriends. A waitress at a sushi joint. A biker he met at a lakeside retreat. The aspiring singer selling her CDs along Commercial Drive.

I turn to Paulo. "How long do you think she'll last?"

He doesn't answer, just looks around the kitchen. At the matching stainless steel refrigerator and stove, upholstered stools along the breakfast bar, a curio cabinet housing three different kinds of porcelain tea sets. Iris is different from all the others.

Papa was waiting for me outside the campus last week. His pressed clothes told me he had a job. The clean nails hinted at a girlfriend. "When will you get a phone?" I told him.

"Is that the hello I get from my little girl?"

He offered to treat me at a nearby café where I ordered the most expensive latte. On the small overhead TV, there was a news story about Muhammad Ali's funeral. The camera panned a bird's eye view over the slow procession on the streets of Louisville. People cheered, waved American flags, threw flowers at the hearse.

"Muhammad Ali liked magic," I told Papa as we waited for our drinks. "Ha?"

"He had a personal magician who taught him some tricks. Paulo told me."

"Just like your dim brother to believe stories like that."

As we sipped our drinks, Papa didn't tell me he was in love. Or that he wanted my help to impress a new girlfriend. Instead, he told me he was proud of me for pursuing my passion. "Culinary arts. I've always known you have my fine taste." He mentioned a new restaurant by the Seawall where he would take me one day. To be heaped upon with such expression of fatherly pride and adoration was as strange as it was rare, stirring a yearning I didn't know

I have. That was how I ended up in Whole Foods this afternoon, buying ingredients for a romantic three-course dinner for two.

Beside me, Paulo checks his watch. "My shift starts at eight." He glances at the scene outside, wondering when he could shed his damask vest, dark pants, and button-down shirt for his 7-Eleven uniform. His long sleeves are folded from wrist up to prove he has nothing to hide.

"You're leaving me here with them?"

He frowns. "You planning to be here all night?"

We don't talk about Mama, who is probably just starting her overnight shift at the geriatric ward downtown. "I have plenty of men in my life," she jokes during breakfast of Spam and fried eggs before heading to bed. She talks about octogenarians whom she has to undress and help to their bathroom routines, whose loose skin and aching joints she massages with pain-relief ointments and topical hydrocortisone. I sometimes wish I worked with her, to ease her nightly burden and perhaps harden my own shell against the sight of our proud, able-bodied father turning dingy and thinning. To Mama, he is more helpless than his aging patients.

Our conversation at the café last week annoyed me but also left me feeling vaguely hopeful. Our father has had many girlfriends. He has asked Paolo and me for favours before. But he has never asked a favour about a girlfriend. It was Iris who made him do it, pushed him past a comfort level. Who knows what else is possible? Life has been known to allow miracles. Out there, in the fairy-tale backyard, our father is already behaving like a better man, well-dressed and soft-spoken. When he calls Paulo for another trick, he does so with a snap of fingers, as if summoning a well-trained butler. My brother, grateful for any willing audience, grins and heads outside. He spreads his deck of cards in a fan on the table in front of Iris.

Main course is roasted bass and asparagus. Iris is a healthy eater, according to Papa.

Will he change his ways for her? Or will she lay a path on which to guide him through? Ever since we reunited with Mama from Manila, it has seemed as if Papa doesn't know what to do with himself. He refuses to work for anyone, but he doesn't have the networks here that helped his printing business back home. The foul words he called out as a form of affection to friends have become just foul words, the way he squared his shoulders during an argument is now just hollow swagger. The way he is behaving around Iris right now hits me with a strange kind of homesickness, as if we are back home and we are children again, except that he has transported this strange woman with us while Mama is out on some prolonged errand.

Paulo walks in with the empty salad plates. His forehead is beaded with sweat, eyes dancing with excitement. Like a boy who has been playing in the streets. "It's hot under those torches." He clears the plates and puts them in the dishwasher like he is in his own kitchen.

"I forgot to get ice cream," I blurt out, as if he could conjure a missing ingredient on the spot. A panic seizes my chest for ruining the grand plan of closing the evening with peach melba. The peaches have been poached, the raspberry sauce is simmering. I check Iris's freezer for a substitute but only find a tub of coco yogurt, its contents too runny.

"You sure you need it?"

"Well."

The oven timer goes *ding!* The bass fillets are ready. They are golden and crisp, but the flesh will be tender on their tongues. Paulo gapes, impressed, as I carefully lay the fish and seasoned asparagus spears on dinner plates already adorned with grapefruit-flavoured salsa.

The dinner plates are huge — I have to use my elbows as I bring out the main course the way I have seen waitresses at Earls do it. Iris is talking about Muhammad Ali. "I think of him during my cardio kickboxing class. Float like a butterfly, sting like a bee." My shoulder stiffens, hearing Papa's voice in my head. "Cardio kickboxing? What kind of a half-assed workout is that?"

But he reaches across for Iris's hand. "Impressive. But sweetheart, let me tell you something about Muhammad Ali."

Iris leans forward, smiling.

"He is a true renaissance man. Did you know that he's into magic too? He has a personal magician teaching him tricks."

I almost dump the fish on his lap but settles for banging the plate in front of him. "Incredible," Iris says, but she is admiring my father, not the fish. It *is* hot under those torches. There is a sheen of perspiration on Iris's bare shoulders. My father dabs his forehead and nose with her serviette. I linger for a moment, waiting for them to taste the food, but Iris keeps talking about her gym routine. Her favourite is a ninety-minute yoga class followed by a sauna session. I'm starting to melt beneath the torch.

Iris notices me just when I turn to leave. "Stay for a little bit," she chirps, but I pretend not to hear. Inside, Paulo notices my darkened face, my quick strides. "Where are you off to?"

"I'm getting ice cream."

Then I am out on the streets, away from the dreamlike house. It is cooler out front, bringing the jarring clarity of a bad idea. Paulo and I have been fooled. Used. My brisk steps turn into a jog. I can go home, leave them wondering. But I don't do that, promising one thing and doing something else.

I learned to cook the summer Mama left for Canada. I wasn't trying to be a good daughter. Preparing meals just made the days less long. It divided the day into three parts. Breakfast. Lunch. Supper. Just simple dishes everyone can make. Fried galunggong, crisp from head to tail, the way I liked it best. Ligo sardines cooked with onions and kangkong. Sinangag with leftover rice and a lot of garlic. Corn and malunggay soup. In my culinary program, my classmates talk of family gatherings around elaborate feasts and secret recipes, trips to farmer's markets or hours in a backyard garden with a grandparent who taught them how to unleash the potency of fresh harvests. I have no such story to tell. My father merely made up our shared fine tastes. He would have starved Paulo and me with his horrible cooking. He was proud of his overfried minced pork and innards, which he served to his drinking friends who brought cases of Red Horse. His adobo was always too sour, never able to grasp the right blend of soy sauce and vinegar. I tried to fix it once, pouring a bit more soy sauce into the simmering pot when he stepped out of the kitchen. Turned out, Paulo had thought of doing the same. We never figured out who snuck into the kitchen first, but the dish had ended up so salty, it was inedible. Our oblivious father had shrugged and said he'll use more vinegar next time.

I reach a Safeway and meander through the aisles, searching for the right way to feel. Everything is too bright, promising something merry in boxes and packs. Cereals and potato chips. Candies and crackers. Jams and condiments.

In the dairy section, I take too long deciding between the store brand ice cream or a pint of something dairy-free with dubious ingredients. After grabbing an eight-dollar tub of Chapman's Vanilla, I wander over to the produce section where it's more spacious, chilled air drifting from the refrigerated display of vegetables.

In a lecture, we were shown pictures of fruits and vegetables before the development of agriculture. Purple carrots with gnarly roots. Bananas and watermelons laden with seeds. Primeval gourds with rough peels and meagre flesh. It took thousands of years before our ancestors learned to till land, willing it to offer up sweeter and juicier crops. The ancient tribes, whose days revolved around hunting and gathering, had to use rocks to break through scaly membranes and hard shells, relying on their senses and wits to tell food from poison.

It fascinates me, the life of prehistoric humans, as trusting of the world's abundance as they were cautious of its elements and beasts. They knew to stick together, their numbers more essential to their safety than any material possessions. I picture them crossing narrow isthmuses and navigating steep ranges, thriving along coasts and within caves. They leave their mark on places, not the other way around. They are strong and happy, free of complicated cares.

A STRANGE FIGURE meets me at Iris's door. Before I can cry out, I recognize Paulo, who has metamorphosed into a 7-Eleven clerk. He looks worried, as if his showman's garb has been confiscated by a fairy godmother with a curfew, exposing him to be a mere servant.

"What took you so long?" he hisses.

"Huh?"

"They're fighting."

I follow him to the kitchen, dark now. The scene in the backyard looks staged, a picture of carelessly abandoned elegance. The twin flames of the torches are bright against the dusk. There is no one at the table, just shadows playing on the linen and dinner plates. Judging from the remains, they have been so close to a different ending, a different life.

"They're upstairs," Paulo says, even though the angry voices through the ceiling have made that obvious.

"How did it start?"

Paulo tells me that things were going well until the topic of Robert Hall came up. Our father declared that his carelessness was to blame for the fate he suffered in the hands of the Abu Sayyaf. Iris was horrified. He couldn't have known, she insisted. He was a grown man who did his own due diligence, just happy to visit a land of warm, hospitable people. Paulo then mimicked our father's condescending snort. "Served him right for being so stupid, vacationing in that region."

"Maybe they'll get past it."

Paulo stares at me like I should know better. We both should have known better. "I'm late for work," he finally sighs. "You know, you don't have to stay." Lugging his backpack, bulky with costume and props, he leaves Iris's home.

As children in Manila, we were adept at finding the places in our small house that were farthest from wherever our parents were fighting. Paulo's room at the end of the hall was best when the action was in the living room. From there, the faults and flaws our parents flung at one another were strangers' noises, could easily have been the neighbours'. They yelled about missed tuition fees, our late mealtimes, a bad word Paulo or I was heard using. I often wondered if they had been happier before we were born.

Once they started, I would let myself in as Paulo shuffled cards. We didn't talk as I watched him play round after round of solitaire. If they fought in their bedroom, Paulo and I snuck out to the backyard, vanishing ourselves between flanks of damp laundry drying on the clotheslines.

I feel around for a light switch. Once it's bright, I see Paulo has wiped the counters and the glass stovetops clean. The two dessert bowls with seashell-patterned rims gape expectantly. There is a barely perceptible flutter in my chest, leftover thrill from the excitement of building a classy three-course meal. I thought of the recipes and ingredients for days, meticulously planning the interplay between textures and tastes.

Upstairs, my dad raps at a door. *Bang! Bang! Bang!* The polished copper pots hanging from the ceiling shake a little.

"Go away!"

I can pack up the peaches and pureed raspberries. Take the ice cream home, enjoy it myself. But it doesn't feel right, leaving out the sweet conclusion, the grand plan fragmented. I hunt around for a ladle.

Iris shrieks. "Get out of my house!"

"Don't yell at me!"

"You work for some pyramiding company. Verdaviva was debunked by the FDA!"

"What do you know about working, you trust fund princess!"

Everything is finished between them, but they fight like there is a way out.

When Mama left for Canada, our father wrote her lengthy emails. During the long-distance calls, Mama kept reminding us to be kind to him. When Papa wept at night, I slept, pained and comforted by his devotion. Six long years passed before we saw her again. Against the cool interiors of YVR, our mother looked much older. Her sentences had a lilt, syllables softer on her lips. She embraced Paulo and me together, our grown bodies awkward, getting reacquainted with the childlike need. She and Papa hugged for a longer time. Then we pushed our luggage carts out into the cold, giddy with hope.

The desserts are ready, but I still don't feel like going home. The yelling upstairs has receded, just hateful words I can't make out now. I start to feel like an intruder in that beautiful kitchen. Maybe they can still patch things up, come downstairs holding hands, smile tearily at the dainty bowls of peach melba. At the thought, my stomach recoils, as if from spoiled food.

The flames outside sway and sway.

Moments later, my father emerges at the top of the stairs. It's too dark to see his face, there is only the defeated slump of a shadow descending. Our eyes meet when he steps into the light, the silence brimming with unspeakable truths. Wounded, we have both surrendered, but neither releases the other from the trap of our bitter stares.

NATHALIE DE LOS SANTOS

Over the Rainbow

I.

July 1975.

Someone helped Maya to her feet when she came to. Her eyes stung. She let out a wet cough and clutched her spinning head. The person holding her said something about gas, or spray. Someone gave her a bottle of milk. She splashed the milk into her eyes and let out a gasp. She saw that her tuition money envelope was empty on the registrar's counter window.

Panic hit her. Her tuition. She ran out on the street, even if she knew the thieves were long gone. Her head pounded against her temples, her eyes sore. The person who helped her earlier called from behind.

"You okay? I can give you a ride home," he offered.

She gently declined and made her way to the car. Inside, she sat for a long while, gripping her steering wheel. Maya knew she couldn't stay in Bohol with her parents now. Maya glanced at the empty envelope on the passenger seat. The future she planned was stolen.

When she arrived home, the smell of honeysuckle wafted in her nostrils as she walked through the flowers in their garden. She heard her parents singing inside as usual. "Over the Rainbow" by Judy Garland.

She snuck into her room as they sang. On her desk were Annie's letters. Her sister's last letter asked her to come to Canada, dated six months ago. She didn't want to go. Maya took off her purse and went outside to lie on the balcony. Maybe she could ask for money, or maybe she could work before she went back to school. She tried to find a way to stay. But even her parents wanted her to go. They told her there'd be more over there for her: there would be better job opportunities, better medicine and social support, and better people. But Maya didn't know anyone, except Annie, Danilo, and Joseph. She couldn't imagine a world without her mom and dad.

As the sun set, the fireflies started to fly around the trees by the house. Maya thought of the comets she saw sometimes while she lay out here, white balls of light in the distant sky. Her mind drifted away from her fears. She thought of the men in the fields whistling at her when she first learned how to drive. Not many women learned, but her mother and father were very proud of her once she got her licence. She remembered when her brother Joseph bought her a radio when she was little, and she thought there were tiny people inside. Her father was so mad when he found her with a screwdriver and the radio disassembled on her lap.

Her mother called her, waking her. "Maya? When did you get home?" Her mother knelt by her and saw her tears. "What's the matter?"

Her mother was still as Maya told her what happened. In her mother's dark eyes, there was a bitter understanding. She held Maya's shoulder with a tight clasp, her face stoic.

"I thank the Lord that you aren't hurt," her mother said, gently. "Life is full of change and heartbreaks. It never stops. If the blanket is short, learn how to bend."

THE DAY CAME to go to Canada quickly, even if Maya did the application with the hopes of being rejected. She was only a year from finishing school and she left an impression in her interview with her perfect English. She wasn't sure why she was asked what the capital of New Brunswick was, because she would never be going there.

When she entered the kitchen, her dad was sitting at the table. He was drawing a cat on a sheet of paper. When he saw her with her suitcase, he rolled it up and gave it to her.

"I'll crush it." Maya shook her head, but he packed it for her anyway.

Her mom walked into the kitchen. "Eat or you'll be late."

As she sat down to eat, her dad opened her suitcase and placed his cat drawing inside.

"Be happy and try to marry an Americano. Naka-jackpot," her dad joked.

Her mom made a frustrated noise at her dad, then told her: "If you go anywhere, bring your sister."

Her Tito Ton honked as he pulled into the driveway. "Come on. Traffic will be bad."

"It's always bad," Maya called out through the window.

Her mom and dad followed her out. Her dad loaded her suitcase in the back.

"You'll do good, I know you will." Her dad embraced her.

Her mom kissed both of her cheeks. "Ask Mary to guide you."

Maya said about a million goodbyes before she went into the car. Maya looked out through the back window and waved, her two parents standing in the dirt driveway. The feeling of leaving finally hit her suddenly.

When's the next time I'm going to see you? How long will we be apart? Does this new life have to be forever?

Though they were the sizes of miniatures now, she saw her dad hold her mom in the driveway, her mom curling in his arms. She felt her eyes well up with tears.

"Hey, eyes forward," Ton joked. "Think about what you're gonna do."

She remembered what she told herself in the nights leading up to this. Maya would make their lives better and send money home. She held on to that.

HER BROTHER WAS three hours late. When Joseph approached her at the airport in Vancouver, she shrank, not recognizing him at first. But when he greeted her by name, she knew his voice. She was just on her second cup of coffee and halfway through her bag of candy she bought at the kiosk. The table was covered in colourful chocolate and candy wrappers.

"Sorry I'm late." Joseph chortled at her pile of wrappers. "Jesus, Maya. Where does it all go?"

Maya shrugged as she swept the candy wrappers off the table. Outside, the cool air of night kissed Maya in the parking lot. This place had a cold that bit at your ears, she had never felt this kind of cold before. He led her to an ancient Chrysler. He caught her expression.

"Don't worry, I'm saving up for a Ferrari."

She snorted and entered the passenger side. He turned the key once and the car sputtered. His second turn had the car rumbling and they set off.

Joseph started: "You know, Annie is something else. She went to Hawaii before you came, to see her boyfriend. We need the money for you, not her stupid vacation."

God, Maya just got here and there already was drama. She listened to his ranting about Annie's spending habits until Joseph pulled over. They went to an apartment complex where a woman sat on the front steps. Maya didn't recognize her at first, but like her brother, as soon as she heard her sister's voice, she knew this was Annie. The last time she saw Annie, Maya was probably nine or ten.

"I thought you were kidnapped!" Annie shouted. "What took so long?"

"He was a *little* late," Maya joked.

Joseph took her luggage upstairs without a word. Annie guided Maya up, but then noticed the bag of candy in Maya's hands.

"My God Maya, did you buy all these?"

"It's so good."

"You won't be able to fit in the door if you don't stop." Annie gave the bag a disgusted look.

Maya cradled the bag protectively as she stepped into a small den. They all sat around the couch.

"Give Maya the money," Joseph barked.

"Not right now, Jo. We gotta go to Danilo's, he's been waiting for us."

"You can give Maya her —"

"So she can bring it to Danilo's and get pickpocketed? He lives near Joyce, remember?"

That seemed to silence Joseph. Annie asked Maya about their parents on the car ride home.

"They're all right. They were excited about me coming here. Papa told me to find an American to marry."

Annie snorted. "But you're in Canada. Maybe one day we can move to the States. It's nice there."

"Get your boyfriend to sponsor you," Joseph interjected.

"Aye." Annie turned away from him.

Joseph parked, and Maya noticed Danilo's home had no grass on the front yard — just gravel and a small walkway. It was a two-level house. The bottom had a white door with two tinted windows by its side and a wide window to its right. The second floor had a railing that enclosed a sundeck and patio doors, with another set of windows on the left.

"They call this kinda house a 'Vancouver Special.' " Joseph explained.

Danilo's wife greeted them when they entered and led them to the living room. Maya was surprised at how small the home was compared to her parents' home. Maybe it was because Danilo had boxes everywhere.

Danilo was watching hockey when they entered, and he waved at Maya. "What took you so long?"

"There was a bunch of traffic coming into Vancouver," Joseph answered.

"You mean you were on Filipino time," Danilo jabbed at him, then a buzzer went off on the TV. Instantly, Danilo shouted, "Go CANUCKS!"

Joseph sat next to him, clapping at the goal.

"There's food." Danilo's wife pointed to the dining room table.

Maya grabbed a paper plate and loaded her plate with garlic fried rice. She also grabbed a cup of Sprite before she went to join her brothers. When she sat on the leather couch, it seemed to exhale out as she sank into it.

"How do you like Canada?" Danilo asked.

"It's nice." Maya finished chewing her bite. "How do I send money back home?"

Joseph replied pointedly, "If you send money back home, everyone will start asking ma and think you're rich —"

Annie interrupted, "You go get a money order at the bank. Make sure the money is USD. Then you mail it."

"Wouldn't it get stolen?"

"Lots of money get stolen. It's called *a golden elbow*. They forge your signature. Tita Ligaya has seen it with her own eyes. They use steam to open the envelope by melting the glue, take the money, seal it, and it's delivered empty —"

Danilo noticed Maya's fidgeting and interrupted, "You'll want to send it to our cousin in Cebu instead of Bohol. She can do the money exchange there. If you don't register your mail, it will take forever, like three months. If you register, the fastest is a month."

"How do you know if it gets there?"

"Someone's gotta sign for it when you register. It's worth the seven bucks, don't risk it."

All of these things made Maya tighten. Annie noticed this time. "I'll help you."

ANNIE HELPED MAYA get a job as a lab technician at the hospital. After a while, she saved up enough to send back home. Maya called her cousin Rosa in Cebu.

Rosa agreed and said, "We'll convert it at the black market."

Maya thought of the large grey buildings with long lineups. The black market was a private company, not a bank. She heard stories of Filipinos buying U.S. dollars from the black market to go travelling abroad, only to find out it was fake money.

Rosa continued her pitch, "It'll be fifty-three pesos or fifty-five to your dollar, instead of just fifty. It's worth it. May I have the difference?"

Unsure, Maya agreed. A day later, Maya stood in line inside the Canadian Imperial Bank. She stayed close to Annie and gripped her bank card in her hand. She asked the teller for two thousand in USD, but the limit was one thousand per order. He told her she could send two orders if she'd like.

"Why don't you send five hundred and send more later?" Annie said behind her.

Maya took her advice. Annie brought her to Canada Post after. The seven dollars to register her mail did nothing for her anxiety.

As two weeks passed, she imagined some thief steaming her envelope open, then forging her signature, all the money disappearing from her bank account. The impossibility of justice clouded her thoughts. She tried to believe she could only be robbed once. The dark part of her wondered why she even tried. But she sent the second money order with the same leap of faith.

After a month passed, Maya always felt too sleepy to eat breakfast. Maya didn't want to burden Annie, so she kept her fears to herself. Annie had been making batches of soup and bone broth to save up for a new purse. Annie beamed when she brought home an orange box with *Louis Vuitton* written on it. Maya looked enviously at the beautiful leather bag printed with the LV logo and its stars.

"I'll get an LV hat one day too." Annie put the bag around her shoulder proudly and waltzed around the apartment.

Besides saving, Maya used her money to buy phone cards.

Her mom chastised Annie's new purse. "Save for a house, anak."

"I *am*. Did you forget that I own this apartment?" Annie defended.

"How much was that thing?" her dad asked, half-jokingly.

"I'm just having fun!" Annie handed the phone over to Maya.

Though Maya and Annie called their parents every two weeks, Maya wondered what they were doing all the time. She wondered if Tito Ton was somewhere in traffic yelling at someone, while listening to peaceful flute music on the radio. She also listened to her parents' favourite karaoke song over and over: "Over the Rainbow." Her sister had a little ukulele at home that her boyfriend had bought her. Annie told Maya all about her trip to Hawaii with him, the trip that Joseph complained about. Maya was envious of all the good food and the tour Annie took at the pineapple plantation. One day, she would go, Maya thought. For now, Maya taught herself by ear how to play "Over the Rainbow" in her lonely hours. During the minutes of the song, it was the only time she felt like she was allowed to feel the things inside. It allowed her to remember. One memory that always came back to her was waking up in the morning, seeing her dad sketching by the window, just before they all ate.

"Come on, eat na, Maya."

She was afraid of forgetting their home. Maya would cry in private, because she felt like an insignificant, distant planet revolving around her family back home.

Every day at work she would cheerily deliver specimen results. The doctors called her sunshine. Smiling was hard but being sad was too easy. One day she couldn't hide how she felt and wasn't as talkative.

"Who are you and what have you done with Maya?" a doctor joked. "Where's your smile, sunshine?"

At this, she found her smile and felt embarrassed. "Sorry, sir."

One night after work, she noticed a note from Annie saying to call Rosa. Her stomach twisted. As she called, she stared at the drawing of a cat her dad gave her on the fridge, the only thing she unpacked. She lived out of her suitcase, not quite accepting this place as her home yet.

There was no answer. She called her parents instead with her last couple of minutes on her phone card. Her mom answered, static crackling in the background.

"Hello, it's Maya ..."

"Oh Maya! We got the money. Thank you, anak, we appreciate it."

Maya cheered, teary eyed. The weight inside of Maya vanished, replaced by a renewed resolve.

Her mom asked, "Did you eat?"

An automated message spoke, "You have five minutes."

"No. I'm out of minutes, ma."

"Eat, call later!"

"Yeah, I will," Maya said, wiping the tears out of her eyes.

"We love you so much and miss you!"

Maya thanked the Lord and asked Him to keep them all well. She prayed for life not to change in the blink of an eye ever again. She promised to work hard, build a house for her parents back home, and live with them again one day.

(Author's note: In 1985, Manila Express Cargo opened in Vancouver, BC, making money remittance and mailing to the Philippines easier.)

II.

October 1995.

The cold air bit at Katherine's ears. She felt her little pink rain boots sink into the mud, and she glanced at the endless fields, dotted by pumpkins. Her mom pulled down her toque past her ears.

"Vid," her mom called to her dad, who was still in the car, "can you get Kay's gloves?"

"What's that, Maya?" her dad responded.

"Kay's gloves,"

"Oh. Nic, can you get it?"

Kay's sister, Nicole, came out with her gloves. "Put it on, silly."

"Where are we?" Kay asked.

"Abbotsford," Nic answered.

"Hello lovelies. Make sure to pick a big pumpkin today!" An elderly woman walked past them.

Kay recognized the elderly woman: she was her friend James's grandma. She had glittering green eyes and reddish skin. Kay liked her because she always gave them candy at school. Kay didn't meet either of her grandmas in the Philippines before they passed away. She had only met her grandpa from her dad's side, who lived on the east coast. He was a funny old man who liked bananas and perfume. He always told her to be proud to be Filipino. When Kay's other grandpa died, her mom spent hours in her room, door shut. Nic and Kay would play tag and cards outside her door, calling for their mother to join them. Sometimes she did, sometimes she didn't. Their mom never talked about how her mother and father passed to Kay. Only once had Kay heard her say, "Our house back home is empty now."

In the present, Kay took her sister's hand as they walked into the muck, their dad following close behind. The smell of pine trees and fresh earth wafted into her nostrils. The air was cool and crisp.

Kay found a big pumpkin all right: she wrapped the entire length of her arms around it in an embrace. She tried to pick it up but only got it a couple inches off the ground before dropping it with a thud. "Pa! Pa! Over here! Paaa!"

Her dad came over and swooped up the pumpkin with no issue, and she glanced up at him in awe.

When they drove back, he said simply: "We have to go to the mall and pick up a couple of things. Your titas are coming."

When they arrived at the mall, whatever their dad had to buy was overshadowed by Nic running into the music shop first.

"Pa, can I please, please, *please* get this?" Nic waved a Backstreet Boys album at him. "*Please!*"

"Wait one second." Their dad went to the sound booth, put on the headphones, and selected a random track. Their dad responded, "They're singing about getting down and moving around ... Is this song about sex?"

"What? I don't know," Nic said, completely beet red now.

The grin on his face told Kay that her dad was messing with Nic. He stuck his tongue out at her and they went to the cashier, their dad still whistling the tune of the song.

Shortly after they arrived home, their dad began to cook. He started chopping onions and garlic. Kay hoped it was pancit and wondered if he was going to put those jumbo shrimps she liked in them. She realized she had to look nice for her aunties. Kay went into her room and found her ruby red slippers that her mom got her last Christmas. She loved The Wizard of Oz and would sing all the songs with her mom. When the doorbell rang, she bounded down the hall and her titas Rachel and Mary came in. They were always so well-dressed, she admired their fresh makeup, sweet smells, and large hairdos. They were so glamorous and beautiful. Her mom was never excited to see them. She seemed to stand like a ghost as she let them in and they walked past her with a simple hello, then went over to embrace Kay's dad.

"We got you your perfume!" Mary boasted, placing a bright pink bag onto the table.

"And I got this Estée Lauder kit," Rachel piped in. "What are you cooking?"

"Pancit canton," he responded.

"Why not bihon?"

"Do you want to eat or not?" he joked.

Mary sat and opened a tabloid, and the cover was of O.J. Simpson. Her mom walked in to help their dad with cooking.

Rachel shook her head and started, "First O.J. goes off scot-free, and can you believe all those Blacks marched too? Scary."

"Marched for what?" their mom asked as she helped their dad grab more ingredients.

"How do you not know?" Mary shot.

Their mom didn't answer. She gave their dad the noodles and then went down the hall.

"She doesn't keep up with much," their dad offered.

"I have to remember not everyone is educated like we are," Mary said, then turned to Kay. "Does she teach you anything about what's going on, Kay?"

"She tells me lots of stories of growing up in Bohol. Did you know that she could shoot a bow and arrow at my age!"

Her aunts restrained a laugh. "Did she tell you about the aswang too?"

"What's that?"

"Evil spirits and monsters."

"Oh yeah, she told me about how people believed in Santelmo —" Kay couldn't finish because her titas just let out roaring laughter at what she was saying.

"You don't need to learn about that, you're Canadian," Mary scoffed. "You can't even speak Tagalog."

"I can say kumusta ka! And na-naw ... uhm, nawawala ako!" Kay struggled on that last one.

"You sound like you have a Chinese accent when you talk." Mary twisted her nose. "It's better you learn English anyway."

Kay deflated, this was one of the few ways her family reminded her she was not Filipino enough. Her dad asked his sisters to try his noodles. Kay joined in and she loved the citrusy taste that came with each bite.

"That's kalamansi, the real deal. Sarap." Tita Rachel gave Kay another scoop.

"Thanks," Kay said as she stuffed her mouth.

"Isn't she cute? You have our family's skin." Rachel pinched her cheek. "So light and pretty!"

"Just like her papa." Her dad ruffled her hair.

Kay's spirits lifted. She liked the compliments about her fair complexion: it made her feel special. Kay giggled and ran away from Rachel's pinches. Kay went down the hall to meet her mom in the living room. Her mom was cleaning the pumpkins they picked.

"Take off your shoes first." Her mom pointed.

Kay peeled off her ruby red slippers, her feet pressing against the cold tile. Her mom smiled at her when Kay slid in next to her and started to draw the face with a Sharpie.

Her mother cut the top of the pumpkin out. Kay reached in, squirming, squealing as she extracted the pumpkin guts, dropping it onto a pile of newspapers her mom readied. Her mom gave her a little child-friendly knife and

Kay sawed away. Nic joined them halfway and began cleaning her pumpkin. When Kay was done, her mom placed a candle into the pumpkin.

"Do they do this in the Philippines too?" Kay asked curiously.

"I didn't do this," her mom answered.

"Tell me stories about the aswang, ma." Kay held on to her toes in excitement, swaying back and forth. "Tita told me what it meant."

"Yes, I heard. I know they think I'm uneducated, but I sent everything I had back home." Kay was confused but her mom continued: "I built my parents a house and helped my family, but I guess it doesn't matter to *them*."

Kay or Nic didn't really have a response, so their mother sighed. She turned on the TV instead. The two parked themselves in front of the TV. Their mom sat on the couch as well and watched cartoons with them for the rest of the afternoon.

When their mom left, Nic turned to Kay and pulled a pack of cards from her pocket.

Nic snickered. "I got these tarot cards, don't tell."

"Why?" Kay asked quietly, excited to be part of a secret.

Nic made a cross with her two fingers and hovered them above the deck. "The priest would *burn us*. Ask it a question and draw three cards."

Kay thought of the future and only drew two: the World and the Hanged Man. The Hanged Man was upside down and was hanging from his foot, his money falling from his pockets. The World was a nude woman holding two sceptres. Before she could draw the next card, their mom came back, and Nic slid the cards off the table.

"Come help." Their mom waved them over, and they went into the kitchen.

They saw their dad sitting by the table with a giant metal mixing bowl. His fingers were covered in sticky, wet pieces of ground meat and chopped veggies. Kay instinctively knew to sit at the end and start unpeeling the spring roll wrappers for their lumpia. She always peeled it off the edge really slow to avoid tearing. Her first one had no such luck and she tore a small tear-shaped hole in the centre.

"What is this?" Nic waved it at her. "Fired."

Nic rolled the lumpia because she was more coordinated than Kay. Her dad scooped the meat mix with a spoon onto the wrappers before Nic rolled. Her mom heated up the oil in the pot and waited for their first batch of lumpia to fry. As soon as they started frying, the crackle and pop of the pan filled the room. In the distance, Kay heard her titas howl in the living room as they chittered about everything.

Their dad placed a postcard on the table with a grin. "Guess where we're going next spring?"

Kay saw a palm tree and a white sandy beach before Nic scooped up the postcard and squealed, "Hawaii!"

"I wanna see!" Kay reached for the postcard.

Their mom smiled at the stove. She placed the cooked lumpia from pan to serving plate.

III.

June 2021.

"*Konichiwa. Ni-hao!* Are you Japanese?" a man catcalled at Kay on the street.

"Sure," she responded, half-there since she was on her phone.

Kay recently got into kali, also known as arnis or escrima, which was the national martial art of the Philippines. Her latest Instagram post detailed her recent trip to Bowen Island with Isabel. During a rainstorm, she decided to do kali in the woods. In the picture, she stood drenched, mid-Redondo with her bamboo kali stick. The caption read: *reconnecting with my roots, so proud to be filipinx!*

Some butthurt side of the Internet decided to descend upon her, and a handful of people in the Philippines were @-ing her account like wildfire. Her pronouns were also she/they in her bio.

I AND THE MAJORITY OF FILIPINOS WOULD APPRECIATE IT IF FILIPINX WOULD STOP BEING USED

TAGALOG IS A GENDER-NEUTRAL LANGUAGE ALREADY IDIOT

LOOK AT THESE DESPERATE "FILIPINX" REACHING FOR A CULTURE THAT'S NOT THEIRS

KALI IS OUR TRADITION, IT IS NOT FOR SOME DUMB AMERICAN LIKE YOU

"Speak Eng-rish?" the catcaller asked, following her.

I just spoke to you in English, Kay rolled her eyes. She sped up her walk and lost him eventually. She took a seat at an outdoor patio by the Vancouver Art Gallery. She waited for Isabel. She sanitized her hands, then her phone, with a wet wipe.

She remembered her kali instructor's words: "In typical gyms, I'd have to leave one half of myself at the door. Here, you bring both selves: the warrior, the sun, and the intuitive, the moon. Do not leave that other half at the door."

DO WHATEVER YOU WANT, BUT I DON'T TRUST SOMEONE WHO IS WHITEWASHED
THE X IS PERFORMATIVE SJW BS
FILIPINX IS A WORD ONLY FOR THE OPPRESSED, NOT FOR US TRUE FILIPINOS

Kay thought more about the *x*. Maybe one day this word would change and language would shift. Maybe it would stick like Pinoy and Pinay, which Filipino-Americans coined in the 1920s. The *x* was there to break down the feminine and masculine -*a* and -*o* that the Spanish introduced into Tagalog and unweave the machismo threaded into what was once a gender-neutral language. Filipinx also represented her love for Isabel. Also, she felt that if she called her work Filipino, some people would maybe assume that she lived in the Philippines, which she didn't. On a dorky note, the *x* also reminded her of "xoxo" or when you pair something together like "JLo x Ben." Or when you use an *x* as a kiss at the end of a text message. She saw the word "Filipin♥" when she read the *x*.

YOU'RE TOO WESTERNIZED, NEOCOLONIST

"Hey." Isabel appeared. She had chestnut brown hair and a soft, goofy face.

"You need to take my phone away from me."

"How bad is it?"

She shook her head. "How was work?"

Isabel described the impending amount of overtime coming her way because of a patch update to her company's mobile game. But Isabel stopped. "No seriously, are you doing okay?"

Kay let out a sigh and showed Isabel the comments.

> ADMIT THAT YOU'RE A LITTLE BROWN BROTHER
> YOU CAN GET BAYBAYIN TATTOOS, SAY CATCHY FILIPINO PHRASES, BUT YOU ARE AMERICAN
> WE'RE NOT A "MOTHERLAND" LIKE CHINA. YOU'RE NOT ONE OF US.
> I DON'T TELL ANYONE HOW TO IDENTIFY BUT PILIPINX IS A MISGUIDED WORD
> SHE/THEY? WHERE'S THE OTHER PPL DUMB BITCH?

Isabel's response was: "What kind of nationalist bullshit is this?"

"They just see this *x*. I'm not human to them. It's like they're saying: 'Don't tell me how to identify but let *me* tell *you* how *not* to identify.' "

"Are they in the Philippines or here?"

"Mostly the Philippines. Even my relatives can be like this, they remind me how I'm not Filipino enough when I don't know something about our culture. But then some people here believe I'm not Canadian just by looking at me. When I'm asked, 'Where you from?' it implies that. Who am I then?"

Kay sighed. "But, maybe all of this is coming from the same place of hurt?"

"Um. That's too kind of you, Kay. These trolls are just pathetic little ball-less shits spewing bigoted garbage. Attacking you and policing other people's behaviour is the best they can do."

Kay handed Isabel her phone. With each notification and buzz, it felt like a flash of lightning with a large rumble to follow. But even if Isabel took the phone from her, she couldn't cut the wires running around her head.

"Should we check in on your dad?" Isabel asked.

"Sure, he hurt his knee from a bad fall."

"Okay, let's go to papa bear."

Isabel led them to her beat-up Jetta she parked near the convention centre. While Isabel drove, Kay asked her, "Do you know *The Red Shoes*? The fairy tale?"

"It's about the girl who puts on these red shoes that make her dance non-stop?"

"At first she's happy but then she finds out she can't stop or take them off." Kay nodded. "I recently read an interpretation where the addiction to the dance is what happens when you are soul starved over meaning. I understand where my soul starved growing up here, Belle. I just want to share what I learn with other people. I feel like I'm dancing joyfully while I do kali, and less so when I'm met with unkindness online. Social media are my red shoes. I'm starting to feel like this dance I give my life to changes nothing."

Isabel said softly: "People who hate on others don't think of their targets after they're done spewing. But people who are like-minded and who want to connect can't find you if you're hiding out of fear."

Kay was comforted by that but continued: "The Canadian education system taught me nothing about the Philippines, let alone even Canada's real past. I was in university when I realized how messed up this country is to our First Nations communities. When I learnt about the Oka Crisis, it blew my mind. Why would our country send the army to stop a protest, a protest where people wanted to save their homes from becoming a golf course expansion? I realized I knew nothing, so I started to wonder about myself, about my family."

Isabel sighed. "You know how they found those bodies of children recently at Kamloops? The knowledge of the abuse and murder at the residential schools here is not new. It just took this terrible discovery to make people understand. I don't understand how people are still finding excuses. The right to get medical care for your child and to take care of their bodies when they pass is crucial to a family's grief journey. I can't even, Kay. These kids died alone, with no explanation or care given. I always wonder: what can we do?"

"I don't even know where to start."

"I'm glad you took kali."

Her virtual kali class was her light during the pandemic. She remembered her instructor's words as she did the twelve basic strikes, "Your ancestors' trauma and their thwarted dreams, your trauma from casual cruelty, on and on it goes ... Say this: *It ends with me.*"

Many Filipinx classmates were curious about where their family had come from, the history they never learnt, and wanted to know who they were in the world. In silence and anonymity, Kay had found herself. She did not understand why the people in the Philippines hated them so much. She would apologize to no one.

When they arrived at her parents' apartment, her dad was lying on the bed and greeted her, "Did you eat?"

"Yup, I'm good."

He got off the bed with a wince. He headed to the living room.

Kay asked, "Did you go to physio yesterday?"

"The taxi wouldn't come here, said it wouldn't be worth it, so I walked."

"Are you serious?" Kay was livid. Sure, the physio was only a five-minute walk, but not to someone with a knee problem.

"Don't worry about it, anak."

Kay really had to buy a car, but the lease would make her budget tight. She could ask Isabel to drive him, but she didn't know how to explain to her dad about her relationship with Isabel yet.

"Here, I made some fish." Her dad made it to the kitchen.

"No, it's okay ..." But he was already warming the food.

This was her dad's love language. When they had full lockdown and couldn't see each other in person, he'd message her "Did you eat?" or "What did you eat?" Kay sat at the table and saw her phone. Isabel was in the washroom, so she must have left it there. She glanced at her notifications.

YOU ARE A PRODUCT OF YOUR PARENTS' TREACHERY TO OUR COUNTRY

Her mom greeted her, but Kay barely heard her. The words came out of Kay's mouth before she thought about them: "Why did you come here, ma?"

"I didn't want to come here. I lived out of my suitcase for a year because I didn't want to unpack."

"Why?"

"My tuition was stolen from me, then your tita brought me here."

"Stolen? What happened?"

"I got sprayed by a thief while I was paying my tuition."

"*What?*"

Her outrage seemed to encourage her mom. Her mom was about to speak but then Kay's phone buzzed.

"Answer it," her mom said politely.

ENJOY THAT SILVER SPOON IN YOUR MOUTH

It ends with me, Kay thought.

"Go on." Kay powered off her phone and assured her mom. "It's nothing."

Maya's eyes lit up at Kay's undivided attention. As Maya spoke, Kay could still see the light of her mother's stars, even if they were long past.

VINCENT TERNIDA

Acacia

I DREAMT THAT *you visited again to take care of your acacia tree. Your father visited as well when he died. He would come in my dreams and make me feel guilty for abandoning you both. When you died, you started haunting me too. Now you're haunting me again. Tell me what you want me to do, so you can finally be at rest.*

WHEN CONSTABLES STORM and Katigbak asked me about a certain Hiroki Marquez, I realized they were talking about you. It wasn't an auspicious day at all, just another cold autumn night at my flat in New West. After a lifetime of work, I was able to afford my own place as well as a retirement home in Legazpi City. When I retire in a couple of years, I will rent out this room and collect my pension in a sunny place. When the storm season hits, I will vacation anywhere else in the world, funded by my hard work.

For the two decades since you moved out, I never heard from you, not a single letter, an email, or even a Facebook message. You were never on social media, all I heard were rumours going around that you were Romeo Galang's business partner. I did not believe them, you were a good boy. Misunderstood, but still a good boy. I admit when you were young, there were not many pinoy kids to play with, and you were stuck with that adik-adik couple, Romeo and Sadie. Romeo's mother always hated us because we were different from them and you eventually pushed them away. Then one day, *you* pushed me away. I admit I was a tough aunt, but I took care of you like any real parent would. When I heard that Romeo had been killed like a dog in an unnamed alley, I said he deserved it. After you died, he dragged your name through the mud. I hoped his death would reveal the shit he deflected to good boys like you.

The police were polite. The petite yellow-haired officer was accompanied by that Bicolano boy from Burnaby, Jejomar's kid. He grew up nice and handsome, but still flat nosed and short like his dad. I was glad he got his mestizo complexion from his mother, but all the real puti probably still see a brown man. You were taller than him, and more handsome, too.

"Good evening," I said.

"Good evening po," Katigbak said, being all polite and courteous. If that puti woman wasn't around, he would've taken my hand to his forehead and made mano. "We have questions about Hiroki Marquez," Storm said.

The puti woman didn't take care of her skin. She gets paid a lot, she should invest in some moisturizer. In ten years, she will be losyang. She probably drinks too a lot, I could see the bilbil through her uniform.

"I'm sorry, I don't know who that is," I said. "Would that be all? I'm very busy."

"Miss Martinez," Katigbak said. "We're here to ask about Angelo. When was the last time you saw him?"

I was jealous of my brother and his live-in partner who had a healthy baby boy. I thought he would be deformed as they were both heavy drinkers. My brother met his girlfriend at a beer house, where he was a heavy regular drinker and she was a waitress. Little did I know that she had another racket on the side. Gil worked at a tobacco factory all day and drank his earnings. When he got himself a jowa, I worried for him.

All my life, I wanted out of that shithole called Maynila. There was not a lot of opportunity to go around unless you finished accounting. Unless you were rich or educated, women either worked in service, as pokpoks, or both like your mother. I got denied entry to the U.S. when I was in Hong Kong with my shitty bogus visa. I tried to enter the U.S. for missionary work. The plan was to TNT for a few years, marry an American, some dumb white guy, and get rich. I ended up being barred from entering the country. Then you were born.

"Angelo Martin Martinez," the puti woman asked. Martin was your father's middle name. Angelo because you were your mother's angel. Martinez was the name we all shared.

"That's impossible, he's dead."

I was about to cry. Katigbak sympathized, but Storm was more on her guard. "Can we come in?" she asked.

Part of me didn't want to reveal my dirty apartment, though the law-abiding part of me easily complied. The puti woman would be difficult to get off my back, but Katigbak already fell for my charms. Like father, like son.

"What's going on?"

"Someone reported that Angelo visited you," Storm said.

"How can he? He's been dead for years."

Storm appeared suspicious. "Is that so? Because we have multiple sources and witnesses saying that you claimed that Angelo visited you."

"You trust rumours? Why are you so interested?"

"Witnesses say that Hiroki Marquez, the killer of Romeo Galang, looked exactly like Angelo."

I reluctantly opened the door, my hands were shaking. The puti woman noticed this but kept her poker face.

"Please come in," I said.

Katigbak waffled awkwardly by the entrance. Storm walked around with an agenda. She seemed to have a mental list of what to search for. Immediately, she marched toward my garden near the veranda.

"*Acacia confusa*," said Storm, noticing the tropical tree in my collection.

"Wow," I said.

"It's getting bigger than the pot. Do you have plans of moving it?"

"I'll figure something out." I didn't expect the question. Angelo used to deal with the plants, I kept them because he loved them. Storm noticed the plants right away; it was like she was searching for them.

I had an opportunity to migrate to Canada in the late 80s. They were looking for skilled workers for their caregiver program. I thought about jumping on that chance and hopefully crossing over to the U.S. when it was possible. I turned in my application and the waiting game began. I really hoped that my blacklist in the U.S. would not affect my application. The good news was that it didn't affect it, they probably overlooked it, but I didn't want to question fortune.

While waiting for my visa, I stayed with your family in Maynila, in that cramped apartment in Cubao. Your mother took you to your section —

One-Acacia. At the end of the day, your father asked me to pick you up. Your mother suddenly disappeared. She didn't take any bags, she just vanished into thin air.

At the time, we thought there was foul play involved, as it was a year after the EDSA Revolution, and the crime rate was up. We called up her family and we reached out to people in her province. She just disappeared. We even asked her agency in Japan as she was due back after her leave. They were silent. You were a small, chubby kid. You cried at the principal's office. They asked if I was your mother, and I was tempted to answer yes.

"Tita," you began. "Where is Mama?"

"From now on, call me Nanay," I said.

"But isn't Nanay Mama in Tagalog?"

"Mama is still Mama, but I'm your Nanay."

A few months after that, my Canadian entry visa was approved. When I moved to this remote barrio called Maple Ridge, I immediately sent in my petition to sponsor you as my dependent. As much as I loved my brother, he was also a useless drunk.

I lit a cigarette to calm my nerves. I was surprised, they were clove cigarettes. When I quit smoking about three years ago, I stopped buying packs. They were expensive at thirteen bucks a pack; the budget ones were almost like breathing in ash. I wondered why this pack was in my possession. Right now, I would take anything.

"Can I get you something to drink? Because if you don't mind, I would like a cup of coffee."

"I could use a coffee. You good with coffee, Johnny?" Katigbak shrugged. "We'll have two coffees."

I was proud of my kitchen, but I wasn't necessarily a good cook. I would chastise you when you complained about my cooking. I may have deterred you from pinoy cuisine for good as I would use sour broth mix for chicken tinola, chicken tinola mix for sinigang, and I would make adobo way too sour. You were like your mother, you liked food bland.

I designed the kitchen with you in mind. Maybe you would show up and live with me for a bit, I would cook for you, and you would appreciate your

Nanay's cooking. I expected you would return to me after all those years of absence. In the past, you didn't touch your dinner and I would spank you in my frustration. After a while, you ate it quietly.

I refused to let you go to pinoy gatherings for the sole reason of eating someone else's food. If you couldn't appreciate my cooking, nobody else could force pinoy cuisine on you. Maybe it backfired, because after a while, you would be making your own sandwiches and microwaving your instant dinners. You eventually refused to touch adobo, kaldereta, sinigang, and all the other traditional dishes I cooked. You would take your beating, but you refused to touch my cooking in the end. I should've seen that you were already pushing me away that early in life.

I brewed a pot of coffee for the cops. I had a few minutes until I could calm down and answer their questions. You were dead for a while, I was at your funeral. It's probably sheer coincidence the Hiroki guy looked like you. Puti people can't tell the difference between Pinoy, Tsino, or Hapon — they look at our eyes, see that it is singkit, and just think "Asian."

Once the coffee pot finished brewing, I poured them into separate cups. I placed the cups on the table. "How do you take your coffee?"

"Double-double," Katigbak said.

"Black," the puti woman said.

I dropped two lumps into Katigbak's cup and poured a generous amount of cream. It might've been a double-quadruple and he seemed to like it, taking a lot of sips.

Puti pulis was still on guard. Would anything break through the wall she put up?

"Could you tell us about the break-ins in your apartment?" Storm asked.

"Nobody's here but me," I said.

"We've received complaints from your neighbours," Storm pressed the issue. "Some nights, there's someone who waits by the back entrance, a suspicious gentleman. There are reports of the same gentleman leaving your apartment."

"I don't know what else I can tell you," I said. "It's just me in the house. It must be somewhere else. If something is stolen, I would have contacted you."

"Was anything stolen then?"

"No! I just told you!" I felt my eyes tearing up. "Oh, I'm so sorry, give me a moment ..." I took a breath and wiped my eyes. Storm set her cup on the table.

"Failure to cooperate with the police is a criminal offence," Storm said. "Are you sure that you're not keeping anything from us? We cannot help you if you withhold any information."

I remember you bringing back an acacia sapling home for a project — an *Acacia confusa*, you said, endemic in Australia and an invasive species in Hawaii. You never brought in other living things like stray cats (I was deathly allergic) or worse, rats or snakes. Yet I didn't even know where you got that plant. When you said acacia, I remembered your grade one section. I didn't know how you felt, but that affinity for the plant was possibly the same as your separation anxiety from your real mother. I was not a cheap substitute, I loved you like a son.

You really liked plants, always talking about horticulture and the conditions of soil. I thought you would take agriculture after high school, but you went to Vancouver, and I never saw you alive again. For some weird reason, however, I knew you visited me in my dreams. The other day at the supermarket, Myrna from Meats and Abby from Deli confronted me about their boss Romeo Galang being found shot dead.

"Kapatid, you heard what happened to Romeo?" Myrna asked.

"Yeah, that adik-adik who kept working here and getting fired? He deserves it." Myrna and Abby met me with awkward silence.

"I heard someone who looks like Angelo shot him," Abby interjected.

"And where did you hear of this, aber?"

"Jaime heard it from Kit," Myrna said.

"You can stop this bullshit tsismis right now, *my Angelo* is dead! He's a good boy. Even beyond the grave he visits me. In fact, the other day he came over and was taking care of his plants. You're telling me some multo killed your precious Romeo? How dare you torment a grieving mother!"

I was never part of the tita club. It was because of Romeo Galang's punyeta mother. She and her caregiver gang did not want me around. I got into Canada through the caregiver program, but I ended up doing other work in a couple of months. I'd rather work the cash register than slave away in some hospice, make hugas the puwet of some old puti shit. Puta and her friends think I'm too good for them. They never invited me to their parties, but they invited you, and you never told me until you complained about my lumpia.

After that, I forbade you to be friends with Romeo and that girlfriend of his. I forbade you to do a lot of things. Looking back, I regret all the rules I established, because you never listened to me. Eventually, that tarantado Romeo Galang murdered you and had the audacity to pay for your funeral. I was glad that Hiroki Marquez killed that bastard.

I mean to take care of your plants. I buy them fertilizer, larger pots, more soil as you instructed before you left me. Your sapling is now a large plant, it keeps growing, and some days I notice it has been moved to larger pots. Now it sits in the living room facing the view of Fraser River. The plant is watered, trimmed, or moved into a better pot. If I couldn't take care of you when you were under my care, I could at least give the plants the same care as I would you.

Katigbak was back on Storm's side. He was her partner after all. He was here to drop my guard, but like father, like son, they flirt for a bit, but they never go all the way. I sipped my coffee and turned my attention to the puti woman. She was in charge, she just needed Katigbak to get them through the door. If I was more taray I would ask the snivelling shit to step out.

"I couldn't have children," I said. "So, I sponsored Angelo from the Philippines. He lost both his parents at a young age, and I felt sorry for the child."

"You're his legal guardian?"

"Yes," I said. "Until he turned eighteen."

"Did you keep contact?"

"No," I said. "He moved to Vancouver. I never heard from him after that."

"Ten years ago, you attended his funeral."

I paused and said, "Yes."

"The report was that Angelo Martinez was slain by Sanjan Ratanaruang of a rival gang."

"Romeo Galang is the real killer," I said. "The casket was empty when we had the funeral. Romeo killed him and was blaming this Thailand man. My Angelo is coming back to visit me, he told me his real killer!"

"So, you're saying, the ghost of Angelo breaks into your apartment and talks to you?"

I covered my face and cried. Katigbak touched Storm's arm and whispered into her ear. She shook her head and gave him a pained look.

"I apologize, I'm sorry for your loss." Storm paused and massaged her temples. "How long has this been going on?"

"Probably three years? No, five years now. If there were complaints, why check now? You didn't check back then."

"Because now, a man is dead and it has become relevant again ..." Storm paused, I could tell she was losing her cool.

Katigbak turned to her again. "Take a breath, Sharon."

He then faced me. "I'm sorry about this, Miss Martinez," he said. "We're saying that Angelo may be a person of interest, we're aware of his deceased status, but at the moment we don't have a lot of leads. The prime witness said that Hiroki Marquez is the killer and other witnesses who've seen this man are saying that he bears a striking resemblance to Angelo."

"Well, I'm sure that Hiroki Marquez and my Angelo are not the same person. My Angelo has a common face. He didn't live long, and he had a sad life. Could you just leave him alone?"

Katigbak stopped writing. He looked at Storm and she shrugged.

"All right, if you hear or remember anything else with regards to your trespassing case, please call us at our non-emergency line."

He left a business card and both he and Storm left the apartment building. I smoked another cigarette and thought of you. I believed after all this time that Romeo killed you and that your ghost was haunting me. When Gil died years ago, he appeared to me here in Canada. It made me sponsor you and his ghost stopped haunting me. What would make your ghost rest? You stopped visiting after a while. I thought that was because your spirit had been put to rest. Romeo's death was restitution.

That night, I stirred from my sleep. There was activity in the living room. I got up and put my slippers on. I took care not to make a sound. Was it your ghost visiting again, Angelo? Oh, my beautiful child.

I slowly opened the door and peered outside. The acacia plant was in full activity. It was being watered; it was being trimmed. As I peered outside, just the same way that I checked every night I dreamt you were there. No, your ghost was there. You are dead, Angelo Martin Martinez. There is no way the dead can come back to life unless they're Jesus.

You saw me leave my bedroom and stopped taking care of your plant. You faced me and smiled. I was glad to finally see you again.

"Nanay," you said. "This will be the last time you'll see me."

You walked over to me and held me in an embrace. You were so warm. "My business is done here," you said. "Rest easy, Nanay, you earned it." You vanished and I stood there, alone. I went back to sleep, knowing that your spirit rested easy.

Contributor Biographies

Editors

Teodoro Alcuitas is the publisher and editor of *Philippine Canadian News*, an online paper linking the Filipino diaspora. He founded *Silangan*, the first Filipino newspaper in western Canada, in 1976. He lives in Vancouver, British Columbia.

C.E. Gatchalian is the author of six books and co-editor of two anthologies. He is a three-time Lambda Literary Award finalist and received the Dayne Ogilvie Prize in 2013 from the Writers' Trust of Canada. Originally from Vancouver, British Columbia, he now lives in Toronto, Ontario.

Patria Rivera is a poet and writer who has authored four books and two chapbooks of poetry. Her first poetry collection, *Puti/White*, was shortlisted for a Trillium Book Award for Poetry, and she was the recipient of the Global Filipino Literary Award for Poetry. She lives in Toronto, Ontario.

Contributors

Jim Agapito hosts *Recovering Filipino*, a podcast from CBC Manitoba featured on CBC Radio One, in which he reconnects to his Filipino heritage through self-discovery. Jim is a Filipino writer, producer, and filmmaker from Winnipeg, Manitoba. Jim's passion is storytelling, and his specialties include producing, screenwriting, and directing documentaries, short films, and music videos. He has worked in the Canadian film and television industry and with several independent production houses since obtaining diplomas in journalism from Durham College. When Jim isn't working on his multimedia projects, he writes, boxes, wrenches on his motorcycle, and sings in a punk band.

Hari Alluri (he/him/siya) is a migrant poet of Pangasinan, Ilokano, and Telugu descent who lives, loves, and writes on the unceded Coast Salish territories of the Musqueam, Squamish, and Tsleil-Waututh peoples, and Kwantlen, Katzie, and Kwikwetlem lands of Hənq̓əmiņəm̓-speaking peoples, a.k.a. New Westminster, British Columbia. Siya is author of *The Flayed City* and the chapbook *Our Echo of Sudden Mercy*. Recipient of the Vera Manuel Award for Poetry, among other prizes, grants, fellowships, and residencies, his work appears through these venues and elsewhere: *Apog̱yu, Marias at Sampaguitas*, *Michigan Quarterly Review*, *Poetry*, *poetry in canada*, and — via *Split This Rock* — *Best of the Net*. @harialluri.

Christine Añonuevo (she/her/hers) is a community organizer, writer, and educator who has worked in rural and remote communities across British Columbia and internationally in Ukraine, South Africa, and Japan. Her poetry has been shortlisted for *Prism International*'s Pacific Poetry Prize, *Malahat Review*'s Long Poem Prize, and *Room Magazine*'s Poetry Contest. She is completing her PhD in Human and Health Sciences at the University of Northern British Columbia. She lives in the unincorporated community of South Hazelton, British Columbia.

Kaia M. Arrow (she/her) is an artist, educator, and advocate. Kaia uses her writing to process and portray her experiences as a neurodivergent, sick & disabled, queer, Filipina settler. She applies structural understandings of power with an anti-colonial and anti-capitalist approach to her life and art. Kaia is privileged to be a part-time wheelchair user and full-time shit disturber. She dreams of supportive communities for all. Kaia writes from her apartment in Tkaronto (colonially known as Toronto), which she shares with her Bunny and her partner, Peter. She carries lineage from fierce and tender ancestors in Pampanga and Aklan.

Isabela Palanca Aureus, from Toronto, Ontario, grew up in San Juan and San Mateo, Isabela, in Northern Philippines. A lover of books, she graduated from the University of Toronto, specializing in English. Isa's Filipinx-Canadian pride was nurtured during her tenure as board secretary and, later, board chair at Kapisanan Philippine Centre for Arts + Culture. This work led to her board advisory and associate producer role at Carlos Bulosan Theatre. She usually writes about technology and business as a product marketing leader. Isa's favourite story is the one she is still writing with her two sons, Leon Victor and Anders Noel, and her husband, Leon.

Leon Aureus is a writer, actor, director, producer, and community leader dedicated to creating and supporting proud and diverse stories. He is currently the artistic producer of Carlos Bulosan Theatre, a founding member of fu-GEN Theatre, and the associate producer of the inaugural theatrical run of *Kim's Convenience*. As a playwright, Leon adapted the novel *Banana Boys* for the stage, and he wrote and directed the children's play *Kaldero*. He also co-wrote the plays *People Power* and *In the Shadow of Elephants* and is a Dora Award–nominated actor and filmmaker with multiple credits in theatre, television, and film.

Jennilee Austria-Bonifacio is the author of *Reuniting with Strangers: A Novel Told in Stories* (Douglas & McIntyre), which was a finalist for the Jim Wong-Chu Emerging Writers Award. As the founder of Filipino Talks, she is a speaker and school board consultant who builds bridges between educators and Filipino families. After completing her Masters in Immigration and Settlement Studies, she studied at the Humber School for Writers and completed a residency at the Banff Centre for Arts and Creativity. Born and raised in Sarnia, Ontario, she now lives in Toronto. Follow Jennilee at @jennilee_a_b, or visit https://jennileeaustriabonifacio.com for more.

Jellyn Ayudan is a recent graduate of the University of Regina with an honours degree in English. She currently works at University of Regina Press as an editorial intern. Born in Pateros, Metro Manila, Philippines, she now resides in Treaty 4 lands in oskana kâasastêki (Regina, Saskatchewan) with her close-knit family and their dogs, Max and Rocky.

Hannah Balba was born in the Philippines and immigrated to Richmond, British Columbia, in 2001. Inspired by her deep involvement with Filipino community groups in Vancouver, her research interests centre around Canadian foreign domestic worker movements, with a special emphasis on the socio-economic impacts of caregiver programs on Filipino-Canadians. She holds a BA in History from the University of British Columbia, and she will begin her legal studies as a JD candidate in September 2023. She speaks Tagalog.

Monica Anne Batac (she/they/siya) is a teacher, community organizer, and PhD candidate at the School of Social Work at McGill University. Monica identifies as a second-generation Filipina/x in the Canadian diaspora, born and raised in Tkaronto (Toronto). She is currently residing between Whitehorse, Yukon; Montréal, Québec; and Winnipeg, Manitoba. Monica's writings include *Growing Up Pinay*, published in 2020 as part of the *Home is in the Body* anthology by ANAK Publishing, and "'Failing' and Finding a Filipina Diasporic Scholarly 'Home': A De/Colonizing Autoethnography," published in 2021/22 in the academic journal *Qualitative Inquiry*.

Alexa Batitis is a second-generation Filipino-Canadian writer living in Ottawa, Ontario, where she was born and raised. She holds a Bachelor of Arts degree in English Literature from Carleton University and a diploma in Professional Writing from Algonquin College. Alexa's published works include poetry, fiction, and non-fiction. She is a proud federal public servant and amateur astrologer, and hopes to visit the Philippines one day. She lives with her husband, Shane, and their two cats, Kiwi and Kochi.

Mila Bongco-Philipzig has published five children's books, four of which are bilingual (Filipino-English). She also translated two children's books from Filipino to German, which were included in the Frankfurter Buchmesse 2022. Mila has poetry, personal essays, and articles published in various magazines, anthologies, and podcasts in the Philippines, Canada, and Germany. In 2021, Mila was an Edmonton Arts Council's Featured Artist for Asian Heritage Month and the first featured reader for Edmonton Public Library's Multilingual Storytime. When she is not writing or painting, Mila is busy organizing community events, running long-distance, and helping various organizations promote human rights and social justice.

Davey Samuel Calderon (he/they/siya), from Vancouver, British Columbia, is a director, performer, writer, producer, drag artist, dramaturg, and settler on the unceded lands of the Hən̓q̓əmin̓əm̓ and S̲kw̲x̲wú7mesh speaking peoples. He is the co-founder of New(to)Town Collective, an emerging theatre collective. His work has been on stages (*Big Queer Filipino Karaoke Night!*), film (*RUN!*, part of the shorts program of the 2018 Vancouver Queer Film Festival), and other mediums (contributor to *Canadian Theatre Review, Drag!*, vol. 185, Winter 2021). Currently, he is Playwrights Theatre Centre's Dramaturg, Public Engagement.

Shirley Camia is the author of four collections of poetry. Her 2019 collection, *Mercy*, was a finalist for the High Plains Book Award, and her 2017 book *Children Shouldn't Use Knives* was shortlisted for a ReLit Award. Her work has appeared in publications such as *The New Quarterly* and *The Ex-Puritan*.

Isabel Carlin is a librarian and archivist in the occupied territories of the Musqueam, Squamish, and Tsleil-Waututh Nations (so-called Vancouver, British Columbia). They are a Filipinx poet and activist who writes and struggles for the national democratic revolution in the Philippines. Their research and writing focus on the intersections of imperialism, resource extraction, record-keeping, and class struggle.

Rachel Evangeline Chiong is an author, poet, and happy person. Kabangka, a Canadian-Filipinx not-for-profit, was named after her poem, which encapsulated the values and hopes of the community. She has published a comic book based on her poem "Dark Magic" with illustrator and absolute lad Sven (@svencomicsart). Currently, she is working on her fantasy YA novel, *Doctor Daniri and the Mythical Beasts of the Mundo*, which was awarded the Ontario Arts Council recommender grant (2021–2022) and long listed on Voyage's First Chapters Contest (2021).

Karla Comanda is a Vancouver-based poet, playwright, editor, translator, educator, and arts administrator. Her poems have appeared in *Contemporary Verse 2*, *filling Station*, *decomp*, *Poetry is Dead*, *Room Magazine*, and others. She is the 2017 recipient of the Asian Canadian Writers' Workshop's Jim Wong-Chu Emerging Writers Award for Poetry. She has taught writing workshops for the UBC Philippine Studies Series, Vancouver Public Library, Migrante BC, La Salle University - Ozamiz, Co.ERASGA, and other organizations and institutions. In 2019, she hosted the Sinag-Araw Writing Workshop, a poetry workshop series created for Filipino youth in the diaspora.

Kay Costales is an author and poet represented by Lesley Sabga of the Seymour Agency. She is based in Toronto, Ontario. Her poetry collection, *the EMOTIONS series*, is available now, and her debut novel, *WHEN THEY BECKON*, will be released by City Owl Press in late 2023. As a child of immigrants, it is important for her to always provide Filipino diaspora representation in her stories regardless of genre. You can usually find her constantly daydreaming about monsters, magic, and romance.

Gemma Derpo Dalayoan was a high school teacher in the Philippines and immigrated to Canada in 1976. She finished a BEd and a master's degree in English as a Second Language (ESL) at the University of Manitoba. She was one of the founders and a three-time president of the Manitoba Association of Filipino Teachers' Inc. (MAFTI). She served as vice-principal of three schools in the Winnipeg School Division from 1994 to 2004. She has received several awards for her community work and is the author of four books. She lives in Winnipeg and is currently finishing a memoir.

Ariel de la Cruz (they/he/siya) is an educator and care worker based in Toronto, Ontario, Canada. Currently, they are a doctoral student in the Department of Performing and Media Arts at Cornell University in Ithaca, New York. Their current research project focuses on alternative modes of care performed by tomboy and transmasculine caregivers across the Filipinx labour diaspora. They hold a BSc with Honours in Neuroscience and Psychology as well as a MA in Women and Gender Studies from the University of Toronto.

Adrian De Leon is an award-winning writer and public historian. His most recent books are *barangay: an offshore poem* (Buckrider Books, 2021), which was named one of the best Canadian poetry collections of 2021 by CBC Books, and *Bundok: A Hinterland History of Filipino America* (University of North Carolina Press, 2023). He teaches Asian-American studies in Los Angeles at the University of Southern California and will soon move to New York University to teach U.S.-Philippine histories.

Nathalie De Los Santos is a writer and creative based in Vancouver, British Columbia. She created *PilipinxPages*, a bookstagram featuring Filipino/a/x authors. She has written for or appeared in interviews for the following publications and festivals: *Kapwa Magazine*, TFC, *Marias at Sampaguitas*, *Ricepaper Magazine*, *Gastrofork*, *Chopsticks Alley Pinoy*, CBC, Cold Tea Collective, Sampaguita Press, *Filipino Fridays* podcast, *Stories with Sapphire* podcast, UBC's Games in Action conference, and LiterASIAN Writers Festival (2020). She is also the creator of the podcast, *Filipino Fairy Tales, Mythology and Folklore*. She is the author of *Hasta Mañana, Alice's Order* and is working on a Filipino fantasy novel, *Diyosa Mata*.

Sol Diana is a spoken word artist and teacher born and raised on the traditional, ancestral, unceded, and occupied lands of the Musqueam, Squamish, and Tseil-Waututh First Nations. He is of mixed Filipino and Scottish background and credits the Filipino artists he grew up around as his biggest influences. Sol's passion lies with empowering youth through art and education. His biggest hope is for a future where diasporic Filipinx youth are connected as a cohesive, safe community; their voices are heard; and their humanities are affirmed.

Erica Dionora is a Filipina poet and illustrator. She grew up in Saipan, Northern Marianas Islands, and migrated to Canada in 2008. Erica studied Publishing at Centennial College and completed her MA in Creative Writing at the University of Gloucestershire. She is currently based in Scarborough, Ontario, where she is working on a collaboration for an illustrated poetry book.

Based in Toronto, Ontario, **Carolyn Fe** is a trilingual actress (English/French/Tagalog), award-winning singer-songwriter-lyricist, former contemporary dancer-choreographer, and in a former life owned and operated a science and technology human resources firm. Her continuous pursuit of artistic evolution adds new instruments to her creative portfolio as a published writer and emerging playwright. Some TV/streaming credits include Lola in Nickelodeon's *Blue's Clues & You!*, Madame Z in the award-winning French series *Meilleur Avant*, and voices on animated series on DreamWorks' *Pinecone & Pony* and PBS Kids' *Work It Out Wombats*. More of Carolyn at https://linktr.ee/TheCarolynFe.

Renato Gandia, born and raised in the Philippines, emigrated to Canada in 1997 when he was twenty-seven years old. He studied theology and holds a Master of Divinity degree. He worked as a journalist for daily newspapers in Alberta for several years. He became a Canadian citizen in 2007. He currently works as a communications advisor in the oil and gas industry. He lives in Calgary with his husband and their fourteen-year-old dog.

Kawika Guillermo is the author of *Stamped: an anti-travel novel* (2018), which won the Asian American Studies Book Award for Best Novel, as well as the queer speculative fiction novel, *All Flowers Bloom* (2020) and the prose-poetry book, *Nimrods: a fake-punk self-hurt anti-memoir* (2023). Under his patrilineal/legal name, Christopher Patterson, he is an associate professor in the Social Justice Institute at the University of British Columbia in Vancouver and is the author of the books *Transitive Cultures: Anglophone Literature of the Transpacific* (2018) and *Open World Empire: Race, Erotics, and the Global Rise of Video Games* (2020).

Award-winning playwright & author, **Primrose Madayag Knazan** (she/her) has been featured at Winnipeg Jewish Theatre, Royal Manitoba Theatre Centre, the Winnipeg International Writers Festival, CBC Radio, the Winnipeg Fringe, and the Tales from the Flipside Festival of new Filipinx-Canadian Plays. She won the bi-annual Canadian Jewish Playwriting Competition and her plays have been published by Scirocco Drama and Playwrights Canada

Press. Her debut novel, *Lessons in Fusion*, won the Manitoba Book Award for Young People, and was nominated for both the Manitoba and Saskatchewan Young Readers Choice Awards, as well as the Manitoba Book Award for Best New Book.

José Romelo Lagman hails from Angeles, Pampanga. He graduated cum laude from the University of Santo Tomás (Manila) with a BS in Mathematics degree in 1989. He has since worked as a computer programmer in the Philippines, Malaysia, U.S., and Canada, arriving in Toronto as an immigrant in January 1994. José is also an internationally published sports and travel photographer. He started writing during the pandemic lockdowns, and he is nearly finished with his first novel — a multilingual historical fiction piece set in Manila in the tumultuous 1890s.

Yves Lamson is a second-generation Filipino-Canadian writer who takes from the Philippine oral tradition to spin tales of fantastic creatures. He also enjoys writing around the historical elements of the islands he is wistful and wondrous for. He is a writer by profession, but at the core, he is a storyteller. Interested in preserving the intangible histories, he writes the stories down as a tool to not forget, to keep the precious things safe.

Grace Sanchez MacCall (she/her) was born in Manila, grew up in Calgary, and went to university in Vancouver. She currently splits her time between Toronto, where she lives and writes, and Tatamagouche, where she tries not to do anything at all. Her work has appeared in the *Capilano Review* and *Hamilton Arts and Letters*. She is a founding member of the Eastwood Writers Collective and is currently working on a novel. Her writing explores themes of power, culture, construction of knowledge, inequality, and strategies of resistance.

Lorina Mapa was born in Manila in 1970 and at the age of sixteen moved with her family to Washington, DC. In 1990 she graduated from the Kubert School of Comic and Graphic Art in New Jersey, where she met her husband, artist Daniel Shelton. They have four children and live in Hudson, Québec. Her graphic novel *Duran Duran, Imelda Marcos, and Me* was nominated by the American Library Association as a Great Graphic Novel for Teens. Lorina was featured on the CBC's 2017 list of Writers to Watch and nominated for the Joe Schuster Award for best writer.

Deann Louise C. Nardo is a poet, interwoven artist, and cultural worker living and napping in Tiohtiá:ke/Montréal, Québec. They work as mycelium: connecting, decomposing, metabolizing, and regenerating nutrients for/with their community. Their practice thrives on the thin line where questions live and curiosity flowers.

Christopher Nasaire is a queer writer, editor, and visual artist. He writes fiction and creative non-fiction. He co-wrote *buto/buto: bones are seeds*, a community-led theatre production staged in Vancouver in 2022. As a visual artist he works with photography and illustration. Born and raised in Mindanao, Philippines, he lives in Burnaby, British Columbia.

Rafael Palma (he/him) is an English major at Brandon University, with a minor in Creative Writing. He was born and raised in the province of Laguna, in the Calabarzon region. As a kid, he read science fiction and fantasy novels and started writing short stories in his elementary days. He immigrated to Brandon, Manitoba with his family when he was fifteen and continued his studies. He discovered Western Poetry in high school and has been writing poetry ever since. He follows the styles of Margaret Atwood, Mary Oliver, Sylvia Plath, and Robin Morgan, his favourite poets.

Marc Perez is the author of a poetry chapbook, *Borderlands*, from Anstruther Press (2020). His first full-length collection, *Dayo*, is forthcoming from Brick Books in Spring 2024. His work has appeared in *Event Magazine*, */temz/ Review*, *decomp journal*, *Contemporary Verse 2*, *Prism International*, and *Vallum*. He lives in Vancouver, British Columbia.

Remilyn "Felix" Policarpio is a Filipino transmasculine artist, musician, educator, and storyteller. The oldest of four siblings and first in his family to be born on Canadian soil in Toronto, and inspired by a thirst for learning, he grew up reading encyclopedias for fun. He attended the Iona School of the Arts, specializing in instrumental works there before later transferring to visual arts. He moved to Ottawa in 2015 to study philosophy, stopping short due to mental illness but continuing his work as an educator. Felix currently resides in Britannia, Ottawa, lurking around as a member of the Haunted Walk.

Leah Ranada's stories have been published in *On Spec*, *Room Magazine*, *Santa Ana River Review*, *emerge 2013*, and elsewhere. Her writing is informed by her childhood in Metro Manila and eventual move to Vancouver in 2006, where she made writing her permanent home. She now lives in New Westminster, British Columbia. In 2013, she attended the Writer's Studio (TWS) at SFU. She released her debut novel, *The Cine Star Salon* (NeWest Press), in 2021. You can read her blog at https://leahranada.com.

Alma Salazar Retuta, MD, a veterinarian and a doctor of medicine, works in Calgary, Alberta, as a physician. She came to Canada in 2011 with her husband and five children. She loves cooking, reading, camping, and singing. She also adores babies and children. She hopes to uplift the lives of close family members by assisting them to come to Canada to build a new life here.

In her brief life, **Rani Rivera** (1981–2016) experienced moments of darkness and light. She worked among the marginalized in two of the neediest neighbourhoods in Toronto: first, at St. James Town, where she organized after-school activities for children and youth, and later, at the Community Place Hub in the Weston and Mount Denis area. She enrolled in the English program of the University of Toronto on a bridging scholarship. Her poetry collection *All Violet* was published by Caitlin Press (Dagger Editions) in 2017. For a review of Rivera's posthumous collection, *All Violet*, please go to: http://themaynard.org/views/rivera0218.php.

Aileen Santiago (she/they) is a teacher in Toronto, Ontario, with a background in languages, literacy, and social justice education. Born in the Philippines to Filipino and Chinese parents and coming to Canada at the age of seven, Aileen has some understanding of what it feels to straddle diverse cultures, embrace shifting identities, and the discomfort of learning how to unlearn. Her ongoing journey of reconnecting to her Philippine Taga-Ilog and Chinese Fukien roots has led her to curriculum writing projects, poetry performances, building the Fil-Can Educators Network, and research in anti-racist and decolonizing pedagogies. She shares her story as a racialized settler who is always ready to learn in community with others.

Angelo Santos is a writer, filmmaker, and physiotherapist who spent his formative years living in many places around the world — namely, the Philippines, the Middle East, the United States, and Canada. He now lives in Oakville, Ontario. Angelo's work has been published in various outlets including *Ricepaper Magazine* and *filling Station*. He is currently working on a collection of essays.

Carlo Sayo is a cultural worker engaging in diverse artistic disciplines such as visual and installation art, poetry, new media, and performance work. Drawing from experiences as the child of Filipino immigrants who left the Philippines during the Martial Law era of the 1970s, Carlo's creative endeavours delve into themes of culture, identity, migration, and settlement. His work is rooted in community building, striving to foster a greater understanding of the Filipino settler experience on unceded territories. Born in Montréal and later moving to Vancouver during Expo 86, Carlo's imaginative spirit grew partly from being a child of the 1980s. As a youth, Carlo grew up in and around the Kalayaan Centre, a Filipino community centre based in Vancouver's downtown eastside that was the heart of Filipino political activism in the late 1990s and early 2000s. Alongside his artistic pursuits, Carlo takes immense pride in being a devoted parent to two curious children.

Maribeth Manalaysay Tabanera a.k.a. **Kilusan** (siya/sanda/any pronouns) is a Tagalog Visayan filipinx non-binary multi-hyphenate artist, educator, and community organizer. They were born and raised on Treaty 1 Territory (Winnipeg, Manitoba) and spent thirty-five years based in this community.

They have presented their work as an educator, dancer, and DJ at events all over Turtle Island (North America). In September 2023, Maribeth will begin the Master of Education in Social Justice Education program at the University of Toronto in Tkaronto (Toronto, Ontario). For more information about them, please visit: https://maribethtabanera.com.

Born and raised in Manila, Philippines, **Steffi Tad-y** is a poet and writer based in the territories of the Musqueam, Squamish, and Tsleil-Waututh Nations, also known as Vancouver, British Columbia. Her chapbook of poems *Merienda*, published by Rahila's Ghost Press, was nominated for the 2021 bpNichol Chapbook Award. In 2022, she published her debut book of poetry, *From the Shoreline*, with Gordon Hill Press. Steffi's poems often reflect on kinship, diasporic geographies, and formations of the mind.

Vincent Ternida is the author of the novella *The Seven Muses of Harry Salcedo*. His essays, articles, and poetry have appeared in several publications, including *Polyglot*, *British Columbia Review*, *rabble.ca*, *Rappler*, *Voice and Verse Poetry Magazine*, and *PR&TA Journal*. His short story "Elevator Lady" was long listed for the CBC Short Story Prize in 2019. He is currently completing a short story collection. He lives in Vancouver, British Columbia.

Acknowledgements

Much thanks to the Canada Council for the Arts, for financially supporting this project.

A big thank-you to the team at Cormorant Books — Marc Coté, Sarah Cooper, Barry Jowett, Luckshika Rajaratnam, Marijke Friesen, Sarah Jensen, Fei Dong, Basil Sylvester, Diyasha Sen — for their warmth, openness, and enthusiasm.

Gratitude to Daniel Gawthrop for connecting us with Cormorant.

Thank you to Leonora C. Angeles, Darlyne Bautista, Ida Beltran, Robert Diaz, and Eleanor Guerrero-Campbell for voicing their steadfast support for this project at a crucial time.

And finally, a shout-out to the late Jim Wong-Chu — legendary author, activist, and co-founder of Asian Canadian Writers Workshop — for helping plant the seeds for this anthology before his passing. While we wish Jim were still with us to see this book come to fruition, his nurturing spirit lives on in its every page.

We acknowledge the sacred land on which Cormorant Books operates. It has been a site of human activity for 15,000 years. This land is the territory of the Huron-Wendat and Petun First Nations, the Seneca, and most recently, the Mississaugas of the Credit River. The territory was the subject of the Dish With One Spoon Wampum Belt Covenant, an agreement between the Iroquois Confederacy and Confederacy of the Ojibway and allied nations to peaceably share and steward the resources around the Great Lakes. Today, the meeting place of Toronto is still home to many Indigenous people from across Turtle Island. We are grateful to have the opportunity to work in the community, on this territory.

We are also mindful of broken covenants and the need to strive to make right with all our relations.